The Dark Side of Creativity

Edited by

David H. Cropley
University of South Australia

Arthur J. Cropley
University of Hamburg

James C. Kaufman
California State University at San Bernardino

Mark A. Runco
University of Georgia, Athens

CAMBRIDGE UNIVERSITY PRESS

CAMBRIDGE UNIVERSITY PRESS
Cambridge, New York, Melbourne, Madrid, Cape Town, Singapore,
São Paulo, Delhi, Dubai, Tokyo, Mexico City

Cambridge University Press
32 Avenue of the Americas, New York, NY 10013-2473, USA

www.cambridge.org
Information on this title: www.cambridge.org/9780521139601

First published 2010

Printed in the United States of America

A catalog record for this publication is available from the British Library.

Library of Congress Cataloging in Publication data
The dark side of creativity / [edited by] David H. Cropley ... [et al.].
p. cm.
Includes bibliographical references and index.
ISBN 978-0-521-19171-5 – ISBN 978-0-521-13960-1 (pbk.)
1. Creative ability. 2. Good and evil. 3. Criminal intent.
I. Cropley, David. II. Title.
BF408.D36 2010
153.3′5–dc22 2010014625

ISBN 978-0-521-19171-5 Hardback
ISBN 978-0-521-13960-1 Paperback

THE DARK SIDE OF CREATIVITY

With few exceptions, scholarship on creativity has focused on its positive aspects while largely ignoring its dark side. This includes not only creativity deliberately aimed at hurting others, such as crime or terrorism, or at gaining unfair advantages but also the accidental negative side effects of well-intentioned acts. This book brings together essays written by experts from various fields (e.g., psychology, criminal justice, sociology, engineering, education, history, and design) and with different interests (e.g., personality development, mental health, deviant behavior, law enforcement, and counterterrorism) to illustrate the nature of negative creativity, examine its variants, call attention to its dangers, and draw conclusions about how to prevent it or protect society from its effects.

David H. Cropley is Deputy Director of the Defence and Systems Institute at the University of South Australia, where he is also Associate Professor of Engineering Innovation. His interest in creativity and innovation is centered around the role that they play in the design and development of products, processes, systems, and services of a technological nature, for which functionality is as important as form in determining the value of creative solutions. Cropley co-authored the book *Fostering Creativity: A Diagnostic Approach for Higher Education and Organizations* (2009) with Arthur J. Cropley and has published articles in the *Cambridge Journal of Education*, the *International Journal of Technology and Design Education*, the *Creativity Research Journal*, and the APA journal *Psychology of Aesthetics, Creativity, and the Arts.*

Arthur J. Cropley is Emeritus Professor of Psychology at the University of Hamburg and previously worked at the UNESCO Institute for Education in Hamburg. He is currently a visiting professor of psychology at the University of Latvia. He has published extensively in a wide range of journals and is the author, co-author, or editor of 25 books, which have appeared in a total of 12 languages. He was the founding editor of the *European Journal for High Ability* (now known as *High Ability Studies*).

James C. Kaufman is an Associate Professor of Psychology at the California State University at San Bernardino, where he directs the Learning Research Institute. Kaufman is the author or editor of 16 books, including *Creativity 101*, *Essentials of Creativity Assessment* (with Jonathan Plucker and John Baer), *International Handbook of Creativity* (with Robert J. Sternberg), and *Applied Intelligence* (with Robert J. Sternberg and Elena Grigorenko). He is a founding co-editor of the official journal for the American Psychological Association's Division 10, *Psychology of Aesthetics, Creativity, and the Arts.* He is also the associate editor of *Psychological Assessment* and the *Journal of Creative Behavior*, editor of the *International Journal of Creativity and Problem Solving*, and the series editor of the Psych 101 series.

Mark A. Runco is E. Paul Torrance Professor of Creativity and Gifted Education at the University of Georgia, Athens. He also has taught at the University of Hawaii, Hilo, and California State University, Fullerton. He is a Fellow and Past President of Division 10 of the American Psychological Association and founder of the *Creativity Research Journal*, of which he remains editor-in-chief. Runco is currently co-editing the second edition of the *Encyclopedia of Creativity.*

For John Baer, colleague and friend, who has shown me the good side of creativity in all that he does
James C. Kaufman

For Colin, Moe, and Howie, friends whose scholarship is apparent throughout this volume
Mark A. Runco

For AJ, without whom ...
David H. Cropley

Contents

Contributors

PINO G. AUDIA
Dartmouth University

JAMES R. AVERILL
University of Massachusetts

ARTHUR J. CROPLEY
University of Hamburg

DAVID H. CROPLEY
University of South Australia

RUSSELL EISENMAN
University of Texas–Pan American

LIANE GABORA
University of British Columbia

LORRAINE GAMMAN
Central Saint Martins College of Art and Design

LUIS DANIEL GASCÓN
University of California, Irvine

JACK A. GONCALO
Cornell University

AMIHUD HARI
Technion – Israel Institute of Technology

DAVID K. HECHT
Bowdoin College

KEVIN HILTON
Northumbria University

NANCY HOLMES
University of British Columbia

KEITH JAMES
Portland State University

JAMES M. JASPER
CUNY Graduate Center

JAMES C. KAUFMAN
California State University, San Bernardino

ELMA P. NUNLEY
ACT Counseling Center

MAZIAR RAEIN
National Academy of the Arts, Oslo

MARK A. RUNCO
University of Georgia, Athens

DEAN KEITH SIMONTON
University of California, Davis

JENNIE KAUFMAN SINGER
California State University, Sacramento

ROBERT J. STERNBERG
Tufts University

AISHA TAYLOR
Portland State University

LYNNE C. VINCENT
Cornell University

MARIA N. ZAITSEVA
Cornell University

1

The Dark Side of Creativity: What Is It?

ARTHUR J. CROPLEY

FAILURE TO RECOGNIZE THE EXISTENCE OF THE DARK SIDE

In everyday usage as well as scholarly discussions, it is almost axiomatic that creativity is good. Indeed it cannot be denied that it often leads to beneficial advances in art and literature, science, medicine, engineering, manufacturing, business, and other areas (the bright side). Unfortunately, the enchantment with creativity is so intense that, as James, Clark, and Cropanzano (1999) complained, people, including researchers "... typically ignore the fact that a great deal of creative effort is done in service of negative ends" (p. 212). James, Clark, and Cropanzano argued that this has led to an absence of consideration of negative creativity or, as the editors of the present volume would put it, a failure to come to grips with the dark side of creativity. This means that little has been worked out about the "... triggers, processes, outcomes ..." (p. 212) of the dark side. The result is obvious: Approaches to recognizing the dark side, avoiding circumstances that foster its growth, discouraging its manifestation, redirecting it, protecting against its negative consequences, and the like, are not well developed. The purpose of this book is to increase both awareness of the dark side and understanding of the forms and processes of negative creativity, begin to develop the necessary conceptual framework, and set in motion a discussion of how to deal with it in practical settings.

In pursuing this goal, the book contains chapters by people from disparate fields of study (e.g., psychology, criminal justice, sociology, engineering, education, history, and design) and different areas of focus (e.g., personality development, mental health, deviant behavior, law enforcement, and counterterrorism) in order to illustrate the nature of the dark side of creativity, examine its variants, draw attention to its dangers (although even the dark side has its bright side), and draw conclusions about how to prevent negative creativity or protect ourselves against it. Examples of practical programs are found in several chapters, including those by Gamman and Raein, Sternberg, Hilton, D. H. Cropley, and Hari.

THE BRIGHT SIDE OF CREATIVITY

Creativity is widely seen as so good that in his seminal discussion, from which the title of this book is derived, McLaren (1993) points out that it has a "quasi-religious function" (p. 139). He cites Tsanoff, who referred to creativity as involving "some divine principle," (p. 137) and Plato, who wrote of "divine influence" (p. 137). Nietzsche (1947, p. 407) argued that creativity involves "*deification* of existence [emphasis added]" and is above all moral considerations. Gammel (1946, p. 140) emphasized that for many people creativity is the new way of finding solace in an imperfect world in which religion no longer offers such consolations. This tone of almost religious fervor was already present at the beginning of the modern creativity era. Bruner (1962) saw creativity as the last bastion of the human spirit in an age in which electronic devices are taking over most noncreative functions: It thus marks the boundary between the human being and the intelligent machine. Discussions along these lines have not infrequently argued that creativity is a principle of nature and that it is, by definition, a universal beneficial force fostering growth and rebuilding in all organic systems.

In addition to the inherent spiritual goodness just outlined, various writers such as Rogers (1961), Maslow (1973), and May (1976) also emphasized that creativity is good for the individual. It was typically associated with positive personal properties such as flexibility, openness, courage, or high ego strength. As a result, it is often thought to be connected with favorable psychological development of the individual, such as achievement of a high level of self-actualization, personal fulfillment, or improved mental health. The making of art or production of works of prose or poetry has often been assumed to be therapeutic for people suffering from mental health problems or incarcerated for criminal offenses (see Chapter 10 by Singer). Cropley (1990) attempted to develop a model of the mechanisms through which creativity has beneficial effects on mental health. By contrast, Gabora and Holmes (Chapter 15 in this volume) discuss the pros and cons of the argument that creativity may even be *bad* for mental health, citing Coleridge's warning in *Kubla Khan*, "Beware!"

Discussions such as those just outlined have tended to equate creativity with artistic creativity: fine art, literature, music and dance, and the like.

More recently, however, it is also commonly being seen as good in that it fosters material prosperity: D. H. Cropley (Chapter 19 in this volume) cites José Manuel Barroso, President of the European Commission, who in a 2009 speech identified creativity as essential for collective and individual well-being, long and sustainable economic growth, and answers to the current financial, economic, and social crisis. As Oral (2006) put it, creativity is vital "for shaping ... future orientations and actualizing reforms in political, economic and cultural areas" (p. 65). Other business-oriented writers, such as Buzan (2007) or Florida (2004), see creativity as the key to meeting the challenges of the early twenty-first century arising from technological advances, social change, globalization, and now the global financial crisis.

This view of creativity as crucial for social and economic well-being goes back at least to the Chinese Emperor Han Wu-di, who reigned until 87 BCE. He was intensely interested in giving innovative thinkers high rank in the civil service because of their importance for the well-being of the society, and he reformed the method of selection of mandarins to achieve this. Both Francis Bacon (1909 [1627]) and René Descartes (1991 [1644]), two of the founders of modern science, saw scientific creativity as involving the harnessing of the forces of nature *for the betterment of the human condition*. Cropley and Cropley (2005, p. 169) refer to practically useful creativity that serves society by leading to the production of useful objects, devices, machines, or processes as "functional" creativity, contrasting it with aesthetic or artistic creativity.

THE DARK SIDE

McLaren (1993) contrasted the extremely positive view of creativity just spelled out with the facts of its misuse in, for instance (a) advertising, where it is employed to promote the sales of, among other things, unhealthy food or dangerous products, (b) entertainment, where it is used to promote repulsive values, glorify crime, and so on, (c) politics, where it has been used to promote, for instance, racial hatred, or (d) science and technology, where it is applied to developing and building weapons of mass destruction (see the discussion of the development of such weapons in Chapters 4 and 5 in this volume), or polluting the environment. Interestingly, McLaren pointed out that the harm generated by technological creativity is not confined to physical destruction. He refers to eighteenth- and nineteenth-century figures such as Coleridge, Dickens, and Victor Hugo, who already then were warning of the destructive *social* effects of technological innovation. To these can be added (e.g., James, Clark, & Cropanzano, 1999) negative use of creativity in (e) business or production, for instance, to evade regulators or to steal competitors' secrets, (f) social life or at work, for instance, to avoid work, curry favor, gain unfair advantage, or steal from an employer without being detected, (g) crime in general (e.g., Cropley, Kaufman, & Cropley, 2008), (h) war, and (i) terrorism. The dark side of creativity is so pervasive that we can paraphrase Graham Greene's words in his book *The human factor* (1978, p. 130): "... it is the *creative* person we need most to fear [emphasis added]."[1]

The variety of settings in which what James, Clark, and Cropanzano (1999) called "negative" creativity can manifest itself is large. At an every-day level it is seen when, to take those authors' example, a person finds creative ways to get others to do the hard work in a factory. This may be regarded by observers as no more than annoying cunning. More obviously dark, however, is the application of creativity to manipulate other people or to profit at other people's expense, without regard to possible negative consequences for the people concerned: An obvious, legally permitted example would be the use of creativity to persuade children to eat foods that are harmful to their health (as in advertising). Another example is the field of crime. As Gamman and Raein argue in Chapter 9, "resourceful offenders" (p. 161) constitute a group "whose creativity is rarely acknowledged" (p. 158). As they point out, some "criminal 'projects' may exhibit the 'wow' factor" (p. 158), and represent paradigm-breaking creative breakthroughs. They mention the Great Train Robbery, which is often cited in the relevant literature as an example of a criminal breakthrough with the "wow" factor. Ronald Biggs, probably the most famous of the Great Train robbers, showed enormous ingenuity in escaping and evading capture for many years, until old age and physical infirmity persuaded him to surrender. Eisenman (Chapter 11 in this volume) gives simple examples in the form of brief case studies of the use of creativity by prisoners in the correctional system to manipulate supervisory personnel to their own advantage, for instance to make it easier for them to smuggle drugs, whereas Singer (Chapter 10 in this volume) gives the example where prisoners creatively use unusual materials to make, for instance, a knife.

Most obviously dark is the application of creativity with the conscious and deliberate intention of doing harm to others, the harm being the main purpose of the creativity, not just a spin off. This is what Cropley, Kaufman, and Cropley (2008) called "malevolent" creativity. Intentional negative

[1] In fact Greene wrote "educated" person.

creativity may be seen not only in some crime, but also in business, as well as in war. Fully intended negative creativity may be widely applauded as positive by one side (often the victors), even though it is devastatingly negative for the other. One example from war is Nelson's highly effective novel tactic of sailing inshore of the French fleet at the Battle of the Nile in 1798. The tactic caused the loss of 12 out of 14 French ships of the line and death or captivity for thousands of French sailors, results that were adjudged good by the British but bad by the French. Another example is the dropping of the atomic bomb on Hiroshima and Nagasaki in 1945 (see Chapter 5 in this volume), which was greeted with delirious gladness by some – especially allied soldiers whose lives it may well have saved – but ultimately killed hundreds of thousands of Japanese civilians.

Unfortunately, even creativity intended to be entirely benevolent may have a dark side in the form of unintended or unforeseen negative consequences: For instance, the discoveries of Jenner and Pasteur, although extremely beneficial for all humankind, laid the foundation for germ warfare. McLaren (1993) gave the example of the building of cathedrals in the middle ages: These may still stand as creative triumphs of architecture and civil engineering that add beauty to the world even today, but their dark side is that they often caused great misery and hardship to the poor at the time of their construction. At a more down-to-earth level, in 1935 the cane toad (*Bufo marinus*) was introduced into the sugarcane fields of the Australian state of Queensland as a novel way of combating the gray-backed cane beetle and the frenchie beetle, great pests for the sugar industry at that time.

The deliberate introduction of a natural enemy to combat the pest was novel at the time and well intentioned. It promised an environmentally friendly remedy that avoided, for instance, the use of harmful pesticides.[2] Now, however, the toad itself has become a major environmental threat in Australia and is slowly spreading throughout the country, where it is a serious danger to the survival of native Australian fauna. Because it is extremely poisonous, it has no natural enemies (no predator can eat it), and it is extremely cunning, so humans find it difficult to hunt or trap. Introduction of the toad was a novel and well-intentioned approach to combating insect pests, to be sure, but it is ultimately having negative effects, despite the good intentions.

[2] Unfortunately, the novelty proved to be ineffective mainly because the cane toad is a ground feeder, whereas the beetles just mentioned live well above the ground on the plant's foliage! This fact, however, is not relevant to the present discussion.

Even where an undesirable outcome is foreseeable, negative creativity is not necessarily the result of deliberately evil intentions. Some people may even create evil despite generally having benevolent motives. They may, for instance, be unable to, unaware of, or unwilling to anticipate the dark side of their work, deliberately or subconsciously blinding themselves to negative consequences. This may occur, for instance, because of their fascination with what they are doing, or because they are deceived or coerced by factors such as the prospect of money and fame or the manipulation of a despotic government. Zaitseva (Chapter 4 in this volume) gives an example of how this happened with some participants in the Soviet Union's program for the development of weapons of mass destruction.

INHERENT NEGATIVE ASPECTS OF CREATIVITY

The traditional approach of psychological research on creativity (e.g., Barron, 1955; Rhodes, 1961) has examined it in terms of the 4*P*s (Person, Product, Process, and Press). Discussion in this chapter has focused until now on the *results* of the creativity, that is, on the *P* of Product, or on the *intention* or *motivation* of the creative individual, that is, on one aspect of Person. However, as was pointed out in the opening paragraph, some writers have argued that creativity is above such considerations. Runco (Chapter 2 in this volume) focuses on a different *P*, namely, Process. He points out that creative processes are neither inherently good nor inherently bad. The dark side is a property of, for instance, human motivation or the use made of products, not of the process of creativity itself.

Negative Aspects of Process

However, as I argue (Chapter 16 in this volume), not only Person and Product but also Process has an *inherent* dark side, independently of the motivation of the people involved or the nature of the product. Process involves procedures such as seeing the known in a new light, producing multiple answers, shifting perspective, giving surprising answers, and opening up risky possibilities (often referred to as "divergent" processes). Gamman and Raein (Chapter 9 in this volume) sum up divergent processes as involving "rejection of mechanical approaches" (p. 157). While it is true that processes such as these are in themselves neither good nor evil, it is clear that under certain circumstances they lead more or less automatically to disruption and introduce intolerable levels of uncertainty. In

Chapter 16 of this volume, I give the example of the classroom; Cropley and Cropley (2009) described the case of the French mathematician, Evariste Galois, who was expelled from secondary school despite being a brilliant and, as we now know, highly creative mathematics student who wanted to learn, admired his mathematics teacher, and produced excellent work in math lessons. Galois was not a more or less innocent victim of unreasonable attitudes, values, or demands of those around him but contributed substantially to his own downfall. He was simply too divergent to fit in. In Chapter 9 Gamman and Raein give another educational example: The adoption of the "nonmechanical" processes described above can be associated with failure to master "mechanical" processes, such as making fine distinctions, adhering to strict rules, or being accurate, all necessary for acquiring skill in reading. As a result, a one-sided preference for "nonmechanical" processes in itself increases the likelihood of dyslexia, which in turn increases the likelihood of difficulties in social functioning stretching all the way to crime.

In Chapter 7 Goncalo, Vincent, and Audia draw attention to another dark aspect of the creative process: Past creativity may actually block further creativity. For instance, successful production of effective novelty in the past may lead a person to continue to work along a particular line of attack that has ceased to be novel in the present. Furthermore, as Amabile (1983) and Csikszentmihalyi (1996) pointed out, a product is only publicly acclaimed as creative when it is accepted by those who are knowledgeable in a field and it becomes integrated into the field. Thus, almost perversely, creativity not infrequently changes the current paradigm in a field and thereafter redefines the norm – on the one hand ceasing to be novel itself (the process of acclamation as creative makes a product familiar and therefore no longer novel, at least to insiders), and on the other hand, not only rendering redundant earlier products that may, in their own time, have been novel, but also destroying the novelty of potential new products by anticipating them or directing attention in a new direction and thus denying new products the seal of approval.[3]

3 One consolation is that a new product can reopen assessment of the creativity of a product previously dismissed as uncreative, for instance, by making observers look at the old product in a new way. An example is the impact of the work of Galois at the time of his early death. He left a body of writing that was judged to depart from the conventional but to lead nowhere because of its lack of a basis in existing mathematical knowledge (i.e., it was judged to involve at best quasi-creativity). Only several years later, when mathematics had advanced sufficiently through post-Galois creativity, was it possible to recognize the creativity of Galois's previously rejected ideas in group theory.

Negative Aspects of Person

Creativity is also connected with negative phenomena in the area of Person, as has been shown repeatedly by many researchers. For a summary, see Simonton (Chapter 12 in this volume) and Gabora and Holmes (Chapter 15 in this volume). Creativity appears to be linked with both cognitive disturbance, as in schizophrenia (e.g., Schuldberg, 2000–2001), and mood disturbance, as in bipolar disorder (e.g., Andreasen, 1987; Jamison, 1993). Simonton examines this relationship in Chapter 12, and concludes that there is some truth to the idea that creativity is connected with mental illness. However, there is no simple, linear causal relationship according to which mental illness would make a person creative (the more serious the illness the greater the creativity) or creativity make a person mentally ill (the more creative the person, the more acute the illness).

Focusing on literary creativity, Gabora and Holmes (Chapter 15 in this volume) examine the "shadowy swamplands of the creative mind" (p. 277). Among other things, they give examples of numerous twentieth-century poets, writers, musicians, and painters who committed suicide. They also review discussions of the question of whether creativity causes psychological disturbance or psychological disturbance leads to creativity. One possible dynamic of the relationship is that creative artists may delve deeply into the unconscious in a process of "deep mining into the darkness" (p. 285), and bring to the surface material that uncreative people – wisely – leave undisturbed. Gabora and Holmes suggest that precisely this process of going where others fear to go may lead to an "allure of darkness" (p. 283) that makes the dark side attractive to some creative individuals as well as to some of the people who admire their work.

The essence of creativity is going against the crowd. The development of an individual identity by each person also involves becoming different from the crowd by "creating" an individual self and a unique identity. Thus, personality development itself can be seen as a creative process. According to Barron (1963) and Moustakis (1977), not infrequently this self-actualization requires resisting pressure from the surrounding society to conform, and Burkhardt (1985) argued that the creative individual must fight against society's pathological desire for sameness. Sternberg and Lubart (1995) called this fight "defying the crowd" and labeled the tendency of certain individuals to resist society's pressure to conform "contrarianism" (p. 41).

However, at some point the process can go awry. The positive, desirable breaking away from the conventional to form a unique personal identity can cross the line and become pathological, leading to maladjustment and neurosis, or manipulation, antisocial behavior, crime, or terrorism. In fact, creativity seems to be inextricably bound up with not only positive but also negative consequences for the individual and society: Gascón and Kaufman (Chapter 13 in this volume) examine personality, deviance, and creativity, looking as they say at "both sides of the coin." Deviance may be perceived as a place where creativity and crime can meet; just as deviance from the norm may lead to creative ideas, so too can it lead to crime. Some of the same personality traits that are associated with criminal thinking are also associated (albeit not as strongly) with creativity. Some concepts, such as mood and impulsivity, illustrate ways that someone primed to be creative may also be more at risk for the dark side. Averill and Nunley (Chapter 14 in this volume) analyze the relationship in a closer and more differentiated way by examining the nature of the link between creativity and neurosis. Essentially, they conclude that neurosis is creativity gone wrong, that is, neurosis is an example of the dark side of creativity.

MORAL DARKNESS

Early in modern thinking, Amabile (1983) emphasized that creativity does not occur in a vacuum but in a social context. It always involves subjective judgments made by observers. These judgments may well involve formalist qualities (e.g., "unity," "harmony," or "complexity") or technical properties (e.g., "high quality of construction," "skillfulness," or "professional finish"), as Slater (2006) pointed out, or practical considerations such as usefulness, practicability, or marketability. However, the approval of external observers also results from a creative work being judged beautiful or pleasing (i.e., aesthetic criteria) as well as admirable and worthy of emulation (moral criteria). Morality, in particular, involves judgments of good and bad, virtuousness and wickedness. According to Sternberg (Chapter 17 in this volume), the moral dimension is essential to any discussion of creativity.

However, even monsters of evil, such as Hitler and Stalin – cases where the moral verdict seems to be indisputable – are regarded by some people as having been great leaders. Sternberg makes the point that both these men introduced high levels of effective novelty (including systems for suppressing opinions differing from their own and previously unknown systems that worked well for murdering people) and had a very substantial impact on their societies. However, those who praise them as great men focus only on the novelty and impact (effectiveness) of what they did. Sternberg argues that people like Hitler and Stalin produce what he calls "originality," to be sure, but that in the absence of moral goodness they cannot be said to be creative. This accords with the intuitive feeling of many people that it is disgusting to refer to such monsters as "creative," despite the fact that they generated effective novelty and, in a strictly formalistic sense, *were* creative.

In the context of this book, creativity without morality is part of the dark side. Nonetheless, different observers' ideas of what is morally good and bad are highly subjective, and may differ sharply from person to person and, indeed, from era to era. Galileo's publication of the thesis that the earth rotates around the sun (and not vice versa) was regarded in his own time as so morally reprehensible as to be heresy and led to years of house arrest. Thus, the moral goodness or evil of effective novelty is not a clear-cut matter: What is needed are guidelines on how to recognize moral creativity. In Chapter 17 Sternberg offers insights into the distinguishing characteristic that renders creativity moral: According to him, the crucial element is what he calls "wisdom." When creativity is tempered by wisdom, it is of necessity moral. The central characteristic of wisdom is concern for the common good: A wise person seeks to maximize the common good, not just to seek his or her own advantage. From an American point of view, the 9/11 attack can then be seen as not displaying wisdom, since its intention was not to serve the common good,[4] and thus can be seen as being immoral and ultimately not creative.

A second aspect of the moral side of creativity is described by Hilton (Chapter 8 in this volume). One person's creativity may inspire another person's antisocial behavior. An obvious example is the copying of evil deeds depicted in imaginative works. Hilton gives the examples of a murder committed using a technique described in the novel *Shibumi* and a double murder committed by copying a scene in a Clint Eastwood film. Thus, an artistic creation that is successful in entertaining, even informing or inspiring readers, listeners, or beholders (the bright side), may simultaneously encourage, promote, or provide models of wicked behavior (the dark side). It seems plausible that the more effective the creativity in such situations, the greater the likelihood that it will promote antisocial behavior, so that, perversely, the stronger the bright side, the worse the dark side. Is such a work moral or immoral?

[4] Nonetheless, it may well have seemed (rightly or wrongly) to the attackers to be advancing the common good of some other ethnic or national group(s), so even wisdom is obviously relative. Disagreement among beholders on what is dark and what is bright does not negate the general principle that creativity can have a dark side.

Hilton mentions censorship as one possible way of curbing this dark effect of creativity but does not recommend it because it is incompatible with individual freedom. What he calls for is reminiscent of Sternberg's recommendation. What is needed, according to Hilton, is "social wisdom" (Chapter 8 in this volume, p. 138), which is based on a "multiperspective community approach" and essentially considers the results of creativity in its social context. He also calls for emphasis on "the hard-won insights of the past," thus incorporating the historical context and the accumulated wisdom of previous generations (as does Sternberg – see following text).

PRACTICAL REMEDIES AGAINST THE DARK SIDE

A number of systematic practical measures are proposed by the authors in this volume. These include an educational approach that emphasizes the teaching of wisdom in the school classroom (Sternberg, Chapter 17). Sternberg sees this as requiring the reading of "classic works of literature and philosophy" (p. 325), discussion in various forms of what has been learned from such works, fostering of "dialogical and dialectical thinking" (p. 326), study of truth, emphasis on serving good ends, analysis by students of the way their own actions have both good and bad consequences, and acceptance by teachers of their own importance as role models. Sternberg gives the example of a program for the teaching of American history based on these principles.

In Chapter 8 Hilton suggests the *Cyclic Countering of Competitive Creativity* (C4) program for developing creative solutions that combat crime. This approach regards criminals as competitors of crime-prevention agencies. It is based on "personas" of criminals constructed from real cases. The purpose of the procedure is to improve critical thinking and analytic processes in designing measures against criminal threats. It is aimed at producing creative solutions to the problem of combating crime by training crime-fighting agencies to look at the situation from a new perspective (that of the "competitor"). It involves role playing in a group setting, each participant being assigned a criminal persona and representing the position of this persona in the group. In alternating cycles, the participants make novel suggestions or act as critics of these suggestions.

Gamman and Raein (Chapter 9 in this volume) make the point that simply labeling crime or terrorism, among other aspects of the dark side, as "deviant" or "abnormal" does not help. They quote Einstein's dictum that problems cannot be solved using the same thinking that created them. What is needed is to understand the nature of the thinking involved, in this case to "think thief" (p. 167). They offer insights into criminal thinking gained from a comparison between artists and "resourceful offenders" (p. 161). Both groups live outside mainstream life and adopt an "entrepreneurial approach" (p. 162) to dealing with it. This is characterized by a willingness to challenge the status quo, the ability to spot and exploit opportunities, resourcefulness, amorality, a willingness to adopt anarchic strategies, risk taking, and openness to the possibilities offered by chance events, among other things. All these characteristics are also linked to creativity, and this fact needs to be acknowledged in designing countermeasures. Gamman and Raein then offer case studies using the *Design against Crime* approach, which considers, for instance, how the behavior of perpetrators could be redirected into morally acceptable channels.

D. H. Cropley (Chapter 19 in this volume) analyzes malevolent creativity in a highly differentiated way in terms of six *P*s (Process, Personal characteristics, Personal motivation, Personal feelings, Products, and Press) involved in the development of products that serve a practical purpose or *solve problems* in an effectively novel way – as an engineer, he is more interested in such "functional" products than in aesthetic-artistic products. He shows that the manner in which the *P*s are involved in functional creativity is paradoxical, but he resolves the paradoxes by mapping the six *P*s onto seven phases in the emergence of an effectively novel product (Preparation, Activation, Generation, Illumination, Verification, Communication, and Validation). He then goes on to derive from this model general principles for blocking the functional creativity of terrorists: This involves especially "phase blocks" and "dimension blocks" (p. 355).

Hari (Chapter 18 in this volume) also treats combating negative creativity – in this case, terrorism – as an exercise in creative problem finding and problem solving in a competitive environment. He looks at this from the point of view of systems engineering and focuses on the "functional" characteristics of creative solutions, especially engineering solutions: effectiveness, novelty, elegance, and generalizability (Cropley & Cropley, 2005). As is the case with all functional creativity, the creativity of counterterrorists requires continuous generation of effective novelty because of the constant and often rapid "decay" of novelty and effectiveness mentioned by D. H. Cropley in Chapter 19 and discussed in more detail in Cropley, Kaufman, and Cropley (2008). Thus, what is needed is an "agile" methodology. In Chapter 18 Hari outlines an approach, based on the *Integrated Customer Driven Method,* for generating effectively novel antiterrorism solutions that both solve the counterterrorist agency's problem and also prevent terrorists from solving theirs: This methodology underlies a training method described by Hari.

CLOSING OVERVIEW

The theories and research here run across a variety of disciplines (psychology, history, sociology, graphic design, and engineering). Approaches range from analyzing past dark side behavior through the lens of its creativity (Hecht, Zaitseva), to arguing that the processes associated with creativity also can be associated with dark or criminal behavior (Cropley, Gascón, & Kaufman), to discussing creativity behind bars (Singer, Eisenman), pointing out how creativity can battle the dark side of human behavior (Hari), to arguing that there is no dark side in creativity (Runco).

What has been interesting in editing this volume is that, in addition to the many exciting chapters received, the subject matter raised a striking amount of interest in other researchers. Many eminent scholars turn out to have held a (sometimes secret) fascination with this topic. Had this book been delayed a year, twice the number of chapters could have been included, spread across twice the number of domains. All four editors of this volume are eager to see more work in this area. The interest is there, and several different theoretical conceptions are in place to serve as starting points. What is needed is more research, more data, and more synthesis of this future research. Particularly exciting is the idea, first discussed in Cropley, Kaufman, and Cropley (2008), that creativity can be used to combat terrorism.

REFERENCES

Amabile, T. M. (1983). *The social psychology of creativity.* New York: Springer.

Andreasen, N. C. (1987). Creativity and mental illness: Prevalence rates in writers and their first degree relatives. *American Journal of Psychiatry*, 144, 1288–1292.

Bacon, Francis (1909 [1627]). *Essays, civil and moral and the new Atlantis.* New York: Collier.

Barron, F. X. (1955). The disposition towards originality. *Journal of Abnormal and Social Psychology*, 51, 478–485.

Barron, F. X. (1963). *Creativity and psychological health.* New York: Van Nostrand.

Bruner, J. S. (1962). The creative surprise. In H. E. Gruber, G. Terrell, & M. Wertheimer (Eds.), *Contemporary approaches to creative thinking* (pp. 1–30). New York: Atherton.

Burkhardt, H. (1985). *Gleichheitswahn Parteienwahn* [Sameness psychosis]. Tübingen: Hohenrain.

Buzan, A. (2007). Foreword. In S. C.Lundin & J. Tan (Eds.), *CATS: The nine lives of innovation* (pp. iv-viii). Spring Hill, Queensland: Management Press.
Cropley, A. J. (1990). Creativity and mental health in everyday life. *Creativity Research Journal*, 3, 167–178.
Cropley, A. J. & Cropley, D. H. (2009). *Fostering creativity: A diagnostic approach for education and organizations.* Cresskill, NJ: Hampton Press.
Cropley, D. H. & Cropley, A. J. (2005). Engineering creativity. A systems concept of functional creativity. In J. C. Kaufman & J. Baer (Eds.), *Faces of the muse: How people think, work and act creatively in diverse domains* (pp. 169–185). Hillsdale, NJ: Lawrence Erlbaum.
Cropley, D. H., Kaufman, J. C., & Cropley, A. J. (2008). Malevolent creativity: A functional model of creativity in terrorism and crime. *Creativity Research Journal*, 20, 105–115.
Csikszentmihalyi, M. (1996). *Creativity: Flow and the psychology of discovery and invention.* New York: Harper Collins.
Descartes, René. (1991 [1644]. *Principles of philosophy.* (Trans. V. R. Miller and R. P. Miller.) Boston, MA: Kluwer.
Florida, R. (2004). America's looming creativity crisis. *Harvard Business Review*, 82(10), 122–136.
Gammel, I. (1946). *The twilight of painting.* New York: Putnam's Sons.
James, K., Clark, K., & Cropanzano, R. (1999). Positive and negative creativity in groups, institutions and organizations: A model and theoretical extension. *Creativity Research Journal*, 12, 211–226.
Jamison, K. R. (1993). *Touched with fire: Depressive illness and the artistic temperament.* New York: Free Press.
Maslow, A. H. (1973). Creativity in self-actualizing people. In A. Rothenberg and C. R. Hausman (Eds.), *The creative question* (pp. 86–92). Durham, NC: Duke University Press.
May, R. (1976). *The courage to create.* New York: Bantam.
McLaren, R. B. (1993). The dark side of creativity. *Creativity Research Journal*, 6, 137–144.
Moustakis, C. E. (1977). *Creative life.* New York: Van Nostrand.
Nietzsche, F. (1947 [1888]). *Werke.* New York: Farrar Straus.
Oral, G. (2006). Creativity of Turkish prospective teachers. *Creativity Research Journal*, 18, 65–74.
Rhodes, M. (1961). An analysis of creativity. *Phi Delta Kappan*, 42, 305–310.
Rogers, C. R. (1961). *On becoming a person.* Boston, MA: Houghton Mifflin.
Schuldberg, D. (2000–2001). Six sub-clinical spectrum traits in normal creativity. *Creativity Research Journal*, 13, 5–16.
Slater, B. H. (2006). "Aesthetics." Available at http://www.iep.utm.edu/a/aestheti.htm#H2. Retrieved on July 30, 2007.
Sternberg, R. J. & Lubart, T. I. (1995). *Defying the crowd: Cultivating creativity in a culture of conformity.* New York: Free Press.

2

Creativity Has No Dark Side

MARK A. RUNCO

Creativity does not have a dark side. Creative products and efforts can be malevolent, but that is apparent in their impact and is not an inherent quality of creativity nor a requisite trait in the creative personality. Claiming that there is a dark side to creativity is much like arguing that hammers are evil because they can be used to dismantle as well as construct things. Creativity is indeed in some ways a tool of humanity, but of course that is merely a metaphor and, as such, only imperfectly applicable. The important point is that the process that underlies all creative things is not moral or immoral, ethical or unethical, good or evil. It is essentially blind. Like a tool, it can be applied in many different ways, some of which are benevolent and some of which are unethical and immoral, but to understand creativity it is best to be parsimonious and leave out what is extraneous, and that includes all possible effects. This chapter develops this view of parsimonious creativity and describes the ostensible dark side as a function of values and decisions that are ancillary to actual creative work.

There is no denying that creative talents have in the past been used in highly unfortunate ways. Many famous examples of this have been described by McLaren (1993), Stein (1993), and the authors of others chapters in this volume. But creativity also provides us with the capacity to adapt and sometimes allows useful and reasonable escape from the immediate environment (for instance, via imagination and fiction). It can be used by artists, engineers, managers, and teachers – and every one of them has the option of using it in benevolent or malevolent ways. Great care must be taken when discussing the dark side of creativity, for much like theories of the "mad genius" (Becker, 1999; Runco & Albert, in press), it could keep someone from encouraging creativity because of the fear that it will lead to insanity or, in the case of its dark side, malevolence.

This chapter defines creativity as a process that can and should be kept separate from the product, just as the causes of any behavior can and should be kept separate from possible effects of that same behavior. Various theories and lines of research are marshaled to support this view, including evolutionary theories, research on divergent thinking, studies of unambiguously creative accomplishment (for instance, Picasso's *Guernica*, Von Braun's missiles), theories of cultural and moral relativity, and research on the development of conventionality. After reviewing these and defining creativity such that a dark side is limited to products and not inherent in the capacity for creativity, questions concerning why and how some people apply their creative talents to immoral and unethical ends (i.e., the ostensible dark side) are briefly addressed.

DEFINING CREATIVITY

A big part of the confusion over creativity is semantic. This was implied in the preceding section of this chapter by the distinction between product and process. For some reason, the separation of these two things is often ignored (Kasof, 1995; Runco, 1995, 2007). This is surprising because behavioral scientists are usually good at distinguishing causes from effects. Clearly, it is most parsimonious and useful to define creativity as process because that is the fundamental causal agent for all expressions of creativity, regardless of their effect or value (e.g., benevolence or malevolence). In other words, it is most parsimonious to separate process and potential from what may result, namely, the effects or products (Runco, 2007). In addition to defining creativity as a universal and yet simple capacity, this approach allows a discussion of the dark side because it is only manifest in products and effects. Although it might be fair to give the process and product perspectives equal respect, products tell us little or nothing about what comes first, which in this case is the capacity or potential for creativity. In this light, the process perspective has more explanatory power than the product approach to creativity.

Interestingly, there are several similar nouns that, unlike the noun "creativity," do not lead to apparent confusion. The best example here is "evolution." Why is it that the noun "evolution" is treated accurately, but the noun "creativity" frequently leads to confusion? Evolution is not accused of being two-faced. Indeed, any description that suggests that the process of evolution can be directional (toward good or bad) is widely recognized as *teleological* and readily dismissed. It is known as the *teleological error.* It would not be too much of a stretch to say that assigning a dark side to creativity is another kind of teleological error.

One explanation for the unfair treatment of the noun "creativity" is that it is inherently deviant, and not surprisingly, the concept of "deviance" is itself widely misunderstood. It is, too often, associated only with unfavorable things. The connotations imply something undesirable. Yet deviance is, in essence, a statistical property. Behavioral scientists should know better than to associate deviance with anything unfavorable given how often they calculate standard deviations and how they correctly interpret them as merely "away from the mean" or "not average." (Of course, "abnormal" also tends to connote unfavorable things, and it too could simply refer to that which is not normal, or away from the norm.) This is a directly germane issue because creativity is always original, and originality requires novelty, uniqueness, unusualness, or (statistically speaking) deviance. Creativity is inherently deviant.

The parallel between creativity and evolution is even more useful not just because they are both blind processes (lacking directionality and teleology) but also because creativity functions much like an evolutionary process (Albert, in press; Campbell, 1960; Lumsden & Findlay, 1988; Simonton, 2008). As a matter of fact, creative capacity must be viewed as a result of evolution; certainly, it gives us a variety of advantages over the environment and for survival. Getting back to their similarity, however, what is most relevant is that both creativity and evolution rely on variation. Neither is complete without some sort of eventual selection, which in the case of biological evolution is *natural selection*. It has been given several different labels in studies of the creative process, including *selective retention* (Campbell, 1960).

Simonton (2008) recently concluded that creative work results from "a Darwinian process of blind-variation and selective-retention (i.e., nonmonotonic variants), rather than a more systematic, expertise-driven process (i.e., monotonic improvements)" (p. 329). Support for his view was provided by judgments of Picasso's sketches from different stages of completion of the painting *Guernica*. These judgments implied a nonmonotonic progression, as would be expected if the work was created in a blind fashion. Interestingly, the nonmonotonic progression was apparent in judgments about the work of art as a whole and in judgments about different elements within the work. Also compelling was the interjudge agreement about the nonmonotonic progression ($\alpha \cong 0.85$), which is particularly impressive because some of the judges were selected because they held anti-Darwinian theories of creativity!

Creativity relies on variation, and that variation is blind or nonmonotonic. Its lack of direction is what allows unpredictable insights. This blindness is not just cognitive. The creative process, at the most basic level, is also free of the values that would be involved if there were a dark side to the process. Values do come into play, but only during a late stage, when there is something to evaluate. They are not effective during variation, generation of alternatives, or creation. They come into play afterward, in judgments and implementation.

Evolution and creativity both must be blind and at least partly random. To claim that they are not blind is in both cases untenable. Creative thinking, for instance, leads to original insights, but if they are original, they are new, and if they are new, they could not be known beforehand. It is therefore difficult to tie the creative *process* to the alleged dark side or its antithesis, be that health or any other beneficial or benevolent result. How, then, does the dark side come about? Here it is useful to consider theories of divergent thinking and problem solving.

DIVERGENT THINKING AND THE DARK SIDE AS OPTIONS AND IDEAS

Theories of divergent thinking are almost as useful as theories of evolution for understanding creativity. Divergent thinking is often tied to the potential for creative thought. It is, however, often misunderstood. It is not a kind of creativity but merely a cognitive process that sometimes leads to creative ideas. *Divergent thinking* is cognition that moves in different directions. It can be contrasted with *convergent thinking*, where correct or conventional ideas and solutions are discovered (Guilford, 1968; Torrance, 1995; Runco, 1991; in press-a, in press-b).

Ironically, divergence per se is not operationalized in tests of divergent thinking. Instead, such tests are scored for *fluency* (the number of ideas), *originality* (novelty or unusual ideas), *flexibility* (the variety of themes within the pool of ideas), and occasionally, *quality*, *appropriateness*, or *elaboration*. Yet, theoretically and logically, divergent thinking can move in all directions. Creative thinking can be divergent in a literal fashion. Thus divergent thinking might lead to mildly conventional ideas, or it might lead to extremely unconventional ideas. Entirely conventional ideas probably are retrieved from long-term memory rather than constructed or created most of the time, but there is no reason that a conventional idea cannot be discovered or constructed anew using divergent thinking.

Of most relevance is the fact that when divergent thinking does lead to unconventional ideas, these ideas may be immoral or unethical. If these ideas are explored and eventually implemented, actions and products that deserve to be described as *malevolent* may result. The results mentioned earlier, from the study of Picasso, suggest that the original divergence is blind rather than malevolent. Other findings from more experimental studies support that same conclusion. Before reviewing those findings, more background on divergent thinking will be helpful.

Visual depictions of divergent thinking often show two lines that diverge from one another and move in different directions. This is a huge simplification. In fact, divergent thinking can take ideation in all directions. Depictions probably are inaccurate because they are two-dimensional, in which case ideation can only move along the abscissa and ordinate. Ideation can go anywhere, in any of the 360 degrees. This is still a simplification; surely, for truly creative thought, three dimensions would be necessary. In fact, given the possibilities of the human mind, what statisticians and science fiction afficionados sometimes call *hyperspace* (with dimensions more numerous than three) would be helpful for understanding creative potential and truly divergent thinking. This is especially true because creative thinking is sometimes preverbal (Tweney, 1996), more metaphorical than literal (Runco, 1996), unconscious as well as conscious (Rothenberg, 1990), more intuitive than conceptual (Bergson, 2002), and more emotional than logical (Gutbezahl & Averill, 1996; Runco & Shaw, 1994). Each of these implies a unique and perhaps orthogonal dimension for ideation. This hyperdimensionality is difficult to describe because I am relying on words to do so, and it may be difficult to conceive because while reading we are forced to be more reasonable than intuitive.

Divergent thinking allows people to generate ideas, but these ideas are merely options or possibilities. Most are quite immature at first, and for many, the value is in that they lead in a fruitful direction via associations (Mednick, 1962). If the person invests the time and resources into an idea, it might be refined and validated and perhaps implemented, in which case it may be malevolent. But that investment and refinement will not occur unless certain decisions are made and the person values certain things. For malevolent creativity, the person no doubt must value dark, immoral, unethical things. This is where studies specifically into the dark side should be directed – at the decisions that are made to invest in malevolence and the values that support them. More on that below.

First, the evidence mentioned briefly earlier can now be reviewed. Some of this comes from studies of divergent thinking and, more precisely, studies of idea evaluation (Runco, 1989; Runco & Basadur, 1993; Runco & Smith, 1992; Runco & Vega, 1992). These studies were motivated by the fact that creative thinking is always defined as (a) original and (b) effective or useful (Cropley, Kaufman, & Cropley, 2008; Runco, 1988). Some sort of evaluation and selection must be involved, especially for the latter. Most divergent thinking tests only allow fluency, originality, and flexibility, not evaluation. For this reason, measures of evaluation were developed and administered to various groups along with standard tests of divergent thinking. The process measured by the new tests was labeled *evaluative* to distinguish it from that assessed by tests already in existence – tests that focus on convergent and critical thinking. These previously existing tests assess how well a person can find or judge an idea or solution as correct or not. Tests of evaluative thinking, on the other hand, assess how well a person specifically judges the originality of ideas. Runco (1989) also described *valuative thinking* because sometimes to judge the originality of an idea accurately, you need to look for what is right (new, novel, unique) and find value rather than look for what is wrong or missing.

Research with various samples of participants has demonstrated that evaluative thinking is very difficult. Indeed, across samples, original ideas are often only recognized about 25% of the time. The highest level of accuracy was 50%. How could divergent thinking be guided if ideas are so difficult to judge? People produce original ideas, but most likely it is because they are truly thinking divergently and in different directions, blind to the best possible direction. At some point, they may evaluate their ideas, but the initial generation of ideas is largely or entirely blind. Note here that the empirical findings from these new measures of evaluative thinking are consistent with the research cited earlier and presented by Simonton (2008).

The valuative process is noteworthy because it says something about the values that are involved in creative efforts. Simplifying some, creative things are always new and original, and thus they are unpredictable. This may be why Bruner (1962) claimed that they had *effective surprise*. Their unpredictability means that they are appreciated only if a person is in fact open to new things. If the person is instead looking for something specific (e.g., the typical or conventional idea or answer), an original idea is unlikely to be appreciated and considered further. This, in turn, implies a few things about what should occur in applied settings, such as a classroom, if creativity is to be encouraged, or organizations if they hope for innovative employees. Indeed, if an educator or manager evaluates ideas and solutions based on particular expectations, he or she will tend to find what is missing or wrong about original ideas. However, if the educator or manager values creative things (and sees the task at hand as an opportunity for creativity), he or she may see something new, something that was not predicted, and for that reason take the time to explore it and perhaps find value in it. This is the *valuation* mentioned earlier. In this light, creative ideas and solutions will only be recognized if originality is a part of the values held by the individual or organization. More will be said later about the implications of the theory presented here and about the tolerance that is important in educational and organizational settings. First, a word about the relativity of values is in order.

RELATIVITY, VALUES, AND CONVENTIONALITY

Valuation to support creativity may require a kind of judgmental relativity. It is useful, therefore, to consider the moral absolutes and moral relativity that have been debated for years. This debate has covered much of the same ground needed to support the judgmental relativity I am associating with creative thinking.

One view is that people living in the contemporary world know more now than ever before, so they are more correct than ever before. The problem with this view, however, is obvious, and this kind of thinking is called either *Whiggist*, after the Whigs who seemed to favor it (Gould, 1991), or *presentism* (Runco, Kaufman, Halladay, & Cole, in press), as in "favoring the present." There is also a similar fallacy that modern Western culture is more advanced than all other cultures and thus that modern Western views and values are the closest to what is ideal. Fortunately, Benedict (1989) and others demonstrated that cultural differences are just differences in kind, not level or advancement. They cannot be evaluated with any absolute values or standards.

These brief reminders about *moral* and *cultural relativity* confirm that variations (among eras, cultures, and standards) must be separated from values and judgments. Variation is just variation, deviance just deviance. After variation or deviance occurs, judgments are possible, but there must first be a result, an effect, or a product to examine and judge. This is not to say that creativity is free of values. It merely suggests that divergence may be blind and values only relevant when judgments are possible.

The idea that values are a part of creativity may be most obvious in the arts. Recently, archeologists discovered a figure carved out of ivory in Germany (Maugh, 2009). This figure was highly newsworthy, although only an inch or two long, because it clearly resembled a voluptuous woman, like Venus. It is approximately 40,000 years old, and thus 5,000 years older than other examples of representational art. One art historian was quoted as saying, "It suggests the same values and ways of seeing the world existed among the earliest humans that migrated to Europe as among humans today" (quoted by Maugh, 2009, para. 7).

The claim that art conveys the values of the artist and his or her culture and era is a basic premise for art historians and individuals studying aesthetics. Aries (1973) was able to infer quite a bit about Western attitudes about death by examining art from across history. Later, he inferred how conceptions of childhood changed, again looking to changes suggested by depictions in artwork from different eras. Admittedly, some values and messages are ambiguous to viewers and sometimes even to the artists themselves (Jones et al., 1997), but this does not undermine the claim that values are a part of artwork – and all creativity. But again, a parsimonious view separates values from the generation of original ideas. This may sound reductionistic, but the evidence supporting blind variations indicates that it would be misleading to blend the two parts of the process into one.

The first part of the process (the generation of original ideas and solutions) can be used by one person toward benevolence and a moment later by the same person toward malevolence. The difference is in the product or implementation, not in the capacity. That capacity for ideation is separate from the uses of the ideas, and given that one person can be both malevolent and benevolent, only the specific uses or products can be judged as benevolent or malevolent. It therefore makes as much sense to separate the values from the other parts of the creative process as it does to separate cognition from affect (Lazarus, 1980; Zajonc, 1980). At most, we might identify people who have a tendency toward malevolent creativity, but this is still a judgment based on products or manifestations of a blind capacity.

One last example of values involved in art should be mentioned. This is from developmental studies of children as they move from a preconventional stage of thought (Kohlberg, 1987), where they are unable to conceive rules and conventions, to conventional thought, where they conform to rules and conventions, and hopefully then to postconventional thought, where they take rules and conventions into account but make decisions for themselves. These stages were first suggested by changes in moral reasoning, but the stages also seem to describe various other developmental trends, including those apparent in divergent thinking (with a fourth grade slump when in the conventional stage), language (with a literal stage), friendships (with peer pressure), and artwork. Rosenblatt and Winner (1988) found that the artwork of young children was highly creative in part because they were preconventional and as such their thinking was highly self-expressive and unconstrained. Conventional artwork, on the other hand, is constrained and representational. It is realistic but often not as creative as preconventional artwork.

One interpretation of this is that the thinking of the preconventional children could diverge more than that of the conventional children. In fact, these stages of development were first conceived to describe moral reasoning (Kohlberg, 1987), and this is, of course, directly relevant to the question of a dark side of creativity. Preconventional children can diverge quite a bit in both their artwork and their decisions when faced with moral dilemmas. Are children malevolent when they hurt someone? If the action leading to the harm was unintentional, a reflection of their immature reasoning tendencies, the act is unfortunate but clearly not a reflection of a dark side. Piaget referred to *subjective* and *objective moral reasoning*, the former taking intentions into account and the latter just the act itself. More recent theories of cognition also recognize the difference between what is expressed and what is possible, as in the case of performance versus competency. Practically speaking, this is one of the first lessons a parent should learn, for their children will make mistakes, and it is much wiser to say "that was not a good decision" than it is to say "you are not a good person because you made that decision." In all these instances, there is a clear separation of the result or product from the process. This separation is vital for understanding creativity. It removes malevolence from the capacity for creativity.

The reference to conventionality suggests a hypothesis for future work. After all, social deviance is likely to peak as the individual moves from conventional tendencies toward postconventional behavior. Ideally, the individual will finally master postconventional thought and behave in a socially appropriate and perhaps benevolent fashion, but he or she may not master that until he or she explores unconventional options, one of which is deviance that is socially inappropriate. Gascón and Kaufman (Chapter 13 in this volume) offered a parallel view when they described how "deviant behavior tends to peak from late childhood to mid-adolescence, and then begins to decrease in late adolescence to early adulthood."

As noted earlier, many of the practical implications of the concept of parsimonious creativity and the ideas about benevolence and malevolence involve decisions and intentions. These are the most reasonable targets for any enhancement efforts. It certainly would help to encourage the postconventional and mindful reasoning that was described earlier. In more entertaining but still useful language, enhancement efforts might target what Barron (1993) called *controlled weirdness*. He obviously recognized that all creativity is deviant and that we cannot have creativity without deviance. This, in turn, reinforces the notion that creativity will only flourish when there is tolerance for deviance, as well as some control of it.

DISPLACED INVESTMENTS

Often the distinction between malevolent and benevolent creativity is easy to see (Cropley et al., 2008). Other times the distinction between malevolent and benevolent creativity is vague and difficult. Even the value of atomic weapons, which required creative problem solving to design, construct, and deliver, can be debated. At first blush, they would seem to be one of the worst inventions in history. Apparently, the presidential administration and military justified the bombing of Hiroshima and Nagasaki in terms of lives saved. The enormity of the bombings is clear, but this justification was offered: Approximately 200,000 lives were lost in order to end the war and thereby save an estimated 600,000 lives.

The theory of parsimonious creativity outlined in this chapter should help when a distinction is necessary. It should be involved in all theories of creativity, including those that attempt to explain the dark side. It will allow us to find what is truly involved in creativity and thereby lead to a reliable scientific theory. It will allow us to separate occasional influences from requisites and correlates from actual causes (Runco, 2010). This is not always easy.

Consider in this regard the theory that creativity requires attributions and benefits from *self-promotion*. There is no doubt that self-promotion is apparent in the lives and work of certain eminent creative individuals. Von Braun, famous for his work on the Nazi V-1 rocket and, after the war, on the Saturn V rocket (which was used subsequently for Apollo missions to the moon), was described as "a cunning self-promoter" (Lord, 2007), and Gardner (1993) concluded the same about Picasso, Freud, Martha Graham, Einstein, Stravinsky, T. S. Eliot, and Gandhi. Kasof (1995) used these findings and theories of social creativity in his proposal that creativity will be enhanced if self-promotion and impression management are practiced! After all, if creativity is influenced by what others think, we can maximize our creativity if we manage the impressions we project.

This is not, however, a parsimonious view of creativity. It confuses the work that is involved in finding original insights with the public reactions to those insights. It confuses creativity with *fame* and *reputation* (Runco, 1995). It is also damaging and very likely would actually undermine creative work. That is so because if self-promotion and impression management are encouraged, nonsocial and personal expressions of creativity will suffer. Self-promotion is a *displaced investment* of one's time and energy (Runco, 1995). The more a person puts into self-promotion, the less he or she has available to invest in actual creative work. Time devoted to self-promotion is time away from creative thinking. It may help one's reputation but not one's creativity.

There are similar benefits to thinking parsimoniously about the dark side of creativity, but before introducing them, another aspect of Lord's (2007) biographic study of Von Braun should be noted. Lord uncovered something about values and creativity. The quotation above from Lord continues as follows:

> Von Braun was a cunning self-promoter, but he made one big mistake – allowing Hollywood to dramatize his life. Titled "I Aim at the Stars," the 1960 biopic is rarely mentioned today without comedian Mort Sahl's suggested subtitle: "But Sometimes I Hit London." ... Of necessity, the movie was mostly fiction. But one section rang true. When Von Braun tells his mother about the deal he cut with Hitler to fund his research, she says, "Long ago, they said witches made a pact with the devil, so they could fly on broomsticks." He replies: "My broomsticks fly without the devil's help. But if they didn't – I guess I'd be willing to sign with him."

This logic can be applied to many instances of *malevolent creativity*. After all, creative individuals are notoriously intrinsically motivated, and this description of Von Braun implies that nothing else may matter to some of them, as long as the work continues. That work may be immoral, but the creative individual could miss that, being so focused on exploring the originality of his or her work. This is the downside of intrinsic motivation.

A parsimonious view of creativity will separate self-promotion and other social effects from the personal determinants of creative insight. It will also separate divergent and original thinking from the values that come into play in judgments of malevolence. Simply put, a person can have the capacity for divergent, original, and creative thought along with the values that lead to malevolent creativity or along with the values that lead to benevolent creativity. Or that person may have less than average capacity for divergent, original, and creative thought along with those same two value orientations (one toward benevolence, the other toward malevolence). The values work with the capacity for creative thought but are extricable from it.

The extreme view of blind ideation holds that values only come into play after ideas are generated. But since ideation is a recursive process, with movement back and forth, from idea generation to idea evaluation and back again (Runco, 1994), it would be inaccurate to say that all options are produced (blindly), and then each of them is judged. This does not fit with the idea of recursion, and it may explain why brainstorming does not work well at all (Rickards & deCock, in press). More realistically, a person probably generates an idea (blindly) and then reacts to it based on values. If the idea has some potential relative to those values, the person may explore that line of thought further. The person will not invest the effort to do so unless it appears to be a valuable line of thought; this kind of investment and effort are necessary because the vast majority of good ideas are found only late and not early when thinking divergently (Mednick, 1962; Milgram & Rabkin, 1980). This is admittedly a brief description of the role of values. Dollinger, Burke, and Gump (2007) and Kasof, Chen, Himsel, and Greenberger (2007) presented much more detailed and compelling explanations.

INTENTIONS AND DECISION MAKING

Implicit in much of this chapter is that creativity depends heavily on intentions and decision making. This same conclusion was reached some time ago by Runco, Johnson, and Gaynor (1997) after reviewing a large amount of research, all of which indicated that creative thinking depends on judgment. It is frequently directed and highly intentional. Gruber (1993) and Runco (1993) later tied intentions to creativity in the moral domain. This conclusion should be underscored because it is so practical. After all, if creative work is intentional and depends on the decisions and subsequent investments one makes, a great deal can be done about it. Presumably something can be done to direct creative thinking toward benevolence and away from malevolence! Keep in mind that this emphasis on decision making and intentions is entirely consistent with the notion presented earlier that the creative process should be kept separate from the results of the process. Intentions and decisions will merely direct the process.

WHAT CREATIVITY IS AND WHAT IT IS NOT

This brings us back to the definition of creativity. The definition presented here looks to parsimony and causality and thus emphasizes the process that underlies all creativity. Admittedly, this view is at odds with several theories and definitions. Most notable are the claims about the dark side of creativity that view products or other manifestations as prerequisites. These define creativity in terms of impact and effects. This may be so because the intent is to be maximally scientific, and this in turn leads to objectivity, which means that things (products) must be studied because they can be counted and quantified. Much headway has been made applying the scientific method to creativity, but much will be lost if the cause is equated with the effect and the creative process is equated with its products.

The parsimonious view of creativity presented in this chapter is also incompatible with the theories that assume that malevolence is a part of human nature (Hobbes' claim about the natural wickedness of humanity, Calvinism, and Freud's *Thanatos* come to mind) and at odds with several psychological perspectives in this same volume. Gascón and Kaufman (Chapter 13 in this volume), for example, suggested (p. 242) that "it would be incorrect to suggest that all creative behavior is deviant, just as it is incorrect to suggest that all deviant behavior is creative." Earlier I proposed much the opposite in part because the role of originality (and thus the value of deviance) means that creativity can be subsumed under deviance, and deviance does not need to be subsumed under creativity. There is no reason to require bidirectionality for creativity and deviance. The fact that all creative things are original means that all creative things are deviant. Recall here the discussion about deviance as meaning only that something is outside the norm.

The different definitions of creativity are at least as obvious when Gascón and Kaufman (Chapter 13 in this volume) proposed (p. 241) that there are four criteria for judgments of creative things: relevance to a particular goal, originality, elegance ("the product is fully worked out or well engineered"), and generalizability. Given the inclusion of originality, it would not be possible to exclude deviance from creativity; but putting that aside, it would seem that a definition of creativity with those four features only applies to a subset of all creative things. It has the same limitations as other social, product definitions. It ignores personal insights and indeed all of personal creativity (Maslow, 1973; Richards, 1990; Rogers, 1954; Runco, 1995, 1996, 2003). It ignores most instances of *everyday creativity* (Lemons, 2005; Richards, 1990). It ignores the creativity of children that may not generalize beyond their own lives, nor indeed beyond any one particular situation.

We might simply conclude that the definition presented here applies to the creative process, whereas the definition (and criteria) of Gascón and Kaufman (Chapter 13 in this volume) applies to products. Yet Gascón and Kaufman themselves wrote (p. 242), "such behavior [benevolent creativity] is the product of a creative problem-solving process and personality is the mechanism through which it is expressed. Though artworks may be creative given that they are crafted employing innovative processes, the cognitive problem-solving process itself is creative." Hence there is disagreement about underlying processes.

Parsimonious creativity requires separation from problem solving. Summarizing earlier arguments for this separation, (a) there are several kinds of problem solving that do not involve creativity (for instance, those that have mundane, unoriginal, convergent, or preexisting solutions), (b) creativity often requires more than just solving a problem (for instance, identifying or defining a problem before solutions are even considered), and (c) some kinds of creativity do not involve any sort of problems (for instance, self-expression, exploration for the sake of exploration, imaginative play) (Runco, 1994). None of this implies that creativity is entirely independent of problem solving. It simply means that they should not be equated. They are extricable, which is necessary for a good scientific theory.

The differences of opinion just reviewed – including the role of deviance, the relationship between creativity and problem solving, and the most reasonable definition of creativity – may seem superficial, as if they are merely semantic. If this were the case, something I suggested long ago would solve all problems and minimize disagreement. My suggestion was to stop using the noun "creativity" in the scientific study of creativity. Clearly, it is ambiguous, sometimes referring to processes (as is the case in this chapter) and sometimes to products (as is required by theories that see a dark side). The solution is to only use the adjective "creative." This would require that there be a specific noun being modified by that adjective; it would require admirable specificity. Scientific studies then could examine creative products, creative traits, creative thinking, creative achievement, creative solutions, and so on. The ambiguity resulting from the noun "creativity" could in this way be avoided.

CONCLUSIONS

The dark side of creativity can be refuted in several ways. The most fundamental argument is that it is parsimonious and therefore scientifically tenable to look at the creative process and at creative capacity (and potential) rather than at eventual creative products. The products are the results of the process and so more like symptoms (an appropriate word for malevolent creativity) than causal factors. Second is that the creative process is blind and only supplies original options and ideas. These are often deviant, but only in the sense of being unusual and unconventional, not in any immoral or unethical manner. The morality of the options can be determined (and an influence, for that matter) only after the ideas are produced, that is, after the generative process that is the engine for creative work.

The idea that the creative process is blind has implications for the clinical question of treating creative persons who suffer from alcoholism, depression, or any sort of psychopathology. Some question the ethics of treating such persons because if creativity is functionally related to the problem(s) or disturbance, treatment may inhibit the creativity and thereby interfere with a positive aspect of the clients' lives or even (in the case of professional artists or others who rely on creative talents) their livelihood. There would seem to be clinical benefits if treatment could focus on the stages in the creative process that are tied to disturbance and avoid the stages that are involved only in creative thinking. There are reasons to believe that this cannot be done, at least with some of the affective disorders (Rothenberg, 1990). Maybe it can be done with the more superficial tendencies of graffiti and art vandalism (Norlander, Nordmarker, & Archer, 1998, 2000; Spooner, 2008).

Creativity will never be fully understood if we view it as problem solving, it will only manifest in products (that come late in the day, if at all, in many creative efforts), and if deviance (statistically speaking) is excluded. The trick is to recognize that creativity is a form of deviance and then determine how and why it is sometimes used in a benevolent way and sometimes in a malevolent way. Once that is determined, efforts can be directed at encouraging the former and discouraging the latter. My suggestion in this chapter was to focus on intentions and decision making when encouraging creativity. Tolerance also was recommended. Clearly, there are ways to support creativity that is likely to be benevolent and unlikely to be malevolent.

REFERENCES

Aries, P. (1973). *Centuries of childhood.* New York: Penguin.

Barron, F. (1993). Controlled weirdness. *Psychological Inquiry,* 4, 182–184.

Becker, G. (1999). Mad genius. In M. A. Runco & S. Pritzker (Eds.), *Encyclopedia of creativity.* San Diego, CA: Elsevier.

Benedict, R. (1989/1934). *Patterns of culture.* New York: Mariner Books.

Bergson, H. (2002/1946). *The creative mind.* New York: Citadel.

Bower, R. (1999). Dangerous minds: Eminently creative people who have spent time in jail. *Creativity Research Journal,* 12, 3–13.

Bruner J. 1962. The conditions of creativity. In J. Bruner (Ed.), *On knowing: Essays for the left hand.* Cambridge, MA: Harvard Univ. Press.

Campbell, D. T. (1960). Blind variation and selective retention in creative thought as in other knowledge processes. *Psychological Review*, 67, 380–400.

Cropley, D. H., Kaufman, J. C., & Cropley, A. J. (2008). Malevolent creativity: A functional model of creativity in terrorism and crime. *Creativity Research Journal*, 20, 105–115.

Dollinger, S., Burke, P A., & Gump, N. W. (2007). Creativity and values. *Creativity Research Journal*, 19, 91–103.

Gardner, H. (1993). *Creating minds: An anatomy of creativity seen through the lives of Freud, Einstein, Picasso, Stravinsky, Eliot, Graham, and Gandhi*. New York: Basic Books.

Gould, S. J. (1991). *Bully for Brontosaurus*. New York: Norton.

Gruber, H. E. (1993). Creativity in the moral domain: Ought implies can implies create. *Creativity Research Journal*, 6, 3–15.

Guilford, J. P. (1968). *Creativity, intelligence and their educational implications*. San Diego, CA: EDITS/Knapp.

Gutbezahl, J. & Averill R. J. (1996). Individual differences in emotional creativity as manifested in words and pictures. *Creativity Research Journal*, 9, 327–337.

Jones, K., Runco, M. A., Dorinan, C., & Freeland, D. C. (1997). Influential factors in artists' lives and themes in their art work. *Creativity Research Journal*, 10, 221–228.

Kasof, J. (1995). Explaining creativity: The attributional perspective. *Creativity Research Journal*, 8, 311–366.

Kasof, J., Chen, C., Himsel, A. & Greenberger, E. (2007). Values and creativity. *Creativity Research Journal*, 19, 105–122.

Kohlberg, L. (1987). The development of moral judgment and moral action. In L. Kohlberg (Ed.), *Child psychology and childhood education: A cognitive developmental view*. New York: Longman.

Lazarus, R. S. (1991). Cognition and motivation in emotion. *American Psychologist*, 46, 352–367.

Lemons, G. (2005). When the horse drinks: Enhancing everyday creativity using elements of improvisation. *Creativity Research Journal*,17, 25–36.

Lord, M. G. (2007). A look at Wernher von Braun, patriarch of U.S. rocketry, Nazi past and all. *Review of Von Braun: Dreamer of Space, Engineer of War*, by Michael J. Neufeld. *Los Angeles Times Book Review*. Available at www.latimes.com/features/books/la-bk-lord23sep23,0,4789920.story?coll=la-books-headlines; accessed September 23, 2007.

Lumsden, C. J. & Findlay, S. C. (1988). Evolution of the creative mind. *Creativity Research Journal*, 1, 75–92.

Maslow, A. H. (1973). Creativity in self-actualizing people. In A. Rothenberg and C. R. Hausman (Eds.), *The creative question* (pp. 86–92). Durham, NC: Duke University Press.

Maugh, T. H. (2009). Venus figurine sheds light on origins of art by early humans. *Los Angeles Times Science*. Available at www.latimes.com/news/nationworld/nation/la–sci–venus14–2009may14,0,181830.story. Accessed on May 14, 2009.

Mednick, S.A. (1962). The associative basis of the creative process. *Psychological Review*, 69, 222–232.

McLaren, R. B. (1993). The dark side of creativity. *Creativity Research Journal*, 6, 137–144.

Milgram, R. M. & Rabkin, L. (1980). Developmental test of Mednick's associative hierarchies of original thinking. *Developmental Psychology*, 16, 157–158.

Norlander, T., Nordmarker A., & Archer, T. (1998). Effects of alcohol and frustration on experimental graffiti. *Scandinavian Journal of Psychology*, 39, 201–207.

Nordmarker, A., Norlander, T., & Archer, T. (2000). The effects of alcohol intake and induced frustration upon art vandalism. *Social Behavior and Personality*, 28, 15–28.

Richards, R. (1990). Everyday creativity, eminent creativity, and health: Afterview for CRJ issues on creativity and health. *Creativity Research Journal*, 3, 300–326.

Rickards, T. & deCock, C. (in press). Understanding organizational creativity: Towards a multiparadigmatic approach. In M. A. Runco (Ed.), *Creativity research handbook* (vol. 2). Cresskill, NJ: Hampton Press.

Rogers, C. R. (1954/1959). Toward a theory of creativity. In H. H. Anderson (Ed.), *Creativity and its cultivation* (pp. 69–82). New York: Harper & Row.

Rosenblatt, E. & Winner, E. (1988). The art of children's drawings. *Journal of Aesthetic Education*, 22, 3–15.

Rothenberg A. 1990. Creativity, mental health, and alcoholism. *Creativity Research Journal*, 3, 179–201.

Runco, M. A. (1988). Creativity research: Originality, utility, and integration. *Creativity Research Journal*, 1, 1–7.

(1989). Parents' and teachers' ratings of the creativity of children. *Journal of Social Behavior and Personality*, 4, 73–83.

(Ed.). (1991). *Divergent thinking*. Norwood, NJ: Ablex Publishing Corporation.

(1993). Moral creativity: Intentional and unconventional. *Creativity Research Journal*, 6, 17–28.

(1994). Conclusions concerning problem finding, problem solving, and creativity. In M. A. Runco (Ed.), *Problem finding, problem solving, and creativity* (pp. 272–290). Norwood, NJ: Ablex.

(1995). Insight for creativity, expression for impact. *Creativity Research Journal*, 8, 377–390.

(1996). Creativity and development: Recommendations. *New Directions for Child Development*, 72, 87–90.

(2003). Education for creative potential. *Scandinavian Journal of Education*, 47, 317–324.

(2007). A hierarchical framework for the study of creativity. *New Horizons in Education*, 55(3), 1–9.

(2010). Parsimonious creativity and its measurement. In E. Villalba (Ed.), *Measuring creativity: Proceedings of European Council meeting on creativity and innovation* (pp. 393–405). Luxembourg: Publications Office of the European Union.

(Ed.). (In press-a). *Divergent and creative thinking.* Cresskill, NJ: Hampton Press.

(in press-b). Divergent thinking. In R. J. Sternberg, & J. Kaufman (Eds.), *Handbook of creativity* (2nd ed.). New York: Cambridge University Press.

Runco, M. A. & Albert, R. S. (In press). Creativity research: A history. In R. J. Sternberg, & J. Kaufman (Eds.), *Handbook of creativity research.* New York: Cambridge University Press.

Runco M.A. & Basadur, M. (1993). Assessing ideational and evaluative skills and creative styles and attitudes. *Creativity and Innovation Management,* 2, 166–173.

Runco, M. A., Johnson, D., & Gaynor, J. R. (1997). The judgmental bases of creativity and implications for the study of gifted youth. In A. Fishkin, B. Cramond, & P. Olszewski-Kubilius (Eds.), *Creativity in youth: Research and methods.* Cresskill, NJ: Hampton Press.

Runco, M. A., Kaufman, J. C., Halladay, L. R., & Cole, J. C. (in press). Change in reputation as index of genius and eminence. *Historical Methods.*

Runco, M. A. & Shaw, M. P. (1994). Conclusions concerning creativity and affect. In M. P. Shaw & M. A. Runco (Eds.), *Creativity and affect* (pp. 261–270). Norwood, NJ: Ablex.

Runco, M. A. & Smith, W. R. (1992). Interpersonal and intrapersonal evaluations of creative ideas. *Personality and Individual Differences,* 13, 295–302.

Runco, M. A. & Vega, L. (1990). Evaluating the creativity of children's ideas. *Journal of Social Behavior and Personality,* 5, 439–452.

Simonton, D. K. (2008). The creative process in Picasso's *Guernica* sketches: Monotonic improvements versus nonmonotonic variants. *Creativity Research Journal,* 20, 329–344.

Spooner, M. T. (2008). Commentary on malevolent creativity. *Creativity Research Journal,* 20, 128–129.

Stein, M. I. (1993). Moral issues facing intermediaries between creators and the public. *Creativity Research Journal,* 6. 197–200.

Torrance, E. P. (1995). *Why fly?* Norwood, NJ: Ablex.

Tweney, R. D. (1996). Presymbolic processes in scientific creativity. *Creativity Research Journal,* 9, 163–172.

Zajonc, R. B. (1980). Feeling and thinking: Preferences need no inferences. *American Psychologist,* 35, 151–175.

3

Positive Creativity and Negative Creativity (and Unintended Consequences)

KEITH JAMES AND AISHA TAYLOR

THE UTILITY OF DISTINGUISHING POSITIVE AND NEGATIVE CREATIVITY

Creativity is important to the lone soul; to groups large, small, formal, and informal; and to whole societies and cultures (Csikszentmihalyi, 1999). To capitalize on creativity, however, individuals, organizations, and societies need to understand how different types of people will respond, as far as creativity goes, to different conditions and tasks (Amabile, 1996).

Virtually all existing empirical and theoretical work on creativity to this point, however, has either explicitly focused on or implicitly assumed only positive outcomes from creativity (James, Clark, & Cropanzano, 1999; McLaren, 1993, 1999). That is, creativity is seen as the production of *beneficial products* (concrete or abstract) by novel means. Discussions of creativity tend to assume that it is always socially desirable. Although a few individuals have mentioned the possibility of negative creativity, that side of creativity has received relatively little research or theoretical attention. Creativity can, though, produce results that are damaging or unpleasant to other individuals, to groups, or to society at large.

Both the most widely used definitions of creativity and the full range of real-world instances of it indicate that creativity does not necessarily produce positive effects. Probably the most widely used definition of creativity is the generation of products or problem solutions that are both *novel* and *useful* (Amabile, 1996; James et al., 1999; Runco, 1991). Usefulness is subjective; what is useful to me could be either useless or harmful to you. Individuals can, and sometimes do, work on developing creative means toward negative ends, such as devising new ways of stealing from a company that will go undetected, finding creative ways to undermine an enemy, or developing schemes for gaining undeserved rewards. Groups and organizations also sometimes seek creative ways of accomplishing negative ends, such as evading regulations, abstracting industrial secrets from competitors, or making money by stealing from or otherwise abusing people (Fritzsche & Becker, 1984; Velasquez. 1982). The recent case of Bernard Madoff and his pyramid-scheme robbery of friends and charities provides an obvious example. If the means to these negative ends are relatively novel and the ends themselves are useful (or desirable) to the actor, then the criteria in this common definition of creativity would be met.

Another standard definition of creativity is that it is a relatively unique idea or behavior that achieves some purpose (goal) or is somehow appropriate to a situation (Weisberg, 1993). Goals can have either a positive or a negative focus. Goals can be hostile or unethical, focused on hurting, cheating, or subverting. Thus, based on the second definition of creativity just given, taking unique approaches to even negative goals of the sort in these examples still would be creative. McLaren (1993) argued that there is a general distorted stereotype about creativity that causes us typically to ignore the fact that a significant amount of creative effort is in service of negative ends. He gives a number of examples, such as technologies like the neutron bomb (or, in U.S. Department of Defense jargon, the "anti-personnel radiation device," itself a creative bit of obfuscation) that certainly have widespread negative implications regardless of their apparent value to those who commission or produce them. For every application of creativity to furthering the exploration of the universe or to curing an illness, there is an application to seizing land from enemies who hold it or to wheedling undeserved money from people (e.g., Bernard Madoff) or to retaliating against someone who has given offense.

The benefits of studying positive creativity are somewhat obvious: understanding of important, basic cognitive and group processes as well as the applied benefits such understanding might promote. The same potential benefits could accrue from studying negative creativity. Research on creativity generally is argued to have value because it will help to give us insight into how to teach, apply, and manage an important resource – human creativity (Amabile, 1996; Csikszentmihalyi, 1999). If it makes sense to try to understand how we might make the positive benefits of creativity more likely, it also makes sense to try to understand how we might minimize its negative manifestations. Where the negative side of creativity has been discussed at all in the literature to this point, the focus typically is purely descriptive (e.g., Amabile, 1989; Maslow, 1970; McLaren, 1993, 1999); virtually no attention has been given to when, why, or how it occurs or how we might minimize it while maximizing positive forms of creativity.

The potential value of better knowledge of negative creativity is clear, however, from events such as the September 11, 2001, terrorist attacks on the people and government of the United States. At the time of those attacks, air transport security systems hijacking-response policies were geared toward preventing the smuggling of guns onto passenger planes along with policies geared toward presumed terrorist goals of extortion or exchange of passengers for political prisoners. The September 11 terrorists, however, had generated approaches to seizing planes that did not involve guns, and their goals in seizing them involved turning them into weapons. Clark and James (1999) cite another example, one in which a computer scientist who had been fired by his company developed (apparently, since definitive evidence was never found because of the very creativity of the method) a novel approach to deleting most of the companies digital files as a means of retaliating for being fired. That example illustrates that negative creativity is potentially relevant to many organizations and types of work, not just to major events such as terrorism.

Better understanding of negative creativity is needed to help identify the types of people most likely to generate such damaging new ideas, the types of circumstances that promote their development, ways of analyzing particular situations for vulnerabilities to negative creative approaches, and countermeasures that might mitigate or prevent the harm that such approaches potentially could produce (James & Clark, 2009; James et al., 1999). Schneier (2000) provides a number of examples, ranging from cell phone manufacturers to operators of state lotteries, of failure to anticipate actual threats to systems or technologies that typically were accompanied by allocation of great time and cost on measures designed to guard against what turned out to be the "wrong" threat. Schneier (2000, p. 288) states the problem of designing security approaches succinctly as: "If you don't know [the real threats against the system], how do you know what kind of countermeasures to employ?" To deal with negative creativity relative to terrorism, the Committee on Science and Technology for Countering Terrorism (CSTCT, 2002, p. 214) of the National Academy of Sciences argued that what is needed is more "unconventional thinking" about both potential terrorist threats and potential responses. Research promoting understanding of influences on and processes of both negative and positive creativity will facilitate those outcomes. In this chapter we seek to analyze the circumstances and individual and collective characteristics that help to determine whether creativity will be directed toward doing good or doing evil.

The assumption that creativity is positive has influenced both laypeople and creativity theorists such that few acknowledge the possibility of negative creativity. In fact, outcome measures of creativity have focused almost exclusively on positive achievements, ideas, or products (James et al., 1999). Similarly, theorists and researchers have failed to attend to the influences that might trigger negative types of creativity. Obviously, the triggers, processes, outcomes, and even fundamental existence of creativity in service of negative ends will be difficult to understand if they are never examined. We also should differentiate negative creativity from unintended negative consequences of creativity intended to achieve positive ends. Murray (2003) discusses how Einstein did not intend to aid the development of nuclear weapons with his early work that is summarized by his $e = mc^2$ equation, yet facilitate it he did. Similarly, the inventors of the internal combustion engine were not trying to achieve air pollution and climate change, but their creative work did, nonetheless, substantially increase those things (Murray, 2003). The negative consequences in the preceding two examples were unintended consequences of efforts undertaken with positive goals in mind. As Murray stated, "What belongs in the hall of fame of unintended consequences … then, are otherwise wonderful accomplishments that inadvertently contributed to some truly awful outcomes."

Some might ask, Is this approach to defining positive and negative creativity scientifically valid? That is, concluding that some creativity is positive and some is negative requires a value judgment, and does that not remove this distinction from the realm of science? Certainly distinguishing between positive and negative creativity does implicate values, but usefulness and novelty are also constructs that always imply some value- or experienced-based judgment. This has not, though, stopped them from being very widely used in theories and research on creativity (see, e.g., Amabile, 1996; Baas, De Dreu, & Nijstad, 2008; Davis, 2009) because there is scientific and applied utility to doing so. We hope, in this chapter, to demonstrate that the constructs of positive and negative creativity also have scientific and real-world utility.

A related criticism would be that if some individual or group has a goal and devises a way of achieving it, this is always positive from the actor's perspective. Yet, from some people's, often most other people's (as with the September 11, 2001, terrorist attacks), points of view, the outcome of some instances of creativity is clearly bad. Thus whether any instance of creativity should be labeled as "good" or "bad" is inherently dependent on the point of view one adopts in examining it. Scientists generally take the perspective of attempting to maximize good outcomes for the greatest possible number of people. From this perspective, creative approaches to achieving goals desired by some individual or group that nonetheless yields substantial harm for others reasonably *can* be characterized as negative. Similar approaches are being taken with other (than creative) individual and team performance outcomes, such as organizational deviance, which is viewed as the flip (i.e., negative) side of organizational citizenship (e.g., Henle, 2005; see also Berry, Ones, & Sackett, 2007, for a meta-analysis of deviance at both the individual and collective levels); social undermining, which is viewed as the opposite of social support (see, e.g., Duffy, Ganster, & Pagon, 2002); and dis-stress, which is viewed as the opposite of eu-stress (beneficial) (Lazarus, 1966).

The negative aspect of some creative effects is clear even from the perspective of the creative actor because some instances of creativity are driven by creators' goals of harming, hindering, harassing, destroying, or achieving unfair or undeserved advantage. Positive creativity, on the other hand, is characterized by intent to achieve some positive purpose by benign or positive means. This attends to the goal aspect of some definitions of creativity and indicates that goals sensibly can be categorized generally on the basis of whether their underlying motivational (i.e., emotional) component is positive or negative. As McLaren (1993) states, creativity "cannot be fully understood, any more than … any other human endeavor, apart from its socio-moral context and intent." Thus positive and negative creativity can be distinguished in part based on the *type of outcome goal* toward which ingenuity is directed. Whereas the goals in positive creativity involve solving problems or improving processes or products, those of negative creativity involve intent to do harm to or to exploit individuals, groups, institutions, or organizations (James et al., 1999). That such outcomes are mediated by the affective tone (Figure 3.1, top box) of the goals is indicated by research showing that situationally induced positive emotional states promote positive creativity (Baas et al., 2008; Davis, 2009). While the relationship of negative affect to negative creativity essentially has not been studied (see, however, James & Clark, 2009, and Lutenberg, 2005), that relationship has not been established empirically. Negative emotions have been shown, though, to trigger a variety of other negative behaviors such as aggression and theft (e.g., Greenberg, 1993; Giacalone & Greenberg, 1997; Miller & Lynam, 2001). So it seems reasonable to assume that goals that are tinged with largely negative affect will trigger negative forms of creativity.

Clearly, the challenge for society is to increase the number and strength of factors that promote positive forms of creativity while reducing the number and strength of factors that promote negative creativity. Doing so requires incorporating the positive/negative dimension into creativity

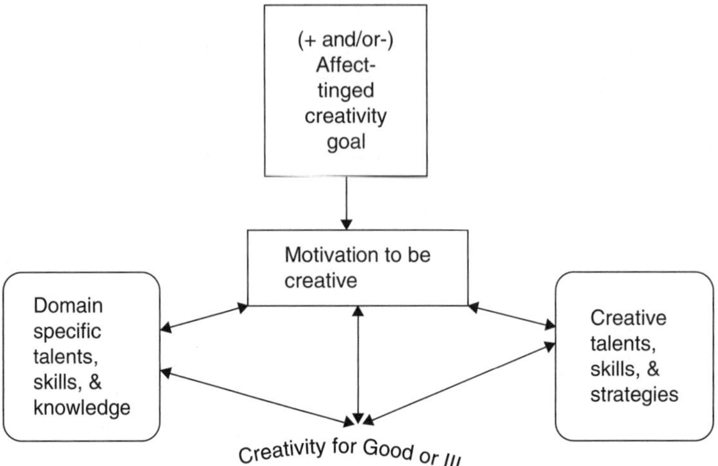

FIGURE 3.1. Modified version of Amabile's model of influences on creative production.

theory and research. Moreover, to the extent that different external or internal factors trigger positive and negative creativity, there will be theoretical and applied value in distinguishing between the two types.

MAJOR POSITIVE ASPECTS OF POSITIVE AND NEGATIVE CREATIVITY

Figure 3.1 takes Teresa Amabile's (1996) model of influences on individual creativity (which also can be applied to collective creativity) and adds the concepts of positive and negative goals to them, as well as adding positive and negative creative outputs as potential results of the creative process. The top three levels of Figure 3.1 show four major factors influencing whether positive or negative creativity will occur. Let us begin with the top-level affect-tinged goal, along with its link to the center box in the subsequent level – that is, "Motivation to be creative." Motivation provides the energy or drive that activates and sustains application of domain (level 2, far left in Figure 3.1) and creative (level 2, far right in Figure 3.1) knowledge, skills, and abilities (KSAs) toward creative (abstract – e.g., problem-solving – or concrete) production (lowest level of Figure 3.1). Goals have been strongly and consistently shown to relate to both the *levels* of motivation that individuals experience and the purposes (i.e., productive outcomes) toward which motivation will be directed (Mento, Steele, & Karren, 1987; Rawsthorne & Elliot, 1999).

Personality can be defined as a particular pattern of goals that vary across individuals, and individuals' idiosyncratic goal patterns substantially influence general thinking and behavioral and emotional tendencies (e.g., Cropanzano, James, & Citera, 1993; Pervin, 1983, 2001). Individuals plainly vary in the types, strength, and configuration of goals held; in ways of thinking about and evaluating the world; and in characteristic moods and emotional reactions. And these three things are related (McCrae & Costa, 1997; Pervin, 2001). Because it devolves from how the mind is organized and involves habitual thought patterns, personality blurs into cognition, even though psychologists and other scientists who investigate creativity generally treat the two separately (e.g., Judge, Bono, Erez, Locke, & Thoresen, 2002; McCrae & Costa, 1997). Similarly, even though there is wide acknowledgment that emotion and cognition overlap substantially, we generally treat emotion as if it were distinct from cognition in studies of creativity because doing so aids theoretical analysis and research.

The consensus view of modern psychologists is that thinking and affect shape each other in reciprocal cycles. Clearly, too, thoughts and emotions influence behavior. Development of, and applications on, goals are in themselves clearly influenced by thoughts and emotions. Goals and what happens during pursuit of them also influence emotions and thinking. So patterns on one of these things tend to reverberate through them all. The pattern of the reverberation is the root of the combination of psychological characteristics and behavior style that we call *personality.* Personality is the distinctive weave of behavioral, affective, thought, and goal patterns that makes for individuality (Eysenck, 1995; Pervin, 1983).

Goals focused on *negative* outcomes (e.g., to damage materials or harm people) can be responses to situations or they can be relatively enduring – that is, dispositional. That individuals differ in general tendencies toward positive or negative emotions is a robust result of decades of research on personality (e.g., Brown & Marshall, 2001; Watson, Clark, & Tellegen, 1988). In particular, the "Big Five" model (i.e., McCrae & Costa, 1997) indicates that human personality can be usefully subdivided into five general dimensions: (O) openness to experience (imagination, curiosity, and intellectualism), (C) conscientiousness (impulse control, planning, and organization), (E) extraversion (sociable and outgoing), (A) agreeableness (altruism and empathy), and (N) neuroticism (psychological maladjustment and more experiences of unpleasant emotions). Openness to experience (positively) and conscientiousness (negatively) are the two "Big Five" factors that have been shown most consistently to be related to (positive, because it is all that has been assessed) creativity (Feist, 1998). Feist (1998) meta-analyzed studies of personality and creativity and found that openness to experience (positively) and conscientiousness (negatively) had the strongest relationships of any of the "Big Five" factors to creativity. The more specific personality characteristics of hostility, self-acceptance, and impulsivity also had notable significant (and all positive) relationships to creative performance in Feist's meta-analysis. The studies analyzed, however, did not include assessment of creativity on both positively and negatively directed tasks.

Neuroticism is a "Big Five" personality dimension that differentiates individuals according to their general inclinations toward positive versus negative feeling states. If our argument for emotion shaping the positive or negative direction of creativity is accurate, individuals generally inclined toward negative emotion also should show more negative than positive creativity, whereas those generally inclined toward positive emotion should show more positive than negative creativity. That is, dispositional affect will influence the type of creativity that individuals are inclined toward and will do so largely by influencing the types of creative goals individuals will tend to develop. Those who are generally more subject to negative affect will tend to develop negative creative goals and engage in negative creative activity. Those who are by nature more subject to positive affect will tend to develop positive creative goals and engage in positive creative activity. This has received little direct research attention (again, because the entire concept of negative creative performance has been largely ignored by scientists), but there is significant indirect evidence supporting it.

Miller and Lynam (2001) report a meta-analytic review that supported a relationship of relatively low levels of the (social) agreeableness dimension of the "Big Five" personality taxonomy to criminal behavior. Bellah, Bellah, and Johnson (2003) provide evidence that individuals who are both relatively low in agreeableness and relatively high in neuroticism exhibit relatively high levels of vengefulness (which Bellah and colleagues define as a tendency to obtain satisfaction from retaliation for real or perceived wrongs done by others). This is congruent with the proposal by James and colleagues (1999) about the potential role of personality tendencies in whether creativity will be directed toward positive or negative ends. In particular, James and colleagues argued that negative dispositional (and/or situational) affect combined with a goal of being creative is likely to produce negative creativity, whereas positive dispositional (and/or situational) affect combined with a goal of being creative is likely to produce positive creativity.

We agree with this possibility, but we want to extend it and add another potential mechanism to it. Our extension (congruent with Miller and Lynam's meta-analysis, as well as with literature on topics such as organizational deviance) is that the negative-affect component of negative creativity probably needs to be directed specifically at outside targets. That is, negative emotions such as depression (i.e., negative feelings directed at self or one's life circumstances) are unlikely to drive negative creativity. We also argue, however, that some negative creativity may be driven primarily not by negative affect toward others but by excessively positive affect (e.g., narcissism or grandiosity) toward self. This is, in fact, congruent both with the positive relationship of the self-acceptance personality characteristics to creativity of Feist's meta-analysis, with Gough (1979) finding that the creative personality tends to include relatively high egotism, and with the literature on sociopaths (sometimes called *psychopaths*), which indicates that some of them have chronic hostility toward others, whereas some lack chronic hostility and are characterized instead by a high general belief in their own importance, value, and deservingness (see Cleckley, 1976 for the classic analysis of sociopathology). Such feelings may, if combined with a creativity goal and appropriate creative and domain KSAs, lead to negative creativity not in service of harming others but in service of gaining positive outcomes for self that are felt to be the psychopath's due by any means necessary.

Creative and Domain Skills in Positive and Negative Creativity

In addition to influencing whether action goals are likely to be directed toward positive ends or toward negative ones, personality also influences the development of and inclination to generally apply creative KSAs (far right side of the modified Amabile model in Figure 3.1). Hayes and Bond (1981; see also Amabile, 1996) stated that dispositional goals that emphasize either creative or noncreative performance are a critical influence on individual differences in creativity. He argued that rather than cognitive abilities, it is motivational differences that distinguish creative from noncreative individuals. Gough (1979) found evidence supporting this in the validation studies for his Creative Personality Inventory (which is derived from the California Personality Inventory, which also can be used to derive scores for the "Big Five" personality factors). Gough found, for instance, that individuals with a relatively high output of real-life creativity (e.g., professional architects) endorsed originality more so and conformity less so than did samples of the general college population. In fact, from the personality perspective, those who are generally creative tend to have originality (novelty) of thinking and action as an overarching goal (Eysenck, 1995; Gough, 1979).

Individual differences in creativity also derive, however, from dispositional differences in creative KSAs. Eysenck (1995), for instance, found that more creative (but "normal") individuals had significantly more close relatives who had been diagnosed with clinical thought disorders than did noncreative people. He argued that creative types possess a genetic predisposition toward the unusual (i.e., novel) thinking patterns that, taken to an extreme, also made some of their relatives clinically insane. Similarly, the openness to experience "Big Five" factor has the strongest positive correlation with creativity, and while it includes some elements of motivational inclinations, it also reflects some distinctive patterns of perception and thinking that aid creativity (Bellah et al., 2003; Eysenck, 1995; Feist, 1998; McCrae & Costa, 1997). Individuals differing on openness to experience differ in their general, relatively stable levels of creative KSAs, such as sensitivity to opportunities in the environment for creative success or ability to generate a large volume of ideas that are potentially applicable to any given problem or situation (Amabile, 1996; Runco, 1991).

Kim (2005) conducted a meta-analysis of studies of creativity and IQ and concluded that the relationship between the two was "negligible." Hetland (2001) conducted 10 meta-analyses of the relationship between training in or practice of various creative arts (e.g., music, dance, visual art) to KSAs in different noncreative cognitive skill domains (e.g., spatial ability, verbal ability, and logical analysis skill). She found that musical training/performance experience had a moderate ($p > .24$, $p < .37$) relationship to spatial ability and that engaging in dramatic productions of literary texts had a moderate relationship to verbal abilities. In the other seven meta-analyses (between, for example, visual arts training or practice and visual-spatial KSAs), the relationships between creative training and practice and noncreative thinking KSAs were nonsignificant. These results substantially support the idea that creative KSAs and noncreative KSAs are largely independent of each other.

Forgas (1995, 2000) affect infusion model (AIM) indicates that those with greater need for cognition are more influenced by affective inputs than are those low in the need for cognition in setting goals, evaluating information, and other aspects of thinking; Cacioppo, Petty, Feinstein and Jarvis (1996) review supporting evidence. The "Big Five" dimension of openness to experience includes need (or desire) for cognition among its components (Eysenck, 1995; McCrae & Costa, 1997); thus individuals high in openness seem to be both more inclined toward creative thinking than those low in it and more susceptible to situational influences on goals and behavioral regulation. It may be that both the personality and circumstantial factors that activate creative KSAs also tend to deactivate algorithmic approaches to information processing and behavioral control (Bellah et al., 2003; James, 1995; James et al., 1999). Such effects may be mediated by certain affective states, including frustration or distress. For instance, several researchers and theorists (e.g., Luchins & Luchins, 1959; Tardif and Sternberg, 1988) have proposed that creativity may be partially the result of feelings of frustration triggered by perceptions that standard approaches are not succeeding in a particular situation. Similarly, James (1995) and James, Chen, and Goldberg (1992) argued that perceived conflicts between personal goals can enhance creativity by redirecting thinking away from more "standard" approaches that are not working in a given situation and toward generation of more novel approaches that might help to address the situation or problem tied to the perceived goal conflict (for a broadly comparable but mechanistically divergent approach, see De Dreu, Baas, & Nijstad, 2008).

Clark and James (1999) found that perceptions of injustice led individuals to generate more creative ideas directed toward a harmful or malevolent goal – what they (and James et al., 1999) termed *negative creativity* – at the same time as it *reduced* creativity directed toward a positive goal. An ability to generate a high volume of ideas for the negative task also partially mediated the effect of perceived injustice on expert-rated negative creativity in Clark and James (1999), but the volume of *positive ideas* participants generated did not mediate (expert-rated) positive originality. James (1995) and Mumford and Gustafson (1988) reviewed research indicating that higher numbers of ideas generated on a task (generally referred to as *fluidity* of thinking) tend to be associated with greater originality of ideas.

It is possible, in fact, that positive affect (and goals) and negative affect (and goals) each can facilitate creative KSAs but do so differentially. Vosburg (1998), for instance, found that the affect-creativity relationship is task-specific. In her study, positive affect was related to the generation of a greater *quantity* of solutions to a problem-solving task, whereas subjects in the negative-affect group showed a greater *quality* of solutions. It was concluded that people in a positive mood adopt a "satisficing" strategy (i.e., constructing a simplified version of the problem and discussing many solutions), and people in a negative mood adopt an "optimizing" strategy (i.e., exploring the criteria of the problem and trying to find the best possible solution). This theory is also supported by the findings of Martin,

Ward, Achee, and Wyer (1993). In their study, people in a positive mood were found to lower their criteria for an acceptable solution and spent less time generating ideas, whereas people in a negative mood raised their criteria and spent more time on task.

While two recent meta-analyses (Baas et al., 2008; Davis, 2009) have indicated that only positive affect facilitates creative thinking, all the studies included in those meta-analyses focused only on positive creative tasks, and most examined fluency or flexibility of thinking as a creative outcome. In line with our general argument for the importance of scientists attending to the possibility of negative creativity, the results of those meta-analyses provide no answer to the question of whether negative goals yield different influences than do positive goals on the functioning of creative KSAs because neither negative creative goals and tasks nor the full range of creative KSAs were included in the line of research included in the meta-analyses. An earlier meta-analysis (Schwenk, 1990) of the effects of the devil's advocacy technique for introducing social conflict into the task-performance process did, in fact, find that devil's advocacy seemed to improve performance on ill-defined (i.e., creative) tasks but not on well-defined (i.e., noncreative ones). The (mix of explicit and implicit) conceptual arguments in that paper were that devil's advocacy produces a sense of conflict (i.e., a type of negative affect) in individuals that helps to break the hindering effects of mental sets and/or the effects of group think on creative tasks. Unfortunately, feeling states either were not measured directly or were measured in inconsistent ways, nor was set breaking assessed directly. But this meta-analysis nonetheless points toward a link between a specific type of negative affect and activation of a specific aspect of creative thinking. In fact, Kaufmann and Vosburg (1997) and Gasper, Lozinski, and LeBeau (2009) found positive mood to enhance and negative mood to reduce strategy biases (which could include mental sets that hinder creative thinking in some circumstances) in problem solving.

The last major box of the model in Figure 3.1, "Domain-specific talents, skills, & knowledge," also has a stable individual-difference component. Domain KSAs such as mathematical aptitude and knowledge, code-writing skill, and fine-motor control have a dispositional – often at least partially genetic – aspect that can be characterized as elements of personality. Domain KSAs are relevant to the distinction between positive and negative creativity mainly in that individual domain strengths will influence the form taken by efforts to engage in positive or negative creativity, as well as the likelihood that such efforts (be they directed toward positive or negative goals) will succeed. Computer virus or "phishing" efforts as forms of negative creativity, for instance, require computer code-writing and other computer KSAs. Note that the domain skills necessary to executing a particular creative goal often can be gotten from other people or from technologies. These domain KSA issues are interesting but largely beyond the scope of this chapter.

To round out the model in Figure 3.1, note the double-headed arrows among the boxes (also an addition to Amabile's basic model, which had only separate one-way arrows from motivation, domain KSAs, and creative KSAs to creativity as an output). These arrows reflect the idea that motivation is necessary for latent domain or creative KSAs to become active, that high levels of a particular domain skill can promote motivation to find ways of making use of that skill, and that creative KSAs can be applied to developing means of regulating one's own motivation, to finding creative approaches to developing and applying one's domain skills, or to mustering external sources of domain skills that one lacks but needs for a particular creative endeavor.

SITUATIONAL ACTIVATION OF NEGATIVE CREATIVE GOALS

To this point we have discussed dispositional goals and their ability to influence inclinations toward either positive or negative actions and toward application of either creative abilities and approaches or noncreative abilities and approaches toward goal attainment. Activation of goals and of creative KSAs also can occur, however, for substantially situational reasons, and individual differences also frequently interact with situational factors to determine goals and motivation (e.g., Pervin, 2001). Figure 3.2 adds individual differences (personality) and situational triggers to the constructs in Figure 3.1, yielding a model of a (negative, in the example in Figure 3.2, with the positive version also possible) "creative complex" (see Jung, 1966, and Mumford and Gustafson, 1988, for related concepts). Hayes and Bond (1981) stated that situational goal setting is often the most critical aspect of creativity and that clear and specific situational goals for creative achievement are an additional major influence on motivation for creativity. Researchers such as Shalley (1991) and Torrance (1962) have found, in fact, that just instructing groups or individuals to "be creative" can increase creativity.

Shalley (1991, 1995) investigated the influence of three types of goals (i.e., productivity goals, creativity goals, and personal discretion) on the creativity of solutions generated to workplace problems. She found that creativity was greatest when subjects were given a goal of finding creative

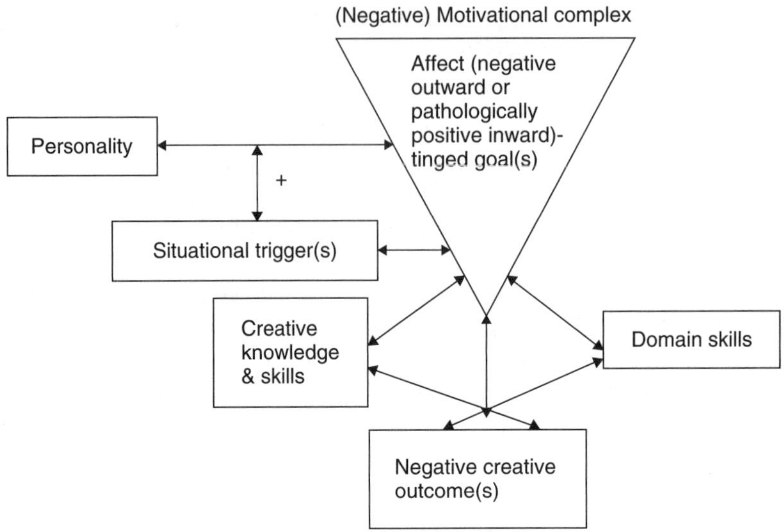

FIGURE 3.2. The psychological creative complex (negative creativity version).

approaches to in-basket problems as opposed to either an injunction to simply "do your best" or a goal of completing many problems quickly. Shalley suggests that goals might function by directing the allocation of both attention and effort. Aspects of performance (e.g., creativity) that are not the focus of attention will, relative to those that are (e.g., quantitative production), tend to suffer.

Clearly, explicit creativity goals, whether derived externally or internally, could be either positive or negative. Thus, if an individual has specific, explicit creativity goals, this will substantially activate the cognitive processes behind creativity; if such goals of being creative are absent, cognitive processes for creativity will be relatively low in activation (De Dreu et al., 2008; James, 1995; Shalley, 1995). If creativity goals are positive, they should channel creative ideas toward positive ends; if they are negative, they should channel creative ideas toward negative ends. An example of an explicit positive creativity goal would be "try to devise a new source of revenue for our company." An example of an explicit negative creative goal would be "try to figure out strategies for undermining public confidence in our competitor's product." James and colleagues (Clark & James, 1999; James, 1995) also have found that creativity can be channeled by situational goals and other factors. Congruent with Shalley's posited attention-allocation process for the influence of creative goals, he also found, however, that the same factors (including salient goals) that increased creativity directed at one valued end led to a diminution of it in other areas. The sections that follow explore such potential situational parallels on affect and therefore motivation for positive versus negative creativity.

Perceived Autonomy/Control

A number of lines of research indicate that independence and perceptions of autonomy (i.e., personal control) are important to creativity. For instance, research on aspects of supervisory styles that facilitate creativity also provides evidence that autonomy seems to enhance positive creativity. Amabile (1988, 1996) and Kanter (1988) concluded that authority systems that give power, respect, and control to subordinates enhance (positive) creativity. Authoritarian styles of leadership appear to be detrimental to creativity, and participative leadership styles appear to facilitate it. Similarly, salient rewards for creative work are argued to increase the perception of external control, and a number of studies have shown that such rewards can inhibit (positive) creativity under certain circumstances (Amabile, 1996; Eisenberger & Cameron, 1996).

Creativity in the works just cited has been defined, however, so as to include only the positive forms shown in Figure 3.1. *Lack* of perceived independence and control is likely, though, to *promote* negative creativity. A great deal of evidence from studies on related issues indicates that perceptions of lack of autonomy/control often trigger negative emotional reactions such as anger and (dis)stress (Cooper, Dewe, & O'Driscoll, 2001; Dollard & Winefield, 1998). Investigations of stressors in organizations, such as excessive workloads, have indicated that high levels of these can impair performance in general and creative performance in particular. For instance, high levels of subjective workload and time urgency seem to have a negative relationship with problem-solving ability (Folkman, Lazarus, Dunkel-Schetter, DeLongis & Gruen, 1986); time pressures also have been linked directly to inhibition of (positive) creativity (Amabile, Conti, Coon, Lazenby & Herron, 1996). Such negative emotions, according to our model, may increase the likelihood of both negative thinking in general and creative goals – by way of activation of negative goals directed at striking back at perceived abuse (Goodhart, 1985; James et al., 1999). Chen, Spector, and Jex (1995), for instance, argue and provide some evidence that perceived (dis)stress influences both perceptions of jobs and behavioral intentions.

Climate/Support/Threat

Positive social climates and feelings of security tend to promote positive emotional states and positive goals; negative social climates and a sense of threat tend to promote negative emotional states and negative goals. The likelihood of positive and negative creativity should follow these emotional and goal effects. And, at least on the positive creativity side, there is evidence that they do. Much research has indicated that more supportive organizational environments yield higher positive creativity in the workplace (Amabile et al., 1996; Ford, 1999; Soriano de Alencar & Bruno-Faria, 1997; Tesluk, Farr, & Klein, 1997).

Although there is little research on negative creative outcomes from poor climates/lack of support, those certainly have been shown to *hinder* positive forms of creativity (e.g., Amabile et al., 1996), which, according to our models and previous discussion, indicates that they also may *facilitate* negative forms of it. Poor support/climates certainly seem to promote negative outcomes such as efforts to undermine individuals or organizations (e.g., Duffy et al., 2002; Henle, 2005). Perceived negative social climates and relatively low social support also have been empirically linked with outcomes (e.g., hidden theft – Greenberg, 1993) that strongly imply relatively high underlying levels of negative creativity. Direct studies are now needed of the role of negative creative thinking in climate/support links to abusive/attacking behaviors.

Perceived Fairness

We discussed previously some of the study results indicating that (perceived) fair treatment seems to facilitate positive creative goals and some distinctive creative thinking skills, whereas (perceived) unfair treatment seems to facilitate negative creative goals and some distinctive aspects of creative thinking. James and Clark (Clark & James, 1999; James & Clark, 2009) have studied the effects of fair treatment on creativity and have assessed both positive and negative creativity. They found that people treated fairly showed increased creativity directed toward positive ends, whereas those treated unfairly showed increased creativity directed toward negative ends. Moreover, these studies provided some evidence that the unfairness impact on increasing negative creativity was mediated by the fluency of negative task-performance ideas but that the fairness-to-positive creativity relationship depended on other cognitive mechanisms.

Intergroup Conflict

Social and cultural diversity may facilitate positive creativity only to the extent that mechanisms (such as strong cultural norms promoting positive interactions among people who are different) also exist for preventing substantial intergroup polarizations (James & Eisenberg, 2006; Whyte, 2000). In fact, norms promoting tolerance of differences have been demonstrated to facilitate positive creativity in schools, societies, and the workplace (Osche, 1990; Simonton, 1995). Otherwise, the sense of uncertainty that can result from high environmental complexity and the intergroup conflict that can result from social diversity can yield negative emotions such as anxiety, fear, and hostility. This may lead creativity to be channeled into such negative avenues as devising schemes for harassing outgroup members.

Strength of systems/strategies of social coordination and integration therefore should interact with diversity levels to influence the direction of creativity. High diversity along with effective systems and procedures to ensure relatively positive interactions and intergroup cooperation will promote positive creativity. High diversity combined with weak integrative systems and procedures, however, will tend to result in negative creativity.

Cultural Influences

Cultures specify for individuals within them both what is considered creative and under what circumstances creativity is appropriate (James, 2005; Mar'i, 1976; Mar'i & Karayanni 1983). Many hints, mainly from case and anecdotal reports, indicate that organizational cultures, group cultures, and societal cultures may channel creativity in a number of ways and that societal and subsocietal cultures often interact to influence individual and group creativity (James, 2005). For instance, Kedia, Keller, and Julian (1992) studied how three of the four major cultural values (power-distance, uncertainty avoidance, and masculinity/femininity) identified in Hofstede's massive international comparison relate to creation of technology in organizations. They studied 808 research and development units in four countries for productivity in creating technologies and new technology-related knowledge. They found support for hypotheses that lower power-distance (i.e., belief in generalized social-status differences among people) and higher masculinity promoted technological creativity (Kedia et al., 1992).

In addition to effects on likelihood of creativity, however, values and norms may help to determine the ends toward which creativity is directed. Regarding the positive and negative types of creativity on which we are focused here, Gundykust and Ting-Toomey (1988) argued that masculine cultures are associated with a greater likelihood of feelings of hostility and anger than are feminine cultures. Fitzgerald provides case-study evidence that highly masculine organizational cultures may promote some negative forms of aggression and outgroup hostility. Maier and Messerschmidt (1998) also linked a highly masculine culture at NASA in 1986 to excessive risk taking, competitiveness, and action orientation that contributed to the *Challenger* explosion. Similarly, organizational cultures that emphasize maximizing profits over all else may increase the likelihood of employee actions that ultimately harm customers, communities, or the ecology.

There also may be some cultural value by situation interactions on likelihood of positive versus negative creativity. For instance, collectivists may experience positive emotions mainly when dealing with ingroup members. They actually may experience greater levels of hostility and competitiveness than individualists in situations of intergroup conflict, negotiation, or resource competition (James, 1995). From this we suggest that relatively high collectivism will interact with whether individuals are involved with ingroup or outgroup members to tend to promote either positive emotion and therefore positive creativity (ingroup situations) or negative emotion and therefore negative creativity (outgroup situations).

Transformational Leadership

Certain types of transformational/charismatic leaders (or what Bass, 1996, called *pseudo-transformational leaders*) sometimes create and use strong identifications for selfish, corrupt, or criminal purposes (Howell & Avolio, 1992). Groups such as terrorists and buccaneering organizations that evade the law or scheme to defraud the public often seem to be led by individuals who have the charismatic and catalyzing effect on subordinates that characterizes *transformational leadership*. Transformational leadership may particularly influence strongly collectivistic individuals who are, by definition, already inclined toward strong identification with groups or organizations to which they belong. Transformational leadership, then, may promote adoption of and success at either positive or negative creative goals and may do so with differential effectiveness across subordinates with different individual-difference (personality) characteristics.

CONCLUSIONS AND IMPLICATIONS

Our primary focus in this chapter has been on the mechanisms behind creativity directed at positive ends versus creativity directed at negative ends. In discussing those mechanisms, we have scattered in references to various different potential outcomes (results or effects) of positive or negative creativity. While such outcomes are not our primary concern here, we should briefly review them more systematically.

Positive creativity historically has been associated with concrete inventions, artistic/literary/musical creation, work-process innovation, improvement of social systems, development of scientific knowledge, problem – large or small – solving, adaptability to changing environments, and the generation and advancement of human cultures. Positive creativity also sometimes has been associated with enhancing individual mental and physical health (even as individual mental disorders have been argued to sometimes promote positive creativity – e.g., Eysenck, 1995).

Negative creativity, we have indicated or implied, is associated with sabotage, theft and other forms of exploitation, undermining or abuse of individuals or social or technical (e.g., computer virus creation) systems, physical harm to individuals or collectives (e.g., terrorism), and the production of dangerous or damaging inventions or materials. The list in the preceding sentence links negative creativity with a variety of forms of potential damage to the health of other individuals or collectives. Its relationship to the health of the producer of the negative creativity is unclear. Negative creativity might yield something akin to "catharsis" that allows for the external release of stress and negative tensions that would be harmful if kept internal. On the other hand, negative creativity may be associated with the undermining of characteristics such as optimism or of mechanisms such as functional self-regulation toward fulfilling (positive) desires, drives, and needs such that mental and physical health would be undermined. James and colleagues (1999) and McClaren (1993) attend further to the outcomes of negative creativity than we can here. This is also clearly an area of knowledge that could be developed profitably in future research and theory work.

The mechanisms of negative creativity, the factors that might trigger them, and the manifestations that they may produce have been considered rarely in the past. A major part of our argument here is that theorists and researchers of creativity should, in the future, include consideration and examination of the possibility of negative creative thinking and action. Creativity theories need to incorporate the positive versus negative dimension, as well as the concept of unintended consequences from creativity, if they are to be complete and valid. Similarly, applied work with individuals and groups should be done with an awareness of the possibility of negative manifestations of creativity, of the potentially inverse relationship of influences on positive and negative creativity, and of the potential negative correlation between creative and noncreative performance. An extension of the possibility that creativity has both positive and negative types indicates that channeling creativity in positive directions may diminish the likelihood that it will be manifested in negative ways. Conversely, inhibiting positive creativity actually may *promote* destructiveness. Providing explicit positive creativity goals and outlets may reduce the likelihood of occurrence of negative creativity (and vice versa). This needs to be tested.

We proposed several factors that may influence both positive and negative creativity. Those factors included personality/individual-difference constructs such as dispositional emotional and goal tendencies, interpersonal factors such as supervisory styles that can promote or reduce perceptions of autonomy and support, social-situational factors such as the presence or absence of intergroup conflict, structural mechanisms such as the presence or absence of procedures for venting negative emotions in more "mundane" (i.e., not negatively creative) ways, and cultural factors such as norms and values. Our ideas about negative creativity, however, are based largely on extrapolations of studies that mostly were actually focused on other issues. There is little direct research on negative creativity, and clearly, much more is needed. In summary, we hope that we have made a reasonable beginning to drawing attention to and developing some specific ideas about an aspect of creativity that seems to have been too much ignored. Much more research and theoretical work are needed for fuller scientific understanding of the positive/negative dimensions of creativity, as well as to, in the words of former Xerox Corporation CEO Paul Allaire, "capture the creative and innovative spirit" for positive individual and social ends.

REFERENCES

Amabile, T. M . (1989). *Growing up creative.* New York: Crown.

(1996). *Creativity in context: Update to "The Social Psychology of Creativity."* Boulder, CO: Westview Press.

Amabile, T. M., Conti, R., Coon, H., Lazenby, J., & Herron, M. (1996). Assessing the work environment for creativity. *Academy of Management Journal,* 39, 1154–1184.

Baas, M., De Dreu, C. K. W., & Nijstad, B. A. (2008). A meta-analysis of 25 years of mood-creativity research: Hedonic tone, activation, or regulatory focus? *Psychological Bulletin,* 134, 779–806.

Bellah, C. G., Bellah, L. D., & Johnson, J. L. (2003). A look at dispositional vengefulness from the three and five-factor models of personality. *Individual Differences Research,* 1, 6–16.

Berry, C. M., Ones, D. S., & Sackett, P. R. (2007). Interpersonal deviance, organizational deviance, and their common correlates: A review and meta-analysis. *Journal of Applied Psychology*, 92, 410–424.

Brown, J. D. & Marshall, M. A. (2001). Great expectations: Optimism and pessimism in achievement settings. In E. C. Chang (Ed.), *Optimism & pessimism: Implications for theory, research, and practice* (pp. 239–255). Washington: American Psychological Association.

Cacioppo, J. T., Petty, R. E., Feinstein, J. A., & Jarvis, W. B. G. (1996). Dispositional differences in cognitive motivation: The life and times of individuals varying in need for cognition. *Psychological Bulletin*, 119, 197–253.

Chen, P. Y., Spector, P. E., & Jex, S. M. (1995). Effects of manipulated job stressors and job attitude on perceived job conditions: A simulation. In S. L. Sauter and L. M. Murphy (Eds.), *Organizational risk factors for job stress* (pp. 341–356). Washington: American Psychological Association.

Cleckley, H. M. (1976). *The mask of sanity: An attempt to clarify some issues about the so-called psychopathic personality.* St. Louis: Mosby.

Clark, K. & James, K. (1999). Justice and positive and negative creativity. *Creativity Research Journal*, 12, 311–320.

Committee on Science and Technology for Countering Terrorism. (2002). *Making the nation safer: The role of science and technology in countering terrorism.* Washington: National Research Council/National Academy of Sciences.

Cooper, C. L., Dewe, P. J., & O'Driscoll, M. P. (2001). *Organizational stress: A review and critique of theory, research, and applications.* Thousand Oaks, CA: Sage.

Csikszentmihalyi, M. (1999). Implications of a systems perspective for the study of creativity. In R. J. Sternberg (Ed.), *The handbook of creativity* (pp. 313–335). New York: Cambridge University Press.

Cropanzano, R., James, K., & Citera, M. (1993). A goal-hierarchy model of personality, motivation, and leadership. In L. L. Cummings and B. M. Staw (Eds.), *Research in organizational behavior* (Vol. 15, pp. 267–322). Greenwich, CT: JAI Press.

Davis, M. (2009). Understanding the relationship between mood and creativity: A meta-analysis. *Organizational Behavior and Human Decision Processes*, 108, 25–38.

De Dreu, C. K. W., Baas, M., & Nijstad, B. A. (2008). Hedonic tone and activation level in the mood–creativity link: Toward a dual pathway to creativity model. *Journal of Personality and Social Psychology*, 94, 739–756.

Dollard, M. F. & Winefield, A. H. (1998). A test of the demand-control/support model of work stress in correctional officers. *Journal of Occupational Health Psychology*, 3, 243–64.

Duffy, M. K., Ganster, D. C., & Pagon, M. (2002). Social undermining in the workplace. *Academy of Management Journal*, 45, 331–351.

Eisenberger, R. & Cameron, J. (1996). Detrimental effects of reward: Reality or myth? *American Psychologist*, 51, 1153–1166.

Eysenck, H. J. (1995). *Genius: The natural history of creativity.* Cambridge, England: Cambridge University Press.

Feist, G. J. (1998). A meta-analysis of personality in scientific and artistic creativity. *Personality and Social Psychology Review*, 2, 290–309.

Folkman, S., Lazarus, R. S., Dunkel-Schetter, C., DeLongis, A., & Gruen, R. J. (1986). Dynamics of a stressful encounter: Cognitive appraisal, coping, and encounter outcomes. *Journal of Personality and Social Psychology*, 50, 992–1003.

Forgas, J. P. (1995). Mood and judgment: The affect infusion model (AIM). *Psychological Bulletin*, 117, 39–66.

(2000). Affect and information processing strategies: An interactive relationship. In J. P. Forgas (Ed.), *Feeling and thinking: The role of affect in social cognition* (pp. 253–280). Cambridge, England: Cambridge University Press.

Fritzsche, D. J. & Becker, H. (1984). Linking management behavior to ethical philosophy: An empirical investigation. *Academy of Management Journal*, 27, 166–275.

Gasper, K., Lozinski, R. H. & LeBeau, L. S. (2009). If you plan, then you can: How reflection helps defensive pessimists pursue their goals. *Motivation and Emotion*, 33, 203–216.

Giacalone, R. A. & Greenberg, J. (1997). *Antisocial behavior in organizations.* Thousand Oaks, CA: Sage Publications.

Goodhart, D. E. (1985). Some psychological effects associated with positive and negative thinking about stressful event outcomes: Was Pollyanna right? *Journal of Personality and Social Psychology*, 48, 216–232.

Gough, H. G. (1979). A creative personality scale for the adjective check list. *Journal of Personality and Social Psychology*, 37, 1398–1405.

Greenberg, J. (1993). Stealing in the name of justice: Informational and interpersonal moderators of theft reactions to underpayment inequity. *Organizational Behavior and Human Decision Processes*, 54, 81–103.

Hayes, J. R. & Bond, S. J. (1981). How social conditions affect creativity. In J. R. Hayes, *The complete problem solver* (pp. 217–238). Philadelphia: Franklin Institute.

Henle, C. A. (2005). Predicting workplace deviance from the interaction between organizational justice and personality. *Journal of Managerial Issues*, 17, 247–263.

Hetland, L. (2001). The arts and academic achievement: What the evidence shows. *Arts Education Policy Review*, 102, 3–6.

James, K. (1995). Goal conflict and individual creativity. *Creativity Research Journal*, 8, 285–290.

(2005). Culture and individual and group creativity in organizations. *Korean Journal of Thinking and Problem Solving*, 15, 77–95.

James, K. & Asmus, C. (2000). Personality, cognitive skills and creativity in different life domains. *Creativity Research Journal*, 13, 149–159.

James, K., Chen, J., & Goldberg, C. J. (1992). Organizational conflict and individual creativity. *Journal of Applied Social Psychology*, 22, 545–566.

James, K. & Clark, K. (2009). Organizational justice effects on positive and negative creativity. *Manuscript under review*, Portland State University.

James, K., Clark, K., & Cropanzano, R. (1999). Positive and negative creativity in groups, institutions, and organizations: A model and theoretical extension. *Creativity Research Journal*, 12, 211–227.

James, K. & Drown, D. (2008). Whether "malevolent" or "negative," creativity is relevant to terrorism prevention: Lessons from 9/11 and hazardous-material trucking. *Creativity Research Journal*, 20, 120–128.

Judge, T. A., Bono, J. E., Erez, A., Locke, E. A., & Thoresen, C. J. (2002). The scientific merit of valid measures of general concepts: Personality research and core self-evaluations. In J. M. Brett, Jeanne M. and F. Drasgow (Eds.), *The psychology of work: Theoretically based empirical research* (pp. 55–77). Mahwah, NJ: Lawrence Erlbaum Associates.

Jung, C. J. (1966). *The spirit in man, art, and literature.* Princeton, NJ: Princeton University Press.

Kaufmann, G. & Vosburg, S. K. (1997). "Paradoxical" effects of mood on creative problem solving. *Cognition and Emotion*, 11(2), 151–170.

Kedia, B. K., Keller, R. T., & Julian, S. D. (1992). Dimensions of national culture and the productivity of R&D units. *Journal of High Technology Management Research*, 3, 1–18.

Kim, K. H. (2005). Can only intelligent people be creative? A meta-analysis. *Journal of Secondary Gifted Education*, 16, 57–66.

Lazarus, R. S. (1966). *Psychological stress and the coping process.* New York: McGraw-Hill.

Lutenberg, J. M. (2005). Negative creativity and psychosomatic diseases. *Revista de Psicanalise da SPPA*, 12, 329–353.

Luchins, A. S. & Luchins, E. H. (1959). *Rigidity of behavior.* Eugene, OR: University of Oregon Books.

Maier, M. & Messerschmidt, J. R. (1998). Commonalities, Conflicts and Contradictions in Organizational Masculinities: Exploring the Gendered Genesis of the Challenger Disaster *Canadian Review of Sociology and Anthropology*, 35, 325–344.

Mar'i, S. K. (1976). Toward a cross-cultural theory of creativity. *Journal of Creative Behavior*, 10, 108–116.

Mar'i, S. K. & Karayanni, M. (1983). Creativity in Arab culture: Two decades of research. *Journal of Creative Behavior*, 16, 227–238.

Martin, L. L., Ward, D. W., Achee, J. W., & Wyer, R. S. (1993). Mood as input: People have to interpret the motivational implications of their moods. *Journal of Personality and Social Psychology*, 64, 317–326.

McCrae, R. R. & Costa, P. T., Jr. (1997). Personality trait structure as a human universal. *American Psychologist*, 52, 509–516

McLaren, R. B. (1993). The dark side of creativity. *Creativity Research Journal*, 6, 137–144.

(1999). Dark side of creativity. In M. A. Runco and S. R. Pritzker (Eds.), *The encyclopedia of creativity* (pp. 483–491). New York: Academic Press.

Maslow, A. H. (1970). *Motivation and personality*, 2nd ed. New York: Harper & Row.

Mento, A. J. , Steel, R. P., & Karren, R. J. (1987). A meta-analytic study of the effects of goal setting on task performance: 1966–1984. *Organizational Behavior and Human Decision Processes*, 39, 52–83.

Miller, J. D. & Lynam, D. (2001). Structural models of personality and their relation to antisocial behavior: A meta-analytic review. *Criminology*, 39, 765–798.

Mumford, M. D. & Gustafson, S. B. (1988). Creativity syndrome: Integration, application, and innovation. *Psychological Bulletin*, 103, 27–43.
Murray, C. (2003). *Human accomplishment: The pursuit of excellence in the arts and sciences, 800 B.C. to 1950*. New York: Harper-Collins.
Pervin, E. A. (1983). The stasis and flow of behavior: Toward a theory of goals. In M. M. Page (Ed.), *Personality – Current theory and research: 1982 Nebraska Symposium on Motivation*. Lincoln, NB: University of Nebraska Press.
Pervin, L. A. (2001). A dynamic systems approach to personality. *European Psychologist*, 6, 172–176.
Rawsthorne, L. J., & Elliott, A. J. (1999). Achievement goals and intrinsic motivation: A meta-analytic review. *Personality and Social Psychology Review*, 3, 326–344.
Runco, M. A. (1991). *Divergent thinking*. Norwood, NJ: Ablex.
Schneier, B. (2000). *Secrets and lies: Digital security in a networked world*. New York: Wiley.
Simonton, D. K. (1975). Interdisciplinary creativity over historical time: A correlational analysis of generational fluctuations. *Social Behavior and Personality*, 3, 181–188.
Schwenk, C. A. (1990). Effects of devil's advocacy and dialectical inquiry on decision making: A meta-analysis. *Organizational Behavior and Human Decision Processes*, 47, 161–176.
Shalley, C. E. (1991). Effects of productivity goals, creativity goals, and personal discretion on individual creativity. *Journal of Applied Psychology*, 76, 179–185.
(1995). Effects of coaction, expected evaluation, and goal setting on creativity and productivity. *Academy of Management Journal*, 38, 483–503.
Tardif, T. Z. & Sternberg, R. J. (1988). What do we know about creativity? In R. J. Sternberg (Ed.), *The nature of creativity* (pp. 229–240). Cambridge, England: Cambridge University Press.
Tesluk, P. E. , Farr, J. L., & Klein, S. R. (1997). Influences of organizational culture and climate on individual creativity. *Journal of Creative Behavior*, 31, 27–41.
Torrance, E. Paul. (1962). *Goals for guiding creative talent*. Englewood Cliffs, NJ: Prentice-Hall.
Velasquez, M. G. (1982). *Business ethics: Concepts and cases*. Englewood Cliffs, NJ: Prentice-Hall.
Vosburg, S. K. (1998). The effects of positive and negative mood on divergent-thinking performance. *Creativity Research Journal*, 11, 165–172.
Weisberg, R. W. (1993). *Creativity: Beyond the myth of genius*. New York: Freeman.
Watson, D., Clark, L. A., & Tellegen, A. (1988). Development and validation of brief measures of positive and negative affect: The PANAS scales. *Journal of Personality and Social Psychology*, 54, 1063–1070.

4

Subjugating the Creative Mind: The Soviet Biological Weapons Program and the Role of the State

MARIA N. ZAITSEVA

INTRODUCTION

Weapons of mass destruction (WMDs) invariably carry negative connotations – death and destruction, human suffering, evil intentions, and so on. Yet the process of creativity involved in designing these weapons, which include nuclear, chemical, and biological ones, is, arguably, much more nuanced and less straightforward than simply the intention to cause harm and to commit murder. The motivations for creating WMDs may include a desire to protect one's homeland from external (and internal) enemies, to deter an attack, and consequently, to prevent mass casualties. On the other hand, the weapons' creation may be motivated by the urge to solve purely scientific problems and dilemmas, such as finding ways to battle the plague or creating vaccines for new strands of anthrax or tularemia, for example. It is possible, then, that malevolent and benevolent creativity coexist during the process of WMD creation, which raises the question of how people involved in this process perceive and internalize their actions.

This chapter will explore these questions through the prism of the Soviet biological weapons (BW) program since the end of World War II. Not only was this venture the most massive in scale (and, arguably, ambition) ever undertaken in human history, but it also necessitated a juxtaposition of two seemingly opposite endeavors: the search for and understanding of lifesaving vaccines and the creation of deadly viruses and bacteria capable of killing a great number of people and livestock. This led to the problem of cognitive dissonance for the majority of Soviet scientists, the resolution of which often was difficult but necessary in order to successfully function within the Soviet system. Furthermore, the examination of the Soviet BW program also reveals the extent to which a political regime can influence and control the creative process needed for the invention of WMDs. The chapter will argue that the totalitarian nature of the Soviet State is key to understanding the intentions and motivations of the participants in the program. The Soviet government was successful in "selling" to its scientists the *malevolent* purpose of the BW program as a *benevolent* enterprise and in channeling and controlling the process of creativity to achieve the ends set out by the state. Some creative individuals later used their cognitive dissonance as an impetus for getting involved in the political reform movement. The chapter will conclude with some thoughts about the extent to which malevolent creativity can be discouraged, especially in the context of weapons creation.

BIOLOGICAL WEAPONS SOVIET-STYLE

Biological weapons lend themselves nicely to the exploration of malevolent creativity because they can be both malevolent and benevolent depending on their ultimate use. A commonly used definition of *BW* identifies them as "microbial or other biological agents, or toxins whatever their origin or method or production, in types and in quantities that have no justification for prophylactic, protective or other peaceful purposes; weapons, equipment or means of delivery designed to use such agents or toxins for hostile purposes or in armed conflict" (www.opbw.org/). In order to defend a state and its population against deadly strains of viruses and bacteria and to come up with suitable vaccines and/or treatments, scientists need to understand and to "master" the very viruses and bacteria that can be weaponized. Even when you develop a new strain of an agent, you may wish to develop an antidote for it as well that could protect your own troops and population in case of exposure in the course of battle. One of the characteristics of the Soviet program was that, by and large, it focused on creating pathogenic strains that were immune to various antibiotics and for which no known vaccinations existed (Wheelis, Rózsa, & Dando, 2006, pp. 143–144). Nonetheless, the Soviet BW program was hidden successfully behind the guise of defensive (even civilian) research and development for several decades of the cold war. The concealment was necessary because the activities of the program clearly broke international laws.

Following World War II, several countries had active BW programs, including the United States, France, the United Kingdom, and the Soviet Union. By the early 1970s, however, international consensus had built for the prohibition not only of the *use* (which was outlawed by the 1925 Geneva Protocol) but also the *development, production, and stockpiling* of BW. This consensus was codified in an international treaty [Biological and Toxin Weapons Convention (BTWC)], which came into force in April 1972. While the Soviet Union had a BW program dating back to the 1920s (Wheelis et al., 2006, p. 134), it was greatly expanded immediately after ratification of the BTWC and lasted until the breakup of the Soviet Union. The timing of the expansion was not coincidental – the Soviet government believed (and, subsequently, convinced its scientists) that the Western countries (particularly the United States) were cheating on their BTWC obligations and never stopped their offensive BW efforts. As a result, the Soviet Union mounted its own version of a biological counteroffensive by devising and implementing the largest BW program in history. Russian President Yeltsin "officially" terminated the program in the spring of 1992. However, some experts have lingering doubts about whether the program actually was stopped or whether it was restarted under the guise of civilian research and continues to this day (Alibek, 1999, p. 258; Steinbruner, 1997–1998, pp. 90–91; among others).

An overview of the Soviet BW program can be found elsewhere (Wheelis et al., 2006, Chapter 6). Not surprisingly, more is known about the defensive rather than the offensive component of the program, yet the latter comprised the bulk of the Soviet BW activities. In some respects, the Soviet program was rather similar to other BW programs because it focused on manipulating various biological agents and viruses meant to deter external enemies or to inflict unacceptable damage on the other side by infecting large numbers of its population and armed forces (Koblentz, 2003–2004; Wright, 1990). However, what distinguished the Soviet BW effort from other similar enterprises was first and foremost its sheer scale and ambition. Agents such as the plague and smallpox were manufactured by the ton, and production and storage facilities were built for the sole purpose of continually churning out massive amounts of biological agents (some were on a standby mode awaiting a "national emergency," in which case agents could be manufactured on a rapid schedule) (Wheelis et al., 1006, p. 141). Second, the Soviet Union focused extensively on the delivery methods and made significant progress in that field, especially with respect to vaccines. Unlike the West, the Soviet Union used aerosol immunizations for both humans and livestock (Wheelis et al., 2006, p. 142). Furthermore, it is believed that the Soviet Union planned to use aerosol delivery for its deadly BW as well – it designed specially adapted multiple-warhead intercontinental ballistic missiles that would deliver the biological agents to the target (Rimmington, 2002, p. 103). Finally, while it is hard to say whether the Soviet program was a "hotbed of creativity" compared with other BW efforts elsewhere, it certainly required its scientists to "think outside the box," especially when it came to manipulating various pathogens. As stated earlier, the Soviet program focused partially on developing strains that would be resistant to any antibiotic treatments, even various types of antibiotics used conjunctively. Some scientists used the so-called binary concept, in which two or more strains were used simultaneously – one for its antibiotic-resistant properties and the other for its virulence (Wheelis et al., 2006, p. 144). Furthermore, sometimes the scientists "capitalized" on accidents that occurred in their labs. For example, when one of the senior employees at one of the research institutes was infected with the Marburg virus in 1988 (he subsequently died), his infected blood was used to create an even more virulent strain of the virus, which was later weaponized (Wheelis et al., 2006, p. 144).

Given the type of work performed by the Soviet scientists, were their incentives purely malevolent, including the infliction of harm and death on millions of people? How did the individuals who were trained as doctors and scientists reconcile the objectives of their vocation with the work that they were ultimately doing for the secret BW program? Did they even know the true nature of their jobs, or did they blindly follow orders from their superiors and not question either the content or the end result of what they were doing? Since the work performed by the Soviet scientists undoubtedly was creative, exploration of the preceding questions helps us to understand how creative individuals fared in a totalitarian society, what kinds of pressures they dealt with, and whether the predicaments faced by the Soviet scientists were purely unique or more universal in nature.

SOVIET BIOWEAPONEERS

To answer some of the questions raised in the preceding section, it is productive to examine some of the intentions and motivations of the participants in the Soviet BW program. Even today, much about the Soviet BW program remains secret. Despite the Russian government's acknowledgment in the early 1990s of the existence of the BW program during the previous two decades, it has not been very forthcoming about the program's particulars, and it still protects any new details relating to the Soviet BW efforts. Despite the secrecy and shortage of open-source materials, a limited number of memoirs have been written by those who participated in the program (Alibek, 1999; Domaradskij & Orent, 2003; Popov & Voronova, 2004) that comprise the core of the data used for the following analysis. The revelations in these accounts range from limited to abundant (only two of the four openly acknowledge the existence of the program), and the authors' retrospective analyses ultimately depend on their overall attitudes toward the Soviet political system, which ranged from staunch support (Burgasov), to ambivalence (Vorobyov), to open critique and condemnation (Domaradskij and Alibek).

The paramount influence of the Soviet regime on the BW program in general and the scientists in particular, including its impact on their intentions and motivations, was undeniable in all the accounts from the participants. The Soviet government, including the Communist Party, held a very tight grip on the direction, content, and implementation of the Soviet BW enterprise. The state handed out assignments for BW work, demanded strict discipline and subordination from all the participants (whose backgrounds were carefully vetted by the KGB before employment was offered), and closely tracked the scientists in both their professional and personal lives. Following ratification of the BTWC, the Soviet program had to remain secret (from both the outside world and from the Soviet population), and the culture of secrecy permeated every aspect of the participants' work (and life in general). In order to minimize any doubts from its scientists, the Soviet regime mounted a forceful propaganda campaign about the urgent need to build up a Soviet BW arsenal to counter the inevitable aggression from the West. As a consequence, the state claimed that the work done by the Soviet scientists was of the greatest order of national security (e.g., it was saving lives, not preparing to take thousands of them). As we shall see, there was indeed some overlap between what the state wanted the scientists to think and what they believed, although the match was not perfect.

Motivations and Intentions

What, then, motivated the Soviet scientists who were part of the Soviet BW machine? Did they intend to create ever more deadly strains of viruses and bacteria for which there was no cure and that could infect and kill millions of people? Did they see their work assignments in purely scientific terms, or did they recognize that they were part of a larger clandestine war machine?

The scientists' motivations fall into two separate categories: personal and ideological. From the personal perspective, the idea of being involved in secret work directed by the state was very appealing to many. There was an element of prestige that accompanied such work, and even though the scientists could not share with their friends or even their families the nature of what they were doing, the very fact that they were recruited by the state for special assignments was exciting in itself (Alibek, 1999, pp. 44–45). Prestige attached to secret work also translated into concrete benefits such as higher salaries, better housing, and access to world-class scientific equipment, which was not available to other Soviet researchers. In a system of perpetual material shortages, cramped living conditions, and meager wages, the inducements offered by the BW program were appealing indeed.

Perhaps the most universal personal motivation was the ability to do interesting scientific work supported by virtually limitless government resources. Both Alibek and Domaradskij, for example, cite this as a primary motivating factor for their initial involvement in the program. The research locations were scattered across the Soviet Union, often in remote corners far away from major cities. Yet, ultimately, location did not matter. What mattered was the content of the research, which, in many cases, was cutting-edge and invariably involved scientific creativity. Some recent research, however, suggests that location might have mattered after all, at least with respect to creativity promotion (Ben Ouagrham-Gormley & Vogel, 2009). Not all Soviet BW facilities were run uniformly, and management styles varied. Some institutions (such as Obolensk) were run more like military organizations with strict discipline and hierarchical rules. The scientists were afforded little scientific freedom and were discouraged from exchanging information, even within the same facility. On the other hand, facilities such as Vector tried to recreate more of an academic environment, where teamwork was supported, information was shared between scientists, and the institute's director was approachable. Innovation and new ideas were more abundant than in Obolensk (Ben Ouagrham-Gormley & Vogel, 2009, pp. 7–10). These findings suggest that different knowledge environments produced different levels of creativity, even in the context of such top-secret and heavily guarded operation as the Soviet BW program.

Yet, even in places where creativity flourished, the involvement in the program had some drawbacks for the scientists. Popov and Voronova (2004) describe the system of "lure and punishment" through which the Soviet state enticed the scientists with the prospect of good salaries, prestige, and interesting work, but "… were they [the scientists] to refuse, they were punished by being given jobs in the hinterlands or in low-level institutions" (Popov & Voronova, 2004, p. 9). Even more consequential was the risk of being labeled as "untrustworthy" by the KGB, which essentially meant being blacklisted by the Soviet secret service agency (Domaradskij & Orent, 2003, p. 185). This, in effect, created a series of "negative" incentives – if you refused to undertake the secret assignments given to you by the party and/or the KGB, you ran the risk of ruining your career and, more generally, faced the prospect of running into trouble with the state at some point in your life. These dilemmas faced not only the Soviet scientists or creative people in the Soviet Union but also the general population. Far from everyone supported the political regime, and some even dared to question it, but that often resulted in "problems" with the state or, worse, a long-term trip to prison or the gulag. The memoirs reveal, however, that there were instances of refusal where the scientists could not bring themselves to knowingly work on BW. Such cases were few and far between, and more often than not, once a scientist entered the program, he or she did not leave (at least until the political events in the Soviet Union of the late 1980s and early 1990s significantly relaxed the state's grip on scientists' activities and allowed them more freedom of choice).

For those who participated in the program, the downside included the inability to publish the results of their research (owing to the secret nature of the work) and heavy restrictions on international travel, either for scientific conferences or for personal reasons (Domaradskij & Orent, 2003, pp. 152–153). The influence of the Soviet regime also was a prominent "negative" motivating factor. The central government dictated the content and direction of work to be done, including the time frame for accomplishing it. As Domaradskij and Orent (2003) put it, "... there was only one way to 'do science' then – the Party's way" (p. 150). In addition, there was a pervasive culture of secrecy in all the research centers, labs, and institutions that were associated with the Soviet BW machine. Over time, secrecy had its effect on the scientists. Alibek, for example, admitted that despite whatever moral dilemmas he might have had with the work he was doing, "... the secret culture of our labs had changed my outlook" (Alibek, 1999, p. 102). He no longer questioned his work or how it agreed with the oath of a medical doctor that he took on graduation from university. In short, secrecy muted the desire to ask questions or to challenge orders that came from above. I will return to this apparent ability to bring together contradictory cognitions later on.

Aside from the personal factors just discussed, the Soviet scientists also were motivated by strong ideological considerations. The Soviet regime provided ample encouragement and propaganda for this set of incentives. As Popov and Voronova (2004) explain, part of the reason that the Soviet BW program got minimal resistance from civilian scientists (let alone the military ones) was due to the Soviet populations' experience in World War II and the suffering that it experienced at the hands of external enemies.

The cold war created new opponents, and the Soviet state set very clear goals for doing whatever was necessary not only to defend the Motherland from an outside attack but also to achieve military superiority over its cold war rivals. The belief that the West, led by the United States, was bent on destroying the Soviet Union was so pervasive that nobody even questioned this "truth," and the participants in the program considered the protection of their homeland from an inevitable attack from the West as part of their professional mission and an overarching goal (Alibek, 1999, p. 31; Domaradskij & Orent, 2003, p. 149; among others). Furthermore, the Soviet scientists were not, apparently, troubled by the fact that the Soviet Union had signed the BTWC in the early 1970s, which prohibited the development and manufacture of the very weapons they were working on. This was due in large part to the secret propaganda engineered by the Communist Party that tried to convince the participants that the United States was most definitely cheating on its BTWC obligations and that it had never stopped its offensive program in the late 1960s (Alibek, 1999, p. 53; Popov & Voronova, 2004, p. 9). This propaganda cultivated a very strong sense of patriotism on the part of the Soviet scientists. They truly believed that their work was beneficial to the country and helped to achieve the goal of strengthening the Soviet Union's military capability. All the participants' accounts prominently cite their patriotic intentions with respect to the BW program, and they called themselves patriots no matter what their eventual attitude toward the Soviet BW machine or the Communist regime in general.

It is hard to say which set of motivations – personal (both positive and negative) or ideological – was more significant in motivating the scientists to take part in the BW program. However, the ideological considerations in particular – patriotism, the defense of the Motherland, protection against the West – raise an interesting possibility of malevolent and benevolent intentions coexisting in scientists' minds. On the one hand, the desire to protect one's country against enemies, to save countless lives of fellow countrymen by averting an attack or at least preventing the annihilation of one's homeland, and to patriotically serve one's government all can be considered benevolent. On the other hand, it certainly can be argued that the intention to create deadly viruses, especially ones for which no known cure exists, with the purpose of killing thousands, if not millions, of people is malevolent, and thus the creativity involved in engineering such deadly agents is malevolent as well.

A further complicating factor in establishing whether or not the scientists' creativity was malevolent, benevolent, or both was the fact that some of them were able to think about their work in purely scientific terms and saw the creation of new weapons as a solution to a scientific problem rather than an act of weapons' creation. Such detachment might have helped some of them to reconcile their work with an intuitive understanding of the end result of the BW program. Domaradskij and Orent (2003), for example, claimed that he and his fellow scientists

> ... were involved in the scientific realm, not the applied aspects of bioweapons work. We thought in terms of creating genetically modified strains, not of creating bombs and missiles filled with weaponized agents. We knew how to create these genetically modified agents in principle. But we thought of them as strains, not weapons. (p. 149)

Domaradskij extended this logic by arguing that "... the creation and development of biological weapons [was] also a scientific problem; without advances in molecular biology and genetics, ... the scientific problems facing bioweapons designers could not be solved" (p. 149). In this statement, Domaradskij clearly attempted to distance himself from those whom he considered "bioweaponeers" but understood that weapons' design was not possible without the work of "pure scientists" like himself. Burgasov echoed this attitude when he claimed that "... it [was] natural, that for development of protection means against bacteriological weapon, we need[ed] to know the characteristics of this weapon, create it, [and] test it (*sic*)" (Popov & Voronova, 2004, p. 7). Such a perspective makes the separation of malevolent and benevolent intentions virtually impossible.

Another tactic for distancing oneself from the world of weapons and war was to believe that the work was purely *defensive* and that it was other people who were doing *offensive* research and development (Domaradskij & Orent, 2003; Popov & Voronova, 2004, p. 7). In fact, the Communist Party wanted most of the participants to think that the entire Soviet BW program was defensive. Furthermore, many scientists in the program knew only of their own specific assignments and had little idea about the larger picture (Popov & Voronova, 2004, p. 9). However, it is very hard to believe that the program's participants who were in positions of leadership (e.g., heads of research institutes or labs, etc.) did not know the true nature of their work or did not understand the offensive component of the program.

The tactic of reformulating the nature of one's work (e.g., calling it defensive research or scientific problem-solving instead of creation of deadly weapons) was part of the process of dealing with cognitive dissonance, or of holding together two contradictory ideas simultaneously, on the part of the Soviet scientists. On the one hand, many of those involved had either medical or scientific training, during which they took an oath to do no harm to their fellow human beings and to save lives. On the other hand, some (but not all) realized that their work within the Soviet BW machine ultimately would lead to many deaths and could cause great pain and suffering. Was the ability to reconcile these cognitions something unique pertaining to creative individuals (such as Soviet BW scientists), or was it a more universal trait acquired by those living in a totalitarian political system? While many of the people (creative and noncreative alike) who did not support the regime had to learn ways to adapt to it, work within it, and even contribute to it, the dilemma of cognitive dissonance affected creative individuals especially strongly.

Creative people in the Soviet Union, including scientists, artists, academics, writers, filmmakers, and others, faced the particular challenge of performing their work in a way that would support, promote, and even glorify the political regime within which they functioned. Some, of course, believed in it fully and unconditionally, and the need to praise Soviet totalitarianism did not present a challenge. For others, who either had doubts about the system or saw its injustices and atrocities, often the only viable option was to continue working without questioning or criticizing the regime. Very few were able to break away from the system by either emigrating or leaving jobs permanently. The "escape" from the problem of cognitive dissonance thus was much harder for creative people in the Soviet Union than for those living and working in nontotalitarian regimes. Immersion in the work for the Soviet system also carried a cost to creative individuals – according to one former Soviet BW weaponeer, long after the program ended, he could not help but continue to think in terms of "bioweapons potential" when tracking new scientific developments.[1] This suggests that some creative individuals got trained to think in a certain way as a result of being part of the program for a long time and could not escape that mind-set even after leaving the BW enterprise.

Interestingly, the ability to deal with cognitive dissonance on the part of creative individuals in a totalitarian system also was an eventual source of strength and inspiration for some who participated in the movement for political change and helped to bring down the very system that trained and controlled their creative minds. In his excellent treatment of some of

[1] Author's personal correspondence with K. Vogel, February 27, 2009.

the causes of the end of the cold war, M. Evangelista (1999) detailed the role played by transnational movements and actors, particularly Soviet and American scientists, in influencing Soviet and American policymaking with respect to disarmament and arms control. Prominent scientists, such as nuclear physicist A. Sakharov, for example, were at the forefront not only of specific disarmament issues but also, in the middle and late 1980s, of the movement for broad political change and freedom. The knowledge acquired by creative individuals from their work (whether in a nuclear lab or a BW facility or by documenting lives of ordinary Soviet people) gave them the ammunition to challenge the system, expose its practices. and call for change. This, of course, is a broad generalization, and not all creative people, including the Soviet BW scientists, led the charge for reform, as will be shown in the next section.

RETROSPECTION: JUSTIFICATION OR REGRET?

When the Soviet BW program came to an end in the early 1990s, some of the former participants felt the need to reflect on their roles in the Soviet BW machine. A select few even put their retrospection on paper, as was the case with the scientists discussed in this chapter. As the Russian government revealed to the outside world and to its own people the extent of its BW program, scientists struggled with moral questions regarding their own involvement. They also had a chance to reflect on the program in general, and these reflections were varied and often surprising. In the end, the attitude toward the program was closely related to one's feelings about the Soviet system in general. With Gorbachev's reforms of *perestroika* and, later, the eventual collapse of the Soviet regime in 1991, Soviet scientists enjoyed increasing freedom to speak their minds about their former work, although many remained cautiously guarded in expressing their opinions – a clear residue of the totalitarian system and the culture of secrecy that did not tolerate dissent or criticism from its subordinates.

The scientists' retrospection ranged from staunch defense, to ambivalence, to harsh criticism of the Soviet BW enterprise. Burgasov, for example, who revered the Soviet totalitarian system and some of its most "infamous" heroes, continued to deny in the early 2000s the very existence of the program and harshly criticized those who revealed any information about it (Popov & Voronova, 2004, p. 4). Vorobyov was much more ambivalent in his assessment of the program, at least in print. It is possible that this was a result of the so-called totalitarian ethics "which subsumes all independent thought, and by which a person should not put his or her personal issues above the duty before and the goals of the state" (Popov & Voronova, 2004, p. 2).

The critics of the program, not surprisingly, were those who either despised the Soviet political system from the beginning (e.g., Domaradskij) or who grew disillusioned with it over the years and condemned the Soviet regime when the cracks in its foundation became too big to repair (e.g., Alibek). Domaradskij's denunciation of the program was twofold: First, he criticized the fact that the Soviet Union poured vast resources into designing weapons instead of promoting "pure science"; and second, he was driven by the agenda of settling personal scores with his former enemies within the program. In effect, Domaradskij's account did not condemn the creative aspect of the program (which he perceived as benevolent) but attacked the program's implementation. Finally, there were a select few who not only grew critical of the system in which they worked and lived for decades but also defected abroad and lived to tell their story to their former cold war enemies. These high-profile defections included V. Pasechnik, who fled to the United Kingdom in 1989, and K. Alibek, who moved to the United States in 1992. Alibek acknowledged that "some of [his] colleagues might consider [his defection] a betrayal. But [he] had come to believe that [his] real betrayal was to have pursued a career that violated the oath [he] had taken as a doctor" (Alibek, 1999, p. 252). The changing political structure offered the possibility of a satisfactory resolution of the problem of cognitive dissonance discussed earlier.

In the end, the scientists' retrospective analyses dwelled little, if at all, on the question of whether their creativity was malevolent or benevolent. More than anything, they tried to reconcile knowledge about the program's true meaning with their own personal involvement in it. The scientists' motivations were a mix of personal benefits (both positive and negative) and ideological considerations supported by the propaganda controlled by the Soviet state. Some clearly knew that the projects they were working on were aimed at killing great numbers of people, but they chose either to turn a blind eye to it, convincing themselves that their particular assignments did not have malevolent intentions, or to believe that they were simply following orders from their superiors that they could not question, let alone refuse. The Soviet regime was instrumental in convincing its scientists that their work was imperative for national security and that it served a noble purpose of strengthening the Soviet military might against the inevitable attack from the West. The government wanted the scientists to believe that they were saving lives rather than preparing to take them.

CONCLUSION

The Soviet Communist Party, in conjunction with the KGB, orchestrated, directed, and oversaw the vast BW enterprise and indoctrinated its scientists into believing that their work was vital to national security of the state and for the protection of the Soviet Union against an attack from the West. The state directed the postings and assignments of scientists and lured them with prospects of higher salaries, good equipment, and interesting research. The culture of secrecy, actively promoted by the regime, added an element of prestige to participation in the program. At the same time, the state punished those who refused to join in or who voiced moral reservations. Furthermore, the government actively spread the propaganda that the Soviet BW program was for defensive purposes only – a lie that many within the program seemed to buy. As a result, some of the participants thought of their work as benevolent, a job that was aimed at saving lives and promoting the security of the state. Even when the scientists could not deny the true intentions of the program or the fact that they were creating deadly agents meant to kill, they often justified their participation by either arguing that their work was patriotic or that they had no choice but to participate for fear of negative repercussions in case they refused.

In effect, the Soviet regime controlled the creative work of its scientists and was able to channel their creativity toward accomplishment of the state's objectives. In the process, it forced the creative individuals to overcome the problem of cognitive dissonance by eliminating opportunities for criticism, freedom of scientific exchange, and availability of alternative attractive employment opportunities. A totalitarian system such as the Soviet one might have had an easier time achieving this goal than its democratic counterparts because it was based on the principles of terror, fear, and subjugation rather than independent thought and freedom of expression. Even though many of the known offensive BW programs prior to signing of the BTWC existed in democracies (the United States, Canada, France, and the United Kingdom), since the signing of the convention in the early 1970s, most of the clandestine BW programs were carried out in authoritarian states (Way and Zaitseva, 2008).

Are there lessons to be learned from the experience of the Soviet BW program and the knowledge, even limited, that we now have about it? In particular, is there anything that can be done to discourage malevolent creativity? In the case of the Soviet BW program, where the role of the state was paramount, one ought to start there. An obvious way to discourage malevolent creativity would be to dissuade states from carrying out clandestine BW research and development through international regimes and norms. To date, however, the BTWC had not proven terribly effective in thwarting BW programs worldwide owing to weak enforcement mechanism and problems with verification. On a more micro (i.e., individual) level, malevolent creativity might be even harder to prevent. While scientists can be encouraged to come up with antidotes to viruses that they are manipulating and creating – something that the Soviet program rarely did – accidental mutations can occur (such as the case with a virulent strand of the Marburg virus derived from the blood of an infected Soviet scientist). Furthermore, the majority of the Soviet BW scientists did not perceive their work as malevolent and, rather, thought of it as something beneficial to their homeland and fellow Soviet citizens. Thus the malevolent creativity often was not intentional, even though the postprogram retrospection suggested that some scientists clearly understood the nature of their work and its end result. Finally, while an appropriate structural context in which scientific freedom was encouraged, ideas openly exchanged, fear of persecution and punishment did not exist, and alternative employment options existed would, theoretically, reduce the risk of scientists engaging in malevolent creativity, such a structure simply did not exist during the Soviet period. What was preset was a system that forced its scientists to overcome cognitive dissonance about the nature of their work and their benevolent scientific or medical training for the sake of professional (and even personal) survival. When a totalitarian regime dictates that you engage in malevolent creativity, more often than not you will and will either not ask any questions or ask them later.

REFERENCES

Alibek, K. (1999). *Biohazard.* New York: Dell Publishing.

Ben Ouagrham-Gormley, S. & Vogel, K. (2009). *Consideration of the social context shaping BW (non)proliferation.* Paper presented at the 2009 International Studies Association Convention, New York, February 15–18.

Domaradskij, I. V. & Orent, W. (2003). *Biowarrior: Inside the Soviet/Russian biological war machine.* Amherst: Prometheus Books.

Evangelista, M. (1999). *Unarmed force: The transnational movement and the end of the cold war.* Ithaca, NY: Cornell University Press.

Koblentz, G. (2003–2004). Pathogens as weapons. *International Security,* 28, 84–122.

Popov, S. & Voronova, I. (2004). Russian bioweapons: Still the best-kept secret? *Nonproliferation Review,* Fall, 1–14.

Rimmington, A. (2002). The Soviet Union's offensive program: The implications for contemporary arms control. In S. Wright (Ed.), *Biological warfare and disarmament: New problem/new perspectives* (pp. 103–148). Lanham, MD: Rowman & Littlefield.

Steinbruner, J. (1997–1998). Biological weapons: A plague upon all houses. *Foreign Policy*, Winter, 85–96.

Way, C. & Zaitseva, M. (2008). *Germ proliferation: A quantitative analysis of the spread of biological weapons*. Paper presented at the Annual Meeting of the International Studies Association, San Francisco, CA, March 26–29.

Wheelis, M., Rózsa, L., & Dando, M. (Eds.). (2006). *Deadly cultures: Biological weapons since 1945*. Cambridge, MA: Harvard University Press.

Wright, S. (Ed.). (1990). *Preventing a biological arms race*. Cambridge, MA: MIT Press.

5

Imagining the Bomb: Robert Oppenheimer, Nuclear Weapons, and the Assimilation of Technological Innovation

DAVID K. HECHT

The atomic bomb presents a number of paradoxes. It ended a brutal war but also decisively shaped decades of international tension. It stands as a monument to human ingenuity but has more than once threatened the species with extinction. It originated in earnest fear of the consequences of a nuclear-armed Nazi regime but ended by setting new standards for the ease of destruction of civilian populations. It offers startling possibilities for both beneficial and detrimental applications. It represents a formidable scientific and technological advance that simultaneously called into question the value of that very kind of endeavor. One of the defining features of late twentieth- and early twenty-first-century worlds, it is often relegated to the back of the mind. Widely bemoaned and regretted, it is assumed to be a permanent fixture of the landscape. And however one defines the idea of "dark creativity" – itself a notion built on a paradox – the atomic bomb would seem to be a near-perfect exemplar of it. The Manhattan Project was a fantastically expensive, logistically daunting, and technologically complex endeavor; its successful completion testifies to the creativity and hard work of numerous leaders and rank-and-file participants. Hans Bethe, one of the leaders of the project, captured some of this spirit with a recollection that of all the laboratories he had worked in, "I have never observed in any of these other groups quite the spirit of belonging together, quite the urge to reminisce about the days of the laboratory, quite the feeling that this was really the great time of their lives" that pervaded Los Alamos (Bethe, 1968, p. 399). This reflected his recollection of wide-ranging intellectual and personal challenge and excitement – and it was this laboratory that created the most destructive weapon the world has ever known.

Rhetoric about the bomb commonly emphasizes its destructive nature. For example, Jonathan Schell's 1982 antinuclear classic, *The Fate of the*

Earth, describes part of a hypothetical explosion in New York City this way:

> ... searing heat would ignite everything flammable and start to melt windows, cars, buses, lampposts, and everything else made of metal or glass. People in the street would immediately catch fire, and would shortly be reduced to heavily charred corpses. About five seconds after the light appeared, the blast wave would strike, laden with the debris of a now nonexistent midtown. Some buildings might be crushed, as if a giant fist had squeezed them on all sides, and others might be picked up off their foundations and whirled uptown with the other debris. (Schell, 1982, p. 48)

The immediate blast and heat of the bomb is only one of the "vast theatre of physical effects" that Schell describes; some of these effects, such as radioactive fallout, potentially can be lethal many miles downwind of an explosion (Schell, 1982, p. 49). Schell's analysis was not even made using effects of the most powerful weapons then existing; this description thus understates the potential consequences. The ubiquity of such imagery in discussions of nuclear weapons in Schell's work and that of other writers is appropriate because it represents a central fact about them. Such prevalence can be misleading, however, as a guide to the overall cultural reaction to the bomb, suggesting that the *only* perceived meaning of nuclear weapons is their destructive power.

This chapter argues that many people could and did find other meanings in the atomic bomb; perhaps surprisingly, Americans did not react to nuclear weapons in a uniformly negative manner. Furthermore, it argues for the importance of external factors in developing the meaning of the atomic bomb. The role of such factors does not preclude appreciation of its intrinsically destructive nature because most images of the bomb were (and are) composites of many different reactions. But the existence of such diverse responses suggests that reaction to the atomic bomb has to be understood as a much more complex phenomenon than simple fear, anxiety, or revulsion against its scientific creators; it also suggests that perhaps other examples of dark and destructive creativity have more complex cultural meanings than is commonly appreciated. The first section of this chapter gives an overview of this multiplicity, exploring reactions to atomic weapons that cannot be understood as purely negative or fearful ones. The second section shows how cultural response to the atomic bomb challenges the notion of technological determinism, calling instead for a more nuanced notion of how technological innovation relates to society and politics. The final sections develop a case study of Robert Oppenheimer, a central figure in both the Manhattan Project and cultural discourse about it. Oppenheimer's rhetoric shows the importance of external factors to contemporary analyses of atomic energy. Perspectives on the bomb may have been shaped by the innate characteristics of the weapons but were not defined by them. Ultimately, this chapter aims to show that public reaction to an invention is an essential category of analysis. A value-laden term such as "dark" has to be understood as a commentary on the reaction to the invention, not just the invention itself.

BEYOND THE DARK SIDE

It is natural to assume that the public reaction to nuclear weapons was negative – that it was the exact inverse of the celebratory tones that generally accompany medical advances, labor-saving devices, and other beneficent examples of technological innovation. Certainly, such negativity – often in the form of fear, anxiety, or revulsion against science – did manifest itself in the initial reactions to Hiroshima and Nagasaki. The American public quickly grasped two essential realities of the atomic age: that further research was likely to lend even more destructive power to these already devastating weapons and that the technology likely would be developed in other countries as well, some of whom might be hostile to the United States. The specter of nuclear apocalypse therefore was on many minds; one editor wrote about the bomb's potentially "unutterably shattering effect upon civilization and the wholesale destruction of millions of human beings" (Boyer, 1985, pp. 13–14). This sort of rhetoric was quite common; another illustration is a *St. Louis Post-Dispatch* editorial that worried that science may have "signed the mammalian world's death warrant and deeded an earth in ruin to the ants" (Boyer, 1985, p. 5). Such apocalyptic fears and their link to views of science run amok were common in the days after Hiroshima, and this is hardly surprising, given the destructive powers that the physicists, chemists, and engineers of the Manhattan Project had unleashed. And links to dark and destructive creativity were explicit; on the very day that Hiroshima was destroyed, an NBC radio broadcast suggested that the new weapon might be "a Frankenstein" (Boyer, 1985, p. 5). This analogy represented a conscious link between the atomic bomb and perhaps the most classic and enduring image of the dark side of scientific creativity.

Such rhetoric, however, was not the only response Americans had to the news of atomic bombs. Science and scientists were frequently celebrated in the years after Hiroshima and Nagasaki; one contemporary author observed that "Physical scientists are the vogue these days," noting that "No dinner party is a success without at least one physicist to explain … the nature of the new age in which we live" (Jones, 1946, p. 425). Celebration of the Manhattan Project was a central reason for this. Most Americans took patriotic pride in the technical and industrial accomplishment, whereas a smaller but still significant group relished its use on Japan in particular. Others expressed gratitude for its assumed role in ending World War II quickly, a sentiment given eloquent expression by Paul Fussell, who was part of an infantry unit that he expected to be involved in a land invasion of Japan in 1945. Fussell recalled the reaction of his unit on hearing the news: "For all the fake manliness of our facades we cried with relief and joy. We were going to live. We were going to grow up to adulthood after all" (Fussell, 1981, p. 29). Looking to the future, many Americans had high hopes for the discovery itself. Some, for example, felt that the immense destructive capability of nuclear weapons would shock the international community into peace. And, as sole possessors of such weapons, Americans assumed that they inevitably would take a leading role in this brave new world. Others focused on potential domestic benefits, imagining that atomic energy would provide a virtually unlimited source of cheap power, thus facilitating rapid social progress. Visions of atomic utopia were not uncommon in the early postwar years; one journalist foresaw: "fantastically cheap power; 'atomic-energy vitamin tablets'; the mining and smelting of various metals through radioactive beams; and the imminent availability of atomic-powered rockets, airplanes, ships, and automobiles" (Boyer, 1985, p. 111). And even deep into the atomic age, images of the mushroom cloud retained surprisingly diverse cultural meaning – as symbols of power, pride, and strength as well as destruction (Rosenthal, 1991).

The most interesting – and perhaps most common – reactions to the atomic bomb are ones that cannot be characterized as wholly negative or positive but are amalgamations of many different impulses. For example, Fred Kirby's hit song, "Atomic Power," noted that this power "was given by the mighty hand of God" – a common mode of expression about the bomb (Kirby, 1946). In this telling, the atomic bomb becomes quite literally outside history, being more reminiscent of divine than human knowledge. But the meaning of this fact varied, even within Kirby's lyrics. On the one hand, likening the bomb to the "mighty hand of God" is a warning, implying a note of judgment and foreboding at having crossed out of safe, terrestrial realms. But the song also celebrates the "joy" of having ended the war and admonishes listeners to use the bomb "for the good of man and never to destroy" (Kirby, 1946). This injunction becomes puzzling in the final stanza, where Kirby notes that "Hiroshima, Nagasaki paid a big price for their sins" (Kirby, 1946). The note of revenge here is clear, but it remains murky what the sin was, who judged them, and whether the price was perhaps too steep. Near the end of the song is a foreboding note as Kirby tells his audience that the nuclear "day of judgment" could come at, quite literally, any moment, without prior warning (Kirby, 1946). In this one song are sentiments of awe, celebration, revenge, worry, and judgment.

Such diversity characterized many reactions to the bomb. Visions of nuclear war offered a curious mix of hope and despair. Although apocalyptic visions were in evidence, some felt that such pessimism was too extreme, and a handful of writers even presented the annihilation of civilization as something that – for all its horror – might have a cleansing effect, leading to spiritual rebirth (Weart, 1988, 220–224). The same was true of the push for international control of atomic energy – briefly but importantly in the world spotlight for perhaps two years after Hiroshima. This idea was variously based in fear of the atomic bomb and hopes that such fear could have a salutary effect on the world by motivating international cooperation. Another example is John Hersey's "Hiroshima" – published in its entirety in the *New Yorker* on August 31, 1946. The article (and book that followed) provides a vivid and often harrowing account of the aftermath of the first atomic bomb, told through the stories of six survivors of the attack. It has been read by generations of students (among others) and stands as a cultural monument to the destruction caused by the first atomic bomb. At the time, however, it had a narrower effect than might be supposed. In his excellent analysis of the piece's reception, Michael Yavenditti notes that "Hersey's work aroused many readers but incited few of them. It enabled American readers to reaffirm their humane sentiments and to examine their consciences, but 'Hiroshima' did not require Americans to question the legacy of the bomb's use" (Yavenditti, 1974, p. 48). Yavenditti's analysis is important for understanding the range of reactions to atomic energy because it demonstrates that the multiplicity of response is about more than a mix of "positive" and "negative." The reaction to "Hiroshima" was more complex than can be captured by such value judgments, and the same is true of attitudes toward atomic energy more generally. It is clear that fear and anxiety are prevalent themes, but it is also clear that they are not sufficient to explain this diversity. There were too many dynamic, confusing, and paradoxical images and meanings of atomic energy to reduce the reaction to one label.

TECHNOLOGY AND SOCIETY

This multiplicity results from an important point about technology and society: External factors as well as internal ones shape the consequences of a particular innovation. This easily underappreciated point is a common theme in history and the history of technology and represents one of the most important disciplinary contributions that those fields can make to the study of the dark side of creativity. Calling a particular invention, discovery, or creative product "dark" assumes that an innovation can have an inherent meaning – in this case, a negative one. But the notion of innate meaning is an ahistorical concept, disregarding the fact that differing contexts can profoundly alter understandings of a subject. Also, the idea that an invention can be inherently "dark" (or inherently anything) sits uncomfortably close to the concept of technological determinism, a tempting but usually fallacious notion that a given technological innovation inexorably causes certain identifiable and definite social changes. Refutations of this abound in the history of technology. Ruth Cowan's book, *More Work for Mother,* argues that technological developments changed the nature of housework but did so through the lens of family and gender expectations; labor-saving technology did not so much reduce the number of necessary domestic tasks as it did alter who was responsible for them (Cowan, 1983, chapter 3). Dorothy Nelkin and M. Susan Lindee make a similar point in their examination of the politics and images surrounding genetic technology, noting that scientific discoveries in this area have no inherent meaning; salutary or damaging effects are products of how they are interpreted and used (Nelkin & Lindee, 1995, p. 106). Evidence of a genetic basis for homosexuality, for example, can have a range of political effects. It can provide the rationale for increased tolerance through acceptance of it as natural or for a latter-day form of eugenics intent on eradication (Nelkin & Lindee, 1995, chapter 6). Both these examples refute any simple notion of technological determinism because social and cultural factors shape perceptions and consequences. In fact, there are few – if any – inventions or theories that inexorably have a given effect. The nature of a discovery might shape but does not determine its cultural meaning.

One of the most interesting things about contemporary reaction to the bomb is that it tries to resist this, being implicitly but powerfully based in assumptions of technological determinism. One of the most common features of the various reactions to the atomic bomb – one that cuts across binaries such as optimism/pessimism and hope/fear – was awe. William Laurence, the only reporter allowed to witness the Trinity test of the first atomic bomb, was an avowed nuclear enthusiast who regularly spoke in florid terms of the revolutionary and awe-inspiring nature of atomic energy. His book, *Dawn Over Zero,* begins with a chapter called "Genesis" that describes the Trinity test as having released an "elemental" flame – one "such as had never before been seen on this planet, illuminating earth and sky, for a brief span that seemed eternal, with the light of many super-suns" (Laurence, 1946, p. 3). Laurence's rhetoric reflected a common pattern. Paul Boyer notes that one of the few common elements of the highly dynamic and varied reactions to the bomb was a widespread agreement that "a fresh page had been turned in the book of human history; that human existence was about to be radically altered" (Boyer, 1985, p. 134). Spencer Weart sounds a similar note. When discussing dreams of world government in the postwar years, he writes: "It was as if nuclear energy were such a cosmic force that it would sweep away history, instantly replacing the web of international tensions with a millennial age of peace!" (Weart, 1988, p. 115). Not all views placed this positive spin on the bomb. But the mechanism of change, as well as its scope, was constant. The atomic bomb was viewed as something outside history, in Weart's phrase, a "cosmic force" that by its mere presence would compel far-reaching and revolutionary changes.

This conception of the bomb's importance – while obviously grounded in its powerful nature – also was conditioned by factors external to it. There is no question that the atomic bomb dramatically raised the stakes of international diplomacy, and it is perhaps natural to look for far-reaching and straightforward consequences from such an overwhelming discovery. However, it is possible to trace the origins of the idea of the bomb as a "cosmic force," and not all of it can be attributed to the visual impact of an atomic explosion or even the wanton destruction it inflicted; the firebombing of Japanese cities was one of the many instances that had greatly increased tolerance for acceptable destruction, even before the end of World War II (Gordin, 2007, chapter 2). The atomic bomb did come to be viewed as a qualitatively different kind of weapon, but external factors as well as internal ones are needed to explain how this happened. A prime example of this – as Michael Gordin has persuasively argued – was that the war-ending strategy of the U.S. government necessitated emphasis on the revolutionary aspects of nuclear weapons. In the summer of 1945, many American strategists believed that the Japanese would not surrender without a "shock" – an attack so devastating in psychological as well as military terms that it would break the country's will to fight (Gordin, 2007). This strategy predated the atomic bomb, which was folded into the shock strategy (Gordin, 2007, pp. 16–17). Once it was, there was a conscious effort to portray the bomb as not simply the conventional (if powerful) explosive many thought it to be but rather as a whole new order of weapon. This novelty, it was thought, would hasten the Japanese surrender. Gordin writes: "A warrant to believe the atomic bombings were uniquely different before the surrender of Japan lay largely in the realm of public relations associated with the shock strategy" (Gordin, 2007, p. 108). This counter-intuitive conclusion is supported by much evidence, including the plans to drop more than two bombs and the logistical preparations for a Pacific War lasting long past August 9, 1945, when Nagasaki was bombed (Gordin, 2007). Neither of these things would have been necessary if the bomb had been viewed as something that would automatically and inevitably, by its mere existence or use, produce a Japanese surrender. Even after the end of the war, there were ample reasons to present the atomic bomb as a revolutionary weapon, not merely a powerful one. Such factors were both cultural (celebrating the achievement) and political (placing the United States in a favorable diplomatic position). Certainly, such factors were not the *only* reasons for this perception of the bomb. But they do suggest that the ubiquity of awed reactions was a product of several factors, external as well as internal.

One of the reasons that awed tones were so pervasive is that the rhetoric of "cosmic force" was adaptable to a wide range of reactions; awe was an intensifier as much as a distinct response. And the near ubiquity of such rhetoric easily can obscure the importance of external factors. In the fall of 1945, President Truman issued one of the most prominent expressions of the idea that the bomb represented an ahistorical force. In a message to Congress on October 3 of that year, Truman said: "the release of atomic energy constitutes a new force too revolutionary to consider in the framework of old ideas" (Truman, 1945). This phrase simultaneously reifies and challenges an idea of the atomic bomb as being outside history. Truman certainly recognized that political choices mattered as to how the atomic age unfolded, and his underlying message here was one of urgency; he felt that "we can no longer rely on the slow progress of time to develop a program of control among nations" (Truman, 1945). But the comment also suggests that the atomic bomb was revolutionary enough that it could change the ordinary rules of political and cultural discourse, in which novelty is always filtered through "the framework of old ideas." However, a moment's thought reveals the logical fallacy in Truman's words: How can anything new be analyzed except using pre-existing notions? Pre-existing ideas represent external factors that, inevitably, must be a part of how an innovation is understood. The next sections explore this idea through examination of the rhetoric of the "father of the atomic bomb," Robert Oppenheimer. Oppenheimer provides a good illustration of the need to consider both external and internal factors because his rhetoric about the bomb was largely filtered through attitudes about science that he wished to promote. Certainly, the technical realities of nuclear weapons had an enormous effect on how he – or anyone else – thought about it. But they did not determine it.

ROBERT OPPENHEIMER

Robert Oppenheimer is one of the iconic figures of American science. Born in New York City in 1904, he studied in Europe and quickly established himself as a brilliant mind working in a revolutionary time for physics. By the end of the 1930s, he had established an excellent reputation as a theoretical physicist and teacher. During World War II, he successfully directed Los Alamos National Laboratory – soon to become the most fabled part of the Manhattan Project. In addition to his gifts as a physicist, teacher, and science administrator, Oppenheimer was a charismatic, intellectually impressive, energetic, and charming presence; the resulting cult of personality that often surrounded him in his professional life became one basis for his emerging status as a cultural icon in the early atomic age. He used his influence to promote two goals: offering advice on the best ways to manage atomic weapons and defending the value of science despite its role in creating such a powerful weapon. In Oppenheimer's rhetoric, these goals were intertwined. He felt that science could help society in the atomic age in a number of different ways and consistently offered thoughts on politics that were steeped in a scientific outlook. In this respect, he was not different from other professionals in the mid-1940s, who tended to see their particular expertise as having special relevance to the problems of the atomic age. Paul Boyer notes this phenomenon, commenting on the "large company of otherwise very diverse post-Hiroshima social thinkers who shared a common conviction," namely, that the revolutionary nature of the atomic bomb "had massively enhanced the social relevance of their particular professional skill, reform cause, or political belief" (Boyer, 1985, p. 165). This phenomenon perhaps can be viewed cynically, but it cannot be ascribed wholly to opportunism. It is natural to see new problems in the light of pre-existing frames of reference, and this is exactly what Oppenheimer did. His rhetoric thus provides an excellent illustration of the importance of external factors – in his case, a certain vision for science – in conditioning reaction to the atomic bomb.

Certainly, Oppenheimer's views took into account factors that seem to be an innate part of the reality of the atomic bomb. His many eloquent pronouncements on the subject leave little doubt that he was haunted by the magnitude of the new creation. One of his most famous quotes captured this awareness: "In some sort of crude sense, which no vulgarity, no humor, no overstatement can quite extinguish, the physicists have known sin, and this is a knowledge which they cannot lose" (as quoted in *Time*, 1948, p. 77). The phrase "known sin" is the eye-catching one, and it served as a welcome suggestion that Oppenheimer keenly felt the moral and ethical consequences of nuclear weapons. Two other phrases are also evocative of how Oppenheimer conceived of the dark side of the atomic bomb – as something persistent and enduring. "No overstatement can quite extinguish" this knowledge, he said – nor could vulgarity or humor. Such attempts might go a long way toward obscuring the ominous aspects of nuclear weapons, but they could not "quite" do so. This is a less sensational idea than the image of knowing sin, but it dramatically emphasizes permanence. It was simply "a knowledge which they" – and here Oppenheimer might well have said "we" – "cannot lose." On another occasion, he said that not only were the bombs already devastating but that they also could readily be made "more terrible" and probably "terribly more terrible" (as quoted in *Time*, 1945, p. 30). Awareness of the power of nuclear weapons – and of the potential for even more powerful weapons to be created – played a central role in his reaction to the atomic bomb.

But such technical facts were not wholly determinative of his views. Oppenheimer had a deep belief in the inherent value of scientific work, and he rejected the notion that the atomic bomb should cast doubt on such faith. For example, in a November 2, 1945 speech in Los Alamos to his former colleagues on the Manhattan Project, Oppenheimer offered a lengthy list of justifications for making the atomic bomb, culminating with the thought that

> But when you come right down to it the reason that we did this job is because it was an organic necessity. If you are a scientist you cannot stop such a thing. If you are a scientist you believe that it is good to find out how the world works; that it is good to find out what the realities are; that it is good to turn over to mankind at large the greatest possible power to control the world and to deal with it according to its lights and its values. (Oppenheimer, 1945, p. 317)

In this formulation, the process of finding out "how the world works" was good. It was external factors – the "lights and values" of humankind – that would determine whether the atomic future unfolded positively or negatively. Scientists must feel, Oppenheimer contended here, "that it is good to find out what the realities are." If the realities are troubling, so be it. Ultimately, neither the facts discovered nor the investigative process can determine the social meaning of any particular piece of "how the world works." To a large extent, such rhetoric served a particular professional and personal purpose for Oppenheimer: It absolved science (and scientists) of blame for the new weapons. But it also reveals an understanding of nuclear technology that recognizes, but is not defined by, its destructive nature. Oppenheimer's rhetoric throughout the postwar years provides an illustration of how an external factor (faith in science) interacted with an internal one (destructive power) to produce a distinct and nuanced reaction.

A SCIENTIFIC VISION FOR THE ATOMIC AGE

Not only did Oppenheimer's faith in science survive the atomic bomb, but he also often argued for its increased importance. Technical expertise was an obvious need, but this was not the basis of his argument. Oppenheimer felt that science provided useful models for how people could confront the nuclear age. For Oppenheimer, science was not only defined by technique, discovery, and theory, but it also was a set of perspectives and attitudes – what his colleague James Conant once called "certain habits of mind" – that would be valuable to society at large (Conant, 1947, p. 11). In Oppenheimer's November 1945 speech at Los Alamos, he suggested: "As scientists I think we have perhaps a little greater ability to accept change, and accept radical change, because of our experiences in the pursuit of science" (Oppenheimer, 1945, p. 318). In this formulation, an ability honed through "the pursuit of science" was seen to have utility to nonscientific questions. Such open-mindedness was only one virtue of science that Oppenheimer felt could be widely applicable; another was its community-based international character. He thought that this "may be one of the most helpful things for the future," and he proposed extending, indeed "more or less forcing," international exchange of scientists (Oppenheimer, 1945, pp. 324–325, 321). In this example, Oppenheimer sees the nature of the scientific community as a model for the increased international collaboration that many observers felt was self-evidently necessary in the atomic age. Oppenheimer felt that more than the physicists' technical expertise could be useful to a world learning how to deal with atomic energy. He argued that science provided a way of living, of being in the world, that held important lessons for nonscientists.

In addition to general points about science, Oppenheimer felt that specific attributes of atomic energy could be marshaled to make international control of nuclear weapons more feasible. But this utility was not what was commonly supposed, that of increased urgency or motivation for such change. Oppenheimer argued that there was "some danger in believing" that the atomic bomb constituted a "new argument" for increased international cooperation:

> ... the point is not that atomic weapons constitute a new argument. There have always been good arguments. The point is that atomic weapons constitute also a field, a new field, and a new opportunity for realizing preconditions. I think when people talk of the fact that this is not only a great peril, but a great hope, this is what they should mean. (Oppenheimer, 1945, p. 319)

This is a very different argument for the beneficial effects of atomic energy on diplomacy that was current at the time, which focused on questions of urgency. Oppenheimer himself could sound this theme, noting at one point that "the peoples of this world must unite, or they will perish" (as cited in Smith & Weiner, 1980, p. 311). But Oppenheimer's emphasis here was different. It can be considered a "positive" rather than a "negative" approach because it focuses on what the atomic bomb makes possible rather than on what it demands. It suggests that part of the atomic bomb's relevance to world politics is not a fear that needed to be molded into constructive action but rather a hope borne of the new possibilities that it contained.

One such new possibility was that atomic energy was "a new field, in which the position of vested interests in various parts of the world is very much less serious than in others" (Oppenheimer, 1945, p. 319). The mere fact of the novelty of atomic energy made it easier rather than harder to use it as what he called "a pilot plant for a new type of international collaboration" (Oppenheimer, 1945, p. 320). Any pre-existing field would carry with it – by the simple fact of its established institutions and norms – obstacles that would have to be overcome in designing international control over matters that formerly had been left to nations; atomic energy faced fewer such obstacles. Furthermore, one of the only pre-existing facts about nuclear history – science's centrality to it – also was helpful. Because of that precedent, Oppenheimer suggested, "it is to my mind hardly thinkable that the international traditions of science, and the fraternity of scientists, should not play a constructive part" (Oppenheimer, 1945, p. 319). He also felt that technical aspects of this new field would be helpful. In a 1948 article – written after hopes for international control of atomic energy had become bleak – he bemoaned this failure by citing a missed opportunity that lay in technical considerations. "The development of atomic energy," he wrote, "lay in an area peculiarly suited to such internationalization, and in fact requiring it for the most effective exploitation, *almost on technical grounds alone*" (Oppenheimer, 1948, pp. 245–246; emphasis added). Technical facts about atomic energy could be seen as helpful to the cause of peace, at least in this one respect.

Oppenheimer's specific thinking here is a little hard to follow – reflecting both the subtlety of the idea and its less than convincing nature. He identified one basic fact about atomic energy – that research into peaceful and military applications had so many areas of overlap as to be virtually inseparable from a policy point of view – and argued that this fact would help to solve two related problems in setting up a system of international control (Oppenheimer, 1946). One was "the absence in the world today of any machinery adequate to provide such control" (Oppenheimer, 1946, p. 11). The United Nations existed in 1946 but was still a fledgling organization, and no other precedent existed for the kind of power that an international atomic authority would need. The second was the very thing that he would ultimately identify as helpful – the fact that peaceful and military atomic research were so technically close. This appeared to be highly problematic as well because it closed off the option of simply banning weapons research and allowing investigation into peaceful uses.

However, Oppenheimer had a rationale for how atomic energy could address both obstacles simultaneously. He said that the establishment of an international agency "will be a step that, once learned, can be repeated, a commitment that, once made in one field, can be extended to others. If this is to happen, the Development Authority will have to have a healthy life of its own; it will have to flourish, to be technically strong, to be useful to mankind, to have a staff and an organization and a way of life in which there is some pride and some cause for pride" (Oppenheimer, 1946, p. 14).

This is a hopeful vision for the international community. And while his vision here could, in theory, begin with a first step in any field, he felt that atomic energy was a particularly promising first step. He continued:

> This would not be possible if there were nothing of value to do with atomic energy. This would not be possible if the prevention of atomic armament were its only concern, if all other activity was technically so separable and separate from atomic armament that it could remain in national hands. In the long struggle to find a way of reconciling national and international sovereignty, the peaceful applications of atomic energy can only be a help. (Oppenheimer, 1946, pp. 14–15)

Since it was not possible to separate the peaceful from the military, Oppenheimer argued, it made sense to see what benefits could be derived from their conjunction. And he saw at least a possibility that by expanding the international agency to be a vibrant, forward-looking research institution, the agency could serve as what he earlier called a "pilot plant" for the production of the kind of international community and collaboration needed to prevent war. Certainly, the creation of this kind of international agency could have taken place regardless of the technical facts of atomic energy – that is, even if peaceful and military research could be separated. But the fact that they could not be separated *necessitated* thinking along these lines because there would be no other way to create a system of international control. And it therefore provides an example of how technical facts could point the way toward alleviating rather than exacerbating international tensions and an incipient arms race.

There are many interesting questions that could be asked about Oppenheimer's ideas from the perspective of the history of the interaction between science and policy. As an episode in the reaction to the atomic bomb, however, one of the central realities it illustrates is how external factors influenced this response. In his November 1945 speech at Los Alamos, Oppenheimer had argued that "the very existence of science is threatened, and its value is threatened" (Oppenheimer, 1945, p. 316). During the early atomic age, the institutions of science were anything but threatened because national security needs and consumer demands kept money flowing. But Oppenheimer's lament was centered on the virtues and underlying value of science, and it was these that he wished to defend. Oppenheimer genuinely believed that science was a broadly beneficial enterprise. In one 1950 article he invoked Thomas Jefferson – a man he admired deeply – to suggest the value of science, saying that "Jefferson is confident that an increased understanding of the world will lead to progress; he is convinced that the barbarisms of the past cannot stand up against enquiry and understanding and enlightenment; he is confident in man and sure that as men know more they will act more wisely and live better" (Oppenheimer, 1950, p. 171).

This is a rousing defense of science's value in more than just technical ways, and it was not uncommon for Oppenheimer; these are Enlightenment values, which several historians have noted were defining for him (Schweber, 2000). In this context, they demonstrate the intellectual tools that Oppenheimer brought to his analysis of the atomic bomb. His ideas for how to make atomic energy serve positive ends were interesting and did have a logical basis. But they were about his views on science, not simply his reactions to the atomic bomb. One cannot be separated from the other.

THE ATOMIC BOMB AND EARLY COLD WAR POLITICS

Oppenheimer's scientific vision sketches out one kind of external factor that helped to shape views of the bomb: the role of pre-existing ideas and intellectual frameworks. There are other important external factors, however; one such example is political context. By 1948, hopes for the international control of atomic energy had all but vanished. Oppenheimer wrote that year of "my own view that none of these proposals has any elements of hopefulness in the short term" (Oppenheimer, 1948, p. 251). Oppenheimer was distressed by this development, and in his postmortems on the subject, he clearly identified political choices, not technical realities of atomic energy, as the cause. The main example of this was an uncooperative Soviet Union; the U.S. proposal would have required not only "a reversal of past Soviet policy" but also "a repudiation of elements of Soviet political theory" that would have amounted to a profound and potentially destabilizing set of domestic changes (Oppenheimer, 1948, p. 245). This analysis – with which most of Oppenheimer's contemporaries as well as cold war historians would agree – locates the blame for the emerging arms race in politics and diplomacy, not in the necessary consequences of the weapons themselves. Nor did he fully exempt the United States, pointing out places where Americans' preoccupation with its internal debates precluded "the objective of making the heads of the Soviet state in part, at least, party to our effort" (Oppenheimer, 1948, p. 248). In a 1953 article, Oppenheimer went even further, noting the "many almost inevitable, yet often tragic, elements of weakness, disharmony and disunity" in the West that contributed to the inability to foster international agreement (Oppenheimer, 1953, p. 526). Arms control may have been trumped by an arms race, but the heightened tensions of the burgeoning cold war – not simply the fact of the bomb itself – were responsible for this.

Oppenheimer continued to advocate policy ideas steeped in his scientific vision, but the changes in how he did so provide further evidence that the political context was the main factor in undermining optimistic visions for arms control. In a September 1947 speech, for example, he advocated specific steps that still could be taken. He felt, for example, that "the distribution of isotopes, all of which can be produced by other methods, and which are primarily chosen for their value in biological research, is an extremely prudent step" (Oppenheimer, 1947, p. 36). This was akin to "painting some slight stroke in the picture of the world as we would like to see it in the future" (Oppenheimer, 1947, p. 36). He also argued, here and elsewhere, for keeping scientific inquiry as open as security allowed both for the goodwill created and to help solicit needed ideas. But his 1948 *Foreign Affairs* article left little doubt as to his analysis of the overall utility of such pragmatic short-term measures: "But such arrangements ... significant though they may be for our future welfare, cannot pretend, and do not pretend, to offer us real security, nor are they direct steps toward the perfection of those cooperative agreements to which we rightly look as the best insurance of peace" (Oppenheimer, 1948, p. 252). He still proposed strategies based in science and technology, but in a more limited way than he had done in the more open political climate of just a few years earlier. His ideas and ideals were the same. It was a changed and increasingly tense political context – not a different assessment of technical facts – that lowered his hopes.

Further evidence for this comes from the decreasing cultural authority granted to scientific advice on policy questions. While the purely technical advice of scientists was still demanded, Americans increasingly were deciding that neither science nor its practitioners had any special insights to offer to the host of social and political problems caused by atomic weapons. In fact, the political shortcomings of the early atomic scientists' activism belied Oppenheimer's notion of their special capacity; Paul Boyer has argued that scientists' "intellectual orientation, with its emphasis on defining and rationally confronting arbitrarily delimited problems" was poorly equipped to confront the "maddeningly tangled and amorphous" world of politics (Boyer, 1985, p. 101). Events of the early cold war – such as reports of espionage and the 1948–1949 crisis in Berlin – helped to establish the Soviet Union and international communism as the biggest threats to American well-being. These were clearly areas about which scientists could offer few special claims to expertise. Even seeming victories for the atomic scientists' movement were often limited. One such success, for example, was successful lobbying against the May-Johnson bill, which would have placed control of atomic energy under military auspices. However, as Jessica Wang has noted, "civilian control did not guarantee a commitment to civilian goals" (Wang, 1999, p. 25). Certainly, money flowed to science like never before during the early cold war owing to its ever-deepening connection to national security; this made the professional lives of scientists easier and more profitable than they had been before the war. Quite quickly after the demise of the US proposal for the international control of atomic energy, however, science-based prescriptions for how to conceive of political problems lost their prominent, if tenuous, cultural foothold.

The marginalization of science from policy – which Oppenheimer and his colleagues deplored – serves as further illustration that it is politics, not technology, that conditions the meaning of a particular innovation. Certainly, the extraordinary power of nuclear weapons created a very strong possibility that they would be viewed as destructive. But such a perception was not *mandated* by the technical facts – it was a result of political responses to those facts. It is the interaction of the technical and the political – or factors internal and external to the bomb – that jointly created the perception of it as an exemplar of dark creativity. This is something that Oppenheimer himself realized, noting in 1948:

> Thus, if we try to examine what part atomic energy may play in international relations in the near future, we can hardly believe that it alone can reverse the trend to rivalry and conflict which exists in the present-day world. My own view is that only a profound change in the whole orientation of Soviet policy, and a corresponding reorientation of our own, even in matters far from atomic energy, would give substance to the initial high hopes. (Oppenheimer, 1948, p. 252)

Oppenheimer is not arguing that the changes in U.S. and Soviet policy would result in a peaceful world, although he may well have thought that. Instead, he is arguing that changes in such policy will allow atomic energy to play the role that he had originally envisioned. It is obviously possible to imagine changes in the political orientations of nations so profound that no other factors are needed to produce peace. But such hopes are as fanciful as predictions that atomic weapons, by themselves, would shock the world into renouncing war. More likely, changed international conditions would have resulted in a context into which specific interventions – such as the ones Oppenheimer proposed – could work.

By 1953, the political context had changed yet again – intensifying many of the worrisome trends of the late 1940s. The Soviet Union had developed its atomic bomb, both superpowers were working on thermonuclear weapons, China had become communist, the Korean War was being fought, and the prominence of Senator Joseph McCarthy in the United States marked perhaps the height of antiradicalism in the United States. Oppenheimer himself would shortly become a victim of this cresting anticommunism, stripped of his security clearance the following year for policy disagreements and a leftist past. Amid this highly charged context, a State Department panel on disarmament concluded in 1953 that "fundamentally, and in the long run, the problem which is posed by the release of atomic energy is a problem of the ability of the human race to govern itself without war" (Rhodes, 1995, p. 15). This suggests both the specific role technology plays and the importance of looking beyond it to understand its impact. It foregrounds a vexing problem that is inherent to nuclear weapons: the fact that they make wars too destructive to continue to play their traditional role in settling international disputes. But there are myriad ways that this could change and myriad opinions that could be offered about the ultimatum humanity faced. In Oppenheimer's November 1945 speech at Los Alamos, he had noted that atomic bombs were ultimately "not too hard to make," which meant that "they will be universal if people wish to make them universal" (Oppenheimer, 1945, p. 319). By 1953 it was clear that people had decided – not as a "wish" in the common sense but as a set of conscious choices – to set out on a course to "make them universal." These choices – and the arms race that followed – darkened the atomic age. The terrifying nature of the atomic bomb therefore is a commentary on both the weapon itself and the choices made about it.

REFERENCES

Bethe, H. (1968). J. Robert Oppenheimer, 1904–1967. *Biographical Memoirs of Fellows of the Royal Society*, 14, 391–416.

Boyer, P. (1985). *By the bomb's early light: American thought and culture at the dawn of the atomic age*. New York: Pantheon.

Conant, J. (1947). *On understanding science: An historical approach*. New Haven, CT: Yale University Press.

Cowan, R. (1983). *More work for mother: The ironies of household technology from the open hearth to the microwave*. New York: Basic Books.

Gordin, M. (2007). *Five days in August: How World War II became a nuclear war*. Princeton, NJ: Princeton University Press.

Fussell, P. (1981). Thank God for the atomic bomb. *The New Republic*, 185, 26–30.

Jones, J. (1946). Can atomic energy be controlled? *Harper's*, 192, 425–431.

Kirby, F. (1946). Atomic power. On *Atomic platters: Cold war music from the golden age of homeland security* [CD]. Hamburg, Germany: Bear Family Records.

Laurence, W. (1946). *Dawn over zero: The story of the atomic bomb*. New York: Knopf.

Nelkin, D. & Lindee, M. S. (1995). *The DNA mystique: The gene as cultural icon*. New York: Freeman.

Oppenheimer, J. R. (1945). Speech to the Association of Los Alamos Scientists. Lecture Presented at Los Alamos, NM [transcript]; Smith, A. & Weiner, C. (1980). *Robert Oppenheimer: Letters and recollections* (pp. 315–325). Cambridge, MA: Harvard University Press.

(1946). Atomic energy. Lecture presented at George Westinghouse Centennial Forum [transcript]; Oppenheimer, J. R. (1955). *The open mind* (pp. 3–17). New York: Simon & Schuster.

(1947). Atomic energy as a contemporary problem. Lecture presented at Washington, DC [transcript]; Oppenheimer, J. R. (1955). *The open mind* (pp. 21–41). New York: Simon & Schuster.

(1948). International control of atomic energy. *Foreign Affairs*, 26, 239–252.

(1950). The encouragement of science. *Science News Letter*, 57, 170–172.

(1953). Atomic weapons and American policy. *Foreign Affairs*, 31, 525–535.

Rhodes, R. (1995). *Dark sun: The making of the hydrogen bomb*. New York: Simon & Schuster.

Rosenthal, P. (1991). The nuclear mushroom cloud as cultural image. *American Literary History*, 3, 63–92.

Schell, J. (1982). *The fate of the earth*. New York: Knopf.

Schweber, S. (2000). *In the shadow of the bomb: Oppenheimer, Bethe, and the moral responsibility of the scientist*. Princeton, NJ: Princeton University Press.

Smith, A. & Weiner, C. (1980). *Robert Oppenheimer: Letters and recollections*. Cambridge, MA: Harvard University Press.

Time Magazine. (1945). Terribly more terrible. *Time*, 46, 30.

(1948). Eternal apprentice. *Time*, 52, 70–72.

Truman, H. (1945). *Message to Congress on the Atomic Bomb*. Speech presented in Washington, DC [transcript]; retrieved June 16, 2009, from www.atomicarchive.com/Docs/Deterrence/Truman.shtml.

Wang, J. (1999). *American science in an age of anxiety: Scientists, anti-communism, and the cold war*. Chapel Hill, NC: University of North Carolina Press.

Weart, S. (1988). *Nuclear fear: A history of images*. Cambridge, MA: Harvard University Press.

Yavenditti, M. (1974). John Hersey and the American conscience: The reception of "Hiroshima." *Pacific Historical Review*, 43, 24–49.

6

The Innovation Dilemma: Some Risks of Creativity in Strategic Agency

JAMES M. JASPER

> *Ipse docet quid agam; fas est et ab hoste doceri* [The enemy himself teaches me what to do; it is good to be taught by him]. Ovid

The study of strategic interaction, in which players hope to influence the actions, beliefs, and feelings of others, has long been dominated by game theory. As a branch of mathematics, and a mostly normative one at that, game theory has had enthusiasts, but most social scientists have rejected or ignored it. Sociologists in particular have dismissed it without even knowing much about it. As a result, they have rejected the study of strategy altogether. Since sociology is my main discipline, since I see both insight and limitations to game theory, and since I believe that strategy is central to a great deal of social life, I have tried hard to develop a softer alternative to game theory (Jasper, 2004, 2006). This entails a fuller, more realistic recognition of emotions, cognition, and social context. And one of my hopes in doing this work has been to better understand the creativity of social action, especially the creativity found in social movements (Jasper, 1997).

In strategic settings, creativity has several characteristics that may not hold elsewhere. For one, it arises out of interaction as players act and react to one another; we must lay aside the popular image of the creative genius who first imagines new possibilities and only then presents or promulgates them. In addition, creative moves and techniques are likely to have an array of both positive and negative consequences, but these normally will be distributed unequally. One player may receive all the benefits, another all the harm. More often the distribution is somewhere between the two extremes. Strategic innovations normally are intended to benefit the creators, of course, but at the expense of others, especially opponents. In some cases we can see malevolence as a motive behind this innovation; more often the player in a strategic engagement is simply doing his or her job and *aiding* his or her team. Only a moralist operating on what Max Weber called an "ethic of ultimate ends" can condemn such creativity out of hand without tallying the full range of consequences. This chapter will examine unintended sources of harm to both the innovator and bystanders not initially involved in the strategic interaction.

In my own research on strategic engagement, I have so far tried to identify tradeoffs or dilemmas (even when choices are not explicitly recognized as dilemmas, they are usually still there as underlying tradeoffs) that strategic players face across a range of different institutional arenas, including families, politics, international relations, markets, and organizations. Similar dilemmas await what I call *simple players*, individuals, and *compound players*, made up of a number of individuals and ranging from small teams up through nations. Compound players always face challenges of coordination that simple players do not because compound players are always *arenas for conflict as well as players in conflicts.*

One central tradeoff/dilemma is the *innovation dilemma*: New strategic techniques can be especially effective because they catch other players off guard, but they have risks. For one, your own team may not be able to pull off the innovation because they themselves are not used to it either. With familiar tactics, you are at least aware of whether you have the know-how and resources to carry them off. If familiarity with your characteristic moves gives confidence to your opponents, it also reduces anxiety on your side. In trying some new line of action, you may overreach, for instance, trying to change cultural understandings more rapidly than audiences can understand or accept. As Thorstein Veblen pointed out, there is a liability to taking the lead and advantages to lagging behind, thanks to this tradeoff between surprise and competence.[1] In this way, *strategic creativity always entails risks* for the creative player as well as for others. In this chapter, I explore some of the destructive effects of strategic innovation for the player that innovates as well as for others.

The innovation dilemma has a number of forms and dimensions that can be formulated as distinct dilemmas. The innovation dilemma is a twist on the *engagement dilemma*: Opening a new interaction has risks that are hard to anticipate or measure – one reason that both compound and simple players usually prefer known habits to new ventures (Jasper, 2006, p. 26; Tilly, 2006). Even those who think that they are starting from an advantaged position may lose that advantage for a number of reasons: Apparently

[1] As Arthur Stinchcombe (1965) put it, there is a liability to newness: Most new organizations fail, forced to do too many things at once: create new social roles, attract new customers or audiences, and develop new technologies.

weaker players may outmaneuver you; new players may enter the interaction, perhaps with greater resources or other advantages, or you may have mis-estimated your relative advantages. The innovation dilemma has similar risks, especially because any move that you invent can be copied by other players. They also may themselves invent new moves that block your innovation. What is more, many innovations have to do with creating new arenas, which are necessarily open-ended in their dynamics and outcomes. Almost every strategic arena is too complex for any player – even the most powerful – to manage completely. The invention of a new technique – a tactic or a technology – stimulates unpredictable reactions that often harm the creator.

The innovation dilemma often raises a related challenge, which I call the *sorcerer's apprentice dilemma* (Jasper, 2006, p. 97). Any routine you invent to accomplish things can take on a life of its own, eventually shaping your ends as well as your means. If you have invested a lot in the old ways (psychically and financially), you may be reluctant to drop them. You will tend to pursue the ends that you think you can attain with these particular means. You grow fonder of and more efficient with these means, so you tend to favor them over alternatives. Experts in the new procedures may arise who reinforce both effects. As in the original fairy tale, the very power of your creation means that you cannot always control it. (I have used the term "tastes in tactics" to get at how we may come to value certain means above and beyond their efficacy: Jasper, 1997, chapter 10). Thus, if the engagement dilemma suggests that one source of risk in creativity lies in the reactions of others, the sorcerer's apprentice dilemma suggests that it also may lie in the new invention itself.

In both cases, the innovation dilemma is linked to the very general *risk dilemma* (Jasper, 2006, p. 18): *Prudent* choices involve low risks but low potential payoffs; *enterprising* choices entail high risks and high potential payoffs. If the engagement dilemma suggests the perils of unknown factors in strategic interaction – Machiavelli's *Fortuna* or Clausewitz' fog of war – then the risk dilemma recognizes outcomes whose likelihoods can be estimated to some extent. We may know these probabilities precisely or only vaguely, but at least we are aware of their possibility. Greater risks are often associated with greater potential gains, as well as greater potential costs and losses – the distribution of likely outcomes is bipolar. Players' choices about how much to risk are based on culture, cognition, emotion, personality, and institutional incentives. These affect how creative players will try to be.

In certain kinds of strategic settings, these related dilemmas are especially prominent. In situations of competition and conflict, one player's advance comes at the expense of others, and most strategic creativity is *intended* to disadvantage others. Here, drawing on international relations theory, we see the *security dilemma*: Even the most defensive moves may be interpreted as threatening by others, who then respond in kind. The original player sees these new moves as threatening, and so on in turn, until there is some kind of arms race (although the innovations need not involve arms). The practical innovations are accompanied by emotions of fear and anger, leading to a spiral of mutual suspicion and hostility. According to political scientist Robert Jervis (1978, p. 169; see also Hertz, 1951; Jasper, 2006, p. 137), "many of the means by which a state tries to increase its security decrease the security of others." Even actions that were not intended originally as threatening (or even seen as strategic in some cases) can be perceived that way by others. These spirals often result when strong rivalries already exist because they focus attention on the conflict and carry hostile emotions. Nothing catches a player's attention like the "power of the negative" that a threat carries (Jasper, 1997, chapter 5, 2006, chapter 2). Competitive arenas influence how players frame and judge the creativity of others.

FLEXIBILITY AND COMMITMENT

Creativity is an extreme form of flexibility. Strategic engagement, like much of social life, is a complex interplay between flexibility and rigidity. In any given situation, there are advantages and disadvantages to each. If you have the resources for extensive reconnaissance, you can maintain your flexibility as long as possible while you gather information. You can look at several options before deciding on one and closing off the others. You also try to work out ways to take only tentative steps down any given path of action, investing few resources in the initial steps until you believe they are the right ones. "People make small investments and build a small structure to collect relevant information," says Arthur Stinchcombe (1990, p. 5). "If the news is good, they make bigger investments and develop a larger structure to collect relevant news; and so on. Uncertainty is transformed piecewise into risk." Flexibility and options are crucial components of strategic action.

I try to get at this interplay through the *planning dilemma*, another aspect of innovation: Too much advance planning and preparation may leave you unable to respond flexibly during an engagement; too little planning and preparation leave you without routines and resources to deploy (Jasper, 2004, p. 13). Although Karl Weick (1979, p. 215) claims that "organizations continue to exist only if they maintain a balance between flexibility and stability," I believe that this balance shifts over time according to strategic imperatives. Creativity is helpful at certain times and harmful at others.

You can be flexible and creative along different dimensions of strategic action: in your tactics, your allies, your arenas, your own identity, your rhetoric, and even your goals. An inability to adapt to new information or circumstances in any of these areas puts more pressure on the other ones. There are fewer "degrees of freedom" for solving any given strategic problem. If you have unquestionable commitments to your allies, your own identity, and your tactics (say, a belief in Gandhian nonviolence), you must work harder to find the right arena where you can put that combination to work. Once you make firm commitments on several dimensions, your opponents know better what to expect of you and can prepare more thoroughly.

But so can your allies. Unpredictable creativity carries as many risks as incompetence does (itself a form of unpredictability, often misinterpreted as canniness by opponents). Allies who joined you because of your basic moral commitments may defect when they see you waffling on those – or when they see you suddenly sell out other allies. (The traitor's problem is that even his or her new allies may dislike and mistrust him or her.) Politicians who seem willing to do anything to win an election lose the confidence of those who care about other goals.

Some players have the flexibility to entirely re-create themselves in response to changed circumstances. France provides an interesting example in the Corps des Mines and the Corps des Ponts et Chaussées, prestigious professional organizations of engineers closely attached to the state. Originating in the Napoleonic era, they were concerned originally with mining and with bridges and roads, respectively. As these pursuits grew less important with industrialization, both corps entered entirely new (industrial) fields in order to remain at the commanding heights of French policymaking and economic development. The Corps des Mines became experts in industrial production and especially energy (including, later, nuclear reactor engineering), allowing it to seize the important posts in the Ministry of the Environment when it was formed. The Corps des Ponts et Chaussées went into urban planning and transport. Both corps seemed to abandon their own reasons for being but in fact merely demonstrated their primary goals to be the power, prestige, and wealth of the corps and their members (Suleiman, 1978).

Even though unwavering commitments on certain dimensions place strains on the others, they also give a strategic campaign its purpose, its sense of identity, without which, why should people sign on? Inflexibility sometimes can be a direct strategic advantage in other ways, too. Your opponents may realize that you are playing a different game than they are. If they are protecting their material interests while you are obeying God's will (say they are the liquor industry defending against moral crusaders), this may signal a stubbornness on your part that would lead you to ignore many of the costs of your strategies. It may make you unpredictable rather than rational in a manner recognizable to your opponents (who may follow a stricter economic calculus of costs and benefits). If you are oblivious to normal strategic calculations, this may make it harder for your opponents to predict your moves. It is like a game of chicken in which one side is willing to die.[2]

LEARNING AND CREATIVITY

If flexibility is one concept closely related to creativity, learning is another. *Strategic learning* is the ability to make inferences from experience and to adjust predictions and actions that are not working. Because mistakes especially command attention, they are the primary teachers, drawing on the negative emotions of threat. Prior success, on the other hand, while it may yield useful confidence, easily slips into complacency. It would be best to learn from the mistakes of others, as Ovid said, but the emotional motivation is rarely there. Without mistakes, there would be little strategic learning or creativity.

Complacency discourages learning and flexibility. You can grow complacent if you have considerable resources [the reason for the common tradeoff between resources and intelligence (Flyvbjerg, 1998)] or if you have a history of success. Success can blind you to the need for learning – often until it is too late to learn what you need to. Thanks to the sorcerer's apprentice tradeoff, expertise in the usual ways of doing things can blind you to new ones, especially to new technologies. Although economists advise us to ignore sunk costs (about which we can do nothing), this is difficult psychologically. "As they develop greater and greater competence in using existing technologies, knowledge, routines, forms or strategies," says James March (1994, pp. 239–240), "decision makers become less and less willing or able to change to newer ones that offer long-run superiority.

[2] On the other hand, moral stubbornness may make you more predictable because you do not respond to changing material incentives. Economists have argued that this is the evolutionary purpose of many emotions, such as righteous anger, that signal that you are dependable beyond the pursuit of narrow self-interest (Frank, 1988).

They become better and better at an inferior practice." Knights did not immediately put aside their horses for pikes and bows. We see here an underlying tradeoff between the short run and the long run (Jasper, 2006, p. 83).

Most learning involves borrowing from others, copying what has worked for them, but occasionally someone invents a new way of doing something or a new thing to do. This creative process is necessarily a bit mysterious – combining gifted individuals, certain kinds of interactions, available resources, suitable incentives, and more (Ganz, 2009). Certain kinds of individuals and certain kinds of organizations tend to be more strategically creative than others. According to Marshall Ganz, writing about union organizing, *leaders* tend to be more creative when they are motivated by the intrinsic rewards of their positions rather than by salaries (especially when they have some personal commitment to the cause), when they are plugged into a number of social networks on which they can draw, and when they have had experience with diverse strategic repertories from which they can derive tactics. Creativity tends to be found in *organizations* with regular and open deliberation, attentive audiences to whom decision makers are accountable, and diverse resource flows (important partly because they involve the players with diverse other kinds of players in their immediate environment). For both individuals and organizations, creativity is enhanced by immediate and solid feedback, the ability to see things in a broad context, and diverse kinds of local knowledge (Ganz, 2009).

In his work on creativity in the arts and scholarship, Mihaly Csikszentmihalyi (1996) seconds some of these points and adds others. Creative individuals tend to be totally absorbed in their activity. This is more obvious for a musician or dancer, but a strategic player, too, must absorb the explicit and implicit rules of his or her arenas so fully that they become second nature to him or her. Since strategic arenas are also arenas of human interaction (unlike mathematics, say), good strategists are rarely as distant or weird as (Csikszentmihalyi implies) creative artists frequently are, although political activists, as artists of moral voice, sometimes can appear a bit kooky, rejecting as they do many of their society's commonplaces (Jasper, 1997, pp. 222ff). Csikszentmihalyi also says that some domains of thought are more open to creativity than others, and it is tempting to say the same about strategic arenas. But the parallels between art/thought and strategy become weak here. When resources flow from society into a realm of artistic endeavor, increased activity levels result in innovations. But when resources flow into a strategic arena, the purpose is often to check the creativity of one side (those relying on intelligence more than resources, typically).

There are tighter parallels between strategic engagement and collaborative arts such as jazz or improvisational theater. In trying to understand the creativity of the these arts, R. Keith Sawyer (2003) observes an emphasis on process rather than product, considerable unpredictability, the attachment of meaning to an action only after the fact and only collectively, complex forms of communication, and the emergence of new actions and processes. Systems of strategic engagement and small groups of performers are similar in how tight their interactions are. But, again, there is a difference: The creation of art perhaps can go wrong, but when it does, the consequences are not as devastating as they are in many strategic systems. And collaborative artists do not have to worry about opponents monitoring their activity for mistakes and vulnerabilities.

Knowledge gained the hard way, by a player learning from his or her own mistakes, can be adopted by other players: the easy way. Most innovations are easily copied [although not all: Dissemination depends on resources, personnel, investments, and social networks, as Joseph Schumpeter argued (1942)]. With strategic action, there is considerable symmetry. What is valuable for one player to know is also valuable for other players to know (if not to adopt, then at least to anticipate). This is one reason that defectors, who take know-how with them to another team, are so valuable. This symmetry means that in most cases *the creativity of one player usually gives it only a temporary advantage*. There is pressure to take advantage of one's own innovation as quickly as possible despite the risks of the innovation dilemma.

If your creativity stimulates counterinnovation by opponents, you may end up with a net loss. For instance, sporadic initial protests against plans for nuclear reactors in the United States during the 1960s – the creation of a new political debate – frequently were successful, but the much larger antinuclear movement that emerged in the 1970s stopped no plants at all. The difference? Recognizing the threat posed by a growing, national antinuclear movement, the nuclear industry and electric utilities (their customers) counterorganized, grew more stubborn and pugnacious, and brought their enormous resources to bear on the controversy (Jasper, 1990, p. 109). This is the kind of result against which the engagement dilemma warns. The inventors of a new political issue caught their opponents off guard, but their very success aroused too much attention – and countermeasures – from opponents.

Not only can strategic creativity directly backfire like this, but it also can trigger sequences and spirals that work to the disadvantage of *all* players involved and many bystanders. In many engagements, learning from others is too slow. Players must act in the absence of careful observation and experience. Strategic engagement is unpredictable, and creative moves have any number of unanticipated consequences. This is true of all social life, but when there are other players trying to twist what you do to their own advantage, unforeseen results multiply – hence the engagement dilemma. One player's initial advantage may give way to everyone's disadvantage. This kind of case, usually portrayed as an unanticipated relationship between individual decisions and collective outcomes, is the stuff of much economics and game theory (e.g., Schelling, 1978). We'll look at two cases of anticipated consequences which suggest not a contrast between individual and collective but a set of risks arising from strategic engagement over time. The creation of new techniques had devastating consequences – immediately in one case, gradually in the other.

BALL BEARINGS

In war, we see clearly how one side's strategic creativity can (and is designed to) lead to the other side's destruction. But some military innovations generate harm to those not previously involved as weapons grow more devastating and affect "noncombatants." Indeed, one of the commonplaces in theories of modern warfare is that there is no longer a clear distinction between the professional militaries fighting the war and the production, transportation, and communication systems that sustain it – or the civilians who work in those industries and also (presumably) support the war. The idea that modern war must be total war is often attributed, in an interpretation especially popular with the Allies of World War II, to Carl von Clausewitz, who had postulated, "War is an act of force and there is no logical limit to that force."[3] Whatever its etymology, the idea that modern war involved all citizens helped to inspire fascist regimes (and their close cousin, Stalin's USSR) to make that awful prediction a reality by mobilizing production and education to the end of "national glory" – and setting off a deadly – if creative – escalation of war in the process.

Even after the carnage of the Great War, World War II represented a new peak of destruction. The 55 million dead were more than in all other wars

[3] Basil Liddell Hart especially promoted the idea of Clausewitz as the "apostle of total war," a view that the British military historian and strategist could see repeated in the Nazis. This clash-of-civilizations view was good propaganda but nonetheless ironic given Clausewitz's actual support for British-style democracy in his own Prussia. See Bassford (1994).

combined (Boot, 2006, p. 299). More strikingly, the proportion of casualties who were civilians rather than combatants was far higher than in previous wars. (The armies actually managed to reduce their own casualties from wounds and disease by a large amount.) The foremost reason for both developments was the use of strategic bombing against industry and cities rather than against narrowly defined military targets. The concept of strategic aerial bombardment was, according to historian Allan Millett (1996, p. 331), the only innovation of the interwar period that "represented a truly new approach to war-waging." It may rank as the most destructive innovation of all time – so far. The reason is that each air force that tried *precision* bombing against military targets soon replaced it with *area* bombing against civilian populations.

The idea that modern warfare would entail this kind of mass bombing had already developed by World War I. An Italian general, Giulio Douhet, through popular writings in the 1920s and 1930s, argued that only bombing could break the kind of stalemate that World War I had become. He believed – erroneously it turned out – that incendiary bombs and poison gas, dropped on large cities, would cripple the morale of a nation's citizens. No air force adopted Douhet's terrible vision as official doctrine. In the United States, for instance, interwar instructors at the Air Corps Tactical School emphasized attacks on economic infrastructure rather than on civilians per se (Schaffer, 1985, p. 28), and it remained official U.S. doctrine to avoid the latter even as real practice diverged.

The Luftwaffe started it. Dunkirk was evacuated at the end of May and beginning of June 1940, and the French surrendered two weeks later. Having concluded a pact with Stalin the previous August, Hitler turned his attention to Britain, where the pugnacious Churchill had become prime minister. Operation Sea Lion, an amphibious invasion scheduled for mid-September (before bad weather set in), required that the Luftwaffe establish air dominance so that it could protect the German landing fleet. This meant destroying large numbers of Royal Air Force (RAF) fighter planes without losing too many Luftwaffe fighters, which would be needed to cover the invasion.

Initially, Luftwaffe fighters were sent in small squadrons to lure RAF fighters into combat. When this failed to have the desired effect, bombers were sent over Britain escorted by fighters – although this put the escorts in the devastating position of simply waiting to be attacked. Bombing was aimed at military targets such as radar installations, aircraft factories, and airfields. On the night of August 24, however, a number of bombs were dropped on London, setting the East End on fire – possibly an unintentional action by a group of bombers simply unloading their ammunition on their way home after failing to find their targets. The very next night, the RAF began bombing raids on Berlin.

In retaliation, and perhaps believing that most RAF airfields had been knocked out of commission, the Germans began massive urban raids on September 7, involving more than 400 bombers. London was bombed day and night, with the docks of the East End especially targeted.[4] But the RAF fighters, no longer facing raids on their own airfields, recovered quickly and put up strong resistance, forcing the Luftwaffe to give up morning raids and then to switch exclusively to nighttime, when precision bombing was impossible. On September 17, Hitler indefinitely postponed Operation Sea Lion, although the raids on London continued (Macksey, 1990; Overy, 2001). In a few weeks, both sides had adopted a terrible new tactic, the mass bombing of cities.[5]

A number of emotional dynamics lay behind the escalation. Historian John Lukacs has described this period as a personal "duel" between Churchill and Hitler. The dictator expected the British to capitulate and saw Churchill as the only reason they did not. In reaction to one of Churchill's pugnacious speeches, according to Lukacs (1990, p. 168), Hitler "was insulted by it. The unbending nature of Churchill's rhetoric angered him." Hitler hoped to persuade the British people of the virtues of peace, portraying Churchill (ironically) as out of touch, a madman. His bombing campaign had the opposite effect. Instead of splitting the coalition that was Britain, he cemented it, helping Churchill to rally support.

Part of Hitler's initial aggressive innovation reflects his extreme choice when faced with the risk dilemma, in the form of the engagement dilemma. Risk taking and initiating engagement give a player confidence. Hitler was supremely confident in his own military powers, believing that Germany would prevail in the Battle of Britain. "Fascists," remarks Michael Mann (2004, p. 22), "were too aggressive for their own good – especially in their

4 That the initial August 24 raid hit the strategically important East End suggests that it may not have been altogether accidental, but no one knows for sure. I thank Tami Biddle for help in pinning this down.

5 The Luftwaffe's precision-bombing campaign failed partly because of Germany's poor handling of the planning dilemma. Precision bombing requires extensive information about an opponent's industrial infrastructure and air defenses. The Germans had gathered this intelligence assiduously for France and Poland but not for Britain, which it apparently had not considered a likely opponent until Churchill became prime minister (Corum, 1997, p. 283). Planning requires and encourages the gathering of relevant information; creativity may take a strategic player down new paths about which little is known.

keenness for war. They were chronically overconfident about what the [fascist] new man could achieve." Initially, that confidence paid off with quick victories, and Hitler might have been able to keep his gains were it not for a number of unforeseeable events (especially Churchill's becoming prime minister, the Japanese attack on Pearl Harbor, and the resulting entry of the United States into the war). Only in retrospect does Hitler's angry assault on Britain look like a case of fatal overconfidence because other players responded strongly enough to make it into that. The destructiveness of his tactical innovation emerged immediately, but it turned back on him only slowly.

The flip side of overconfidence in your own team is underestimation of other players, because confidence consists of relative comparisons of competence. The Nazis cultivated the idea that Germans were hard, ruthless warriors, men of action rather than words, who could concentrate their force in the person of a leader who embodied the nation. Conversely, they saw parliamentary democracies as too soft to redirect their economy to full war production, too divided by parliamentary norms of respect. Göring jeered that the Americans were only capable of making "cars and refrigerators" (Miller, 2006, p. 77).

Now it was Britain's turn to overestimate the effect of area bombing on civilian morale, just as Hitler had done. The British, ignoring their own experience during 1940 (in which mass bombing had increased national solidarity, not damaged it) and understandably eager for revenge, were quick to broaden their own bombing in Germany. In the face of considerable resistance from Luftwaffe fighters and flak from the ground, the RAF switched almost immediately to nighttime raids. Specific factories could not be seen at night, but the lights of large cities could. "The [nighttime] bombing was wildly inaccurate and crew losses were appalling," says historian Donald Miller (2006, pp. 5–6). "But killing Germans was wonderful for British morale – payback for the bombing of Coventry and London, and England had no other way to directly hurt Germany."

Official British policy changed more slowly. The War Cabinet, studying precision-bombing raids conducted during the spring and summer of 1941, found that only one in five crews had come within five miles of their targets, despite crew claims to the contrary (Biddle, 2002, p. 195). The following winter, as a result, "the morale of the enemy civilian population and especially industrial workers" became a "primary object" for bombing (Schaffer, 1985, p. 36). Policy followed reality. Precision bombing had been a fantasy, impossible to carry out. At least area bombing could be executed, even if its expected effects were just as much of a fantasy (a form of the sorcerer's apprentice dilemma). But the new policy was not made public.

For the American bomber units, the Eighth Air Force, which began combat operations out of Britain in August 1942, explicit policy and considerable effort by commanders resisted the switch from precision to mass bombing of targets throughout Europe, even Germany. The Americans had a new invention no other air force had, the Norden sight, which they expected would give their bombers far more accuracy than German or British planes. Plus the American Flying Fortresses and B-24 Liberators were so heavily armed, planners believed, that they could protect themselves on long missions without accompanying fighter planes. Technical superiority, the Americans were sure, would allow them to be more precise and thus more humane, and privately and publicly they compared themselves explicitly to the brutal Germans (and more implicitly to the British). Seeing themselves as superior, they did not think that British and German mistakes held any lessons for them. They would have to make their own mistakes, the usual spur to creativity.

On the basis of their confidence, the U.S. Army Air Forces (USAAF) concentrated on German military targets in the midst of friendly populations in France, Belgium, and the Netherlands. By landing only one bomb in five within a thousand feet of their targets, the U.S. bombers managed to kill thousands of those civilians, perhaps still friendly but increasingly appalled and angry (Schaffer, 1985, p. 39). Later, in the months leading up to D-day, operational commanders secured a compromise with their political superiors: They would adopt oil facilities as a secondary target. This allowed them to aim at military targets that happened to be near oil depots so that "stray" bombs might hit the latter as a bonus. Lower-level commanders and flight crews found many similar ways to conduct mass bombing under the official guise of precision bombing.

In Italy, the USAAF took pains to compile lists of cultural sites that should not be bombed – except with special permission or in case of military necessity. Arbitrary choices and "accidents" abounded: Florence was hit despite being on the most-prohibited list; the ruins of Pompeii were bombed for no apparent military reason; and the Monte Cassino Abbey was pulverized, along with the remains of Saint Benedict it contained, because some soldiers thought they saw a radio antenna sticking out a window and feared Germans might be using it to direct their artillery. When, six days after Rome was bombed in September 1943, King Victor Emmanuel ousted Mussolini, the area bombing raids seemed vindicated. Partly as a result, no restrictions at all were placed on the subsequent bombing of Budapest,

Bucharest, or Sofia in an (unsuccessful) effort to propel their three Eastern European nations out of the Axis.

The bombing of Germany raised the same issues: Could precise military targets be struck? Would civilian morale collapse under mass bombing? Could industrial production be crippled? Despite the experience with Italy, few thought that German noncombatants would fold easily or that, even if they did fold, this would necessarily cripple the undemocratic regime. Unsurprisingly, commanders who believed that selective bombing would contribute more to winning the war also praised its moral superiority over mass bombing. Their opponents argued that civilian morale would collapse under sufficient strain, saving military lives and shortening the war, also a kind of moral position. Both sides were committed to an image of modern society and especially the economy as fragile. But as historian Tami Biddle (2002, p. 9) says, "Modern economies and societies proved surprisingly robust, capable of coping, responding positively to stress, and, ultimately, withstanding tremendous punishment."

The Americans thought they had found a fatal pressure point in the German economy, a factory complex around Schweinfurt that manufactured half the Germans' ball bearings. An intelligence officer confidently briefed some of the pilots: "Three months [from now] there won't be a single engine operating in the whole country" (Miller, 2006, p. 193). The attack in mid-August 1943 saw 16 percent of the bombers shot down; in a follow-up raid two months later, 198 of 291 bombers were either shot down or damaged (Biddle, 2002, p. 224). There was little effect on German production. Although some American commanders insisted that these raids hurt German morale, it was clear that precision bombing was not working. Increasingly, as the British had done, the Americans defined cities as military targets, an escalation into mass bombing that would peak with the utter devastation of Dresden in February 1945.

Ball bearing factories were hard enough to hit, but the USAAF's public relations campaign had raised expectations far higher. The media repeated the boast that Americans could drop a bomb into a pickle barrel with their Norden sites, elaborating the feeling that British bombing had simply been inept. Thus, for audiences back home, the USAAF continued to insist that it used precision bombing and concealed its real targets in its own official statistics with the new category of "industrial areas," which included cities, urban areas, and government buildings as well as factories and railroads (Biddle, 2002, p. 259). A media scandal erupted when, after the Dresden raids, U.S. newspapers reported that a British commander had admitted that the Allied forces were targeting German population centers (Schaffer,

1985, pp. 98ff). The irresistible promise of precision bombing was crafted especially for politicians and voters back home who might influence appropriations – the same rhetorical package Americans would get from Donald Rumsfeld and George W. Bush 60 years later.

Some of the factors that drew the United States into the dark innovation of indiscriminate area bombing were *technical*, especially the impossibility of accurately sighting targets through cloud cover. Others grew out of *interactions* with opponents, including the lack of long-range fighter escorts or effective protection by their own gunnery. And we should not underestimate interactions of the USAAF with other players *on its own team*. Foremost was an intense rivalry with the other forces, even in the resource-rich situation of a popular war. The bombing wing needed to show a return on the huge technological investment it represented, especially so as to maintain the service's independence. Given the fierce rivalry common between different military forces – no doubt due to the necessarily different ways of fighting wars on land, sea, and air – innovations usually entail funding increases. The force gaining the resources favors the innovations for that reason (a twist on the sorcerer's apprentice dilemma), but its rivals almost inevitably oppose them. Like all compound players, a nation's military is as much an arena for conflict as it is a player in external wars. The U.S. public, another domestic audience that admired precise technology and force and disliked heavy military casualties, also had to be placated (or misled).

The USAAF ran afoul of the planning dilemma. Military planners had such confidence in their heavily armed bombers' ability to defend themselves that they did not produce sufficient fighter escorts and ignored altogether the need for long-range escorts (even though a solution was available in the form of disposable fuel tanks that could be added to existing fighters) (Biddle, 2002, p. 207). Flexibility instead had to take the form of secretive mass bombing campaigns.

Some of the devastating bombing of World War II can be explained by a common emotional dynamic of direct conflict: The goal shifts from winning in the arena to punishing one's opponent. The latter is demonized and hated, and self-righteous punishment and revenge take over as motives. Hitler's fury at British resistance – not to mention his patent insanity – led him to initiate massive, indiscriminate bombing campaigns. British thirst for revenge made it easy for them to return the favor. American anger over Pearl Harbor, combined with racism, led them to broad air raids more easily in the Japanese than in the German theater of war. This construction of the opponent as essentially evil can lead to this kind of escalation and shift in goals (on the political importance of villains, heroes, and victims, see Jasper and Young, 2006). Emotions play a central role in decisions here, one key to how creativity can be deployed for destructive purposes.

The Germans brutally captured the emotional essence of mass civilian bombing with their V-1 and V-2 rockets, which began falling on London a few days after D-day: V stood not for "Victory," but for *Vergeltungswaffen*, "vengeance weapons" (Lukacs, 1990, p. 212).

The premise behind area bombing was that civilians were a central part of the opposing side, and if their morale cracked, it might bring down the entire alliance. This is a common – if destructive – idea in politics, sports, protest, and other strategic arenas: Go after the weak link.

Another factor was the sheer will to believe. Biddle (2002) has documented the gap between rhetoric and reality. Although she tends to view the overconfidence behind strategic bombing as a malfunctioning cognitive heuristic, strategically, the rhetoric served many purposes. Although the enormous bombing campaigns had little effect on the Allies' opponents' will to fight, the rhetoric satisfied other players, namely, those on the air forces' own side: the politicians and public and other forces whose support was necessary for funding and autonomy for the air forces, as well as other nations observing the war. On the horns of the *Janus dilemma* – between attending to external players and attending to one's own team – it was in many ways a triumph for the latter choice.

If the United States was drawn only reluctantly into bombing large swathes of German cities, it had no hesitations when it came to Japan. Racism, less appreciation for Japan's cultural monuments, a thirst to avenge Pearl Harbor (parallel to Britain's vengefulness for German bombing campaigns), and awareness of the special vulnerability of the country's wooden housing all played a role. Firebombing was planned from the start, and the momentum of attacking Japanese civilians continued right through to Hiroshima and Nagasaki. Only afterward, and only in small circles, did some sense of regret or at least distress over atomic weapons set in, leading some political elites to work hard to transform the atomic bomb into a peaceful benefit as a form of penance. This enthusiasm for civilian nuclear energy is the background for our other case.

SELLER'S REMORSE

We turn now to a three-way interaction among government agencies, manufacturers of nuclear reactors, and electric utilities, with particular attention to the rivalry between two of the manufacturers, General Electric (GE) and Westinghouse. Established immediately after World War II, the U.S. Atomic Energy Commission (AEC, 1947–1974) saw its mission as the promotion of nuclear energy and only secondarily its regulation. It financed some reactors, offered free uranium fuel, and – most importantly – insured reactors against accidents in the Price-Anderson Act of 1957. None of this persuaded managers of electric utilities that nuclear reactors were competitive with coal-fired plants because indeed they were not.[6]

What primarily changed their minds, in 1963, was GE's sale of a plant to Jersey Central Power and Light for $66 million, known as a "turnkey" contract because GE would arrange to build the entire plant and simply hand over the key to the utility. This was the first time that a utility claimed it was building a nuclear reactor because it was cheaper than a coal-fired plant; others had been described as experiments. GE's main competitor, Westinghouse, immediately began to offer turnkey deals as well, and within three years, the two companies sold a dozen plants this way. In addition, the companies (quickly joined by several others) began to sell plants whose prices were not fixed in advance, setting off what critics would dub "the great bandwagon market." Of new orders for electrical generation, nuclear power represented only 17 percent in 1965 but 36 percent in 1966 and an astounding 47 percent in 1967 (Walker, 1992, pp. 33–34). More strikingly, the bandwagon had the effect of "forcing" this new technology: GE was soon offering gargantuan reactors of 1,100 MW, at a time when the largest operating reactor had a capacity of only 200 MW – and there had only been a few years of experience with that size. "Through the late 1960s," comments Steven Cohn (1997, p. 23), "there were no operating experience data from which to derive cost estimates for commercial-sized nuclear plants." There was insufficient time for these companies to make enough mistakes to learn from. This aspect of the rivalry ended only when the AEC intervened to cap licenses at 1,300 MW. A new technology and accompanying industry had been created.

Despite widespread (but not unanimous) enthusiasm at the time, the great bandwagon market quickly turned into a nightmare for almost all involved, and within a decade, the U.S. market for reactors was dead (it has yet to revive even today). Between them, GE and Westinghouse lost as much as a billion dollars on the turnkey contracts, a sum not recouped in the 10 years of free-flowing orders after Oyster Creek. Electric utilities, making calculations on the basis of the early contracts, were misled

6 For this case study I draw primarily on Cohn (1997, chapter 2), Jasper (1990, chapter 3), and Walker (1992, chapter 2).

into ordering plants whose costs spiraled out of control. Regulators – and even more the public – were saddled with reactors that were much riskier than they needed to be (one reason for rising costs were the safety features that had to be retrofitted during construction). Safer passive designs were ignored in favor of the light-water technologies of these two companies (originally designed to be compact enough to power Navy submarines, not to be safe). Nobody won from forcing nuclear technology along so fast.

How did this happen? The main factor was the intense competition between the two initial reactor producers, GE and Westinghouse. Their rivalry was long-standing, stretching back to the origins of the two companies in the late nineteenth century: GE was Thomas Edison's creation, always at the cutting edge of innovation, whereas George Westinghouse established his company by buying and producing other people's inventions. As GE embraced nuclear energy, the more cautious engineers at Westinghouse felt obliged to follow. As early as 1948, the director of the AEC's Argonne Laboratory complained that this rivalry was rushing reactor choices (Hertsgaard, 1983, p. 23). But the hubris of the turnkey contracts was, more specifically, the result of new chief executives who took over at both companies in 1963: a former light bulb salesman at GE and a financial analyst at Westinghouse. Neither was an engineer, and neither knew anything about nuclear power. But they were extremely enthusiastic about it, confident that the turnkey offers were the beginning of a giant, profitable industry (Jasper, 1990, pp. 45ff).

The companies' enthusiasm for nuclear reactors had additional roots. Both had worked closely with the military during and since World War II, developing nuclear expertise, the trust of AEC officials, and credibility among utilities. They also had diversified into uranium mining, milling, enrichment, and other aspects of the uranium fuel cycle. GE and Westinghouse worried that they would lose these advantages if they did not soon create a viable commercial industry, as they had been trying to do since the mid-1950s. They had enormous advantages over other companies that were testing the nuclear industry – as many as 20 in the early 1950s – and needed to use those advantages to drive others out of the race. [They succeeded in this, narrowing the field to four or five after the turnkey episode (Cohn, 1997, p. 33).] On top of this, GE and Westinghouse had slightly different reactor designs, the boiling-water reactor and the pressurized-water reactor. If either one became the industry standard, the other company might be forced out of the race.

GE and Westinghouse faced a version of the risk dilemma over whether to pursue a riskier strategy that might have a large payoff or to stick with safer bets. But the dilemma remained more of a tradeoff than a conscious choice because managers at neither company saw nuclear energy as particularly risky. The risks and costs of *not* pursuing nuclear markets aggressively seemed greater, especially because they included losing market share and profit to a traditional rival. It is easy today to see the bounded rationality that inflated optimism about nuclear technology 50 years ago (parallel to the inflated optimism about strategic bombing). Players at the time could not realize how large a risk they were taking.

Strategic players are audiences for each other's words and actions, and a number of players were crucial in constructing nuclear optimism as a paradigm of thought. The Congressional Joint Committee on Atomic Energy was filled with enthusiasts: Who else would serve on such a technical committee?[7] The AEC also was filled with enthusiastic engineers. Critics were limited to a handful of local protestors, as I mentioned earlier, a far cry from the national protest movement that would emerge in the 1970s. Electricity producers should have displayed greater skepticism, especially after the turnkey contracts ended, because they were the ones who would pay the open-ended costs. At the time, however, these utilities also were run by self-assured engineers with little economic analysis beyond an assumption of a steady annual increase in demand for electricity. [When GE, displaying its hubris, offered to pay the Tennessee Valley Authority (TVA) $1,500 per hour of peak demand whenever its Brown's Ferry reactors were not functioning, the TVA revealed its own overconfidence in its ability to operate electric generators – and turned the offer down (Pringle and Spigelman, 1981, p. 269).]

Confidence is an important asset for a strategic player, giving it energy and enthusiasm, leading it to try things it otherwise would not, suggesting a sense of inevitability to its projects, and calming performance anxieties (Jasper, 2006, pp. 108ff). But the dark side, the risk, is overconfidence: Precautions are not taken, projects are launched with inadequate information, and competitors are underestimated. Experts such as engineers are especially prone to overconfidence, thinking that the world is under their control when it is not. When powerful strategic players, such as dominant corporations or fascist dictators, suffer from overconfidence because of their strength, I call this the *titan's hubris* (Jasper, 2006, p. 112). It is a frequent source of creativity's dark side.

[7] Actually, the answer is that legislators would serve on a technical committee if they had strong feelings about the topic, negative as well as positive. At the time, there were plenty of nuclearphiles but few nuclearphobes in the U.S. Congress. This would change after the 1970s.

Were GE and Westinghouse too focused on their traditional rivalry to plan their strategic moves objectively? In situations of intense rivalry, as we saw with war, players' goals often shift from winning the rewards of an arena to punishing their rival. Westinghouse might have minded less if another company were threatening to get the jump on it, but it could not tolerate the idea that GE was beating it to the nuclear draw. I call this the dilemma of *players or prizes?* (Jasper, 2006, p. 149). One can focus on winning the prizes available in a given arena or on punishing rivals no matter what the arena – and no matter what happens to the prize as long as the rival does not attain it.

In essence, "regulators" trying to promote technological innovation were joined by manufacturers who – for strategic reasons – claimed to have already had major cost breakthroughs. These two sets of players convinced a third group, utilities purchasing the reactors, to radically change their vision of electric production costs. This persuasion is reminiscent of nothing so much as Solomon Asch's (1955) famous experiments in which confederates ganged up on the subject to persuade him to see the relative lengths of lines as different than they really were. New technologies were being developed without objective assessments.

CONCLUSIONS

If the Luftwaffe's first bombing of London were indeed an accident, it would be a perfect symbol of strategic innovation, in that it may not have been meant quite as it was understood by its victims. However, the misunderstanding rarely matters because it leads to an escalation anyway. Each side, demonizing the other, interprets the other's actions in a sinister or threatening light and adopts what countermeasures it can. War and economic competition are especially likely to generate these spirals, but they occur in personal interactions as well. Every innovation feels threatening and leads to countermeasures. (A bit of paranoia in either player can accelerate the spiral.)

Rivalries exacerbate several destructive trends. They focus strategic attention – but by arousing negative emotions. They create a sense of threat and anxiety [the emotion that Marcus and colleagues (2000) find startles voters out of their routines and forces them to pay closer attention] and often spiral out of control. Rivalries can especially invoke issues of a player's identity and survival, precipitating a crisis that can be solved by taking risks. In this case, the same sense of threat that inspires creativity can lead to too much creativity.

In all these cases, there was creativity without sufficient learning. The nuclear manufacturers did not have time to learn how to operate giant reactors. The British air forces refused to learn from the Luftwaffe's failure to bomb Britain into submission, and the Americans failed to learn from either of them. Whether through hubris or complacency, they pushed ahead into uncertain territory.

Examples from other fields also demonstrate the innovation dilemma. Richard Nixon developed a "Southern strategy" that won him the 1968 presidential election but also set in motion a process that eventually transformed the ideology and composition of the Republican Party. Nixon got what he wanted but probably would not have been entirely happy with the party that resulted, with Sarah Palin its reductio ad absurdum 40 years later. Trade unionists and other protesters look for ways to disrupt economic (and sometimes other) systems – the weak link that is the equivalent of the ball bearing factory. They sometimes win big concessions, unless their targets can find other ways to get things done (making the ball bearings less important). In this example of the dilemma I call *naughty or nice?* a player must gain important and irreversible gains in the short run because it will face repression from authorities or broader damage to its reputation in the longer run (Jasper, 2006, p. 106; Piven, 2006). The reaction even may destroy the player that creatively initiated the interaction.

Holger Herwig (2001, p. 115), a military historian writing about the rise of the modern battleship, comments, "Revolutionary change maximizes uncertainty and risk. Success is never guaranteed. New weapons demand new habits, new thinking, and new training. Enemy unpredictability, weather, friction, and the uncertainties inherent in battle are quite daunting enough without inviting further confusion through novelties of uncertain value." The same innovation dilemma lies behind creativity in any number of strategic arenas: There are sizable payoffs but sizable risks, sometimes capable of threatening the survival of the player or even of the arena. Each strategic player has sufficient agency to try to change the world, but other players have enough agency, in turn, so that the original innovation rarely turns out as hoped.

REFERENCES

Asch, S. E. (1955). Opinions and social pressure. *Scientific American*, 193, 31–35.

Bassford, Christopher. (1994). *Clausewitz in English: The reception of Clausewitz in Britain and America, 1815–1945*. New York: Oxford University Press.

Biddle, Tami Davis. (2002). *Rhetoric and reality in air warfare*. Princeton: Princeton University Press.

Boot, Max. (2006). *War made new: Weapons, warriors, and the making of the modern world*. New York: Gotham Books.

Cohn, Steven Mark. (1997). *Too cheap to meter: An economic and philosophical analysis of the nuclear dream*. Albany, NY: State University of New York Press.

Corum, James S. (1997). *The Luftwaffe*. Lawrence, KS: University Press of Kansas.

Csikszentmihalyi, Mihaly. (1996). *Creativity*. New York: HarperCollins.

Flyvbjerg, Bent. (1998). *Rationality and power*. Chicago: The University of Chicago Press.

Frank, Robert H. (1988). *Passions within reason: The strategic role of emotions*. New York: W. W. Norton.

Ganz, Marshall. (2009). *Why David sometimes wins*. New York: Oxford University Press.

Hertsgaard, Mark. (1983). *Nuclear Inc*. New York: Pantheon.

Hertz, John. (1951). *Political realism and political idealism*. Chicago: The University of Chicago Press.

Herwig, Holger H. (2001). The battlefleet revolution, 1885–1914. In MacGregor Knox and Williamson Murray (Eds.), *The dynamics of military revolution 1300–2050* (pp. 114–131). Cambridge, England: Cambridge University Press.

Jasper, James M. (1990). *Nuclear politics: Energy and the state in the United States, Sweden, and France*. Princeton, NJ: Princeton University Press.

(1997). *The art of moral protest: Culture, biography, and creativity in social movements*. Chicago: The University of Chicago Press.

(2004). A strategic approach to collective action: Looking for agency in social movement choices. *Mobilization*, 9, 1–116.

(2006). *Getting your way: Strategic dilemmas in real life*. Chicago: The University of Chicago Press.

Jasper, James M. & Young, Michael. (2006). Political character types. Paper presented at the Annual Meeting of the American Sociological Association, Montreal, August.

Jervis, Robert. (1978). Cooperation under the security dilemma. *World Politics*, 30, 167–214.

Lukacs, John. (1990). *The duel: The eighty-day struggle between Churchill and Hitler*. London: Ticknor & Fields.

Macksey, Kenneth. (1990). *Invasion: The German invasion of England, July 1940*. London: Greenhill Books.

Mann, Michael. (2004). *Fascists*. Cambridge, England: Cambridge University Press.

March, James. (1994). *A primer on decision making*. New York: Free Press.

Marcus, George E., Neuman, W. Russell., & MacKuen, Michael. (2000). *Affective intelligence and political judgment*. Chicago: The University of Chicago Press.

Miller, Donald L. (2006). *Masters of the air*. New York: Simon & Schuster.

Millett, Allan R. (1996). Patterns of military innovation in the interwar period. In Williamson Murray and Allan R. Millett (Eds.), *Military innovation in the interwar period* (pp. 329–368). Cambridge, England: Cambridge University Press.

Overy, Richard. (2001). *The Battle of Britain: The myth and the reality*. New York: W. W. Norton.
Piven, Frances Fox. (2006). *Challenging authority: How ordinary people change America*. Lanham, MD: Rowman & Littlefield.
Pringle, Peter & Spigelman, James. 1981. *The nuclear barons*. New York: Avon.
Sawyer, R. Keith. (2003). *Group creativity: Music, theater, collaboration*. Mahwah, NJ: Lawrence Erlbaum.
Schaffer, Ronald. (1985). *Wings of judgment*. New York: Oxford University Press.
Schelling, Thomas C. (1978). *Micromotives and macrobehavior*. New York: W. W. Norton.
Schumpeter, Joseph A. (1942). *Capitalism, socialism, and democracy*. New York: Harper Torchbooks.
Stinchcombe, Arthur. (1965). Social structure and organizations. In James G. March (Ed.), *Handbook of organizations*. New York: Rand McNally.
(1990). *Information and organizations*. Berkeley, CA: University of California Press.
Suleiman, Ezra. (1978). *Elites in French society: The politics of survival*. Princeton, NJ: Princeton University Press.
Walker, J. Samuel. (1992). *Containing the atom: Nuclear regulation in a changing environment, 1963–1971*. Berkeley, CA: University of California Press.
Weick, Karl E. (1979). *The social psychology of organizing*, 2nd ed. Reading, MA: Addison-Wesley.

7

Early Creativity as a Constraint on Future Achievement

JACK A. GONCALO, LYNNE C. VINCENT, AND PINO G. AUDIA

Most organizations, particularly those in volatile environments, recognize the need to stimulate creativity in their workforce because new and useful ideas can be highly profitable (Shalley & Perry-Smith, 2001). It is not surprising, then, that employees or teams that manage to develop a highly creative idea are rewarded with greater pay, recognition, and status (Merton, 1968). However, a highly successful creative idea also may lead to frustration, unmet expectations, and failed attempts to replicate success by producing poor imitations of one's early work. In other words, early creativity may constrain future achievement as people buckle under the weight of their past success.

There is abundant evidence that success can stifle creativity from biographies of eminent novelists. For instance, Ralph Ellison never produced another novel after the *Invisible Man* despite years of broken promises (and book contracts) that never materialized. It would appear that Harper Lee did not even make such an attempt; she retired shortly after writing her Pulitzer Prize–winning novel, *To Kill A Mockingbird.* This decision may have been a rational one on her part because even prolific writers seem to have trouble replicating early career success. For example, there was a 32-year gap between Norman Mailer's iconic first novel, *The Naked and the Dead* (1948), and his next critical and commercial hit, *The Executioner's Song* (1980). Furthermore, the constraining effects of creativity are not restricted to writers but may be a consequence of success in many fields. For instance, Art Fry, the scientist who invented the Post-It Note, also has been constrained by early success because all his subsequent inventions, such as the Post-It Flag, are incrementally related to the original Post-It idea.

Almost from the inception of research on creativity, there has been a focus on the highly creative individual and an attempt to identify the traits (Helson, 1996) and social contexts (Amabile, 1983a, 1996) that give rise to creative achievement. However, there is relatively little research to address the question of how creativity can be maintained once it has been achieved. The answer to this question may seem obvious because one might reasonably assume that the best predictor of future creativity is a prior record of creative achievement (Simonton, 1999). However, if early success in creative endeavors is indeed constraining, as the anecdotal evidence suggests, then there may be considerable implications for managing creativity in any organization that desires a consistent stream of original ideas. For example, it is likely that people who generate a highly successful idea will more easily garner resources to continue their work (Merton, 1968). However, if early success stifles creativity over time, then organizations unwittingly may be throwing good money after bad.

In this chapter we develop a theory in which past success may constrain future achievement through three psychological mechanisms that can be described broadly as (a) cognitive, (b) affective, and (c) social. The rest of the chapter proceeds as follows: We begin by reviewing recent empirical evidence to suggest that past success stifles creativity over time. We then discuss the psychological mechanisms that may explain these effects. Next, we extend our ideas to the group level to argue that groups also may be constrained by past success, but the debilitating effects of success may be moderated by the attributions that groups generate to explain it. Finally, we conclude by proposing strategies that organizations, mindful of the constraints imposed by past success, can use to cultivate creative ideas from their most successful members.

SUCCESS AND CREATIVITY: GENERATING INSIGHTS FROM ORGANIZATIONAL LEARNING

In order for an idea to be considered creative, it must satisfy two criteria (Amabile, 1983b; Stein, 1974). First, the idea must be *useful* in the sense that it provides a solution to a problem. For example, the Post-It Note was a creative idea in part because it offered a solution to a nagging problem: Notes that were taped to a desk or computer with a conventional adhesive were impossible to remove without either tearing the note to pieces or leaving a stain. However, the Post-It Note was creative not merely because it was useful: It also satisfied the second criterion of *novelty.* Art Fry recognized a new use for an adhesive that everyone regarded as useless because it did not really stick.

Most research on creativity is concerned with identifying the process leading to the genesis of a creative idea. For instance, current research would suggest that Art Fry's creativity is due in part to his personality (Helson, 1996), his cognitive processes (Ward, 2004), his social networks (Perry-Smith & Shalley, 2003), and other features of his social context such as the organizational culture of the firm in which he was employed (Flynn & Chatman, 2001). Our aim is to carry this sequence one step further and ask, Whatever happened to Art Fry *after* he invented the Post-It Note? To rephrase the issue at a more general level: Although there is a great deal of research to address the question of where highly creative ideas come from, there is less research to address the question of how past success influences subsequent creative endeavors.

We have attempted to address this gap by analyzing the effect of past success on creativity over time in a sample of inventors who generated patents in the hard-disk drive industry (Audia & Goncalo, 2007). We found that highly successful inventors generated more patents than their less successful colleagues, but they generated patents that become increasingly incremental over time as they produced new ideas that closely resembled their earlier work. In other words, much like the creative writers who were constrained by early success, inventors in this industry were "boxed" in by their earlier work and continued to generate patents that were variations on their initial patents.

These findings may seem puzzling in light of existing theories of creativity, especially the seminal research on scientific creativity that suggests that people who generate more ideas also will generate ideas that are more divergent and have more impact on their field (Simonton, 2004). An underlying assumption of this perspective is that the sheer number of ideas generated by an individual is positively correlated with the novelty or divergence of those ideas (Dennis, 1966; Simonton, 1977). For instance, some scientists have been found to produce their most highly cited work during periods of peak productivity (Simonton, 1984, 1985), leading to the argument that quality is a probabilistic consequence of quantity (Diehl & Stroebe, 1987; Simonton, 1997).

The notion that past success constrains creativity over time, however, would be predicted by theories of organizational learning – a theoretical framework that has not been integrated with the creativity literature but is used widely to understand innovation at the organizational level of analysis (Audia & Goncalo, 2007). Our ideas about the effects of past success on subsequent creativity were developed by integrating insights from these two streams of research that emerged from different fields but share several underlying assumptions. Like the research on creativity, theories of organizational learning distinguish between two types of solutions that reflect either *exploration*, defined as "the pursuit of new knowledge, of things that might come to be known," or *exploitation*, defined as "the use and development of things already known" (Levinthal & March, 1993, p. 105). The distinction between exploration and exploitation parallels the categories that researchers of creativity use to distinguish between ideas that are more or less creative. For instance, like divergent creativity (e.g., Kirton, 1976; Sternberg et al., 2003), exploration involves the search for knowledge that departs from an established direction, the potential generation of a completely new principle, and breaking with accepted modes of thought. And, like incremental creativity, exploitation involves continuity with existing solutions, improvement through modification, and generating ideas within an established framework. Exploration/exploitation is also similar to Guilford's (1956) influential distinction between divergent thinking, which reflects thinking that moves outward from a problem in many different directions, and convergent thinking, which involves thinking that moves toward a single solution.

Although the theory of exploration/exploitation is intended to explain firm-level effects, it is a potentially useful analogue for understanding the creative process, especially because of the high degree of overlap on key concepts. However, unlike the research on creativity that has largely ignored the effects of success, a firm's record of past performance is a central feature in theories of organizational learning. According to March (1991) and Levinthal and March (1993), because organizations are sensitive to the risks inherent to the search for new ideas, they are most likely to take the risks inherent to exploration when they are still searching for but have not yet found an adequate solution. However, once a successful or adequate solution has been identified, they are likely to prefer exploitation over exploration because exploitation of knowledge that has proven to be effective guarantees more certain results and therefore reduces the risk that their efforts will lead to dead ends.

Applying this framework to creativity leads to the prediction that success in creative endeavors should favor creativity that results from exploitation, that is, from using new combinations of familiar knowledge or from refining previously used combinations. By exploiting things they already know, these individuals should be more prolific in terms of their ability to generate a large number of new ideas because, to the extent that people draw from familiar knowledge, they should be not only faster in the execution of the creative idea but also less likely to encounter unforeseen obstacles that can stifle the creative process. Ideas that diverge from the status quo not only may turn out to be wrong, as March (1991) emphasizes, but they also may encounter resistance because they are initially perceived as deviant (Moscovici, 1976).

> ***Proposition 1:*** *Past success will cause people to be more prolific in terms of the number of ideas they are able to generate over time.*

A second prediction suggested by the exploration/exploitation framework is that although people who experience success are more likely to generate more ideas (Simonton, 1999), these ideas should be increasingly incremental over time and therefore less divergent. Every person working in a given field is faced with an enormous array of information that may be combined and recombined until a particular idea is deemed to be worthy of "selection" (Campbell, 1960; Csikszentmihalyi, 1999). Novel combinations are more likely to result from what Simonton (1999, 2004) termed a "flat associative hierarchy" in which a given stimulus (e.g., new information) may trigger a wide range of potential associations between existing ideas.

While associations between ideas may occur at random, this combinatorial process is subject to at least three different constraints: (a) the ideas that are considered, (b) the extent to which ideas are combined in a random way, and (c) the specific criteria used to differentiate a creative combination from an uncreative combination (Simonton, 1999, 2004). Drawing on this terminology, research on the exploration/exploitation tradeoff suggests that past success may operate as a constraint on the process of generating new combinations by focusing an inventor's attention excessively on the building blocks of creativity (e.g., ideas, knowledge) that have already been used in the past. For instance, once an inventor experiences success with one idea, all subsequent ideas may be framed narrowly from that perspective.

> ***Proposition 2:*** *Past success will cause people to generate ideas that are increasingly incremental over time.*

CREATIVITY AS A CONSTRAINT: IDENTIFYING THE PSYCHOLOGICAL MECHANISMS

Although organizational learning provides a useful framework for generating predictions about how past success may influence subsequent creativity over time, it does not specify the psychological mechanisms that may explain these effects. Theories of organizational learning were developed to explain exploration at the firm level of analysis, and although that research stream provides a logical foundation for understanding the effects of past success on creativity, it is at best a metaphor and not a fine-grained depiction of the psychological process itself. In this section we extend existing research by proposing potential cognitive, affective, and social mechanisms that mediate the effects of past success on creativity over time.

Past Success and Cognitive Frames

The constraining effects of past success may be explained, at least in part, by the phenomenon of cognitive framing, which suggests that when people have experienced success with a particular strategy, they often become narrowly focused on implementing that particular strategy to solve new problems (Duncker, 1945; Luchins, 1942). This type of mental block is called "negative transfer" (Bartlett, 1958), and it has been found to deter the generation of novel solutions in a variety of situations, such as negotiations over time (Bareby-Meyer, Moran, & Unger-Aviram, 2004), factory operation after a change in accident-monitoring devices (Besnard & Cacitti, 2005), firms acquiring targets from different industries (Finkelstein & Haleblian, 2002), and firms changing their strategies following a radical environmental change (Audia, Locke, & Smith, 2000).

Perhaps the best illustration of this mental block comes from Duncker's (1945) series of classic experiments on functional fixedness. Duncker gave his subjects three cardboard boxes, matches, thumbtacks, and candles and asked them to mount the candle vertically on a screen to serve as a lamp. However, half the subjects received the objects inside the cardboard boxes, whereas the other half received the objects and the boxes separately. The correct solution to the problem was to tack the box to the screen and use the matches to melt the wax and attach the candle to the box and then light the candle. The problem was much more difficult to solve for those who received the objects in the boxes because they fixated on the boxes as merely containers and were unable to rethink the purpose of the box as a support instead of just a container. In other words, the past experience of seeing a situation in a certain way constrained the heuristics used in the creative process by limiting subjects from generating novel solutions.

The classic work on cognitive framing is foundational to modern theories of creative cognition. According to Ward (2004), creativity results from the application of mental operations such as analogies to existing knowledge structures. People store a wealth of information in the form of ideas or concepts, and creative solutions emerge when pieces of prior knowledge stored in memory are combined in a novel way (Smith, Ward, & Finke, 1995). Ward (1994) demonstrated the constraining effects of experience on creativity in a study in which he asked participants to draw an alien from another planet that was "beyond their wildest imagination." Instead of drawing radically different creatures, participants drew figures that conformed to the basic features of earth animals such as bilateral symmetry (Ward, 1994). The constraining effect of past experience also was demonstrated in a brainstorming study in which subjects were asked to generate new ideas; half the subjects were given examples to get them started, and the other half were given no examples (Smith, Ward, & Schumacher, 1993). The researchers found that the groups that were given examples generated less creative ideas than the groups that were given no examples because their "new" ideas followed the examples too closely (Smith et al., 1993). These blocking effects may have considerable negative consequences for creative idea generation because people will suggest ideas that follow existing solutions too closely (Smith, 2003). Therefore, we predict

> ***Proposition 3:*** *A highly creative idea will constrain future creativity because all subsequent ideas will be framed narrowly from the perspective of the initial idea.*

Affective Consequences of Past Success

The negative consequences of past success may have an important cognitive component; however, this is not to say that emotions also may not play a central role. The experience of success has been shown in numerous studies to be associated with feelings of happiness that can carry over to different situations and last a very long time (Lyubomirsky, King, & Diener, 2005). In other words, success is an affectively significant event, and the emotions that emerge following the experience of success may in turn have an effect on creativity over time. Therefore, in this section we consider how positive and negative affect may explain the constraining effects of success.

Research in both the laboratory and field settings has demonstrated that affect can have important effects on individual creative performance (Barsade & Gibson, 2007). However, there are two very different perspectives on the link between affect and creativity that lead to competing predictions. Some research suggests that creativity is enhanced by positive affect, whereas other research suggests that creativity is enhanced by negative affect. Because there are two clearly opposite predictions about the role of affect in creativity and little research to reconcile the two perspectives, it is possible to advance competing arguments that might be generated from each perspective.

On the one hand, research has suggested that positive affect can facilitate creativity by enhancing cognitive and motivational processes (Hirt, Levine, McDonald, & Melton, 1997). Numerous studies conducted primarily by Alice Isen and colleagues (1999) have shown that positive affect induces individuals to generate more novel associations, use broader categories, and solve problems more creatively. Increasing the number of available cognitive elements and increasing the extent that those elements are considered as relevant information to the problem should increase cognitive variation, which should result in increased creativity (Clore, Schwarz, & Conway, 1994). Therefore, Isen (2001) argued that positive affect promotes efficient but not careless decision making by allowing connections between ideas to be more accessible and visible, encouraging broad focuses on problem solving, and encouraging flexible thinking.

There is evidence that individuals are motivated to preserve positive affect and therefore avoid tasks that potentially could cause negative affect (Isen, 1987, 2001). After the initial warm glow of success wears off, people might be motivated to recapture their initial levels of positive affect, but they may encounter frustration as they attempt to generate another equally creative idea. This process could lead to a downward spiral of decreasing affect that simultaneously could reduce creativity in two inter-related ways. First, as people are frustrated in their attempts to recapture their initial level of success, the advantages of positive affect for facilitating problem solving and flexible thinking are less and less likely to be realized. Second, the simplest way to recreate the affect associated with success might be to imitate the initial and highly successful idea while avoiding the exploration of newer and unrelated ideas that have an uncertain probability of success. Therefore, we predict

> ***Proposition 4:*** *Frustrated attempts to recreate the positive affect associated with early success can lead to a downward spiral of positive affect and creativity over time.*

On the other hand, there is also research to suggest that negative affect can facilitate creative performance. The notion that negative affect can stimulate creativity stems in part from a positive correlation found between depression and creative achievements in a study that examined individuals across a variety of professions (Ludwig, 1992). While other research supports this finding (Post, 1996), Feist (1999) noted that the association seems to be strongest in fields involving artistic rather than scientific creativity. Negative affect might be valuable because it could act as a signal that one's situation is unsatisfying (Martin, Ward, Achee, & Wyer, 1993). For instance, Zhou and George (2001) found that negative affect stemming from dissatisfaction could, in certain situations, signal to an individual that change is required. This signal can increase employee voice behavior and increase the desire to create new solutions and methods that will resolve the problem that is causing the dissatisfaction. Moreover, negative affect might encourage set breaking, the ability to abandon typical cognitive processes and patterns (Luchins & Luchins, 1959; Zhou & George, 2001).

From this perspective, positive affect is assumed to signal to the individual that a situation is satisfying or that a goal has been achieved (George & Zhou, 2002). Therefore, initial success with a highly creative idea might lead to complacency and inaction (George & Zhou, 2002), and negative affect might be necessary to signal the need to explore new solutions and abandon old methods for solving problems. Therefore, we predict

> ***Proposition 5:*** *The stifling effects of past success on creativity will be mitigated by the experience of negative affect because negative affect signals the need to change direction and explore new solutions.*

Past Success and Role Constraints

In previous sections we argued that success constrains the way people think at a cognitive level insofar as success with a creative idea may lead to cognitive frames or affective states that hinder creative problem solving. A limitation of this perspective is that it largely ignores the role of the social context, and research has clearly shown that certain features of a person's task environment may have important effects on creativity (Amabile, 1983a, 1997; Amabile et al, 1996). In this section we move beyond purely intrapsychic explanations to consider how past success also may lead to the development of social roles and social networks that constrain peoples' ability to see old problems from a new perspective. In other words, it is possible that success may cause constraints from "within," or one's cognitive processes, but also from "without," in the form of situational constraints. For instance, returning to the case of Art Fry, after the success of the Post-It Note idea, he achieved a kind of notoriety that would be akin to being forever typecast as the "Inventor of the Post-It Note." The question is whether a highly creative idea can create an identity that can be difficult to break out of to create something new.

According to role theory, role identities determine a person's interpretations of the people, situations, and event that the individual encounters in various social situations. A role identity is how a specific role provides meaning or definition to one's self (Burke & Tully, 1977). Others' perceptions, self-judgment of others' perceptions, and affect connected to that perception contribute to the formation of a role identity (McCall & Simmons, 1978). For example, in organizations, role identities may emerge from feedback from coworkers (Woodman et al., 1993) and supervisors (Scott & Bruce, 1994) and can significantly influence employees' behaviors. One's role identity encourages role performances (Markus & Wurf, 1987), and role performances, in turn, allow individuals and their traits to be identified and categorized by others (Burke, 1991). Role identities can be constructed retroactively (Weick, 1995) and can be developed over time as the individual interprets and internalizes various inputs and role activity (Grube & Piliavin, 2000).

The formation of a role identity is relevant to creativity because individuals may adopt the behaviors and actions associated with the role identity, thus constraining and restricting the depth and breadth of their behaviors and actions. Through feedback about the self from social interactions and individuals' self-perceptions, a role identity provides an internalized set of role expectations (Riley & Burke, 1995). For instance, if the individual is a teacher, he or she will act in accordance with the expectations of others and himself or herself of how a teacher should behave. That individual will become less willing to act in a manner that is beyond the established parameters of how a teacher is expected to act. In a similar manner, if a person develops an identity that is strongly connected to a single creative idea, he or she might maintain that identity by generating subsequent ideas that are highly related. Therefore, we predict

> ***Proposition 6***: *A highly creative idea will create a related "role identity" that will in turn constrain peoples' ability to generate ideas that are inconsistent with that identity.*

Role identities also may impose constraints through the kinds of networks that people form to share knowledge and information. Not only do people try to behave in a way that is consistent with a role identity, but because role identities allow an individual to be easily categorized by others, people also may seek out the focal individual to discuss related ideas, thus narrowing and strengthening the role identity over time. For example, after Art Fry became known as the "Inventor of the Post-It Note," people might seek him out to discuss ideas related to adhesives or to office supplies, thus constraining his access to new sources of knowledge and information.

This dynamic could be understood from the perspective of social networks. Network ties can facilitate creativity if they provide people with access to novel sources of information that can be used to generate new ideas. For instance, *weak ties*, defined as ties with comparatively lower levels of closeness and interaction frequency, facilitate creativity by providing diverse and nonredundant information (Perry-Smith & Shalley, 2003). Weaker ties allow for exposure to various sources of information, to domain-relevant information, and to different perspectives. Therefore, weak ties may facilitate the generation of alternatives and encourage autonomous thinking (Perry-Smith, 2006). In contrast, a network consisting of strong ties provides a dense network that may allow information to flow quickly and may encourage the development of shared attitudes, opinions, and beliefs. Consequently, conformity also may occur, which would limit creativity by reducing autonomy. A strong role identity connected with a highly creative idea may constrain future creativity because network ties will form to people who are interested in knowing about, discussing, or extending one's earlier ideas. Therefore, we predict

> ***Proposition 7****: A strong role identity connected to a highly creative idea will lead to the formation of redundant ties that will constrain subsequent creativity.*

PAST SUCCESS AND GROUP CREATIVITY: WHEN THE EFFECTS OF SUCCESS DEPEND ON HOW YOU EXPLAIN IT

Up to this point we have focused our analysis on the individual level to explain how past success might constrain a person's creativity over time. It is possible, however, that group creativity also may be constrained by past success. In this section we extend our theorizing to the group level to investigate the question of how past success might impact group creativity. Although most research on creativity has been conducted at the individual level, over the last decade there has been increasing interest in creativity resulting from the collaboration of several people working interdependently (Sutton & Hargadon, 1996; Paulus & Yang, 2000), especially as organizations have moved to team-base work structures (Ilgen, 1999). The current interest in group creativity can be traced to Osborn's (1953) classic book, *Applied Imagination,* in which he laid out a set of specific brainstorming rules such as "do not criticize" that were intended to reduce evaluation apprehension (Camacho & Paulus, 1995) and make people feel more comfortable to share their ideas with the group. Following Osborn's emphasis on the quantity of ideas that surface during brainstorming sessions (1953), modern brainstorming studies measure creativity by assessing the extent to which groups are able to generate a large number of ideas that are different from each other (Brophy, 1998). Groups that generate a large number of ideas also generate more high-quality ideas by building, combining, and improving on the solutions suggested by other group members (Diehl & Stroebe, 1987).

Extrapolating directly from the individual level, we would predict that a group's history of past success also would constrain their ability to generate creative solutions. However, the effects of past success may be less straightforward at the group level and may depend on the causal attributions that groups generate to explain their past success. Goncalo (2004) proposed a theoretical framework in which attributions at the group level may reflect either (a) the collective attributes of the group as a whole or (b) the unique contributions made by individual group members. This distinction draws on research that has examined attributions that are generated in the context of close relationships (Newman, 1981). For instance, married couples may attribute causality either to each person in the relationship (e.g., you are emotional, and I am stubborn) or to the relationship as a unit (e.g., we lost that spark we used to have). Translated from the dyadic to the group level, a team may attribute causality either to the group as a whole (e.g., we are cohesive) or to specific individuals (e.g., Joe is punctual, Jane is knowledgeable, and Jim is a good researcher).

These attributions are important because they moderate the effects of past success on subsequent group performance, especially creativity and the quality of group decision making (Goncalo, 2004; Goncalo & Duguid, 2008). Existing research suggests that attributions may influence performance through two potential mechanisms. First, attributing success to the group as a whole may send a subtle but important message: Each member's contributions are neither identifiable nor separable from their teammates'. Research on social loafing suggests that people are less willing to exert effort on behalf of their team when they do not feel that their contributions to the group are identifiable (Williams, Harkins, & Latane, 1981). The temptation to free ride on the efforts of others is often invoked as an explanation for the consistent finding that face-to-face groups generate fewer creative ideas than individuals who work alone (Diehl & Strobe, 1987). In order to explore a wide range of alternatives, a group must focus its attention on a broad range of information (Kasof, 1997) and ultimately search for new solutions that extend beyond an existing train of thought (Mednick, 1962). Groups that lack the motivation to search beyond the most obvious solution to a problem are unlikely to generate divergent solutions (Amabile, 1983a).

Second, group-focused attributions may increase conformity pressure by emphasizing that success was caused by the collective effort of a group of individuals whose contributions were indistinguishable from one another. When people are faced with a unanimous majority, they often will ignore the evidence of their own senses and adopt the majority position even when it is obviously incorrect (Asch, 1956). This pressure to conform originates from the desire to be liked by others (Deutsch & Gerard, 1955) and the tendency of groups to reject those who do not fit (Schachter, 1951). A long tradition of research on social influence has shown that one of the most powerful ways to create conformity pressure is by calling attention to what the majority of people are doing in a given situation (Asch, 1956; Cialdini, Reno, & Kallgren, 1990). This principle was illustrated more recently in a series of studies showing that conformity to a group norm increases substantially simply by making the norm salient to people (Cialdini et al., 1990). Applied to attributions, this research suggests that explanations focused on the group as a whole (e.g., we are cooperative) make salient how most people behaved prior to a successful outcome, thus creating pressure to conform to their behavior in a subsequent setting.

While a certain level of conformity pressure is necessary for a group to accomplish its goals (O'Reilly & Chatman, 1996), it may cause the group to perform poorly on tasks that require the group to generate new and different ideas (Peterson & Nemeth, 1996). Conformity pressure, by suppressing dissenting opinions, prevents people from reflecting on and possibly reconsidering their own views (Nemeth, 1986). Excessive pressure toward agreement may prevent people from diverging from a common line of thought to consider multiple different perspectives on an issue (De Dreu & De Vries, 1996; Nemeth & Rogers, 1996). Consequently, the group tends to view a problem from only one narrow perspective and ultimately to come up with less divergent solutions (Schulz-Hardt, Frey, Luthgens, & Moscovici, 2000).

There is evidence from a series of experiments to support the predictions suggested by this attributional framework (Goncalo, 2004; Goncalo & Duguid, 2008). In these studies, a group is given false feedback about its performance, and the members then are asked, "What is it about (your group/the individuals in your group) that allowed you to do so well on the previous task?" The groups that attributed their success to individuals generated more ideas that were more divergent and rated as more novel than groups that attributed their success to the group as a whole (Goncalo, 2004). Individually focused attributions also caused groups to consider a wider range of alternatives prior to making a decision and to share more unique information that was then used to make more accurate decisions than groups that attributed their success to the group as a whole (Goncalo & Duguid, 2008). Video coding of the group's process of working together provided support for the role of conformity pressure to explain the effects. Individually focused attributions caused groups to express more disagreements and to take more time to explore divergent perspectives than group-focused attributions.

This emerging stream of research suggests that past success also may constrain creativity at the group level. However, this effect may depend on how groups explain the causes of their success. The negative consequences of success can be reversed by redirecting attributions from a focus on group-level explanations to a focus on the unique contributions made by individual group members. Attributions that link group success to individual achievement permit the possibility that people can stand out by making their own unique contributions (Beersma & De Dreu, 2005; Goncalo & Staw, 2006), thus reducing the stifling effects of conformity pressure. Therefore, we predict

> ***Proposition 8****: The constraining effects of past success on group creativity are moderated by causal attributions.* ***8a:*** *Success attributed to the group as a whole constrains creativity, whereas success attributed to the individual stimulates the expression of creative ideas.*

CONCLUDING THOUGHTS

In this chapter we have proposed a view of creativity as a double-edged sword. On the one hand, a highly creative idea may bring fame and fortune to the creator, but over time, a highly creative idea also may cast a very long shadow. While some people manage to maintain their creativity over time, history is littered with examples of creative people who began their careers in the stratosphere and ended them in the bottle. Although there is empirical and anecdotal evidence to support the view that creativity may constrain future achievement, there has been little research to identity the psychological mechanisms that explain these negative effects. We extended current research by proposing (a) cognitive, (b) affective, and (c) social processes that may mediate the link between past success and creativity over time.

Given the potentially negative consequences of past success, it is important that managers understand how to manage their most creative employees so that they do not become boxed in by their own ideas. The results of Audia and Goncalo (2007) suggest that the negative effects of past success, at least at the individual level, may be mitigated by encouraging collaboration. Collaboration may allow people to "break set" and view problems from a new perspective and expose people to new information that can be used to generate creative ideas. This solution also may have limitations, however, if role identities based on highly creative ideas create social constraints that lead to collaborations between people with similar perspectives. However, by understanding the mechanisms that explain the negative effects of past success, organizations will be in a better position to develop effective interventions and to continue to profit from their most creative employees.

REFERENCES

Amabile, T. M. (1983a). The social psychology of creativity: A componential conceptualization. *Journal of Personality and Social Psychology*, 45, 357–376.

(1983b). *The social psychology of creativity*. New York: Springer-Verlag.

(1997). Motivating creativity in organizations: On doing what you love and loving what you do. *California Management Review*, 40, 39–58.

Amabile, T. M , Conti, R., Coon, H., Lazenby, J., & Herron, M. (1996). Assessing the work environment for creativity. *Academy of Management Journal*, 39, 1154–1185.

Art Fry and the Invention of Post-it Notes (2005); available at www.3m.com/about3M/pioneers/fry.jhtml. Retrieved July 20, 2005.

Asch, S. E. (1956). Studies on independence and conformity: A minority of one against a unanimous majority. *Psychological Monographs*, 70, (whole no. 416).

Audia, P. G. & Goncalo, J. A. (2007). Success and creativity over time: A study of inventors in the hard-disk drive industry. *Management Science*, 53, 1–15.

Audia, P. G., Locke, E. A., & Smith, K. G. (2000). The paradox of success: An archival and a laboratory study of strategic persistence following radical environmental change. *Academy of Management Journal*, 43, 837–853.

Barsade, S. G. & Gibson, D. E. (2007). Why does affect matter in organizations? *Academy of Management Perspectives*, 21, 36–59.

Bartlett, F. C. (1958). *Thinking*. London: Allen & Unwin.

Bareby-Meyer, Y., Moran, S., & Unger-AviramE., (2004). When performance goals deter performance: Transfer of skills in integrative negotiations. *Organizational Behavior and Human Decision Processes*, 93, 142–154.

Beersma, B. & De Dreu, C. K. W. (2005). Conflict's consequences: Effects of social motives on post-negotiation creative and convergent group functioning and performance. *Journal of Personality and Social Psychology*, 89, 358–374.

Besnard, D. & Cacitti, L. (2005). Interface changes causing accidents: An empirical study of negative transfer. *International Journal of Human-Computer Studies*, 62, 105–125.

Brophy, D. R. (1998). Understanding, measuring and enhancing individual creative problem solving efforts. *Creativity Research Journal*, 2, 123–150.

Burke, P. J. (1991). Identity processes and social stress. *American Sociological Review*, 56, 836–849.

Burke, P. J. & Tully, J. C. (1977). The measurement of role identity. *Social Forces*, 55, 881–897.

Camacho, M.L. & Paulus, P. B. (1995). The role of social anxiousness in group brainstorming, *Journal of Personality and Social Psychology*, 68, 6, 1071–1080.

Campbell, D. T. (1960). Blind variation and selective retention in creative thought as in other knowledge processes. *Psychological Review*, 67, 380–400.

Cialdini, R. B., Reno, R. R., & Kallgren, C. A. (1990). A focus theory of normative conduct: Recycling the concept of norms to reduce littering in public places. *Journal of Personality and Social Psychology*, 58, 1015–1026.

Clore, G. L., Schwarz, N., & Conway, M. (1994). Affective causes and consequences of social information processing. In R. S. Wyer and T. Srull (Eds.), *The handbook of social cognition*, 2nd ed. (pp. 323–417). Mahwah, NJ: Lawrence Erlbaum Associates.

CNET news.com. Available at http://news.com.com/HP-Compaq+A+fight+to+the+finish/2009-1001_3-852197.html. Accessed June 30, 2005.

Csikszentmihalyi, M. (1999). Implications of a systems perspective for the study of creativity. In R. J. Sternberg (Ed.), *Handbook of creativity* (pp. 313–338). Cambridge England: Cambridge University Press.

De Dreu, C. K. W. & DeVries, N. K. (1996). Differential processing and attitude change following majority and minority arguments. *British Journal of Social Psychology*, 35, 77–90.

Dennis, W. (1966). Creative productivity between the ages of 20 and 80 years. *Journal of Gerontology*, 21, 1–8.

Deutsch, M. & Gerard, H. B. (1955). A study of normative and informational social influence upon individual judgment. *Journal of Abnormal and Social Psychology*, 195, 629–636.

Diehl, M. & Stroebe, W. (1987). Productivity loss in brainstorming groups: Toward the solution of a riddle. *Journal of Personality and Social Psychology*, 79, 722–735.

Duncker, K. (1945). On problem solving. *Psychological Monographs*, 58, entire issue.

Feist, G. J. (1999). Affect in artistic and scientific creativity. In S. W. Russ (Ed.), *Affect, creative experience and psychological adjustment* (pp. 3–18). Philadelphia: Brunner/Mazel.

Finkelstein, S. & Haleblian, J. (2002). Understanding acquisition performance: The role of transfer effects. *Organization Science*, 13, 36–47.

Flynn, F. J. & Chatman, J. A. (2001). Strong cultures and innovation: Oxymoron or opportunity? In S. Cartwright, C. Cooper, C. Earley, J. Chatman, T. Cummings, N. Holden, P. Sparrow, and W. Starbuck (Eds.), *International handbook of organizational culture and climate* (pp. 263–287). Sussex, England: Wiley.

George, J. M. & Zhou, J. (2002). Understanding when bad moods foster creativity and good moods don't: The role of context and clarity of feelings. *Journal of Applied Psychology*, 87, 687–697.

Goncalo, J. A. (2004). Past success and convergent thinking in groups: The role of group-focused attributions. *European Journal of Social Psychology*, 34, 385–395.

Goncalo, J. A. & Duguid, M. M. (2008). Hidden consequences of the group-serving bias: Causal attributions and the quality of group decision making. *Organizational Behavior and Human Decision Processes*, 107, 2, 219–233.

Goncalo, J. A. & Staw, B. M. (2006). Individualism-collectivism and group creativity. *Organizational Behavior and Human Decision Processes*, 100, 96–109.

Grube, J. & Piliavin, J. (2000). Role identity, organization experiences, and volunteer performance. *Personality and Social Psychology Bulletin*, 26, 1108–1119.

Guilford, J. P. (1956). The structure of intellect. *Psychological Bulletin*, 33, 267–293.

Helson, R. (1996). In search of the creative personality. *Creativity Research Journal*, 9, 295–306.

Hirt, E. R., Levine, G. M., McDonald, H. E., & Melton, R. J. (1997). The role of mood in quantitative and qualitative aspects of performance: Single or multiple mechanisms? *Journal of Experimental Social Psychology*, 33, 602–629.

Ilgen, D. R. (1999). Teams embedded in organizations. *American Psychologist*, 54, 129–138.

Isen, A. M. (1987). Positive affect, cognitive processes, and social behavior. *Advances in Experimental Social Organizational Behavior*, 13, 1–53.

Isen, A. (1999). On the relationship between affect and creative problem solving. In S. W. Russ (Ed.), *Affect, creative experience and psychological adjustment* (pp. 3–18). Philadelphia: Brunner/Mazel.

(2001) An influence of positive affect on decision making in complex situations: Theoretical issues with practical implications. *Journal of Consumer Psychology*, 11, 75–85.

Kasof, J. (1997). Creativity and breadth of attention. *Creativity Research Journal*, 10, 303–315.

Kirton, M. (1976). Adaptors and innovators: A description and measure. *Journal of Applied Psychology*, 6, 622–629.

Kuhn, T. S. (1970). *The structure of scientific revolutions*, 2nd ed. Chicago: The University of Chicago Press.

Levinthal, D. A. & March, J. G. (1993). The myopia of learning. *Strategic Management Journal*, 14, 95–112.

Lewin, K. (1952). *Field theory in social science*. New York: Harper & Row.

Lyubomirsky, S., King, L., & Diener, E. (2005). The benefits of frequent positive affect: Does happiness lead to success? *Psychological Bulletin*, 131, 803–855.

Luchins, A. S. (1942). Mechanization in problem solving. *Psychological Monographs*, 54, entire issue.

Luchins, A. S. & Luchins, E. H. (1959). *Rigidity of behavior*. Eugene, OR: University of Oregon Books.

Ludwig, A. M. (1992). Creative achievement and psychopathlogy: Comparison among professions. *American Journal of Psychotherapy*, 46, 330–356.

March, J. G. (1991). Exploration and exploitation in organizational learning. *Organization Science*, 2, 71–87.

Markus, H. & Wurf, E. (1987). The dynamic self-concept: A social psychological perspective. In M. R. Rosenzweig and L. W. Porter (Eds.), *Annual review of psychology*, Vol. 38 (pp. 299–337). Palo Alto, CA: Annual Reviews.

Martin, L. L., Ward, D. W., Achee, J. W., & Wyer, R. S. (1993). Mood as input: People have to interpret the motivational implications of their moods. *Journal of Personality and Social Psychology*, 64, 317–326.

McCall, G. & Simmons, J. L. (1978). *Identities and interaction*. New York: Free Press.

Mednick, S. A. (1962). The associative basis of the creative process. *Psychological Review*, 69, 230–232.

Merton, R. K. (1968). The Matthew effect in science. *Science*, January 5, 56–63.

Moscovici, S. (1976). *Social influence and social change*. London: Academic Press

Nemeth, C. J. (1986). Differential contributions of majority and minority influence. *Psychological Review*, 93, 23–32

Nemeth, C. J. & Rogers, J. R. (1996). Dissent and the search for information. *British Journal of Social Psychology*, 25, 67–76

Newman, H. M. (1981). Communication within ongoing intimate relationships: An attributional perspective. *Personality and Social Psychology Bulletin*, 7, 59–70.

O'Reilly, C. A. & Chatman, J. A. (1996). Culture as social control: Corporations, cults and commitment. In L. L. Cummings and B. M. Staw (Eds.), *Research in organizational behavior*, Vol. 18., 157–200.

Osborn, A. (1953). *Applied imagination: Principles and procedures of creative problem solving*. New York: Charles Scribner's Sons.

Pakes, A. & Shankerman, M. (1984). The rate of obsolescence of patents, research gestation lags, and the private return to research resources. In Z. Griliches (Ed.), *R&D, patents, and productivity* (pp. 73–88). Chicago: The University of Chicago Press.

Paulus, P. B. & Yang, H. C. (2000). Idea generation in groups: A basis for creativity in organizations. *Organizational Behavior and Human Decision Processes*, 82, 76–87.

Perry-Smith, J. E. (2006). Social yet creative: The role of social relationships in facilitating individual creativity. *Academy of Management Journal*, 49, 85–101.

Perry-Smith, J. E. & Shalley, C. E. (2003). The social side of creativity: A static and dynamic social network perspective. *Academy of Management Review*, 28, 89–106.

Peterson, R. & Nemeth, C. (1996). Focus vs. flexibility: Majority and minority influence can both improve performance. *Personality and Social Psychology Bulletin*, 22, 14–23.

Post, F. (1996). Verbal creativity, depression, and alcoholism: An investigation of one hundred American and British writers. *British Journal of Psychiatry*, 168, 545–555.

Riley, A. & Burke, P. J. (1995). Identities and self-verification in the small group. *Social Psychology Quarterly*, 58, 61–73.

Schachter, S. (1951). Deviation, rejection and communication. *Journal of Abnormal and Social Psychology*, 46, 190–207.

Schulz-Hardt, S., Frey, D., Luthgens, C., & Moscovici, S. (2000). Biased information processing search in group decision making. *Journal of Personality and Social Psychology*, 78, 665–669.

Scott, S. G. & Bruce, R. A. (1994). Determinants of innovative behavior: A path model of individual innovation in the workplace. *Academy of Management Journal*, 37, 580–607.

Shalley, C. E. & Perry-Smith, J. E. (2001). Effects of social-psychological factors on creative: the role of informational and controlling expected evaluation and modeling experience. *Organizational and Human Decision Processes*, 84, 1–22.

Simonton, D. K. (1977). Creative productivity, age and stress: A biographical time-series analysis of 10 classical composers. *Journal of Personality and Social Psychology*, 35, 805–816.

(1984). Creativity, productivity and age: A mathematical model based on a two-step cognitive process. *Developmental Review*, 4, 77–111.

(1985). Quality, quantity and age: The careers of 10 distinguished psychologists. *International Journal of Aging and Human Development*, 21, 241–254.

(1997). Creative productivity: A predictive and explanatory model of career trajectories and landmarks. *Psychological Review*, 104, 66–89.

(1999). Talent and its development: An emergenic and epigenetic model. *Psychological Review*, 106, 435–457.

(2004). Scientific creativity as constrained stochastic behavior: The integration of product, person and process perspectives. *Psychological Bulletin*, 129, 475–494.

Smith, S. M. (2003). The constraining effects of initial ideas. In P. B. Paulus and B. A. Nijstad (Eds.), *Creativity: Innovation through collaboration*. Oxford, England: Oxford University Press.

Smith, S. M., Ward, T. B., & Finke, R. A. (1995). Cognitive processes in creative contexts. In S. M. Smith, T. B. Ward, and R. A. Finke (Eds.), *The creative cognition approach* (pp. 1–7). Cambridge, MA: MIT Press.

Smith, S. M., Ward, T. B., & Schumacher, J. S. (1993). Constraining effects of examples in a creative generation task. *Memory and Cognition*, 21, 837–845.

Stein, M. I. (1974). *Stimulating creativity*, Vol. 1. New York: Academic Press.

Sternberg, R. J., Kaufman, J. C., & Pretz, J. E (2003). A propulsion model of creative leadership. *The Leadership Quarterly*, 14, 455–473.

Sutton, R. I. & Hargadon, A. (1996). Brainstorming groups in context: Effectiveness in a product design firm. *Administrative Science Quarterly*, 41, 685–718.

Ward, T. B. (1994). Structured imagination: The role of conceptual structure in exemplar generation. *Cognitive Psychology*, 27, 1–40.

(2004). Cognition, creativity and entrepreneurship. *Journal of Business Venturing*, 19, 173–188.

Weick, K. E. (1995). *Sensemaking in organizations*. Thousand Oaks, CA: Sage.

The whole story: A NOTE-able achievement. Available at www.3m.com/us/office/postit/learn_history_story.jhtml. Accessed September 12, 2004.

Williams, K., Harkins, S., & Latane, B. (1981). Identifiability as a deterrent to social loafing: Two cheering experiments. *Journal of Personality and Social Psychology*, 40, 303–311.

Woodman, R. W., Sawyer, J. E., & Griffin, R. W. (1993). Toward a theory of organizational creativity. *Academy of Management Review*, 18, 293–321.

Zhou, J. & George, J. M. (2001). When job dissatisfaction leads to creativity: Encouraging the expression of voice. *Academy of Management Journal*, 44, 682–696.

8

Boundless Creativity

KEVIN HILTON

From an open-minded perspective of creativity knowing no bounds, this chapter discusses some darker aspects of creativity and the role of ethics in responsible design practice and considers the potential need to engage with unethical perspectives in order to "design" more responsibly. This chapter also describes how "Cyclic Countering of Competitive Creativity" (C4), as a critical design process, enables effective engagement with the likes of crime and terrorism.

The intention is to first discuss perspectives on the darker side of creativity in recognition of there being naturalness to it that comes as a condition of human beings' reflexive use of knowledge and to propose that the value of the perceived "good and evil" achieved through creativity is in its balance. This includes an acknowledgment that worldviews and our use and abuse of socioeconomic and technological opportunities can tip that balance in ways that create a need to correct through cessation or redirective practices (Willis, 2008).

When there are no bounds to creativity, creative processes may equally identify and apply opportunities for good or evil, although the concept of good and evil is a human construct relating to helping or harming. We may claim that conscious perception of good and evil enables virtuous behavior, yet either outcome may be achieved by either thoughtful or thoughtless responses to opportunity in more complex situations. At times, to appreciate the nature of a given situation, an understanding of consequences requires higher levels of thinking – systems thinking (Checkland, 1981). Even so, group debate to aid the systemic thinking and the decisions taken, on later reflection, still may prove to be questionable if the problems remained ill informed or ill structured (Simon, 1996).

The categorizing of thoughts and actions and an understanding of what influences the process of decision making (Lehrer, 2009) may serve to simplify our perception of complex situations, enabling quicker and more appropriate decisions to be made. The categories of *good* and *evil* may be viewed by some as separating humans from beasts, as if in some way it makes us more virtuous than animals, such that we should not condone acting like animals. Yet, as Bohm (1996) pointed out, animals rarely kill one another through their violence, but also that following a conflict, animals would appear to show no further concern. Whereas humans, through maintenance and development of "shared memories" (Whittaker, 2007), can keep conflict alive sometimes for hundreds of years. Sternberg (2005) noted that stories can be created and successfully passed on to generate hatred and commitment to false beliefs. It could be said, however, that even apparently more reasonable beliefs may serve to threaten the order of things, for example, the fear of crime when there is belief but no actual evidence supporting the fear and its resulting behaviors. If we are to design more responsibly, we need to question our beliefs. In discussion of wisdom, Pascual-Leone (1990) makes the point that wisdom is not about *believing* but *questioning*, and reference is made to the Book of Job in the Bible, where God praises Job for challenging him.

Whatever worldview an individual lives by, it can be argued that there is a spectrum to our experiences of love and hate and pleasure and pain that is part of life. As MacIntyre (1998) noted, Chrysippus had argued that one perspective cannot be conceived to exist or be experienced and fully understood without experience of the other. Similarly, it is proposed here that we also cannot effectively counter dark creativity without experience of it. Any approach to gaining such experience, however, requires consideration and balance. Mental and physical harm are possible from knowing and applying what is known. Some people, in their investigation of the unethical can become fascinated, risk altering their perspective on life, and even fall into practice. Not everyone is suited to the investigation of the unethical. Ethical review therefore serves to question and monitor intent and actions in order to avoid further harm and should be part of any crime-prevention process.

Ethical review cannot, however, be relied on to predict every negative consequence, and the review process itself may be considered negative if it cannot reach timely decisions, resulting in the opportunities being lost and situations possibly worsening. It also could be argued that if everyone considered the possible negative consequences of their actions, innovation, in terms of change and diversity, would be reduced as we sought to prevent further opportunity for unethical behavior. In such a scenario of conservative sensitivity, even simple creations such as thriller novels might be censored to the point of ceasing to thrill with their accounts of characters' alternative ways of thinking and responding to situations of opportunity or threat. It might be argued that it is the dark side within us that enables us to understand the threat of the dark deed.

Nevertheless, for most individuals, this cognitive engagement ends at the experience of being thrilled. In some cases, however, the dark individual may be inspired. Trevanian (1979), author of *Shibumi*, described, in an author's note, how he was deeply saddened to find that someone had been killed after their murderer had been inspired by a technique described in his novel. In a previous case, described by Katz (1988), the murderer had been inspired by a scene in a Clint Eastwood movie, where a prostitute had been forced to drink drain cleaner and had died swiftly. In this case, the script was not realistic, as the murderer found. His two victims screamed in agony for some time before he decided to finish them with a gun. Effective scriptwriting may require consideration of the darker needs of the villain in order that the author may entertain his or her audience, accepting that this may inspire fantasy and, in some cases, unethical behaviors. This is often done by writers and editors considering whether a story line really needs the proposed scenario or form of description. Nevertheless, what might be most creative and effective for the story line may in a few cases have an impact on the real world.

This is part of the argument for heavier censoring of programs, films, and video games. However, the counterargument relates to the nature of those minds that become inspired to enact and develop such behaviors. Eron (1982) concluded that while violence on television may be followed by aggressive behavior, aggressive individuals preferred to watch violent television. With a dark mind, inspiration can turn everyday objects, such as a newspaper or a paper cup, into lethal weapons (Trevanian, 1979). In those terms, it is not feasible to censor or design against all threat because we do not have complete control over individual differences (Eysenck, 1994) or free will. As Giddens (1973) proposes in discussion of his theory of the *structurization* of society, society is a human creation and yet beyond human control. It is therefore understandable why any dream of utopia is unreachable because we acknowledge the paradox of diverse human interaction and creative influence.

Everyone is involved in "designing" as a process of creating and organizing new value, but some of us are more capable of effective design than others. This chapter engages the reader with considerations of the *creatives*' role in a responsible design process, actively using "fantasy" for a balanced rather than negative outcome.

MEANING

For any audience to understand and engage in new discussion or the development of new propositions, it is important that the meaning of the key concepts first be defined. Therefore, this section further considers the *meaning* of "boundless creativity," starting with two quotes:

> There were no limits here. Once the bomb had fallen, *anything* could happen. What atomic weapons meant, what the death camps in Europe had meant, was that nothing evermore was sacred. In our day, it had been revealed that human beings are capable of demolishing every imaginable boundary. (Driver, 1991, pp. 43–44)

> Creativity can and does occur naturally, universally, perennially, in all people, in every walk of life, be they primitive or civilized, psychotic or neurotic, "gifted" or "normal". Like evil, creativity cannot be proclaimed the exclusive propensity of some particular portion of the population; nor any specific profession, vocation, personality type, or pathological condition. Creativity – as much as evil – is a congenital potentiality in every individual. (Diamond, 1996, p. 256)

The diversity of our languages maintains and develops differences in our thinking and communication. Many cultures have languages that apply dichotomies such as good and bad and saint and sinner. The Blackfoot Indians, however, as described by Bohm (1996), take a morphological approach to the construction of individual words to fit the object or situation. This suggests a dimensional as opposed to categorical worldview (Hilton, 2006) but acknowledges a need to create labels as references in order to share experience of change. Bohm (1996) also described how, as the meanings of words or concepts shift and set again or new meanings develop, some words may become axiomatic in our cultures, going unquestioned. Thus, while there may be no boundaries to creativity itself, the boundaries and blocks we experience are a result of our core beliefs "blinkering" us from seeing things in more insightful ways. Creative minds can order and arrange available images, memories, ideas, feelings, and reflexes in new ways to arrive at solutions, but the outcomes of such ordering may not always be positive. It is also possible to justify the reason and meaning for actions taken by remembering the context differently.

If this is taking place regularly, enabling the slipping of moral boundaries, for example, then it raises the question, "How can we inform our decisions wisely?" It may be argued that it is more effective to do so not on an individual basis but through a multiperspective community approach – a "social wisdom" that questions and then understands a relationship of its conclusions to the context of its present.

In developing social wisdom, through sharing perspectives, we might see "art" as Bohm (1996) suggested it might be, the "essence of human life" and viewed as the consideration and expression of the confusions that are experienced. By these artistic processes, he suggests, the means and end are the action of "fitting." Our literacy, our understanding, and our application of these considerations and expressions might then relate to how, through our wisdom, we become aware and alert to the "nonfitting." Nevertheless, that which "fits" may change over time and context, so we must question the "fitness," or our wisdom becomes outdated and therefore "unwise." Csikszentmihalyi and Rathunde (1990, p. 25) also suggest the need to guard against *dismissing without question* the ways and beliefs that have come to appear out of date. "To ignore the hard-won insights of the past about issues that are vital for survival is like blinding ourselves on purpose out of false pride."

Holistic questioning would seem to be an effective approach to wisdom. Bohm (1996) said that the meaning of who we are arises from our overall contacts with the whole world we live in, yet, "It is not enough to have holism, it must also be coherent." He went on to point out that the Nazi's had a kind of holistic theory – it just was not coherent.

However, if coherence is proposed but not tested and evidenced, there is the danger that it is merely accepted "as seen." Creative reframing of situations has seen "victims" become "survivors" and "terrorists" become "freedom fighters" (Whittaker, 2007). While such reframing may encourage some people to "let go" of negative frames and "move on," this is also noted to be a method supportive of indoctrination, which in some cases has been found to lead to mimicry of deeds. Similarly, the very act of labeling, in order to share a frame of reference, has been shown to change behaviors such that those who are labeled, in considering the label's meaning and consequences, begin to behave as labeled (Becker, 1963).

The need to understand experiences and perceptions as part of gaining wisdom should not be confused with understanding in order to just accept, or we may become unwisely permissive. In a speech, former British Prime Minister John Major once said: "Society needs to condemn a little more and understand a little less." This suggestion, however, should not be confused with "zero tolerance" (Wilson & Kelling, 1982) or the promotion of intolerance to difference. Both Gibran (1962) and Florida (2007) have described the value of tolerance of diversity to the creative economy.

Thus, to summarize this section on meaning, we may say that creativity is without boundaries because it is a natural process involving situations and experiences that inspire change to the order of things through the development and selection of new value. Creativity equally may result in conflicting categorical perceptions of a significant change as a great good or a great evil. While it may be a challenge for our cultures to perceive creative acts in the same light, it is important for future coherence that we find vehicles for discussion in order to develop and agree to helpful pro-social boundaries. We also should consider that the perception of these boundaries may serve us better as "boundaries to unethical behaviors and their consequences" rather than wider boundaries to creativity that would risk stifling innovation and resilience.

MOTIVATION

Physical and psychological individuality can enable people to experience the same event differently. We may associate pleasure with feeling the warmth of the sun or eating good food and pain with injury or grief. For some, however, pain may be part of a creative pleasure through tattooing and scarification, whereas for others, pleasure may involve vengeful acts or witnessing people in distress. Many of our sexual fantasies, according to Kahr (2007), involve distressing events that may be a result of and response to trauma experienced in childhood. Kahr's empirical research into sexual fantasies in the United Kingdom involved a large number of confidential interview case studies where analysis looked for common links between participants' descriptions of background and their fantasy content and construction. It is proposed that these fantasies develop in the personality as desires but are often very individual in nature, and some individuals may not even be conscious of them. The investigation indicated that many of the originating traumas are the result of ignorance, the nature of which is difficult to avoid, as the nature of life itself.

Nevertheless, it has been found that in many cases the mind may use these negative experiences to enable positive social and sexual connections to be made. The darker side of our self is a natural part of our identity and can be core to the way we perceive and reason as an individual. The creatives' responsibility, then, is to decide on their ethical standpoint and boundaries and find balance with them in a way that strengthens their competitiveness in providing support for human needs. This also applies to each individual, though, as a creative, in his or her self-actualization, involving destructive as well as constructive actions – destroying the status quo and old patterns as a response to the need to investigate and develop new and more appropriate opportunities and thus creating new ways of living (May, 1977).

Designers appear motivated to engage with the challenges of ambiguity because of what has been termed "inquisitive discontent" (Spencer, 2008, p. 10), the need to create positive change, and the inability to accept the status quo. In many ways this links to the work of Csikszentmihalyi (1975) on flow, a motivational, self-actualizing balance of ability versus challenge that otherwise may result in boredom or anxiety. This suggests, in terms of applying inquisitive discontent, that we should encourage the deeper, more mindful questioning of our selves and others in terms of both the status quo and future developments in order to better understand the impact of proposed changes.

Some individuals adopt creative thinking to fulfill scenarios and express their desires and needs. A number of forms of sensation seeking that may be considered deviant or bizarre are covered in the works of Franzini and Grossberg (1995). These include the *frotteur*, who takes advantage of, or orchestrates, situations where he or she can press his or her body up behind another person for sensual contact and gratification, and the *necrophile*, who may take the rare opportunity or else resort to murder to fulfill his or her fantasy need for intercourse with a dead body. Often there would seem to be some alternative interpretation of events and messages taking place, as with the *autoerotic*, for whom warning against the dangers of setting up situations for him or her to be strangled is instead experienced as enticement. This links to what Lehrer (2009) has described about the necessary emotional component of decision making being out of balance for some individuals, bringing about impulsive, irrational decisions as a result of one or more of the decision-making components of the brain not being fully developed and perceiving the emotional needs of the present to be more significant than those of the future or their consequences. This leads to the conclusion that making the subject of autoerotica taboo is the best way to reduce the number of accidental deaths each year.

When *Hustler* magazine and later the *Oprah Winfrey Show* in 1988 attempted to address the issue in the hope that raising awareness could help to resolve the problem of autoerotica, deaths of some of their audiences followed. There was evidence of their connection to viewing these publicized materials, with age ranges between 11 and 38 years, even though there had been a warning that viewing of the *Oprah Winfrey Show* was not suitable for children. Again, such warnings against viewing appear to have been interpreted as enticement. As with cases of individuals with a propensity toward violence making them a keen audience for the subject of their behavior, the danger has become increasing ease of access to content on the Internet, where this accessibility may be interpreted as acceptability of such behaviors.

Katz (1988) suggests that deviants tacitly create their sensual perception of the seduction of crime, possibly as a means of deferring guilt, experiencing the situation as if the object and scene were being provocative. While gangs may consciously take on the role of provocateur as they create modes of dress and body language, developing an image that may convey dread or is a manufactured irritation to get a physical reaction from a competing gang, who then might be accused of starting the fight. Presdee (2000, p. 4) said, "The way that we enjoy violence, crime, humiliation and hurt is part of the equation that needs to be examined and thought through."

The difficulty and unpleasantness of such thoughts, though, often are experienced as guilt. Richo (1999, p. 179) argues that guilt, as a "belief that we are cut off from wholeness," is developed over time as a concept and used as a form of social constraint of freedom and change in reaction to a fear of chaos. This concept suggests that guilt has evolved in the absence of other effective natural controls of creative freedom or else suggests that guilt is purely a code of practice placed within a culture to empower certain others. Although guilt is instigated by the culture, it is actually applied by the self, often without question, who potentially experiences the guilt as if the thoughts or behaviors are known to the social group. We may predict guilt for our considered deviation from cultural expectation as a means of denying ourselves some experiences, even though in some cases these experiences actually may contribute to well-being.

In terms of what specifically motivates individuals to carry out socially unacceptable acts, Whittaker (2007) suggests that many terrorists are motivated by discontent, yet terrorists take a more extreme and violent approach to "creative expression and resolution." Terrorists such as the Tamil Tigers have shown "inventiveness and extraordinary persistence" (Whittaker, 2007), and, in an analysis of motivation for reported "hate crimes," Baumeister (1997) found that they actually seemed to be committed out of some combination of boredom and a desire to show off before one's group.

Bandura, Caprara, Carbaranelli, Pastorelli, and Regalia (2001) noted that ordinary people in adverse social circumstances can begin to feel that they are *allowed* to dehumanize and act cruelly toward others, whereas Wootton, Press, and Davey (2008) and the continuing research on "Design Against Crime" indicated that environmental factors have a part to play in allowance of antisocial behaviors. For example, an urban area that is poorly maintained in terms of litter and lighting may suggest that other activities such as vandalism have a lower risk of leading to personal consequences. Nevertheless, engagement with such activities may lead to taking greater risks elsewhere and realizing new opportunities for sensation seeking or criminal gain.

By developing a clearer and shared understanding of the changing core motivations behind antisocial perspectives and behaviors, it should be possible to provide a more coherent resource for both the primary prevention and secondary countering of unethical acts, including crime and terrorism. Open-minded creative processes will play a part in the development of such understanding.

Wilkinson (2006) makes it clear that both terrorists and counterterrorists will continue to employ creative thinking to consider scenarios of action, where gaps in legislation and process may become sources of threat. Profiling has been employed by counterterrorism in the investigation of terrorist groups and their threats. One method for terrorist profile development is use of the "Sinai attack indicators" (Sinai, 2005). There are similar established approaches to the profile development of criminals and their organizations, for instance, relating to the resourcing and commissioning of crime, as described by Reiner (2007). The creation of such profiles and consideration lists adds active support to the proposals of Ekblom (1997), Downes and Rock (2003), Gill (2005), and Hilton and Irons (2006) that first-hand knowledge of deviant rule breakers and criminals should be acquired to inform the development of preventative change.

In summary, there are many personal, social, and environmental motivations for the development of unethical perceptions and behaviors. Nevertheless, processes of modeling and mapping of these individual differences in motivation can enable more insightful engagement with the prevention and countering of antisocial behaviors. Through an understanding of creative approaches to the maintenance and development of new antisocial behaviors, we will be better informed to identify the root causes and propose more effective redirective practices. It is human nature to identify and procure opportunities to realize our most basic and deepest desires, preferably without consequence or, in some cases even, without fully conscious consideration. However, in time, the consequence of our actions does come to us or our children. While there is a drive to copy some behaviors for particular social acceptances, there is equally a motivation for creative exploration and expression for the individual to take ownership of the experience of these behaviors.

ETHICS

Group discussion of ethical considerations serves to inform socially coherent decisions on the creation of change. Frequently, ethics can, however, be a challenge to discuss in terms of defining the boundaries for our actions with a view to evaluating and prescribing what ought to be (MacIntyre, 1998) because categorizing intentions as either helping or harming can prove overly simplistic, at times leaving us unable to conclude. Responsible design practices take a lead from the social sciences in terms of codes of practice, but there is still room for improvement. Grayling (2003, p. 226) referred to Camus and Sartre for their nomination of "four values that individuals, in creating themselves in the face of absurdity, can impose on the antecedent meaninglessness of existence to give it value: namely love, freedom, human dignity and creativity."

Even if a community agrees on and holds to its ethical standpoint, its members need to appreciate the different standpoints that may be held by outsiders in order to understand how best to engage or disengage with them. A moral compass exercise, as proposed by McEwan (2001), might be used as a means of acknowledging differences in perspective and for then making effective selections for critically balanced engagement and development. However, the success of any process of discussion and decision making depends on effective communication, which beyond openness is influenced by the language used and the communicator's preconceptions.

Jung is noted as commenting about Christianity's attempts to constrain behavior as being "unrealistic" and "an attempt to jump off one's shadow" (Hull, 1954). To suggest that God wishes to punish such behaviors is, as Calvin was quoted in Midgley (1984, p. 103), like saying that God is like "a clockmaker who designs, builds, and winds a clock, and then punishes it for striking." All such perceptions contribute to the ethical meaning behind the language available to consider, discuss, and decide on ethical issues. MacIntyre (1998) discussed Aristotle's concepts of "too much" and "too little" – both being perceived as forms of evil, in some cases recognized by our references to them, including malice, shamelessness, and envy and actions such as adultery, theft, and murder. However, labels such as "anger" and "pity" are insufficient to inform as to whether the behaviors should be condemned because the words lack contextual depth, whereas it seems clearer with words such as "envy" and "malice" that there is an axiomatic expectation that such behaviors should be condemned.

This line of thought would lead us to be wary of being led by the available language and attempt to focus more on the situation behind the unethical behaviors. However, not all individuals interpret situations or react to them in the same way, and not all individuals have the same creative capacities. The capacity to create dark events is still inspired by situation, but then, no one person can be blamed for the often complex situation itself.

The proposition, then, is to predict consequence more effectively, using "dark" creativity perhaps, and then to work to prevent undesirable situations. The preventative solutions may not be as successful, though, if they focus on the development of counterthreats, which, in some cases, may lead only to escalation. Midgley (1984, p. 174) suggests that using threats as a deterrence can only work in two ways, "either as a friendly warning between parties who already trust each other, but have sporadic conflicts of interest; or as a serious, immediate menace from an undoubtedly superior power to a weaker one, which really expects action to follow." The outcome is that the threatening may serve to provide evidence of the very perceptions that contributed to the situation in the first place, thus leading to escalation.

Our responsible creative practices require ethical guidance that undoubtedly involves wisdom and an understanding of its processes for the development of mindfulness of boundaries to the unethical. The "balance theory of wisdom" (Sternberg, 1998, pp. 347–365) defines wisdom as "The application of intelligence, creativity and experience towards a common good by balancing one's own interests with other's interests and institutional interests over the long and short terms."

COUNTERING ANTISOCIAL CREATIVITY

Having considered meaning, motivation, and ethics, this section gives consideration to how we might use antisocial perspectives on object, environment, and behavior to develop and apply countersolutions to antisocial creativity. Aspects of the lives of criminals have been investigated by anthropologists (Hendry, 1999), who have developed insider perspectives, including the influences of age, education, employment, social group, environment, media, and the affects of the antisocial behaviors themselves. There also have been initiatives such as the British Home Office–funded "Design Against Crime," which has involved Central St. Martins, Salford, Sheffield Hallam, and Cambridge universities in the United Kingdom. With collaboration among academics, crime-prevention agencies, and the affected communities, these initiatives have sought to record, consider, propose, and develop solutions to situational catalysts for crime. These investigations and their developments have enabled a much deeper and more practical understanding to be gained of the challenges involved.

An investigation of the conjunction of criminal opportunity by Ekblom (2000) highlighted the need for joined-up thinking, and there is now recognition that partial solutions may succeed only in displacing crime to other areas (Wootton et al., 2008). Where possible, the approach of "design *with*" rather than "design *for*" has been adopted, gaining engagement with all sides of the affected communities in the project work to inform effective design decisions. Also, in the development and selection of design proposals, there has been a further inclusive ethic to provide solutions of value to all rather than propose solutions that may in some way stigmatize or exclude. In terms of crime prevention, then, the intention is to discourage or even remove the dark value or reward of these antisocial opportunities from our communities by a human-centered consideration of need.

It might be argued, since Milgram (1963), that the potential for crime and terrorism, as well as crime prevention and counterterrorism, resides in the majority of us. We only have to consider fictional situations that we have read or viewed where many might feel justice appears to require a violent counterattack to prevent further atrocity. However, if this means supporting the minority, then the counter may be viewed by the majority as terrorism, as on TV series such as Cochran and Surnow's (2001) *24* or Moore's (2004) *Battlestar Galactica*. The natural process and conflict of identifying with characters and situations, however, can be turned to effective use in informing new creative perspectives.

Nevertheless, it is argued that to be efficient in our approach to the use of creative perspectives to counter situations and opportunities for antisocial behaviors, there also need to be critical perspectives and action (Barab et al., 2004). As part of the effective management of creative and critical engagement, it is important that the "vulnerability-led" responses (Durodie, 2002) do not overly focus on the boundless "what-if?" avenues but instead more realistically focus on evidence of "what has?" and "what will?"

Wootton and Davey (2003) built on Ekblom's (2001) causal framework and developed their "crime lifecycle," which supports understanding and engagement with stages in criminal progression, covering both situational and offender attributes. Such an approach supports more informed and critical differentiation between the "what if?" and the "what will?" scenarios.

The "Cyclic Countering of Competitive Creativity" (C4), developed by me, enables further support to the approaches of designing *with* and defining the "what will?" scenarios as part of the critical process of crime-prevention development. The process is facilitated in this context through the perspective of the criminal as *competitor*. The process involves the use of criminal personas to *explode*, or at least critically deconstruct, concept solutions. The name "C4" serves at a metaphoric level, helping to keep the intent of the tool in mind because C4 is a military and security services reference to Compound 4 plastic explosive. Core to the effectiveness of this process is the use of role play to ensure engagement with competitor countering. Personas, rather than profiles, are used for this process.

Profiles, as first developed by Brussel (1968), are "working constructions" of *yet to be identified individuals* using crime-scene data as they are gathered. Profiles are applied as investigative tools to narrow down suspect pools and apprehend the suspect. Nevertheless, it has proven difficult to evaluate their success (Ainsworth, 2000). There are also ethical concerns over the use of profiling. Profiles are not evidence or proof themselves, and inaccurate profiles may lead unquestioning investigators off track. Even with an accurate profile, there likely will be many people who fit the description, so care must be taken not to treat the "suspect" as guilty until proven so.

Personas, as defined by Hilton and Henderson (2008), are "working constructions" of *identified types*. This process uses "open" access to *competitor* reports and direct accounts from the competitors or their associates to develop competitive counterperspectives to be used in team situations as a tool to improve the critical-thinking and analyzing processes in "Design Against Threat." The success of this approach is that it immerses and engages project community members in the development and application of the counterperspectives and more effectively informs the process than the use of assumptions developed from the personal experiences of users alone. There are ethical concerns over this use of personas, however, and users must guard against developing and applying the personas in an unethical manner. The process must challenge and positively change the competition's behavior but not physically or mentally harm the "competition" or their associates or bystanders by either the process of investigation or the role play. Ideally, the acceptable outcomes are responsibly improved, win-win responses to the competition.

In application of the C4 process, each project community member who is tasked to take part in designing and critiquing propositions is required to engage with a single persona. This requires continued persona immersion and role play in preparation for and during the application period. Using "research-developed" personas as opposed to guessed or "assumed" personas (Pruitt & Aldin, 1996) ensures that each individual is more effectively informed and prepared to be competitively creative within a specified context. The critical "countering" nature of the C4 process helps designers and other colleagues to become more objective and less precious over concept proposals. This process also enables a "fail often to succeed sooner" approach (Kelley, 2001) to inform context intelligence and the selection and strengthening of preventative proposals.

Teams of four or five members work well, with each member providing his or her different persona perspectives to the mix. It is the responsibility of each member to focus on his or her own persona, to get into character, and to develop that persona throughout the project period. This means that the personas are to be considered "live" and developing, not set or treated simply as a checklist. Team members are encouraged to generate additional prompts and characteristics as their experience develops, especially "creative prompts," which are the competitive processes and inspirations for countering proposals and arriving at win-lose situations.

In the design process, the personas are applied cyclically. The roles of the *creative* and *critic* are switched as the idea, concept, design, and specification-development stages require designer mode then competitor mode and then counterpropositions in turn. A successful solution is considered to be reached when the competitor "types," represented by the personas, would consider further engagement too risky or not worth the investment of money, time, or effort.

The C4 process does require a period of "coming down" or "returning" following persona application as part of responsible practice; otherwise, it is possible for some individuals who are still not intellectually mature or are susceptible to suggestion to maintain aspects of their persona following use. This might be compared with the way some people's driving becomes erratic following a visit to the cinema to watch a film involving car chases or after playing with a car rally computer game. The emotional element of decision making would, for these individuals, be imbalanced without an appropriate period to "come down" from the experience. This also relates to concerns over the creation and alteration of self-identity through inappropriate role models if negative aspects are maintained for emotional affect and then habituated. As mentioned earlier, not everyone is suited to working with the dark side of creativity.

In summary there are a number of methods for informing the countercriminal processes, and each process has its own merit. C4 as a means of countering antisocial creativity does require an investment of time in developing and applying the personas effectively, but that development provides an immersive experience for the role players. A key aspect of the C4 process is that it should enable the project community to use the potential motivations and means of the *competitions'* behavior against itself.

DISCUSSION

The martial arts were a creative response to threat of attack built on lifetimes of observation and understanding of the mechanics of human strengths and weaknesses. Practitioners learned to create structures within the body that delivered grounded force or fluidity of motion that maximized speed. Others learned about pressure points and joint locks. Still others learned to use daily tools as weapons so that the rice flail became the *Nunchaku* and the seeding drill became the *Sai*. In karate, the practitioner learns his or her style of fighting by different methods: *Kata* involves sets of moves to be viewed as a battle with invisible opponents using predefined attacks, whereas *Kumite* involves a duel with an actual opponent, where skills are tested with a level of unpredictability. There are many other styles of fighting. Each one feels and is applied somewhat differently and requires the practitioner to think differently. In countering antisocial creativity, we also must be prepared to think differently.

Novels and film scripts have taken the themes of competition and fighting further by proposing conspiracy theories. In Black's (1996) *The Long Kiss Good Night*, government funding was used to create a terrorist event to enable terrorism to be seen as an even greater threat in order to further fund, develop, and sustain the country's counterterrorism agencies. Alternatively, there was the plot of Woods' (2001) *Swordfish*, where government operatives actually stole from the electronic banking system to fund terrorism against opposing terrorists. The ethics of such creative scenarios falls under question because of the cost to innocent others perpetrated by the cold logic of such fictitious operatives. Against the reasoning of "sacrificing the few for the good of the many," it is argued that such operations would only create a continuation of the threat and its fear. It is generally not agreed to be ethical to decide the sacrifices of others because consideration of such action threatens to undermine the very quality of life that is to be protected (Wilkinson, 2006).

It is proposed here that instead of creating the potential for escalation by returning the strikes of the competitor with more power and precision, as in karate, the whole dynamics of threat instead might be changed by using the competitor's force of attack to the defender's advantage. Aikido as a self-defense uses the attacker's momentum and direction in such a way that control, and then value in persistence, is lost to the attacker. This may be considered a good metaphor for effective countering of antisocial creativity by design and would suggest that by working with the *threatened* and the *threat*, a more effective resolution might be achieved. This latter scenario describes a reactive process, however. To make it proactive, reflexive processes could use competitor experience to forecast future opportunity for threat and then to determine probability and respond preventatively.

Beyond effective engagement of project community members in "Design Against Threat" processes, further success of redirective practices in resolving or reducing threat could be enabled by the development of social wisdom. The components of wisdom have been found to form six categories. In order of strength, these are

1. "Reasoning ability
2. Sagacity
3. Learning from ideas and environment
4. Judgement
5. Expeditious use of information
6. Perspicacity"

– Sternberg (1990, pp. 145–146)

These components act against subversion to some extent by enabling people to develop a perception of the positive and negative social consequences of theirs' and others' actions. "They seek understanding of what will 'work' not only for them but for society as well" (Sternberg, 1990).

It is not proposed, however, that the development of social wisdom and "Design Against Threat" processes are the total solution to antisocial behaviors. There will continue to be behavioral concerns owing to individual differences and abnormal psychology, as well as inequalities in education (Lehrer, 2009). Natural systemic thinkers may become wiser than those not capable of comprehending complex issues. In this situation, while the wise may be seen to be comfortable with the challenges of ambiguity, the unwise may become anxious and, in an attempt to deal with their anxieties, may be more emotionally prone to turn to antisocial activities as a perceived means of escape.

Nevertheless, there are no guarantees even for the wise because wisdom does not last. As we age, we lose pace with change and become less wise (Meacham, 1990). Life changes such as retirement, loss of loved ones, and possible loss of independence see us disconnect from the community, which disengages the social wisdom. It may be such loss of wisdom that breeds doubt and a "fear of crime" through dark imaginings among the less fortunate.

Without boundaries, or with boundaries unchecked or slipping, today's societies would appear, as Bohm (1996) suggests, to be heading toward physical and mental destruction. The desire for power, actualized by creative or mechanical means, ultimately becomes meaningless. However, this "mess" is not new, only the way our cultures facilitate it through our technologies. The Internet has made it easier to engage in criminal activities in part because the criminal is distanced from his or her victim. The technology acts as a dehumanizing filter. Also, Mann and Sutton (1998) have said, "The Internet is a particularly effective medium for criminal recruitment and the dissemination of criminal techniques."

In addition, the audiovisual entertainments now so readily accessible through the Internet, as well as the television, negatively influence child development because they make it more difficult for children to appreciate the need to read. Without reading skills, their engagement with most academic subjects may suffer, reducing individual's accessibility to more positive opportunities. Performance anxieties have been shown to lead to the development of antisocial behaviors, and as mentioned earlier, there is now sufficient visual information through electronic media to inspire the dark creativity behind some of these antisocial behaviors.

Since the development of social wisdom waxes and wanes with changes in understanding, both locally and globally, we should seek to consider the dark side of creativity from a more constructive perspective, to use it against itself, and to innovate incrementally who the human race is.

CONCLUSION

This chapter has contributed to this discussion of the dark side of creativity by considering the influence of creativity's boundlessness in the context of human beings' interactions, particularly crime and terrorism. It has considered the meaning of boundaries or lack thereof and concluded that each community needs to agree to boundaries that are pro-social. The section on motivation acknowledged that while there will remain some differences in perspective, there are creative means of engaging debate and sharing experience that may even use dark creativity as a redirected vehicle for positive change. Ethics are a key consideration in these debates, but it needs to be understood whose ethics are being questioned, discussed, and approved and to what end. The development of social wisdom was proposed to be a common means of enabling systemic thinking and coherence for contexts of opportunity or threat, but it is important to keep the questioning process alive through social engagement or else the wisdom fades. The discussion of methods of countering antisocial creativity saw that a theme is developing in the context of crime prevention and community safety of engaging in the criminal's perspective, using approaches such as the "crime lifecycle" and C4. In the same way that defender and offender perspectives may be applied in role-play experiences to inform investigation and decision making, it is argued that both the light and dark sides of creativity are necessary for wisdom. Instead of developing only the lighter side of creativity, we must provide some balance by knowing the darker side, acknowledging that not everyone is suited to do so, though. Nevertheless, those who can use these methods of investigating the threats of "what will?" should be better positioned to forecast consequences and propose solutions using the threat itself as the means of developing a wiser future.

It would seem that the way forward for humanity is to acknowledge that the dark side of creativity is in us all, and used in conjunction with the light side, it is proposed to better enable the communication of our needs and experiences. By taking an inclusive approach to "design *with*," providing value to *all*, we should build our wisdom on the ethics of our societies, questioning our propositions, and then look to deal responsibly with the consequences of the things that we do miss on the dark side.

REFERENCES

Ainsworth, P. B. (2000). *Psychology and crime: Myths and reality.* Harlow, England: Pearson Education.

Bandura, A., Caprara, G. V., Carbaranelli, C., Pastorelli, C., & Regalia, C. (2001). Sociocognitive self-regulatory mechanisms governing transgressive behaviour. *Journal of Personality and Social Psychology,* 80, 125–135.

Baumeister, R. F. (1997). *Evil: Inside human violence and cruelty.* New York: Freeman.

Barab, S. A., Thomas, M. K., Dodge, T., Squire, K., & Newell, M. (2004). Critical design ethnography: Design for change. *Anthropology and Educational Quarterly,* 35, 254–263.

Becker, H. S. (1963). *Outsiders: Studies in the sociology of deviance.* Glencoe, IL: Free Press of Glencoe.

Black, S. (1996). *The long kiss goodnight.* Los Angeles, CA: New Line Cinema.

Bohm, D. (1996). *On creativity.* London: Routledge.

Brussel, J. A. (1968). *Casebook of a crime psychiatrist.* London: New English Library.

Checkland, P. B. (1981). *Systems thinking, systems practice.* New York: Wiley.

Cochran, R. & Surnow, J. (2001). *24.* Los Angeles, CA: 20th Century Fox.

Csikszentmihalyi, M. (1975). *Beyond boredom and anxiety.* San Francisco, CA: Jossey-Bass.

Csikszentmihalyi, M. & Rathunde, K. (1990). Psychology of wisdom: Evolutionary interpretation. In R. J. Sternberg (Ed.), *Wisdom. Its nature, origins, and development* (pp. 25–51). New York: Cambridge University Press.

Diamond, S. A. (1996). *Anger, madness, and the daimonic. The psychological genesis of violence, evil, and creativity.* New York: State University of New York Press.

Downes, D. and Rock, P. (2003). *Understanding deviance,* 4th ed. Oxford, England: Oxford University Press.

Driver, T. F. (1991). *The magic of ritual.* San Francisco, CA: HarperCollins.

Durodie, B. (2002). Perception and threat: Why vulnerability-led responses will fail. *Homeland Security and Resilience Monitor,* 1, 16–19.

Ekblom, P. (1997). Gearing up against crime: A dynamic framework to help designers keep up with the adaptive criminal in a changing world. *International Journal of Risk, Security and Crime Prevention,* 2, 249–265.

Ekblom, P. (2000). The conjunction of criminal opportunity – A tool for clear "joined-up" thinking about community safety and crime reduction. In S. Ballintyne, K. Pease, and V. McLaren (Eds.), *Secure foundations: Key issues in crime prevention, crime reduction and community safety.* London: Institute for Public Policy Research.

(2001). Crime reduction: The conjunction of criminal opportunity. Home Office Crime Reduction Toolkits; available at www.crimereduction.gov.uk/cco.htm.

Eron, L. D. (1982). Parent-child interaction, television violence and aggression in children. *American Psychologist,* 37, 197–211.

Eysenck, M. W. (1994). *Individual differences: Normal and abnormal.* Hove, England: LEA.

Florida, R. (2007). *The flight of the creative class: The new global competition for talent.* New York: HarperCollins.

Franzini, L. R. & Grossberg, J. M. (1995). *Eccentric and bizarre behaviors.* New York: Wiley.

Gibran, K. (1962). *The spiritual sayings of Kahlil Gibran.* New York: Citadel.

Giddens, A. (1973). *The constitution of society.* Cambridge, MA: Polity.

Gill, M. (2005). Learning from fraudsters. Research report, Protiviti.Perpetuity Research and Consultancy Ltd., London.

Grayling, A. C. (2003). *What is good? The search for the best way to live.* London: Phoenix.

Hendry, J. (1999). *An introduction to social anthropology: Other people's worlds.* Basingstoke, England: Palgrave Macmillan.

Hilton, K. H. (2006). Modelling complexity of gender as an agent of change. *Systemist,* 28, 116–125.

Hilton, K. H. & Henderson, K. (2008). Developing criminal personas for designers. *British Society of Criminology Journal,* 8, 248–259.

Hilton, K. H. & Irons, A. (2006). A "criminal persona's" approach to countering criminal creativity. *Crime Prevention & Community Safety. An International Journal,* 8, 248–259.

Hull, R. F. C. (Trans.). (1954). *Jung's answer to Job.* London: Routledge & Kegan Paul.
Kahr, B. (2007). *Sex and the psyche: The truth about our most secret fantasies.* London: Penguin.
Katz, J. (1988). *Seductions of crime: Moral and sensual attractions in doing crime.* New York: Basic Books.
Kelley, T. (2001). *The art of innovation.* New York: Currency Doubleday.
Lehrer, J. (2009). *The decisive moment: How the brain makes up the mind.* Edinburgh: Canongate.
MacIntyre, A. (1998). *A short history of ethics.* London: Routledge.
Mann, D. & Sutton, M. (1998). Netcrime: More change in the organisation of theiving. *British Journal of Criminology*, 38, 210–229.
May, R. (1977). *The meaning of anxiety.* Revised edition. New York: W. W. Norton.
McEwan, T. (2001). *Managing values and beliefs in organisations.* Harlow, England: Prentice- Hall.
Meacham, J. A. (1990). The loss of wisdom. In R. J. Sternberg (Ed.), *Wisdom: Its nature, origins, and development* (pp. 181–211). New York: Cambridge University Press.
Midgley, M. (1984). *Wickedness.* London: Routledge & Kegan Paul.
Milgram, S. (1963). Behavioural study of obedience. *Journal of Abnormal and Social Psychology.* 67, 391–398.
Moore, R. D. (2004) *Battlestar Galactica.* Los Angeles, CA: Universal.
Pascual-Leone, J. (1990). An essay on wisdom: Toward organismic processes that make it possible. In R. J. Sternberg (Ed.), *Wisdom: Its nature, origins, and development* (pp. 244–278). New York: Cambridge University Press.
Presdee, M. (2000). *Cultural criminology and the carnival of crime.* London: Routledge.
Pruitt, J. & Aldin, T. (1996). *The persona lifecycle: Keeping people in mind throughout product design.* San Francisco, CA: Morgan Kaufmann.
Reiner, R. (2007). *Law and order: An honest citizen's guide to crime and control.* Cambridge, MA: Polity.
Richo, D. (1999). *Shadow dance: Liberating the power and creativity of your dark side.* Boston: Shambhala.
Simon, H. A. (1996) *The sciences of the artificial*, 3rd ed. Cambridge, MA: MIT Press.
Sinai, J. (2005). Red teaming catastrophic terrorism by Al Qaeda jihadists. *Journal of Counterterrorism and Homeland Security International*, 11. 32–35.
Spencer, N. R. (2008). An investigation into the experience of designing. Ph.D. thesis, Northumbria University, Newcastle upon Tyne.
Sternberg, R. J. (1990). Wisdom: Relations to intelligence and creativity. In R. J. Sternberg (Ed.), *Wisdom: Its nature, origins, and development* (pp. 142–159). New York: Cambridge University Press.
(1998). A balance theory of wisdom. *Review of General Psychology*, 2, 347–365.
(Ed.). (2005). *The psychology of hate.* Washington: American Psychological Society.
Trevanian (1979). *Shibumi.* London: Granada.

Whittaker, D. J. (Ed.). (2007). *The terrorism reader*, 3rd ed. London: Routledge.
Wilkinson, P. (2006). *Terrorism versus democracy: The liberal state response*, 2nd ed. Oxford, England: Routledge.
Willis, A.-M. (2008). Design, redirective practice and sustainment. A keynote address at the 360 Degrees conference, Brighton, UK.
Wilson, J. Q. & Kelling, G. W. (1982). Broken windows. *Atlantic Monthly*, 249, 29–38.
Woods, S. (2001). *Swordfish*. Los Angeles, CA: Warner Bros.
Wootton, A. B. & Davey, C. L. (2003). *Crime lifecycle: Guidance for generating design against crime ideas*. Salford, England: Design Against Crime Solutions Centre.
Wootton, A. B., Press, M. P., & Davey, C. L. (2008). *Design against crime*. Aldershot, England: Ashgate.

9

Reviewing the Art of Crime: What, If Anything, Do Criminals and Artists/Designers Have in Common?

LORRAINE GAMMAN AND MAZIAR RAEIN

The "dark side of creativity" is a slippery concept to explore because the idea of "creativity" is subject to historically changing definitions. This chapter will review some ideas about creativity and, when discussing the art of crime as the "dark side of creativity," will try to avoid positioning "darkness" as "blindness, evil, lack, loss and as the underworld" compared with "light" as "clarity, hope, goodness, rebirth and life." Such stark oppositions often contain quasi-religious meanings, as exemplified by the *Star Wars* movies ("Yes, a Jedi's strength flows from the force. … But beware the desire of the dark side"). Instead, we will discuss the dark side of creativity by

1. Reviewing definitions of creativity and examining dyslexia and what else artists, designers, criminals, and entrepreneurs have in common (Gamman, 2008a)
2. Further explaining how and why ideas about the dark side of creativity are relevant to understanding the emergence of the Design Against Crime Research Centre (DACRC) located at the University of the Arts London – in particular, to understand approaches to design creativity defined as "thinking thief" (Ekblom, 1997) as well as the "criminal gaze" (Gamman, 2008b)
3. Finally, discussing how and why ideas about the "the art of crime", as well as actual crime itself, have informed the discourse of transgression associated with art and design, informing a number of creative outputs that we review

WHAT IS CREATIVITY, AND WHAT DO ARTISTS AND DESIGNERS AND CRIMINALS HAVE IN COMMON?

Creativity is … imaginative processes that produce outcomes that are original (or useful). (Robinson, 2001, p. 116)

During the last decade, the word "creativity" has been used in a very generic sense by management gurus such as Charles Handy and Robert Heller and government ministers such as Andy Burnham to make banal statements: "Our vision is of a Britain in 10 years time where the local economies in our biggest cities are driven by creativity."

Politicians such as Chris Smith (1998), the former culture secretary, and "captains of creativity" such as Richard Florida (2002) regularly pay tribute to the idea of creativity. Creativity is heralded as a panacea to cure the economic decline of Western Europe and America, linked to the expanding market share of the BRIC (Brazil, Russia, India, and China) countries (O'Neill, 2003). The prediction that BRIC's overall gross domestic product (GDP) will eclipse that of Western nations by 2050 was made before the present economic meltdown. Yet the underlying point has not changed. The term "creativity" is often accompanied with the allied concept of "innovation" and is applied as a universal remedy by politicians to address current structural shortcomings of industrial production. Innovation, of course, is creative, but it has been used as an essential interface between creativity and creative resources and the cooperative enterprise structures that exploit creativity to drive profit.

There are so many theories about innovation and creativity as to constitute an evolving history of ideas, now summarized on Wikepedia (2009a). This history demands that we make important distinctions and definitions from the outset; that is, "creativity" is a feature of human behavior and phenomena experienced by many individuals. Moreover, this concept has been examined through the lens of many disciplines, ranging from psychology to management studies, from art to science, and nearly all discourses. Despite so much writing about it, as yet there is no established definition that can be characterized by a single feature. We know it operates across all aspects of human endeavor, often mulled through slow thinking (Claxton, 1997) or arrived at through instantaneous intuitive responses, or "eureka" moments. It is these polarities of creative thinking that make it difficult to define creativity.

Therefore, for the purposes of this chapter, we may be best suited to discuss creativity within the realm of art and design practice. From this perspective, we describe creativity as the ability to conceive – often through unconventional, playful, and sporadic approaches – conceptualize and visualize ideas into diverse cultural forms in order to find or discover previously unexpected conceptions. We also point to the fact that there is an identified link between creativity and dyslexia. Thomas West (1997) developed such a link when he described the ability of highly visual people to conceptualize complex ideas, especially those which enabled them to integrate visual-spatial material. This link between visual-spatial thinking and a rejection of mechanical approaches to learning and adaptability in complex situations evidently allows dyslexics to solve problems in unusual ways that employ unconventional methods. West claimed that dyslexics may well be at the forefront of dealing with technological developments, in using their ability to process complex ideas, and in creating "a whole new literacy" in the process.

Discussions about "innovation" are distinctively different from discussions about creativity. Innovation is the process that takes creative ideas to the market in the broad sense. Not all creative people are able to transform their creativity into innovation, unlike the most skilled criminals or business-focused individuals. Many creatives are also successful at innovation, although some artists, such as Joseph Beuys, for example, despised the idea of innovation and took a high moral approach against the commodification of art. This attitude is still present in some discourses today, although most artists recognize the need to earn an income from their creativity and consequently engage with the system.

Art and design, too, have been linked recently to pragmatic strategies that could help to beat the economic downturn. Creatives are seen to be "often faster at responding to emerging needs, resources, and solutions" (Leadbeater & Meadway, 2008). This account has become very significant in the current global economic recession. In fact, there is an emerging recognition that the creative industries (especially those linked to communities and social enterprises) generate large amounts of fiscal and social capital as well as fast and flexible networks.

Previously, the financial arena generated by the creative industries had been surprisingly under-recognized and unmapped. It is now being vigorously reassessed by governments with a view to catalyzing more activity and creating more gross national product (GNP) in the future. Consequently, a number of influential reports have been published that try to explain creativity and innovation. They include Sir George Cox's (2005) *Review of Creativity in Business*, Professor Mark Brown's (2000) *Report on Innovation* for PricewaterhouseCoopers, The Work Foundation's (2007) Report, *Staying ahead: The economic performance of the UK's creative industries*, and Leadbeater and Meadway's (2008) *Attacking the Recession.*

Among all these voices on the current state of "creativity" and "innovation," two groups are largely ignored. The first are the voices of artists and designers, although this is changing. For example, the account of the difference between "interpretative" and "analytic" innovation put forward by Lester and Piore (2004) and the account of the way artists and fashion designers are able to start different "conversations" that generate creativity and innovation (Oakley, Sperry, & Pratt, 2008) go some way toward addressing the gaps in understanding about how such creatives work. The second group is the criminal class, whose creativity is rarely acknowledged (with the exception of gangster and crime fictions that abound in popular culture), even though real criminals also generate innovation and income. Some criminal "projects" also may exhibit the "wow" factor common to creative breakthroughs and paradigm-breaking audacity. Because criminal activity is often immoral (entirely parasitic as well as illegal), though, it is usually only in fiction that we find celebration. Even then, after focusing on it at length, such fictions often try to reposition criminal innovation as linked to spiritual or moral "darkness" to avoid charges of glamorization.

So how are criminals and creatives similar? What is becoming a little more understood and easier to measure is that individuals within both creative and criminal classes share certain dispositions. For example, the number of those found to be "dyslexic" in art school and prison is similarly high; that is, "16% to 20% of Art & Design students are certified dyslexic" (Raein, 2003). As many as 60 percent of art and design students are argued to have problems linked to visual-spatial learning styles (VLSs) (East Mentoring Forum, 2007). This U.K. study shows that 53 percent of the prison population are dyslexic. Morgan and Klein (2000) also point out that "studies from England, the USA and Sweden suggest that between 30 and 52 percent of the prison population in all three countries may be dyslexic, depending on how narrowly dyslexia is defined." Perhaps it is no surprise that entrepreneurs are also found to be disproportionately dyslexic (East Mentoring Forum, 2007) given that both criminals and creatives often have strong entrepreneurial qualities. Dyslexia has been defined as "... a complex neurological condition, which is constitutional in origin." The symptoms may affect "many areas of learning and function, and may include specific difficulty in reading, spelling and written language, often accompanied by accelerated visual recognition skills" [British Dyslexia Association (BDA), 1995] as well as holistic thinking skills. But there is a negative aspect to measuring dyslexia within traditional quantitative frameworks. Dyslexic juvenile offenders have been found to demonstrate "a low ability in verbal expression accompanied by poor reading skills and writing skills that are measured to be well below average" (BDA, 2004–2005). The BDA also states that "untreated dyslexia" (a term some dyslexics object to because it is a medical definition that has labeled dyslexia as an illness and strips it of its positive advantages), accompanied by poor levels of education, has been found to lead to "delinquent behaviour and to the subsequent development of an anti-social and/or criminal lifestyle" (BDA, 2004–2005).

Crime challenges many societies to face the significant question, "How do we deal with our fellow citizens who unacceptably step outside the boundaries of so-called normal behavior?" Dyslexia is a condition/learning style that may contribute to individuals being labeled inappropriately or even sent to prison.

Heather Symonds, who works with dyslexics at the London College of Communication, University of Arts, explains in an account elaborated via e-mail communication with Gamman and Raein how a dyslexic certainly would be perceived as a criminal suspect under questioning, not being able to easily answer what may be (to the police officers asking) apparently straightforward questions. She points out that dyslexia may mean that the person being questioned is unable to describe events in a clear, chronological sequence or have a rapid recall of names and dates. She also suggests that nervous mannerisms in attempting to recall facts may communicate "guilt" or "criminal intentions," whereas "information anxiety" may be more likely. While we do not wish to reinforce the "pathologization" of dyslexia as a "condition" rather than a learning style, in terms of a discussion of creativity, we feel that more research is needed to enable us to better understand how precisely dyslexia is linked to forms of "transgression" that may lead to creative innovation.

Creatives and criminals may have disproportionate numbers experiencing dyslexia and engaging in transgression, but it is not our intention to use the terms "creative" and "dyslexic" interchangeably. Rather, we wish to explore how criminal behavior might be connected to creative activity. Dyslexia is part of this account and needs to be researched further to understand if it informs or generates creative approaches and minds.

The ability to scan, spot, and exploit a situation is a characteristic that is consistent among some criminals, but it is also a characteristic that is shared by many creatives. As Anthony Julius (2002) has observed, artists and criminals share certain characteristics. The artist is as resourceful and amoral in his or her pursuit of the project as the criminal. The likeness of the artist to the criminal was celebrated by Degas and is a familiar trope in art writing. "A painting calls for as much cunning, roguishness and wickedness as the committing of a crime," Degas commented, and he advised the neophyte artist to be "devious."

Artists and designers may draw on risky strategies associated with crime either literally or metaphorically; Julius summarizes such strategies as "crimes committed by or against art." From the Surrealists to the Situationists, many artistic movements employ anarchic, transgressive, and even criminal strategies as a valid way of making social comment. Such ideas about the role of artistic transgression as a way to challenge the status quo has influenced many generations. However, professional burglars and shoplifters do not aim to make creative statements, even if the way they intuitively review design weaknesses or problems primarily to outwit security systems has a lot in common with creative thinking. Clearly, criminals aim to steal objects or services primarily to transform them into profit (cash tender that is difficult to trace by the authorities). Garwood (2009) indicates that "there is preliminary evidence for seeing the world differently if you have been an offender … because to those with an offender's eye, opportunity is everywhere they go."

Our work with artists and designers from Central Saint Martin's College of Art & Design (CSM), University of Arts London, has enabled us to observe characteristics that seem to have links with what this book is calling the "dark side of creativity." To be more specific, artists and designers are different types of creatives and should be differentiated as such. Designers are required to engage directly with the idea of a "user" or "consumer" because their work has a commercial or social application, whereas artists can make different choices about the types of expressions with which they engage and, while they may have a sense of audience, are not required to address anyone unless they choose to do so. All the best creatives, however, put themselves on the line to generate their own projects (rather than work for commissions) and tend, like criminals, to be risk-inclined in the hope that what they produce can deliver outcomes from which they will derive benefit. The difference is that the best artists and designers appear to have a collective account about the function of their work and often are socially empathetic rather than simply being motivated by profit or selfish logic. However, even this is not always the case; many creatives are also individualistic in the extreme, have well-developed egos, and find different ways of transforming complex feelings about identity via their practice.

In 1966, British artist John Latham used books – intact, painted, cut up, burned – in his work (as materials) to invoke meaning. He set up a 1960s "happening," an event called "Still and Chew." Students turned up to watch Latham chew up pages of art critic Clement Greenberg's *Art and Culture* (1971) taken from the school library. Latham's point was that critics are often parasites; they take few risks and eat artists and give little back. So the happening spat out Greenberg's influential essays into a flask, where the reconstituted text was mixed with sulfuric acid, baking soda, and yeast. Latham let the jar ferment and later was fired for the crime of destroying college property. The documentation of his experiment, from the Greenberg grappa to the letter of his dismissal, is now enshrined in the permanent collection at Museum of Modern Art (MoMA) in New York. Latham's "dark" approach to creativity led him to innovate new ways of making social comment and artistic meanings as well as to generate symbolic capital from his work (Eskin, 2006). The point we are making is that not all criminal events, such as kicking in a bus shelter window or simply destroying what has been made by another, constitute creative innovation delivered by criminals. Innovation in the strict sense of "taking ideas to market" and making money is very different from criminal damage. Professional criminals know this. One drug dealer explained that he could not understand the kids who go around tagging the streets because he could see no financial reward in it for them. So, clearly, we need to qualify again the precise definitions with which we are working. When we say that we observe "creativity" or "innovative capacity" in the behavior of criminals, we are referring primarily to what Ekblom and Tilley (2000) call "resourceful offenders," that is, the behavior of shoplifters, bank robbers, confidence tricksters, identity fraud crews, and burglars who make money and/or meaning from their activities and ideas. Yet this group can be differentiated further. Ekblom and Tilley (2000) further discuss the difference between "expressive crimes," where individuals show off, and engage with performativity (even violence and other destructive behaviors), in order to carve out identities for themselves, and "instrumental crimes," which may allow individuals to pursue excitement and thrills as part of their creative criminal work/identities and, significantly, also deliver profit. In this chapter, when we discuss criminals as creative, we are certainly not talking about maladjusted vandals (and we would not define taggers or street artists in this way) who are so frustrated that they wreck our communities. Nor are we talking about criminals whose activities are linked to violence and murder. Lynn's (1971) research, though limited, is useful to draw on. Lynn differentiates criminal behaviors as

> *Aggressive[s],* who cannot control their impulses and are, eventually, caught and incarcerated;
>
> *Inadequate[s],* who just drift along playing petty confidence tricks for small profits; and
>
> *Creative[s],* many of whom manage to avoid being caught in their law breaking due to their cunningness or talent and so prosper from it.

Creatives and resourceful criminals also seem to share a capacity for what Hudson (1967) termed "divergent thinking." This is the creative elaboration of ideas *prompted by a stimulus or stimuli.*

When analyzing intelligence measurement scales, Hudson found that divergent thinking is harder to assess than convergent thinking, in which the person (who is good at it) is able to produce the "correct" answer. This is so because convergent thinking is linked to issues about reliability and consistency and is consequently easier to document and assess. Convergent thinking is particularly appropriate in science, math, and technology, and while it may help in solving many problems, it may not always encourage the individual to think "outside the box" or to consider whether the problem defined is the right one (i.e., to consider whether or not the "problem" is in fact the problem).

Successful criminals draw on both convergent and divergent types of thinking, although they may not be able to explain or articulate their process (what a designer or artist may be able to achieve through a reflective form of methodology). Some criminals may reflect, but what criminals share with creatives is the idea of "practice" – that they need to get up and "do" something (including running complex projects) to make money, even if they do not draw on formal methodologies to aid them in doing so.

Opportunism and Risk Taking

Kees Dorst (2003), in his account of how designers operate in the world, explains the way artists and designers spend time constantly looking for *opportunities*. An opportunity for innovation or change presents the creative with a possibility to interact with an idea, materials, technology, or a social situation and bring about change, often linked to taking risks. In this sense, a creative is an agent for change (both positive or negative) at a strategic or conceptual level. Linked to opportunities, some creatives also display various forms of ego-driven belief (conviction) that they are able "to do tasks better" than others or feel that they are able to see things differently and make a unique contribution. They may assume that they are "luckier" than others too. Professor Richard Wiseman (2003), in his research into the "luck factor," has pointed out that many people, including some creatives, attribute luck to what is really just a kind of positive thinking. They may be opportunistic in their endeavors and open to the possibility of the accidental and fortuitous incidents that will allow them to exploit an occasion/incident. Such convictions appear to help creatives (and criminals who believe that they can "pull off" the crime) to go forward and try to succeed at their self-appointed task. De Graves (1995) discusses the behavior of women confidence tricksters in this way too but goes on to say how they uniquely create their own scripts when engaging in forms of insincere or dishonest behavior in order to make a living. Their approach is clearly not the same as design thinking, but this trope has much in common with the opportunism we are describing and so demands further exploration.

Sociologist Howard Becker (1963) has written extensively, as have other writers, about the "outsider" phenomenon. The experience of "estrangement" that appears to enable creatives (artists and designers as well as criminals) to locate themselves as "different" or outside the everyday and thus create new opportunities for artistic or design interventions. Processes of "defamiliarization" or "making strange" (Shklovsky, 1917) help these self-defined outsiders perceive everyday reality with fresh eyes. This experience is sometimes common to all of us, particularly when traveling. The main difference is that creatives and criminals, compared with the rest of us, may engage with processes of estrangement as a matter of course, and this may contribute to their innovative path-finding behavior.

Breaking the Paradigm

Seeing the shortcomings of a situation and/or thinking like someone from "outside" (thinking like a thief, for example) allows creatives to observe the limitations in the thinking (or circumstance) that, once understood, can help to resolve and change things. This approach to critical subjectivity is not unusual or even confined to artists, designers, entrepreneurs, and criminals. For example, Einstein was a visual-spatial thinker and, among other insights, pointed out that "we can't solve problems by using the same kind of thinking we used when we created them." His account may help us to better understand the sort of "criticality" that operates within the minds of most creative individuals and invites questions not just about "deviance" or "abnormality" but perhaps also about a deficiency of thinking in others in a given situation. Moreover, this behavioral manifestation also may act as a driver for competitive behavior that expresses itself in many creative individuals and is linked to an entrepreneurial approach involving "critical inquiry that may lead a practitioner to reflective insight" (Friedman, 2002). This reflective approach has enabled many designers, as Donald Schön (1983) has identified, to describe the previously tacit understanding that ideas operate in fluid and fast-moving landscapes. The ability to operate fluently in such landscapes very much depends on the ability to maneuver within and deal with complexity. To join up ideas, situations, events – perhaps via what Sangiorgi, Hemment, and Büscher (2008) have called "strange connectors," that is, the linking of things that one would not expect to be linked. Maintaining a faculty for sense making and adapting has been observed by Mika Aaltonen and Theodor Barth (2005) to be useful as a form of reflection in action that can "create contexts that affect an organisation's ability to learn, adapt and innovate."

Problem Solving

The skills we have described so far may be familiar and useful to creatives everywhere, especially if they are essentially highly pragmatic people. Creatives will solve problems in order to gain access to a state of mind that will deliver their desires and/or an income. However, a mind-set that is creative in its approach also needs to be understood in its cultural context – to make sense of how innovation that follows from creativity may be advanced.

Ronald "Buster" Edwards, who took part in the Great Train Robbery in the United Kingdom in 1963, was an ex-British Army paratrooper, then boxer, and nightclub owner who turned to crime because he wanted quick cash to live what he perceived to be the "good life" (i.e., in order to access the income and status denied him). He was persuaded to turn to train robbery (a security train that was delivering cash), a daring crime that was innovative in the way in which it was organized at the time. As Piers Paul Read (1979) explains, after committing the crime, Buster Edwards found that most of the cash he had stolen was used in trying to avoid being captured by the police. Read goes on to point out that Edwards certainly would have earned more, in the long term, as a window cleaner or tradesman than as a criminal, and life on the run (outside his criminal milieu) was not much "fun." Edwards did not stay a free man for long and was sentenced to 15 years for his crime in 1966. After his release from prison in 1975, he ran a flower stall outside Waterloo Station. When a television journalist interviewed him working at his flower stall, he was asked if he missed his former life, to which he replied, "Of course I do. It was exciting, and this is boring."

The idea that creativity and criminality are commonly linked to the need to *be* different from or outside the "norm" – to divergent rather than convergent thought processes – has been addressed by numerous writers, including Malcolm Gladwell (2008). Creativity is often also equated with nonconformity, in as much as successful creatives, and criminals, are seen as risk-taking, nonconformists, often with different "norms" and drivers than the majority of the population.

Johnson's (1983) account of nonconformity describes high-level creativity as so-called abnormality or, worse, deviance. Our experience in working in an art school is the reverse; it is hard to be deviant in an environment where everyone prides themselves on their differences. The reason we have introduced the account of dyslexia to this discussion is to identify the environments (art school, prison, and business) where dyslexia has been measured and found to be a significant indicator or descriptor, as well as to investigate the evidence about this correlation and to make the case about the different types of thought processes that may be shared by diverse groups.

Art and design strategies embrace both positive and negative ends of the creative spectrum, including the employment of destructive elements. These are drawn on if the artist or designer feels that it is called for in order to attribute meaning or create new artistic values or ways of seeing. Here we need to precisely understand the cultural contexts that may have produced such strategies and how they work. Notions about "deviance" (rather than "difference" or "transgression") may compromise this account, even if such ideas give allure to ideas about, for example, "outsider" art (Wikepedia, 2009b),

Arguments about deviant biology (and about "brain wiring") that also explain links between criminality and creativity are compelling. The literature on deviance is packed full of competing accounts that the disposition to conform or deviate is located in the brain and central nervous system rather than in culture and socialization. Paul McLean (Holden, 1979), for example, has argued that nonconformity is caused by a defect in the central core of the brain and consequently appears to define creative thinkers as "brain-damaged." Holden (1979) concurs and suggests, using Darwinian rationale, that such genetic defects "have social value and a certain amount of non-conformity actually helps the human species to perpetuate itself." Certainly some brain injuries have been associated with the onset of artistic skills in those who had not exhibited them previously, whereas many psychologists suggest that all conformist and creative tendencies and tastes are linked to processes of cultural socialization and politics rather than to genetic brain formation.

Stephen Dollinger (2007) cites psychological studies that indicate that people with conservative tendencies tend to favor simple representational paintings over more ambiguous or abstract art. He points out that "conservatives could be less creative than liberals because of greater threat-induced anxiety (e.g., finding the ambiguity of creative tasks threatening), their greater inclination to follow convention, and/or their devaluing of imagination."

More recent research is delivering new insights and new information about how our brain really works (Coyle, 2009; Frank, 2009). For example, current accounts of the human capacity for empathy, particularly feelings of group or social allegiance (Goleman, 2006), may be useful to understanding some of the issues raised here. Certainly, very creative individuals, unlike criminals and/or psychopaths, often exhibit concern for community values rather than profit. Issues raised by social empathy are now being actively investigated in globally located centers equipped with high-tech machinery and new imaging technologies (e.g., PET, MRI, and SPECT). Many researchers are looking at brain activity to understand how the brain structures choice and creativity. In Los Angeles, for example, Anthonio Damisco is heading up the "Brain and Creativity Institute," located at the University of Southern California. Frank (2009) estimates that there are about 60 further centers around the world and that neurobiological science is on the threshold of a revolution. Consequently, such research is continually changing our views about conditions such as Alzheimer's disease. Debates about autism are also being revolutionized by findings that suggests that damage to mirror neurons may be the reason why some children refuse to look at others, make eye contact, or experience empathy.

While we do not want to link accounts of dyslexia or creativity to biological determinism, given that development of the brain and nervous system is also now more than ever linked to social interaction and experience (Goleman, 2006), we are aware that there are studies under way that may do so in future. For the purpose of delivering this chapter, however, we choose instead to draw on Johnson's (1983) suggestion that the relationship between creativity and criminality should best be examined in social terms by looking at specific social groups, not least because it is more manageable in terms of our research investigation.

Johnson originally suggested that connections between creativity and criminality can be best measured by looking at

1. The creative potential of incarcerated criminals or identified delinquents
2. The correlation between criminal and creative tendencies in "normals"
3. Criminal or psychopathic behavior in creative persons.

Although we have issues with some of Johnson's definitions of "normality," in the next section of this chapter we continue to interrogate points 1 and 2 above primarily to introduce case studies that help us to explore further links between creativity and criminality.

THE DARK SIDE OF CREATIVITY: CASE STUDIES FROM THE DESIGN AGAINST CRIME RESEARCH CENTRE (DACRC)

The DACRC at CSM has endeavored to tap into the potential of adapting creativity into a positive tool for social change and has been linked to several government and independent social design initiatives as well as the successful delivery of design resources and design outputs, some of which have won awards for innovation (Figures 9.1 and 9.2). As a practice-led research centre, DACRC addresses how design can enable individuals to channel experiences and their private frustrations about crime into creativity aimed at public expression via positive design against crime interventions. The "think thief" approach (Ekblom, 1997), the account of the "criminal gaze" (Gamman, 2008b), and the explanation of the design against crime process and methodology (Gamman & Thorpe, 2009) that DACRC has produced have enabled many designers working with design

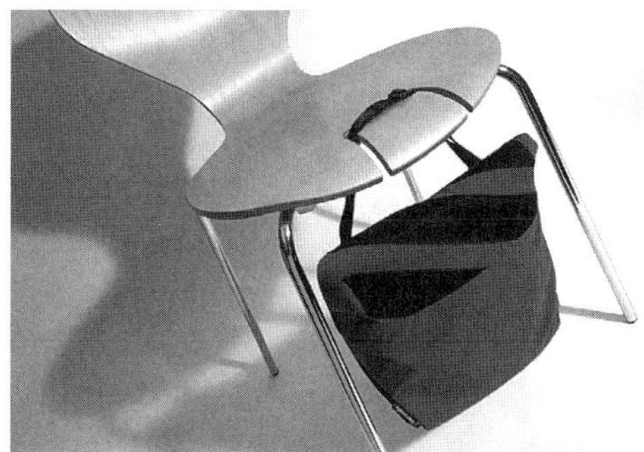

FIGURE 9.1. Stop thief chair.

FIGURE 9.2. CaMden stand (M stand).

against crime to generate design investigations that operate differently from market-led design.

A normal starting point for any form of market design intervention is to receive a brief (a document or verbal expression outlining the client's needs) and to reinterpret it linked to the client's needs. The alternative approach taken by the DACRC has been to consider how the issue addressed originated, or how the perpetrators, that is, the creators of the design problem, and the abusers of products, systems, and services could be "blocked" or their behavior redirected, reduced, or designed "out." This latter design focus is linked to user- and abuser-centered design. It began for DACRC when Professor Lorraine Gamman, who set up the initiative in 1999, became frustrated with market-led design projects. Coincidently, around this same period she had been finalizing the life story of the shoplifter Shirley Pitts as an oral history that formed part of her Ph.D. thesis (delivered in 1999) when it occurred to her to focus on crime in terms of creating briefs for the design students she taught. Gamman says that she was astonished in design terms (and inspired) by Pitt's account of defeating millions of pounds worth of security tags and closed-circuit television (CCTV) systems simply with a carrier bag lined with foil. Evidently, when closed, a foil-lined carrier bag (Figure 9.3) stops the tags from connecting with the alarms, allowing Shirley and many other thieves to get out of the shops without being caught. For Gamman, this raised two questions; the first was, What is wrong with the design of retail environments if it is so easy for professional thieves to get away using such simple solutions? The second was, How did Shirley do it, what prompted her to come up with a design that could outwit millions of pounds worth of security, and how could Gamman encourage designers to draw on such thinking and be more ingenious than thieves?

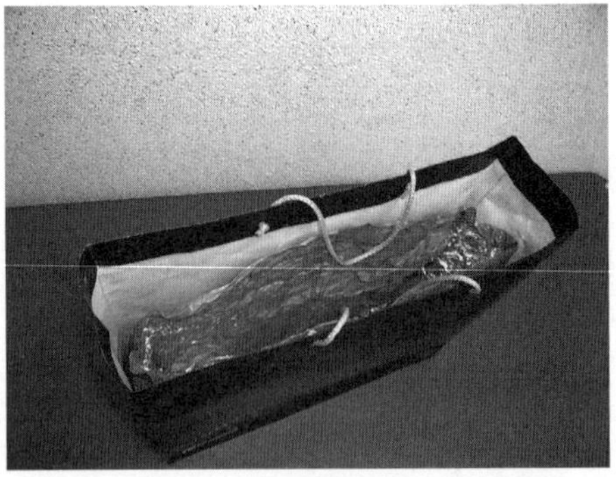

FIGURE 9.3. Foil-lined carrier bag.

The need to reduce costs of staffing and to find ways to inspire or tempt the public to buy things involves troublesome tradeoffs for the retail trade, as well as problems linked to store layout. Many in-store promotions really do work by giving the public easy access to goods so that they are tempted to buy things. However, such strategies also make it easy for thieves, and while such environments and promotions create considerable profits, they also deliver many unanticipated crime vulnerabilities. Criminologists such as Ron Clarke (1995), Paul Ekblom (1997), and Ken Pease (2001) have pointed out that poor design causes crime (not just criminals). Gamman (2008a) has also argued that

1. The design of retails environments is often complicit with criminal intention and needs review.
2. Designers and criminals have a lot in common and a lot to contribute, certainly in terms of understanding how environments might work to be less complicit with crime.

All the writers mentioned suggest that there is a need to understand the mind-set of those who steal. Shirley Pitts, who is the subject of the biography, *Gone Shopping, Shirley Pitts, Queen of Thieves* (1996), is found to be a very creative person, one who was successful at crime, even if the audacity of some of her scams – such as standing in a Harrods shop window pretending to model a mink coat to escape security guards – did not employ all her substantial energy or make her happy. Gamman (2008c) has argued that "Shirley's foil-lined carrier bag in its simplicity may on reflection be far more creative – even if that's an account of the dark side of creativity – than the retro fitted security systems it subverted" (see Figure 9.3). Gamman also suggests that Shirley Pitts could have used her creativity to be anything she wanted, but her circumstances, providing for her family by thieving from the age of seven, prevented this from happening. In between scams, Gamman observes, Pitts frequently drew clothing, faces, and shapes. Also, in order to sell the goods that she stole, she even redesigned some of the clothing with her own accessories. Apparently, Pitts, whom many regarded as stylish, believed that some of the expensive designer clothes she stole, worth many thousands of pounds, did not look "right," so she changed them to suit her customers, whom she "dressed" like a fashion stylist.

DACRC works within design education and industry and visualizes criminal perpetrator techniques and ways of seeing to encourage designers to "think thief." This process may be defined as a form of "alterity" (or "otherness") linked to the philosophical principle of exchanging one's own perspective for that of the "other." Many of us engage with such "oppositional" rather than "preferred" perspectives and readings of films/media during our everyday life; for example, a man reading a magazine aimed at women may receive the information he engages with in a different way from its original intention. The idea of "thinking thief" is aimed at trying to understand the criminal gaze at objects and environments that anticipates opportunity through abuse. With regard to how to think like a shoplifter, Martin Gill (2007) has put such theory into practice and taken shop thieves back to the scene of their offenses and concluded that there are six key decision points that are critical to shoplifting. He suggests that there is the potential for designers to influence offenders' decisions. To stay one step ahead, the list of six questions that designers should consider from the point of view of the thief includes

Why do I choose that store to steal from?

On entering the store, does this look easy?

On searching for goods to steal, can I avoid attracting attention?

On stealing the goods, can I avoid being seen?

On getting away, can I be sure no one is following me and no one will apprehend me?

On selling the goods, will I get money and avoid being traced?

DACRC's strategy of familiarizing designers with criminal thinking while also locating designers within a crime-prevention discourse does not necessarily deliver "problem solving"; rather, it directs designers to intervene as agents for change. DACRC's methodology also acknowledges that not all problems can be solved and that it is also important to understand how social disorder and social disorganization have a role to play in our lives and can be a source of illicit pleasure. For example, the word "graffiti" describes more different types of mark making and creative strategies than the words "vandalism" and "criminal damage" convey. As a consequence of such criminal definitions, enormous public funds are spent cleaning up graffiti linked to zero-tolerance campaigns, but nothing really changes. Each side perceives the problem in criminal terms – one side views marking the walls as a crime, and the other perceives erasing their art as criminal. Such polarization certainly does not lead to resolution of the problem or creative social innovation strategies that could accommodate the compulsions and communication that underli graffiti.

Tony Dunne and Fiona Raby (2001), in their book, *Design Noir*, review the human capacity to enjoy misuse and abuse and the pleasures of illegal activities such as hacking (rather than graffiti). They discuss the "noir" edge of human subjectivity in design terms, specifically the potential of human beings to establish unpredicted or dark relationships with things, namely, electronic objects. Complex emotions, desires, and needs clearly are played out through engagement with objects and environments that have the potential for more than one type of behavior or pleasure. This potential manifests in vastly different ways, from expected types of uses (many of which could be termed "creative") to the way that individuals subvert such usages, as well as preferred readings. Dunne and Raby cite extreme examples of what they mean, from the man who "married" his television to the teenagers who use new mobile phone technologies to bully and intimate each other. The experience of a 15-year-old girl who was driven to suicide after receiving up to 20 silent calls in half an hour is documented. Evidently, she left her suicide note as a text message on her phone.

Like the Dutch design group Droog, whose work questions what design is or could be, Dunne and Raby play with dark emotions in their own work. For example, they discuss the desk that makes it possible for the overwhelmed simply to hide inside it. They argue that "our environments have room for danger, adventure and transgression. We don't think that design can fully articulate the richness of this unofficial world and neither should it. But it can draw inspiration from it and develop new design approaches."

THE DARK SIDE OF CREATIVITY: MORE CASE STUDIES FROM ART AND DESIGN

Artists and designers certainly have drawn on the dark, the strange, and the criminal in their attempts to make meanings in the world. The fashion industry, for example, not only has generated dark imagery (from heroin chic to road-kill shots) but also has encouraged designers to play with transgression, like artists. Consequently, some have used mould and other abject materials to make fashion statements. Such actions are rarely intended to inflict harm on others but instead to make us think by removing us from the realm of the familiar, secure, or routine. While some criminal activities may do something similar, that is, transgress on routine understandings, the difference is that real criminal acts often harm and traumatize us, whereas crimes of the imagination are uncommitted in reality and rarely do similar harm. Artists and criminals, for this reason, may enjoy revealing or interrogating power structures at work in different ways, which takes both ingenuity and, often, courage. Certainly some artists, when they have seen a need, resort to transgressive behavior in order to make statements, often provoking public outrage. From Serrano's *Piss Christ* (1987) to Judy Chicago's image of a vagina and bloody tampon (1971), rule-breaking, taboo-busting art has become the norm even if some of it – such as Marcus Harvey's *Myra* (1995) from the Sensation exhibition, does not really offer much in the way of meaningful social comment about crime.

Some artists go further and engage with real crime to make their point, sometimes bringing into question their moral sanity. Robert Mapplethorpe abused a model he kidnapped and photographed and was taken to court. Sophie Calle (born in 1953) took to stalking in order to expose the vulnerability of individuals being watched or looked at. Andrew Savage allegedly shoplifted and photographed white goods and displayed them in a gallery space to make social comment about issues of ownership. We could add more examples, including artists who are more ambiguous about how they approach crime. The photographer Alan Lodge, known as "Tash" (http://tash.gn.apc.org), for example, engaged with the mechanisms of crime prevention and used CCTV as a form of public theater. He presented a number of short plays and performances to London's Oxford Street surveillance cameras in order to reject the passivity imposed by CCTV and to retrieve power. Dutch artist Jan de Groot (2007) also chose to challenge issues about naming and identity by faking his own death after a rather brutal rejection by his gallery, which informed him that he was "dead as an artist." A press release described in dramatic terms how de Groot jumped to his death from the window of his parents' home. It also went on to claim that his parents were found beheaded in their beds. Subsequently, the police found de Groot and his parents alive and well.

Anthony-Noel Kelly (1997) stole anatomic specimens from the Royal College of Surgeons (RCS) to make gilded plaster casts from them as sculptures. He subsequently caused controversy and outrage when some of the faces were recognized by horrified relatives. His conviction for theft overturned hundreds of years of legal precedent that had said that the body was not property and so could not be owned or stolen. His actions obviously were "criminal," although his credibility as an artist was brought into question not just for the theft of body parts but also for his use of plaster, regarded as an inferior and cheap material and not worthy of artistic presentation (Wildgoose, 2002).

CONCLUSION

We hope that the foregoing discussion will have demonstrated that the account of "creativity" has been linked to a history of competing definitions. Thus in this chapter we have focused primarily on the ways that creativity leads to innovation and income generation. We also have looked at some of the traits creatives and criminals have in common and have suggested dyslexia as an area that needs further research. We also have suggested that artists, designers, entrepreneurs, and criminals share divergent thought processes and, occasionally, similar creative strategies in their work. Opportunism and understanding of risk are a common link. Both groups are known for seizing the opportunity, and their handiwork is everywhere linked to social good or ill. The main difference we have identified between groups is that while they both make a living from their creativity and ingenuity, criminals exhibit less capacity for social empathy and appear more pessimistic and parasitic, using their creativity for selfish ends. Some artists and designers also demonstrate these qualities, but most appear to have more capacity for group-orientated comment or even empathetic behavior, that is, creating more shared social outcomes and meanings than criminals, perhaps because artists often seek to conquer taboos and social prejudices through art, which, they believe, can emancipate us. Most of the creatives from the world of art and design appear optimistic enough to believe that their skills can be put to use to change the world for the better, usually, but not always, within the confines of the law. The task now must be to figure out how to encourage those who force the law's boundaries and whose activities lead to social harm to move "into the light" (to follow the *Star Wars* metaphor through to its conclusion) and understand why their approach is negative (rather than "evil"). The challenge must be to find alternative and better outlets for creative energy than crime presently serves. It is our contention that from Buster Edwards to Shirley Pitts, from graffiti taggers to happy slappers, different lives may be possible – indeed different worlds may be possible – if viable alternatives for creative energy can be found without simply containing or sanitizing passion.

REFERENCES

Aaltonen, M. & Barth, T. (2005). *Complexity as a sensemaking framework for methodology*. Turku, Finland: Finland Futures Research Centre, Turku School of Economics and Business Administration.

Becker, H. (1963). *Outsiders: Studies in the sociology of deviance.* New York: Free Press.

British Dyslexia Association. (1995). *The dyslexia handbook.* Reading, England: British Dyslexia Association.

(2004–2005). *Practical solutions for identifying dyslexia in juvenile offenders.* Report of a Joint Project of the British Dyslexia Association and HM Young Offender Institution. Reading, England: British Dyslexia Association.

Brown, M. (2000). *Innovation survey.* New York: PricewaterhouseCoopers.

Clarke, R. V. (1995). Situational crime prevention. *Crime and Justice,* 19, 91–150.

Claxton, Guy. (1997). *Hare brain, tortoise mind: Why intelligence increases when you think less.* London: Fourth Estate.

Cox, G. (2005). *The Cox review of creativity in business: Building on the UK's strengths.* London: HM Treasury.

Coyle, D. (2009). *The talent code: Greatness isn't born. It's grown. Here's how.* New York: Random House.

De Grave, K. (1995). *Swindler, spy, rebel: Confidence woman in nineteenth-century America.* St. Louis, MO: University of Missouri Press.

Dollinger, S. J. (2007). *Creativity and conservatism: Personality and individual differences* (pp. 1025–1035). Available online at www.sciencedirect.com.

Dorst, K. (2003). *Understanding design.* Amsterdam: BIS Publishers.

Dunne, T. & Raby, F. (2001). *Design noir: The secret life of electronic objects.* Princeton, NJ: Princeton Architectural Press.

East Mentoring Forum. Ltd. (2007). *Dyslexia and mentoring.* London: Mentor CIC.

Ekblom, P. (1997). Gearing up against crime: A dynamic framework to help designers keep up with the adaptive criminal in a changing world. *International Journal of Risk Security and Crime Prevention,* 2, 249–265.

Ekblom, P. & Tilley, N. (2000). Going equipped: Criminology, situational crime prevention and the resourceful offender. *British Journal of Criminology,* 40, 376–398.

Eskin, B. (2006). Books to chew on. *New York Times* (online), March 26. Available at http://topics.nytimes.com/top/reference/timestopics/organizations/m/museum_of_modern_art/index.html?inline=nyt-org.

Florida, R. (2002). *The rise of the creative class: And how it's transforming work, leisure, community and everyday life.* New York: Basic Books.

Frank, L. (2009). *Mindfield: How brain science is changing our world.* Oxford, England: One World Publications.

Friedman, K. (2002). Theory construction in design research: Criteria, approaches, and methods. In David Durling and John Shackleton (Eds.), *Common ground: Proceedings of the Design Research Society International Conference, Brunel University, September 5–7, 2002.* Stoke on Trent, UK: Staffordshire University Press.

Gamman, L. (1996). *Gone shopping: Story of Shirley Pitts, queen of thieves.* New York: Signet Books.

(2008a). *A wry look at design & crime: The dark side of creativity* (video clip). Inaugural lecture by Professor Lorraine Gamman, Cochrane Theatre London. Available at www.designagainstcrime.com/index.php?q=lecturesandpresentations.

(2008b). *A wry look at design & crime: The criminal gaze* (video clip). Inaugural lecture by Professor Lorraine Gamman, Cochrane Theatre London. Available at www.goneshopping.org.uk/archive.

(2008c). *A wry look at design & crime: Shirley Pitts parts 1 & 2* (video clip). Inaugural lecture by Professor Lorraine Gamman, Cochrane Theatre London. Available at www.designagainstcrime.com/index.php?q=lecturesandpresentations.

Gamman, L. & Thorpe, A. (2009). *The design against crime evolved twin track model of the iterative design process.* Available at www.designagainstcrime.com/index.php?q=designmethodology.

Garwood, J. (2009). A quasi-experimental investigation of self-reported offending and perception of criminal opportunity in undergraduate students. In *Security Journal* (pp. 1–15). Basingstoke, England: Palgrave Macmillan.

Gill, M. (2007). *Shop thieves on shop theft: Lessons for retailers.* Leicester, England: Perpetuity Research and Consultancy International.

Gladwell, M. (2008). *Outliers: The story of success.* Boston, MA: Little, Brown.

Goleman, D. (2006). *Social intelligence: The new science of social relationships.* New York: Bantam.

Greenberg, C. (1971). *Art and culture: Critical essays.* Boston, MA: Beacon Press.

Holden, C. (1979). Paul MacLean and the triune brain. *Science, 204*, 4397, 1066–1068.

Hudson, L. (1967). *Contrary imaginations; A psychological study of the English schoolboy.* Harmondsworth, England: Penguin.

Johnson, J. (1983). Criminality, creativity, and craziness: Structural similarities in three types of nonconformity. In W. S. Laufer and J. M. Day (Eds.), *Personality theory, moral development, and criminal behavior* (Chapter 4, pp. 81–105). Lexington, MA: DC Heath.

Julius, A. (2002). *Transgressions: The offences of art.* London: Thames & Hudson.

Leadbeater, C. & Meadway, J. (2008). *Attacking the recession: How innovation can fight the downturn.* London: Nesta.

Lester, R. & Piore, M. (2004). *Innovation: The missing dimension.* Cambridge, MA: Harvard University Press.

Lynn, R. (1971). *An introduction to the study of personality.* London: Macmillan Educational.

Morgan, E. & Klein, C. (2000). *The dyslexic adult in a non-dyslexic world.* London: Whurr.

Oakley, K., Sperry, B., & Pratt, A. (2008) *The art of innovation: How fine arts graduates contribute to innovation.* Nesta Research Report. London: Nesta.

O'Neill, J. (2003). How solid are the BRICs? Dreaming with BRICs and Global Economics Paper 134. Goldman Sachs Economic Research Group, New York.

Pease, K. (2001). *Cracking crime through design.* London: Design Council.

Raein, M. (2003). *Writing PAD primer report.* London: Goldsmiths.

Read, P. P. (1979). *The train robbers.* London: WH Allen/Secker & Warburg.

Robinson, K. (2001). *Out of our minds: Learning to be creative.* Oxford, England: Capstone Publishing.

Sangiorgi, D., Hemment, D., & Büscher, M. (2008). *Everyday imagination, practices, systems: Designing with people for systemic change.* An ICSID initiative of the IDA. Torino, Italy: World Design Capital.

Schön, Donald A. (1983). *The reflective practitioner: How professionals think in action.* New York: Basic Books.

Shklovsky, V. (1917). Art as technique. In *Russian formalist criticism: Four essays.* (Lee T. Lemon and Marion J. Reis, Trans.) Lincoln: University of Nebraska Press.

Smith, C. (1998). *Creative Britain.* London: Faber & Faber.

The Work Foundation. (2007). Foreword by W. Hutton. In *Staying ahead: The economic performance of the UK's creative industries.* London: Department for Culture, Media and Sport.

West, Thomas G. (1997). *In the mind's eye: Visual thinkers – Gifted people with dyslexia and other learning difficulties.* London: Prometheus Books.

Wildgoose, J. (2002). The business of the flesh. *Guardian* (online). Thursday, October 31. Available at http://society.guardian.co.uk/news/story/0,7838,821587,00.html.

Wikipedia. (2009a). Creativity. Available at http://en.wikipedia.org/wiki/Creativity.

(2009b). Outsider art. Available at http://en.wikipedia.org/wiki/Outsider_Art.

Wiseman, R. (2003). *The luck factor.* Los Angeles, CA: Miramax.

10

Creativity in Confinement

JENNIE KAUFMAN SINGER

The number of American citizens who are incarcerated each year has been increasing for over a century. This number has increased dramatically in the last 20 years as the United States has developed a mind-set of crime control as the main goal of its sentencing laws. Other countries share the American use of incarceration to penalize those who break the law and are considered dangerous. However, the United States incarcerates more citizens and for longer sentences than any other developed nation (Schmalleger & Smykla, 2008). Legislation such as the "three strikes law" and the federal "truth in sentencing" law may help American citizens to feel safe, but it has contributed to America having the largest prison population per capita in the world (Walsh & Ellis, 2007). Numbers of both men and women who are in state prisons and jails are increasing every year. The Bureau of Justice Statistics found that on June 30, 2007, over 115,000 women and almost 1½ million men were incarcerated in state or federal prisons. The Bureau of Justice Statistics estimates that over 509 people are sentenced as prisoners per 100,000 U.S. residents. This is an increase from their latest figure at year-end 2006. The Bureau of Justice Statistics indicated that local jails had also increased their populations from 2006 to mid-year 2007 and held over 766,000 individuals who were awaiting trial, serving a sentence of one year or under, or waiting for a prison bed to become available.

With so many citizens in prison or jail, it is important to note the effects of incarceration. Effects can be physical, with diseases such as hepatitis and other air-, saliva-, and blood-borne pathogens finding ample hunting grounds in quarters so densely populated. Effects of incarceration can be economic. Families must survive without a breadwinner to help support children left in single-parent or foster-care situations. When the inmate returns home, problems associated with reentry frequently include economic hardships arising from difficulties in finding employment owing to lack of education, skills, or greatly lowered status in the community (Petersilia, 2006). Additionally, many issues arise from the emotional toll of being confined in a frequently violent and regimented atmosphere.

MALEVOLENT CREATIVITY AND CONFINEMENT

Brower (1999) reviewed the connection between truly creative people (those who would be labeled as such in a dictionary of famous people) and how their creative and innovative thinking became so subversive that these individuals were jailed by their culture. Examples such as moral innovators and political prisoners (e.g., Mohandas Gandhi and Nelson Mandela) along with writers and painters (e.g., Thomas More and Paul Gauguin) were chosen to explore how some famous creative individuals' art or thoughts were progressive and threatening enough for their current society to hold them as prisoners. Ultimately, however, these famous inmates are not the norm in today's prison population, generally a mix of lower-income, undereducated, and substance-abusing individuals. But can current inmates, imprisoned for legitimate criminal activity, display creativity in their actions?

According to Cropley, Kaufman, and Cropley (2008), there is a functional model of creativity that can apply to terrorism and crime. When applied to incarcerated individuals, this model still provides an excellent framework with which to view creativity as an outgrowth of confinement. Unlike the previous notion that creativity had to be beneficial to society, this definition was expanded to include those works beneficial to the individual who created an object or process in order to further his or her unique and potentially selfish needs (or subjective benevolence). Even if the creative product is intended to cause harm, if the object fits certain criteria, the term "malevolent creativity" can apply. Two types of malevolent creativity exist, according to the model of Cropley and colleagues, in the prison setting:

1. *Creative products or behaviors that are used for the inherent and total competition between inmates and staff.* While incarcerated, inmates have certain needs that are difficult to attain. Examples include drugs, weapons for protection and for attacks against dangerous rivals, and other items that may improve their lives (e.g., a way to cook food in their cell). These items are seen as dangerous or as nuisance items by the staff and are deemed against the rules. Some items (such as weapons) are seen as a threat to the safety and security of the institution. The competition for inmates to possess

these items and for staff to eliminate them is a continuous process. Because of the need to increase the innovativeness and usefulness of these products (Cropley and colleagues state that when a product is no longer surprising both the innovative and useful properties of this once-creative product fade), newer and more surprising products are continually invented (along with innovative hiding places) as the older products and hiding places are discovered by staff members. This type of creativity is also what would be termed "functional creativity" by Cropley and colleagues because the products serve a purpose in this battle between inmates and staff, and the "effective novelty" must continually be renewed. Further, generalizability (so that more than one inmate or staff member may use the new creation) is a desirable outcome of the inmate and staff's inventions. Finally, to be the most functionally creative, inmates must become proactive in their approach to inventing ways to build necessary items, hide these items, and develop more creative ways to keep officers from finding their work. Staff must be able to anticipate novel weapons and ways for drugs to enter the institution and then find these creations (such as drugs or knives, known as "shanks") before a violent act can be committed.

2. The other way that inmates have displayed creativity is more in line with traditional creativity as an aspect of self-fulfillment, personal growth, and gaining social approval for works of art, writing, music, and the dramatic arts. Are such works created by inmates truly creative by being "original, effective, or useful in their originality" (Eisenman, 1999)?

According to Brower (1999), inmates have displayed originality and creativity (such as writer Arthur Koestler, referred to later in this chapter) but tend to lack creativity in a general sense [as measured by story telling in response to the pictures presented in the Thematic Apperception Test (TAT)]. Eisenman's (1999) conclusion is that if prisoners are creative, it tends to be in areas that do not require structure and rules. Creativity is more likely to be present in an inmate population when the product or process has a minimal amount of societal rules and restraints because inmates display criminal thinking, which precludes them from being interested in or able to follow a set pattern of social rules. Walters (1990) is a prison psychologist who developed a complex theory of criminal lifestyles that hinges on the thinking patterns of criminals. Two of his tenets: (a) Crime can be seen as a lifestyle that is characterized by a global sense of irresponsibility, self-indulgent interests, and chronic violation of society's rules and laws, and (b) a distinctive thinking style is derived from a lifestyle criminal's decision to engage in illegal behaviors. These two key pieces of Walters' theory support the idea that a lack of creativity on structured activities can be anticipated on the basis of inmates' general style of thinking.

However, using their emotions and ideas in less structured venues inmates should be able to display the creative process and products associated with the general population. Since their emotional state is likely to be negative, this actually may enhance their creative flow because creative writing has been linked with depression, bipolar disorder, and mental illness in general (Kaufman & Baer, 2002). Additionally, those who write most expressively in narrative form are most likely to derive emotional benefits from creative work (Kaufman & Sexton, 2006). As Eisenman (2008, p. 119) states, "Never again should we think of creativity as strictly a good thing. ... we should see that there can be a malevolent side to any achievement or skill."

The Emotional Impact of Confinement

Because of the potential link among emotional state, mental health, and creativity, it is important to explore the impact of confinement on emotions. Mental health problems are common for prison and jail inmates. More than half of all prison and jail inmates surveyed in 2005 were found to have a mental health problem, defined as having a recent history of a mental health problem or current symptoms of illnesses such as depression. Between 20 and 30 percent of jail and prison inmates reported symptoms of major depression. James and Glaze (2006) found that inmates have a significantly higher rate of mental illness than the general population, with inmates who are female, Caucasian, and young being the most common groups diagnosed. Substance dependence also was found to be a significant problem, particularly for those with symptoms of mental illness.

These data enable it to be surmised that inmates tend to be at a higher risk of depression, substance use, and other mental health symptoms than the general population of the United States. Many of the homeless in that country are also mentally ill for a myriad of reasons, including lack of bed space in mental hospitals across the country. These individuals are under increased scrutiny from law enforcement agencies, and frequently are incarcerated because they become problematic or break laws, and law enforcement frequently has no options for containing this type of person other than jail or prison. Thus the mentally ill become disproportionately incarcerated as jails and prisons become the new mental hospitals

(Schmalleger & Smykla, 2008). Other inmates can become depressed as a result of the atmosphere of deprivation or overcrowding in the prisons (Huey & McNulty, 2005).

THE DEFINITION OF CREATIVITY IN A CORRECTIONAL ENVIRONMENT

As mentioned earlier, there are two main ways creativity can be expressed in prison. One method of combating the depression and other negative symptoms that are suffered by inmates is by self-expression. Creativity in the context of a correctional environment is the ability to use what is available in an atmosphere of intimidation and sparse resources to produce a product of some type with the goal of emancipation of the spirit. Creativity takes many forms: It can be the ingenious inventions inmates devise for practical reasons, the artistic products made for soul expression, and even activity sanctioned by the prison as part of a therapeutic program. Finally, creativity can be displayed by inmates in creating and hiding dangerous products and by the correctional staff in uncovering the frequently devious objects made by inmates that can pose risks to the security and safety of the institution. This chapter will explore various methods of creative expression that can be viewed in current penal institutions across the country. The final analysis will examine the ultimate effect inmate projects can have on the individuals involved.

Creativity and Contraband

Very few scientific journals examine or empirically analyze products of inmate creativity. The next sections generally are informed via accounts of such activities that are available on the Internet and in magazines, trade publications, and books written by inmates. This information is very detailed and interesting, even though it is extremely anecdotal. There are some empirical studies on inmate creativity, but they do not focus on functional creativity that is used for malevolent or self-serving purposes. One way that inmates display creativity is by turning everyday items into weapons or other devices that are confiscated by correctional staff because of the potentially dangerous properties these items have in their new form. Examples of functional malevolent creativity include radios that have been altered to have secret compartments inmates use to hide items of value such as drugs. Further examples include a myriad of contraband. "Contraband" is defined as anything not regularly issued to the inmate or something altered by the inmate that cannot generally be bought at the commissary (Payne, 2003). There are two kinds of contraband: *nuisance* (not hazardous to the facility but in excess of what the inmate is allowed to have in his or her cell) and *dangerous* (weapons, drugs, or alcohol). Contraband is often found by correctional staff during regular shakedowns or during intricate sweeps of prison areas such as courtyards, hallways, and cells. The usual contraband items include weapons that are used for self-defense, intimidation, or attacks. Items such as dice made of toilet paper are also counted as contraband and confiscated.

Weapons can be made out of any material and are confiscated immediately because of the danger they pose not only to other inmates but also to staff. In Pelican Bay State Prison, a maximum-security prison in California, staff have confiscated knives, or shanks, made by using a piece of metal cut from a bed frame or cell door or by heating a plastic garbage bag and rolling it until it develops a sharp point (Grube, 2007). Correctional staff also have found weapons made of sharpened vent grates and toothbrushes whittled to a point with a handle formed from bandages (Lesnick, 2006).

One popular inmate blog declared that toilet paper is the "most useful and versatile item for the average inmate" (Bornfool, 2007). The inmate described using toilet paper mixed with toothpaste, water, and other ingredients to make a "penitentiary papier mache" that is soft and moldable and dries hard, allowing this substance to form many items for inmates with creative flow. This inmate described many products made of this papier mache, such as chess pieces, knife handles with custom finger grips, and a fire maker. The inmate described smoking a contraband cigarette or drinking coffee with the aid of a papier mache "donut." The inmate first tightly coils three-fourths of an inch of this material into a donut-shaped object. Next, the donut is set on the metal commode rim and lit on fire. Fire is produced by using tightly rolled pieces of paper and the lead from a pencil inserted into an electrical socket. The lit donut will burn "smoke-free" on the metal toilet seat for up to 15 minutes. The creative inmate notes that "evidence can be flushed" once three to four cans of water have been boiled.

Inmates also have used their creative inclinations to outsmart correctional staff in the mail room. The State of New York Corrections Committee found that inmates were instructing their loved ones to hollow out thick bindings of legal briefs to create a container for sending drugs through the mail (Purdy, 1995). Legal mail is given special status in correctional institutions and is not searched for privacy purposes. After discovering this type of mail scam, institutional procedures were modified. Other institutions have found black tar heroin disguised as legal mail, ironed flat between two pieces of paper with identical legal mastheads, so that the dual pieces of paper appear as one (Grube, 2007). Other findings in prison mail rooms include Christmas cards smeared with heroin and reglued so that they appear unaltered and paper drawings made to look as if created by a child for a parent which were really paper soaked in methamphetamine (Gearhart, 2006).

In California's Pelican Bay, as in most prisons in the country, drugs are trafficked into the prison in the oral and anal cavities of inmates and their visitors. Inmates also hide tobacco in creative places such as Halloween stickers (sent by family members or friends) and in hollowed-out books taken from the inmate library. Prison employee Major David Wedding was quoted as saying that he has a "certain respect" for the "creativity involved" in the contraband activities of the inmates. He said, "If they would channel that into good things, they could probably be useful members of society. This shows they're not dumb people. They're just poor decision makers" (quoted in Lesnick, 2006).

An inmate celebrated on the Internet by the moniker "Angelo" and in a book entitled, *Prison Inventions* (Angelo and Temporary Services, 2003), appears to have used his creative side in a manner more marketable to Internet viewers. His inventions (both those he creates and those he observes and documents) are still considered to be contraband and are confiscated along with weapons in the institutional setting, but he has the artistic flair of a showman. Interviewed in a piece in *Wired* magazine (Shachtman, 2003), Angelo creates immersion heaters to cook, containers made from Chapstick tubes, salt and paper shakers, inmate "weights," ways to create more electrical plugs in a cell, a broom, and many other improvisations that turn his small, spare cell into a more comfortable place to spend time. Angelo was interviewed by Schmidt (2004), who described him as a man who wants to express himself through his writing and art. Along with his more practical inventions, Angelo is also an artist and writer. Angelo does not talk about his conviction, stating that it is a privacy issue.

While the article points out that Angelo is an exceptional artist, Schmidt points out that no more prisoners are good artists than people outside prison. This statement agrees with Eisenman's (2008) study that declares that most inmates lack true creativity. Figure 10.1 shows an invention that Angelo either created or discovered by observing other inmates where he is incarcerated in California. This invention is currently unpublished. The figure was drawn with ballpoint pen on paper, 8.5 inches high and about 5.5 inches wide.

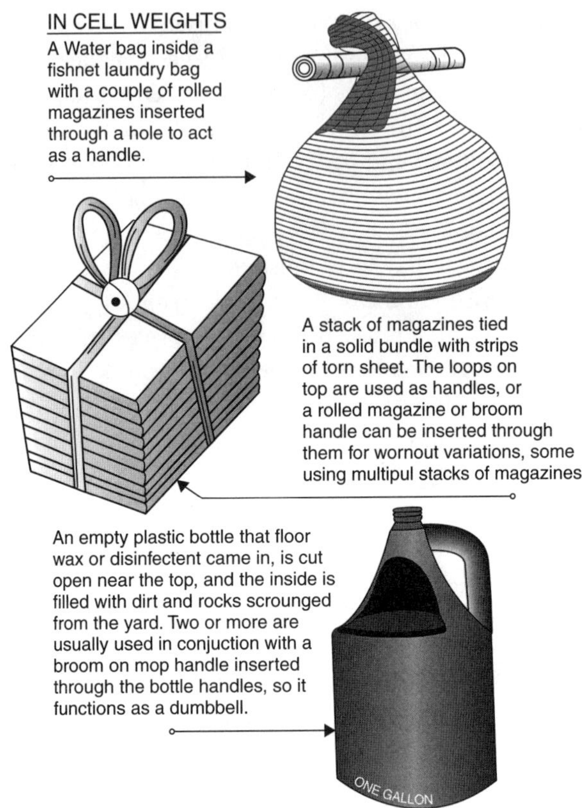

FIGURE 10.1. Angelo in-cell weights, 2006. (*Angelo, courtesy of Temporary Services.*)

Creativity and the Correctional Staff

Continuing the idea of functional creativity as derived from competition (Cropley et al., 2008), Gearhart (2006, p. 24) stated, "Jail staff must be as cunning as the inmates they watch over when it pertains to controlling contraband in a correctional facility." Technological strategies must evolve continually to keep up with inmates' evolving ideas (Ryan, 2000). Gearhart cites examples of correctional staff creativity in the "boss chair" developed to detect hidden metal objects in the body, including an attachable chinrest for the inmate's mouth, when sitting. In addition to expensive trace detectors and scanners developed to locate substances sent craftily through the mail, Gearhart advocated the use of old-fashioned information gathering as well. He found that inmates are good sources of information regarding contraband, and if all leads are followed up, contraband such as drugs and syringes smuggled in after an inmate was allowed to attend a funeral can be located and confiscated. High-security institutions have greater concerns about security risks and use measures such as night-vision cameras and electronic doors to work with the inmates safely (Silk, 2008). All returned library books are automatically scoured for messages or codes, and all incoming items are scanned for contraband. Visits are held behind glass to extinguish the flow of incoming contraband from visitors.

Yet, even in the strictest of environments, contraband flourishes. The minutes of the Georgia Board of Corrections (2007) detail that state's struggle to constantly shake down all inmates so that they are searched for all contraband on their bodies, where they hide objects in all orifices. The officers also have to be aware of other interesting hiding places, such as heater vents, PVC pipe shower rods, the seam of their pants, poles attached to their beds, jars of coffee, and inside their mattress. The goal is the daunting task of always trying to remain a step ahead of the inmates.

THE VARIETY OF ART IN A CORRECTIONAL SETTING

The next descriptions of different types of art created in a correctional setting involves more traditional creative products in that the purpose of these creations is not to harm other individuals but to express oneself in a heart-felt and artistic fashion. The reason these artistic productions still can be considered "malevolently" creative is that the topics of the artistic creations are likely to be negative and focus on a theme of confinement. In addition to using their creative skills for hiding weapons and drugs, inmates display a variety of artistic talent in the prison setting. Institutions manage their talent in a variety of ways, from punishment to public exhibitions of their artwork. Peter Cameron is a former British inmate who began painting in prison and now manages a trust (which manages the Koestler Awards, named for an inmate who was sentenced to death and then survived in the Spanish Civil War), which gives annual awards to inmates in the United Kingdom for their creative endeavors. Cameron, who got his start in the art world after winning a Koestler Award as an inmate, stated, "Making art is a basic human need. We all make art as children, and when we are thrown back on our own resources, we feel compelled to make it once more" (Cook, 2003, p. 41). Art is a way for inmates to feel good about something they do, feel productive, and express emotion in a safe and eloquent manner.

How Artistic Vision Is Expressed

Painting is a popular inmate activity. Some inmates paint using dye from M&Ms or almost any substance that they can find in the prison. An inmate in solitary confinement for almost 20 years painted with a brush he created from plastic wrap, aluminum foil, and his own hair. He used postcards he bought as his canvas (Liptak, 2006). Hanes (2005, p. 44) called inmates resourceful and stated that they use "soap, toothpaste, toilet paper, magazines and food pigment" for art because "where there is a creative passion, the resident will find a suitable material."

An inmate who had been incarcerated for three residential burglaries and had been locked up since 1997 created art for correctional staff with colored pencils and paint remnants made available to him by staff. His art adorns the office walls at Pelican Bay State Prison, and he has created murals and collages of the Iraq war and the World Trade Center in a room used by correctional officers. He also admits to giving inmates tattoos in the yard when he can "get away with it" (Durant, 2006). Even when no materials exist, Brune (1999) states, "Art finds a way to blossom [because] art is necessary the way love is necessary." Marty, an inmate at California State Prison, Sacramento, paints with coffee, Kool-Aid, and crushed chalk.

Some inmates choose to create objects that can be considered art, such as the one crafted by a North Carolinian inmate. He made a Thomas grandfather clock out of paper, Popsicle sticks, and pencils and built entirely with tweezers, fingernail clippers, and a razor blade. The inmate creator of this clock was able to post a picture of his creation, which took four months to build and is purported to "keep great time," on a Web site (www.clockplans.com). Marty, the California inmate, also creates sculptures of soap. As part of a mentoring project in Canada, mentor artists were paired with inmates as their mentees. The mentors sent art and poetry into the prison as fodder for the inmates to then create an artistic response. Greenberg (2000, p. 2) cited a "hauntingly grotesque ceramic doll" as an inmate's response to a mentor's cloth doll wrapped in flannel strips accompanied by a poem about mothers.

Other inmates find solace in words, writing poetry behind bars. One inmate poet, Spoon Jackson, now at California State Prison, Sacramento, and serving a life sentence, learned how to write poetry from teachers in the prison at the California State Prison in San Quentin and at Folsom State Prison. He said that he "slowly transformed" inside and, by reading others' poetry, learned to "get my eyes on" (Jackson, 2007). He found his own voice as an artist, and aside from writing what he terms "organic poetry" in a natural voice, he runs two poetry classes for a program called Arts in Corrections. He invites artists on the outside to collaborate with him to develop plays. Mr. Jackson has written many poems, posts newsletters on his Web site, and is noted on the International Movie Data Base (IMDB.com) for being the subject of a short film, *Three Poems by Spoon Jackson,* where he reads poems via a telephone from the prison. One of his many moving poems is "For However Long":

FOR HOWEVER LONG
winter in the desert
nearly always
the snowflakes melt
before touching the ground
I wonder how it feels
to be in love
and write poetry
to know how a pair
of swans feel together
in their own pond
love, especially when
shared, is limitless
but one love, one heart, alone
what could it be?
a sweet love song on the radio
when there are no lovers
around to hear
one love bird in a tree listen!
if it sings at all
it is slightly off key
I long to lie close to you
on the banks of a glowing lake
eating pizza you made
just for me
sharing some silence, the same silence
blending with nature
at dusk the sun screams over
the lake
and its waters shimmer hello
I long to read you
the poetry you inspire
to have the words embraced
by your heart and soul
to see your face light up

to have you read some for me
to hear the words held
by your breath
spoken by your lips
the lake glistens under
a smiling full moon
it ignites our spirits
to kiss your lips
under its beams
to hold you as flowers bloom
the buds burst and spring
turns to summer
in time the great pyramids
of Egypt
will crumble to the ground
the seven wonders of the world
will not be so wonderful
our bodies, these shells
where we live
will return to dust
yet, I shall adore you
I shall want to kiss
and hold you
for however long
forever is:
Dedicated to loneliness love
Peace and Realness – Spoon

Wally Lamb, an author famous for such novels as *She's Come Undone* and *I Know This Much Is True*, has been helping many Connecticut inmates to produce books of their own writing since 1999. Writing, according to Lamb, is a way to see patterns, "move out of dead ends and find your way out to understand your history and rehabilitate yourself" (Dahlberg, 2006, p. 3). His goal in helping to develop a writing workshop for inmates is to enhance "creativity by choice, not by chance" (p. 3).

The dramatic arts are also a way for inmates to display their creative flair while learning life skills and working in conjunction with others in a teamwork approach that can help them to integrate into the community when they receive parole (Brune, 1999). Kentucky's program, Shakespeare Behind Bars, is housed at the Luther Luckett Correctional Center. The inmates cast themselves in Shakespearean productions and then form a community as they embody their characters. The warden of Luther Luckett is very supportive of this program. A documentary of these inmates was released in 2005.

A nonprofit organization, Prison Performing Arts, in St. Louis, Missouri, incorporates music and other formats such as performance into programs for inmates in jails and juvenile detention centers with the goal of helping them to develop skills that will aid them when returning to the community. Another nonprofit organization, Rehabilitation Through the Arts, in New York State works mainly with inmates at Sing Sing Correctional Facility (Brune, 1999). The inmates write plays, act, design and construct sets, and perform the technical components of play production such as lighting and sound. Correctional officers and administrative staff are directed by the warden at Sing Sing to allow outside guests to attend the last night of the performance.

Finally, inmates display culinary skills in a resourceless atmosphere (Geranios, 2008). Rick Webb, one author of *The Convict Cookbook* (Washington State Penitentiary Convict Charity Project, 2004), a published book of inmate recipes that grew out of a community college course taken by Washington State Prison inmates learning how to make the transition to the outside, stated that cell cooking provides variety and creativity for inmates who have limited ingredients and need to cook without the use of a stove (Gerianos, 2004). "Dave Rivers' Perfect Omelet is made by combining all the ingredients in a plastic bag and boiling. … Donald Dunn's Jailhouse Pizza uses uncooked Top Ramen as the crust and tops it with pizza sauce, cheese spread, some pepperoni or summer sausage and corn chips" (Geranios, 2004). "It's not delivery; it's jailhouse!" says the caption of the accompanying cartoon. Dunn also provided the recipe for the Dope Fiend Sandwich, a treat popular in the King County Jail. It consists of two Grandma's brand peanut butter cookies, with a smashed Snickers bar in between. "These cookies are so named because heroin addicts often come to prison craving sweets," Dunn wrote. Geranios stated that many of the recipes are original, whereas some have been passed down from inmate to inmate for years. *The Convict Cookbook* was paid for by private contributions. The book also includes a glossary of prison slang and facts about and insights into prison life.

Inmate Art in the Public Eye

Like the variety of media used to express their artistic vision, the community at large and prison officials have taken varying attitudes toward inmate art. Inmate art is sometimes put on public display for sale or might be a reason for having inmates caught with unapproved art projects or sales finding themselves sanctioned or punished for breaking prison rules.

Angelo's inventions and artwork were displayed (with diagrams of his inventions) at the Massachusetts Museum of Contemporary Art in North Adams, Massachusetts. The agency Temporary Services chose to work with Angelo on the projects of publishing his book and producing his exhibition because the directors found his work compelling and because they "seek out intense creativity wherever it resides." The directors of Temporary Services feel that true creativity is lacking in the art world and cite the "inventiveness and resourcefulness" of prisoner inventions. Inmate inventions can highlight the "impoverished environment of prison" (Schmidt, 2004).

The varieties of artwork from the winners of the Koestler Awards are displayed in London, and all art is for sale. Critics find that inmates who win the Koestler Award in England paint pictures that display the "untaught candor" of artists not trying to impress art dealers. Some have taken art classes at their prisons, whereas some paint in the isolation of their cells (Cook, 2003, p. 40). Connecticut has an annual art show featuring inmate artists' work from Connecticut's 15 state prisons. The art show can garner negative attention when work from a high-profile inmate is displayed (such as a member of the Kennedy family, Michael Skakel, convicted in 2002 of murdering a teenage girl in 1975). However, in general, inmate art is appreciated by the public. Some images are abstract, whereas others, such as a painting of a group of men and women and tangled telephone cords, bring up images of prison life (Bulger, 2008).

The federal penitentiary in Leavenworth, Kansas, has an annual exhibit and sale that acts as an annual fundraiser for the city of Leavenworth while also allowing the inmates to profit from the sale of their artwork by being able to purchase more art supplies (Crawley, 2008). The "Hidden Art Locked Away" exhibit features the artwork of many inmates, including United States Disciplinary Barracks inmates, with many pieces described as "exceptional." The artwork is priced at the skill level displayed by the inmate, with prices ranging from $10 to a cap of $300.

Los Angeles County's Correctional Services Division's Bureau of Offender Programs and Services solicited artwork from the jail inmates to be donated for their silent auction. Division employees worked hard to find a local framer to frame the artwork, which was described as being of high quality (Dalton & Oliver, 2006).

The infamous Louisiana State Penitentiary in Angola (called Angola) holds a biannual arts and crafts festival featuring handmade work, or "hobbycrafts," as inmates refer to their work. Angola is one of the nation's largest maximum-security prisons, containing over 5,000 male prisoners. Two-thirds of the inmates are serving life sentences. Inmates work at stands displaying their art, consisting of paintings, woodwork, metal work, carvings, toys, leather work, jewelry, glass etchings, furniture, clocks, crocheted items, and other products made from materials gathered using "ingenuity and innovation from the trash, discarded items, or items that are available from the commissary, or prison store" (Schrift, 2006, p. 264). Inmates are able to sell their wares and state that they feel part of America's consumerism: part entrepreneur, part salesman, and part inventor. Most of all, inmates feel that they increase their humanity and sense of integrity by being able to both create and sell their inventions or art at a price. Examples include folded paper cigarette pack art by an inmate named Lonnie and popular leather belts and purses. Other items include birdhouses made from boots with the words "Boot Camp" painted on the top, painted skulls from dead bulls found on the farm, and a game one inmate named Junior worked on for two years called "Serving Time on the River: The Harsh Realities of Prison Life." Although the "harsh realities" range from sexual assault and getting clubbed with a sock full of batteries to being attacked with human feces, Junior claims to sell many at $25 per game (Schrift, 2006).

Connecticut inmates at York Correctional Institution participated in a program called "Time In," a six-month project run by Judy Dworin's Performance Projects and the Women of the Cross. The women involved created performance art from text, lyrics, and movement (Judy Dworin Performance Project, Inc., 2006). Some ex-inmates participated, and the information written by and gathered from inmates was incorporated in the performances of "Time In" at the prison and later in the community. Inmates felt that their experiences were represented by the work.

Books published by inmate authors are sold to the public so that the authors can share their creative products with the public. Spoon Jackson, although he does not have access to the Internet, is able to post a Web page with a newsletter and poetry, and he even has a Web page on MySpace, aided by his sister and his many friends (www.spoonjackson.com). He plans to publish a book of poetry entitled, *Longer Ago.* Jackson is currently working on his memoir, which will be published by the New Village Press in 2010. His co-author is his former poetry teacher, Judith Tannenbaum. Books such as *The Convict Cookbook* and Angelo's *Inmate Inventions* have been published, sharing inmate recipes, lingo, culture, and art with public audiences.

However, inmates generally need to have permission before selling their work. An inmate from Pelican Bay State Prison in California sold 20 of his paintings for $500 each when he mailed them to an art dealer. Despite the fact that he donated the proceeds to the Pelican Bay Prison Project (which used the money to help the children of prisoners at the inmate's request), he was written up for a serious rules violation and may have an extended sentence because the sale was unauthorized (Liptak, 2006).

"Famous" inmates such as Ted Bundy, John Wayne Gacy, and Charles Manson also have produced various works of art during their stay in correctional facilities. Only Manson survives at the current time, and the individuals who were able to purchase paintings while the inmates were alive (Gacy painted macabre clowns and portraits he was often commissioned to paint for money while in prison) try to sell their "murderabilia" on the Internet for large sums of money. These individuals are often criticized for making money from other people's tragedies (Foxnews.com, 2008). There is a Web site (CharlieManson.com) devoted to those who avidly track Charles Manson and his followers' terms in prison, who speak at parole board meetings to keep them all incarcerated for life (Turner, 2007). This Web site features Manson's art (one called "Devil Sketch"), poetry, and song lyrics. Other "murderabilia" are as inartistic as the dirt taken from the grave of the man claiming to be the Boston Strangler and are available on Web sites such as PrisonBoundSerialKillers.com and murderauction.com (Shriver, 2008).

ART PROGRAMS VERSUS ART THERAPY IN A CORRECTIONAL SETTING

"Art therapy" is defined as creative expression used therapeutically to generate insight by a trained therapist. "Therapeutic" is defined as any positive change. In contrast, art programs are led by educators or artists and focus on the creative process or a creative product (Ezell & Levy, 2003). The funding for both art classes as part of an enhanced educational programming and for art therapy as part of mental health rehabilitation has been severely limited because all educational and prison program funding has declined in the past few years. Without firm outcomes from empirical studies finding that these types of programs reduce violence and reoffending behaviors there is little compelling evidence to convince policymakers to spend more money in the creative arts in correctional settings. However, limited evidence from both the educational and rehabilitation ends of the artistic spectrum, along with numerous anecdotal examples of the remedial effects of art in the inmate environment, is worth examining. Grant (2007) states that for some inmates art may be the only productive and positive experience they will have.

Art as Education

Art programs are part of an enhanced educational curriculum, and although they may have a rehabilitative effect on the inmate they are run by artists or art teachers through the institutional education programs. Regular prison staff who teach in prisons also can teach art as part of an overall educational program, but most of the time this activity is not funded. Generally, prison art is taught by outside volunteers funded by nonprofit organizations or by educational facilities and sometimes by inmates themselves. Grady Hillman, a poet and president of the Southwest Correctional Art Network, places artists of various disciplines in prisons. When asked if she or the artists are fearful of teaching in a prison setting, she answered, "I've encountered my share of sociopaths, but it's no worse than teaching in junior high school" (Grant, 2007, p. 1). Teachers who choose this setting feel that inmates are human beings, no matter what they have done, and that being given a chance to engage in creative activities is of prime importance in helping inmates "figure out how to reconstruct their lives" (p. 2). Several universities, such as Auburn University in Alabama, Brown University in Rhode Island, and the University of Michigan in Ann Arbor, give students school credit for teaching art in correctional facilities as part of prison arts programs. The University of Michigan's Prison Creative Arts Project is noteworthy in that university students rigorously learn about themselves, prison issues, working with the prison community, and how the prison community engages with the community at large. The program places students in prisons and juvenile detention centers, where they help to facilitate workshops in collaboration with incarcerated adults, previously incarcerated adults, and juveniles throughout the state of Michigan (Brune, 1999).

In California, grants from nonprofit agencies help to fund the program Art in Corrections now that state funding is limited. Art in Corrections tries to keep art teachers and supplies in all California institutions, from those taught by inmate poets (Jackson, 2007) to outside teachers brought into institutions to teach other forms of artistic expression. Art in Corrections is unusual in that California established a line item for this agency in the state budget many years ago (Brune, 1999). However, some prisons' Art in Corrections classes (such as those taught at California State Prison, Sacramento) are financially feasible because all course instructors are inmates (Jackson, personal communication, 2009).

Other states have nonprofit organizations which directly fund art programs, such as Prison Performing Arts in St. Louis, Missouri, which has incorporated drama, music, and other creative formats into many correctional facilities in the St. Louis area since 1989. Art Behind Bars is an art-based community service program for inmates in the Monroe County Detention Center in Key West, Florida. This nonprofit organization, which is partially funded by the state of Florida, Florida Arts Council, and other organizations, helps to organize inmate art auctions and shows by putting out calls for inmate art donations that fund 400 nonprofit organizations nationwide, and the council stated that it has helped more than 6,000 inmates with their art programming (www.artbehindbars.org). Lynne Bantriglia, who runs the Web page, among other duties, for Art Behind Bars shared the piece of artwork created by an inmate artist shown in Figure 10.2. Tony Gregory was the photographer of the work of art, and Damian Vantriglia designed the graphic setup of the picture.

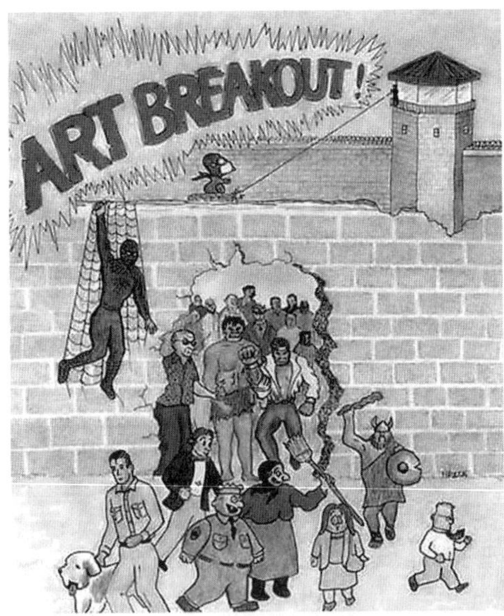

FIGURE 10.2. *Art Breakout* by Joseph Houck for Art Behind Bars. Medium: Colored pencils and pen on paper.

Art as Rehabilitation

Extending the idea of malevolent creativity into a more positive realm, the use of creativity as a tool to help those with pain and guilt is one that has moderate empirical evidence supporting art as a way to rehabilitate criminals and alleviate the secondary despair that can result. Art therapist Will Ursprung at the State Correctional Institution at Grateford, Pennsylvania, stated, "The incarcerated artist's need to synthesize new artistic materials in response to a desolate, restrictive and often debilitating environment speaks to the wonders of creative expression and the resilience of the human spirit against major odds. The art is important work ... [and is] a coping mechanism for survival" (www.cellblockvisions.com).

Many nonprofit organizations work with inmates to help rehabilitate them through the use of art and other creative activities. Resolana is a nonprofit organization that creates programs for women in the criminal justice system. Its mission is to "empower women to break the cycle of incarceration" by integrating "creative and spiritual, therapeutic and pragmatic elements into a holistic approach." Programs include art, music, drama, and movement as therapeutic activities designed to enable nonverbal personal growth through creative self-expression that "promote[s] the integration of memory and affect" (www.resolana.info).

The creators of Resolana cited literature linking high degrees of trauma with female incarceration as reasons why creative activities are particularly appropriate in alleviating traumatic symptoms and aiding rehabilitative healing with incarcerated females. Green and colleagues (2005) found that 98 of 100 women surveyed in a Maryland jail had experienced at least one type of trauma, such as interpersonal violence with a boyfriend or husband or childhood physical or sexual abuse. Green and colleagues explained that because women inmates are more likely to have experienced some type of traumatic event prior to incarceration, different types of programming are necessary to aid their rehabilitation prior to community release. The link among trauma, healing, and creativity forms a more restorative view of malevolent creativity, even though the creative products produced by inmates may not conform to traditionally creative tenets such as innovation, effectiveness, and elegance (Cropley et al., 2008).

Male inmates also experience rehabilitative effects in art as therapy. Hanes (2005) examined the "self-directed" creative activities of males in a county jail. Hanes observed inmates using the "image-making process" and artistic creation to "endure and adjust to their current life circumstances and the jail environment" (p. 44). Hanes examined the themes present in inmate art and found that inmates use images for purposes of inner "escape" fantasies; as a way to play out anger and rage, with art acting as a safe container for their aggressive feelings; and for purposes of redemption and atonement or other feelings inmates may have regarding their confinement or crime. Hanes cited the Christian cross as the most frequently occurring image in the county jail, which he felt represented "suffering, humiliation, atonement, transformation, faith, and the mercy of God giving redemption for the sins of man" (p. 47).

THE IMPACT OF CREATIVE EXPRESSION IN A CORRECTIONAL ENVIRONMENT

There are few studies that empirically state the rehabilitative effect of art therapy or art education programming on inmates. The funding for these programs typically is generated by a wide variety of outside sources, and well-designed evaluation research demonstrating the decrease in recidivism (which is not a criterion for true creativity but is a criterion for gaining funding for empirical research studies) in offending is not present. An evidence-based review of the scientific literature in prisoner reentry programs by Aos, Miller, and Drake (2006) asked the question, Are there corrections programs that work to reduce the reoffending rate of adult offenders? Drug treatment programs, correctional industries programs, basic adult education, and vocational education programs in prison all were shown to reduce recidivism, among many other prison and community programs. However, no studies were found or evaluated relating to art therapy or art education.

The literature that exists on art education and art therapy programs is mainly anecdotal or qualitative in design. Most programs cite positive gains with the few recipients of their rehabilitation efforts, such as Rehabilitation Through Arts in New York. Informal interviews with program staff who have followed 12 ex-participants in Sing Sing's program found that 10 are residents of the New York area, living prison-free lives (Brune, 1999). The director of Shakespeare Behind Bars in Kentucky found no recidivism among the 35 program participants released. It is important to remember, however, that studies with small numbers of subjects and that use personal interviews as the main methodology generate far weaker conclusions than more empirically based studies with larger numbers of subjects.

An older study found more positive than negative or neutral results for art used as part of an educational protocol. In a project funded by the Pennsylvania Department of Education, inmates enrolled in adult basic education and general education development programs were encouraged to create works of art, poetry, and creative writing that were subsequently compiled into an anthology and distributed among other inmates and staff (Hawk et al., 1993). The anthology, entitled, *The Walls That Speak*, generated positive regard for inmates among staff and better staff-inmate relationships and "created excitement, creativity, and a sense of worth" among 23 of 40 participating inmates surveyed (p. 7).

Gussak (2006, 2007) examined the quantitative and qualitative effects of art therapy on medium to maximum-security inmates in a Florida institution. In Gussak's pilot study, he found that using pre- and postsurveys of depressive symptoms and mood, inmates had a decrease in depressive symptoms and an increase in mood after they participated in a four-week art therapy group. Additionally, the 48 inmates who participated in the pilot study had positive results on a socialization scale, improved attitude, and an increased acceptance of each other and their environment. Gussak ran a subsequent study (2006, 2007) where he again used inmates in a mental health setting within a Florida correctional institution. In the second study, intended to improve on the previous study's methodology, Gussak randomly assigned small groups of male volunteers to art therapy or control conditions. He found that inmates who had received art therapy for eight weeks within a mental health unit had fewer symptoms of depression, as measured by the short form of the Beck Depression Inventory (BDI-II), compared with inmates who did not receive weekly art therapy sessions. No increase in social skills or problem solving was detected in the experimental group in Gussak's (2006, 2007) subsequent study. Gussak (2007, p. 446) concluded, "Art supports creative activity in prison and provides necessary diversion and emotional escape."

Ezell and Levy (2003) evaluated an arts program for juvenile offenders called A Changed World with the purpose of reducing recidivism as a result of the juveniles' participation in "culturally relevant" (p. 109) experiential arts activities. Artists conducted workshops for a period of two weeks to two months in a safe, positive environment. In 1996 and 1997, the youths created a touring multimedia exhibit. In year three (1998), they produced a film for television, helping to write the script and also assisting with the filming, musical score, and creation of the accompanying catalogue. Participation was voluntary, with the number of youths varying from 265 in 1996 (with 86 evaluated) to 41 participating and evaluated in 1998. Workshops varied from visual arts, creative writing, music, sculpture, graphic design, murals, photography, drama, poetry, cartoon art, collage, and paper mache. Information was collected from the participants, artists, teachers, and correctional staff, and the juveniles were followed for six months after release for a measure of recidivism. The results of the evaluation found an overall "positive impact" (p. 113) that included lower recidivism rates for participants, a decline in 63 percent of behavioral incidents as measured in years two and three, and positive feelings of staff and the juveniles regarding skills learned as a result of the workshops.

In a new and promising study conducted by Wilson, Caulfield, and Atherton (2008) in the United Kingdom, the long-term effects on those who participated in the Good Vibrations Gamelan in Prisons Project were examined. The project is part of a music charity where percussion music from Indonesia is taught in one-week courses. Positive short-term effects have been shown in those who participated in this program designed to "inspire and empower people" (p. 1). The Wilson and colleagues study assessed the longer-term effects of Good Vibrations by interviewing participants six to nine months after the project was completed. These individuals were assessed for changes in emotions and behavior based on a scale created by the research team. Key findings included improved listening and communication skills, improved social skills and increased social interaction, improved relationships with prison staff, decreased levels of self-reported anger, a greater sense of calmness, and greater levels of openness and engagement with regard to learning activities. The authors recommend continuing and expanding this program (which has already included more than 1,700 people in over 25 different institutions overseas since 2003, according to www.good-vibrations.org.uk) because of positive and sustained changes in the participants. It is important to note that although these studies show significant effects of behavioral change and interest in creativity, the resulting products are not measured for being truly innovative and effective creations that are objectively considered to be of artistic value.

A CONCLUSION REGARDING INMATES' CREATIVITY IN CONFINEMENT

In general, although the value of educational programming in reducing recidivism is well documented (e.g., Aos et al., 2006), Wade (2007) makes the point that the measuring tool used most frequently as an indicator of success is *recidivism rate,* or the rate at which inmates return to custody after receiving educational programming and being paroled to the community. However, Wade also pointed out that since studies use different definitions of "recidivism" and because differential job skills may influence return to crime, learning achieved is a more fair measure of the success of an educational program. Jacobi (2008) makes a pointed case that using creativity in teaching education to juveniles in custody is of primary importance given that most juvenile inmates have had difficulty in more traditional educational settings. Since most offenders, juvenile or adult, are likely to have experienced school failure and are much less likely to be high school graduates than the general population (Schmalleger & Smykla, 2008), the idea of infusing creativity into an educational setting with all inmates is appropriate.

Ezell and Levy (2003) stated that owing to the lack of well-designed evaluation studies measuring the various types of success art programs can facilitate, more evaluative studies focusing on the types of inmates who volunteer for art programs, comprehensive information on the offender's background and crime, and a better definition of positive change can help researchers to more effectively assess the cost-benefit of art programs in juvenile and adult correctional settings. If cost-benefit analyses show that creative programming can both decrease institutional violence and aid all aspects of reentry while reducing recidivism, more art programs will be funded nationwide. Ezell and Levy believe that their work indicates that art programs can generate positive changes for incarcerated juveniles. Gussak's (2006, 2007) work indicates that art as rehabilitation can aid mentally ill inmates in experiencing relief of symptoms and potentially increase their skill development. The work of Wilson and colleagues (2008) shows that music as rehabilitation can increase positive effects for a general inmate population. However, even if studies are able to prove a reduction in recidivism based on inmates' involvement in art programs, there likely will be funding for very few inmates to participate (Petersilia, 2005). Petersilia (2006) stated in her report to the California Policy Research Center, "The politically expedient effort to cut or deprioritize such programs because they 'coddle criminals' has been extremely short-sighted and ultimately threatens public safety" (p. 78).

Although programs that encourage inmate creativity are few in number, it is important to realize how beneficial art can be to incarcerated individuals. Even when inmates create art on an individual basis and do not take part in a structured program, the expression of important themes can be found in their work. Art as a coping style or art as communication ultimately translates to art reinventing and healing the inmate's soul. Even the most utilitarian of prison staff can see inmate art in a positive light. Ultimately, inmate creativity, unless used to create specialized weapons, is a positive force in the incarcerated population that should be nurtured and enhanced. Additionally, inmate creativity, as defined by innovative contraband as well as beautiful and healing art products, can result in a broader definition of malevolent creativity.

REFERENCES

Angelo & Temporary Services. (2003). *Prisoners' inventions.* Chicago: Whitewalls.

Aos, S., Miller, M. , & Drake, E. (2006). *Evidence-based adult corrections programs: What works and what does not.* Olympia, WA: Washington State Institute for Public Policy.

Art Behind Bars. (1994). An Internet site that provides art-based community service to those in need: http://artbehindbars.org/.

Bornfool. *TP.* Available at http://bornfool.blogspot.com/2007/01/tp.html; retrieved June 24, 2008.

Brower, R. (1999). Dangerous minds: Eminently creative people who spent time in jail, *Creativity Research Journal*, 12, 3–13.

Brune, K. (1999). Creating behind the razor wire: An overview of arts in corrections in the US. Community Arts Network. Available at www.communityarts.net/readingroom/archivefiles/2007/01/ creating_behind.php. Retrieved June 24, 2008.

Bulger, A. (2008). Insider art. *Hartford Advocate.* Available at www.hartfordadvocate.com/article.cfm?aid=7810. Retrieved June 27, 2008.

Christian, S. (1990). The clock below has a very interesting history. Available at www.clockplans.com/page17.html. Retrieved June 24, 2008.

Cook, W. (2003). Creative freedom. *New Statesman*, September, pp. 40–41.

Crawley, J. (2008). Inmate art featured in exhibition. *Fort Leavenworth Lamp.* Available at www.ftleavenworthlamp.com/articles/2008/02/07/features/features2.txt. Retrieved June 27, 2008.

Cropley, D. H., Kaufman, J. C., & Cropley, A. J. (2008). Malevolent creativity: A functional model of creativity in terrorism and crime. *Creativity Research Journal*, 20, 105–115.

Cuellar, C. (2008). Resolana celebrates its first anniversary helping women in Dallas County jail. *Pegasus News.* Available at www.pegasusnews.com/news/2008/may/27/resolana-celebrates-anniversary-dallas-county-jail/. Retrieved June 24, 2008.

Dahlberg, S. (2006). Applied imagination: The right to be creative – in schools, in prison and in life. Available at www.appliedimagination.org/. Retrieved June 24, 2008.

Dalton, K.S. & Oliver, J. (2006). Inmate art: Raising money for charity. *Sheriff*, November, p. 30.

Durant, C. (2006). Inmate's art brings color to Pelican Bay. *Times-Standard.* Available at www.times-standard.com/local/ci_3459105. Retrieved June 26, 2008.

Eisenman, R. (1999). Creative prisoners: Do they exist? *Creativity Research Journal*, 12, 205–210.

(2008). Malevolent creativity in criminals. *Creativity Research Journal*, 20, 116–119.

Ezell, M. & Levy, M. (2003). An evaluation of an arts program for incarcerated juvenile offenders. *Journal of Correctional Education*, 54, 108–114.

FOXnews.com. (2008). Chicago man looks to cash in on John Wayne Gacy "Murder-a-Bilia." Available at http://FOXnews.com. Retrieved January 13, 2009.

Gearhart, G. (2006). Controlling contraband. *Corrections Today*, October, pp. 24–29.

Georgia Board of Corrections (2007). *Minutes of Board of Corrections*. Glennville, GA: Board of Corrections.

Gerianos, N. K. (2004, November 12). Dope fiend sandwich anyone? Prison chefs tout creativity in cookbook. *The Standard-Times*, Washington.

Grant, D. (2007). Bringing art behind bars. *American Artist*, 71, 1–2. Available at www.myamericanartist.com/2008/05/bringing-art-be.html. Retrieved June 27, 2008.

Green, B. L., Miranda, J., Daroowalla, A., & Siddique, J. (2005). Trauma exposure, mental health functioning, and program needs of women in jail. *Crime and Delinquency*, 51, 133–151.

Greenberg, B. (2000). Prison project unlocks artistic expression. *Horizons*, 14, 9–10.

Grube, N. (2007). In focus: Pelican Bay's underground economy. *The Daily*, March 31. Available at www.triplicate.com/news/story.cfm?story_no=3374. Retrieved June 24, 2008.

Gussak, D. (2006). Effects of art therapy with prison inmates: A follow-up study. *The Arts in Psychotherapy*, 33, 188–198.

(2007). The effectiveness of art therapy in reducing depression in prison populations. *International Journal of Offender Therapy and Comparative Criminology*, 51, 444–460.

Hanes, M. J. (2005). Behind steel doors: Images from the walls of a county jail. *Art Therapy: Journal of the American Art Therapy Association*, 22, 44–48.

Hawk, K. Bohna, A. E., Riddell, K., & Stark, J. M. (1993). *Anthology of inmate art: Special demonstration project*. ERIC Document Reproduction Service No. ED 368873. Uniontown, PA: Pennsylvania State Departments of Education, Harrisburg, & Bureau of Adult Basic and Literacy Education.

Huey, M. P. & McNulty, T. L. (2005). Institutional conditions and prison suicide: Conditional effects of deprivation and overcrowding. *The Prison Journal*, 85, 490–514.

Jackson, S. (2007). Speaking in poems. *Community Arts Network*, May. Available at www.communityarts.net/readingroom/archivefiles/2007/05/speaking_in_poe.php. Retrieved June 24, 2008.

Jacobi, T. (2008). Writing for change: Engaging juveniles through alternative literacy education. *Journal of Correctional Education*, 59, 71–93.

James, D. J. & Glaze, L. E. (2006, September). *Mental health problems of prison and jail inmates. Bureau of Justice Statistics Special Report* (NCJ 213600). Washington, D.C.: U.S. Department of Justice.

Judy Dworin Performance Project, Inc. (2006). Time in feedback from inmates. Available at www.judydworin.org/pages/timeinfeed.html. Retrieved June 24, 2008.
Kaufman, J. C. & Baer, J. (2002). I bask in dreams of suicide: Mental illness and poetry. *Review of General Psychology*, 6, 271–286.
Kaufman, J. C. & Sexton, J.D. (2006). Why doesn't the writing cure help poets? *Review of General Psychology*, 10, 268–282.
Kornfeld, P. (2008). Prison art in America: Criminal justice and the arts. In *Cellblock Visions*. Available at www.cellblockvisions.com/justice3.html. Retrieved June 26, 2008.
Lesnick, G. (2006). Clever contraband: Sneaky inmates keep jailers on their toes. *Courier Press*, November 21. Available at www.courierpress.com/news/2006/Nov/21/clever-contraband/. Retrieved June 24, 2008.
Liptak, A. (2006). Prison disciplines publicized inmate who makes art using M&Ms. *New York Times*, August 4. Available at http://query.nytimes.com/gst/fullpage.html?res=9800E4DB113FF937A3575BC0 A9609C8B63&sec=&spon=. Retrieved June 27, 2008.
Payne, S. (2003). Creativity not encouraged: Toilet paper dice and other prison innovations. *The Houstonian*, September 9. Available at http://media.www.houstonianonline.com/media/storage/paper229/news/2003/09/09/News/Creativity.Not.Encouraged-460658.shtml. Retrieved June 27, 2008.
Petersilia, J. (2005). Prisons can be cages or schools. *Los Angeles Times*, October 16. Available at http://docs.google.com/gview?attid=0.1&thid=11e70042f99fa7e1&a=v&pli=1. Retrieved December 30, 2008.
(2006). *Understanding California corrections*. Berkley, CA: Regents of the University of California, California Policy Research Center.
Purdy, M. (1995). Officials ponder expansion of drug searches in prison. *New York Times*, December 17. Available at http://query.nytimes.com/gst/fullpage.html?res=9C07E7D61739F934A25751C1A 963958260&sec=&spon=&pagewanted=all. Retrieved June 24, 2008.
Ryan, C. L. (2000). Think staff safety … Think technology. *Corrections Today*, 62, 108–111.
Shachtman, N. (2003, September). Ingenuity helps prisoners cope. *Wired Magazine*.
Schmalleger, F., Smykla, J., & Ortiz, J. (2008). *Corrections in the 21st century*, 4th ed. New York: McGraw-Hill.
Schmidt, J. (2004). The cell block and the white cube. *Big Red and Shiny: An Art Journal*, 1, 1–7. Available at www.bigredandshiny.com/cgi-bin/retrieve.pl?issue=issue01§ion=article&article=SCHMIDT_THE_CELL_BLOCK_131345. Retrieved June 24, 2008.
Schrift, M. (2006). Angola Prison art: Captivity, creativity, and consumerism. *Journal of American Folklore*, 119, 257–274.
Shriver, L. (2008). The US taste for ghoulish "murderabilia." The Guardian (UK), May 29. Available at http://gardian.co.uk. Retrieved January 13, 2009.
Silk, S. (2008). No room for error: Government security. Available at http://govtsecurity.com/public_facility_security/no_room_Error/. Retrieved June 24, 2008.

Spoon Jackson. (2005). An Internet site that presents the text of many of inmate Jackson's poetry and a forum to communicate with Jackson. www.spoonjackson.com/.

Temporary Services. (2004). *Prisoners' inventions: Three dialogues*. Chicago: Temporary Services.

(2005). *Prisoners' inventions*. Chicago: Temporary Services.

Turner, M. (2007). An anti-Manson Web site. CharlieManson.com.

Wade, B. (2007). Studies of correctional education programs. *Adult Basic Education and Literacy Journal*, 1, 27–31.

Walsh, A. & Ellis, L. (2007). *Criminology: An interdisciplinary approach*. Thousand Oaks, CA: Sage Publications.

Walters, G. D. (1990). *The criminal lifestyle: Patterns of serious criminal conduct*. Thousand Oaks, CA: Sage Publications.

Washington State Penitentiary Convict Charity Project. (2004). *The convict cookbook*, 2nd ed. Walla Walla, WA: J. G. Narum.

Wilson, D., Caulfield, L., & Atherton, S. (2008). Promoting positive change: Assessing the long-term psychological, emotional and behavioural effects of the Good Vibrations Gameplan in Prisons Project, November, good-vibrations.org.uk.

11

Creativity and Crime: How Criminals Use Creativity to Succeed

RUSSELL EISENMAN

Criminals can be creative, and this can lead to their being more successful in their criminality. This chapter presents mostly examples and case histories to show how criminals use creativity to succeed. If there were lots of research studies, I would present them, but the evidence comes mainly from my work with prisoners and from information from others who have worked with criminals or their captured cousins, prisoners. Part of being creative is using original and effective ways to get what you want. Depending how you look at it, this could be called "manipulating the environment" or "being manipulative" or "being persuasive." Many people must be persuasive: salespeople, lawyers, teachers, therapists, parents, and so on. The criminals discussed in this chapter were, at times, very good at being persuasive or, as I will usually refer to it, at being manipulative or using manipulation. "Manipulation" has a more negative connotation, implying that it gets others to do things they may not want to do. This fits well with what occurred in the prison. We usually do not think of manipulation as being part of creativity, but any reflection will show that creativity enables a person to get what he or she wants. Thus creativity leads to increased manipulation, whether it is manipulation for good or for bad purposes.

I previously did two studies in which I found prisoners to be low in creativity (Eisenman, 1992, 1999). They seem to have rigid lifestyles in which they do not know how to do anything but be a criminal, respond with aggression to minor slights, and so on. Their thinking seems to be at a low level, at least as far as solving most problems in life. Their Thematic Apperception Test (TAT) stories (Morgan & Murray, 1935) usually showed little creativity. However, I believe that in some instances criminals or prisoners can be high in creativity or at least display creativity in certain instances. Going back to my two studies, I did find that some of the prisoners, if they showed any creativity at all, showed it with regard to TAT stories about crime.

Crime seemed to be their domain, just as science is the domain of a scientist. The scientist might or might not be creative in other domains, such as the arts, writing, baseball, and so on. Even in other sciences, the creative scientist might not be creative. For example, a creative biologist would not necessarily show creativity in the domain of engineering. So it could be that the one area where many prisoners show creativity is in the area (domain) of crime. If you test their creativity in other areas, you might not realize how creative they can be regarding crime.

Crime is, after all, the chosen lifestyle for most of them, at least based on my experience working for about two years in a California Youth Authority prison treatment program. As senior clinical psychologist, I worked closely with young (up to age 25) prisoners, doing much psychotherapy (individual and group) and many psychological assessments, writing parole reports for the Youthful Offender Parole Board, and just talking with the prisoners. A typical TAT story about crime would be like the following one, which mentions phencyclidine (PCP), a very powerful drug that can produce many extreme results, including possibly assaultiveness, disorganized thinking, rapid heartbeat, hallucinations, psychotic symptoms, and so on (Lyons & Martin, 2009).

A TAT STORY TOLD BY A CRIMINAL

This guy is thinking about what kinds of crimes he is going to do. He and his gang take PCP and plan out some crimes, maybe robberies. The PCP helps them to think about things in new ways and leads to all kinds of new ideas about what crimes to commit and who to do them to. They pull off a bunch of robberies, being very smart about it, and do not get caught. They share the proceeds of the robberies and buy drugs, weapons, new clothes, and other stuff.

Note that this story is about crime and reflects the lifestyle of the prisoner, in that, in real life, he and his gang did just the kinds of things mentioned in the story. Note also that they use PCP for purposes of malevolent creativity, that is, to come up with new ways to do evil things that will provide profit for them but hurt the victims. Also, note that in the story they do not get caught. Perhaps noncriminals could tell a somewhat similar story but would be more likely to have society prevail and the criminals caught. In the TAT stories of criminals that I got, they usually get away with their crimes, often after doing some clever or creative things to pull off the crime.

I have some doubts about using PCP to plan crimes. On the one hand, it would help you to think "outside the box," a term that has become something of a cliché but that refers clearly to creativity. On the other hand, it might interfere so much with intelligent thinking that it would lead to poor planning and thus increase the likelihood of getting caught. However, this prisoner and his gang members routinely did PCP before committing crimes, including drive-by shootings of enemy gangs. Usually, they did not get caught. In fact, I found that many of the prisoners in our facility committed many crimes throughout their young lives and usually did not get caught, often going for long periods of time – months, years – without being apprehended. However, since they kept doing crimes, eventually they got caught for one of them and got sent to prison.

THE RED LIGHT FROM THE DOOR

I heard about creative work by some prisoners recently in a nearby prison that eventually led to a successful prison escape. The prison had recently installed a red light warning system on a door. Whenever the door was opened, a red light would go on in the next room, where a guard was stationed. This red light was an important addition because the next room led to a place where the prisoners could climb to the roof and escape, using sheets or something to help them climb down the wall.

Here, creativity from the dark side involved figuring out how to overcome the red light system so that prisoners could escape. The prisoners acted like creative thinkers, finding a problem (the red light) and trying to solve the problem (the dark side of prisoners escaping). The solving involved, in effect, testing different hypotheses to solve this difficult problem and get what they wanted, *namely*, for the guards to ignore the red light and thus allow prisoners to escape and obtain freedom.

Some prisoners decided to crack open the door just a little to see what the guards would do. The guard at the desk thought the door was really closed because he could not perceive that it was slightly open. So he ignored the red light, which was supposed to serve as a warning system. The prisoners decided to keep doing what they did, so every day they would open the door just slightly, and the red light would appear in the room with the guard, but it would be ignored. Finally, the guard tired of the red light, which he assumed was malfunctioning. So he turned off the system. Now, no red light warning was available. The prisoners kept the door open, just slightly, as before. Finally, several prisoners went through that door one day, got to the roof, and escaped.

The prisoners seemed like scientists testing a hypothesis. What would happen if we opened the door just a little, enough to make the red light go on, but perhaps not enough for the guard to notice that the door was open. It worked, and several eventually escaped. This example, by the way, is the reason that prisons, police departments, and bureaucracies in general often demand strict attention to rules. Failing to adhere to a rule, even if it seems unnecessary, can have bad consequences. Of course, this is also one reason bureaucracies are often looked down upon because their rigid rules and the inflexibility of people working there make for instances in which a new approach is demanded, but the old approach is maintained. For instance, a policeman in Dallas pulled over a man at a hospital for going through a red light (Dixon, 2009). The man was trying to get to the hospital to see his mother-in-law, who the hospital had told him was dying. He was taking his wife with him in the car. The policeman demanded that both wait while he checked the driver's license, insurance, and so on. When the driver and his wife did not want to wait and the wife ran into the hospital to see her dying mother, the policemen allegedly pulled his gun on the man and made him wait while he wrote out a ticket. Hospital personnel came out to tell the man that he needed to be inside to see his dying mother-in-law. The policeman would not relent. While the ticket was being written, the man's mother-in-law died.

This can be seen as a lack of creativity on the part of the policeman. Up to the point that the hospital personnel came out, one could argue that he was doing his job. He does not really know that the man's mother-in-law is dying. Once that fact was confirmed, however, he should have been flexible enough to let the man go in – to reconceptualize how he perceived the incident. But he was stuck into seeing the situation as that of a cop dealing with a lawbreaker. Possibly, the situation was exacerbated by the fact that the cop was White and the man and his wife were Black. We will never know for sure, but prejudice can occur in situations such as this and has happened enough to make us wonder.

LUIS, A GREAT MANIPULATOR

Luis (not his real name; all names have been changed) was one of the best manipulators I have ever encountered. He was 17 years old and a member of a Hispanic gang that was heavily involved in selling illegal drugs, mostly cocaine. From what I learned, the drugs he sold originally came from a South American country, usually Colombia or Peru, and went through Mexico, to be delivered to Black gang members, either Bloods or Crips (the two major Black gangs in California), in southern California. The Bloods and Crips then sold the drugs to people wanting cocaine (or other drugs), selling some of their drugs to Hispanic gangs, who then did the same thing the Bloods and Crips did, selling the drugs to people who wanted them. In one of my group therapy sessions, Luis said about a Crips gang member in the group, "He is the one I bought my drugs from."

Luis was a very clever criminal. He used creativity to manipulate people to do whatever he wanted, to further his goals of selling drugs, being a gang member, and being a criminal in general. Thus his use of people was creativity for the dark side. Was it truly creativity, one may ask, or just clever criminal thinking? I believe that clever criminal thinking is often creativity because criminals often employ novel means (or at least something most people would not think of) designed to further their dark, evil purposes. We could argue about where to draw the line for something to be truly creative, but in so many instances what criminals do is extremely clever and effective and could be called "creative."

Luis had turned himself in and asked to be sent to prison. This is very strange behavior, and I never learned why he did it. Perhaps things were too dangerous on the streets, and he was likely going to be killed by another gang wanting to take over the drug trade in his area. This could have been a Black gang or another Hispanic gang. There were few, if any, White or Asian gangs that were major players in the illegal drug trade in California, as far as I could tell. Or perhaps Luis wanted to get credit for being in prison, which is often seen as a badge of honor among gang members. Luis had a beautiful girlfriend, Ramona, who was a professional model. She visited him regularly and encouraged him to stop being a criminal. Perhaps he went to prison to persuade her how good he was and that she should stay with him. However, in one visit I heard Luis tell Ramona, "When I get out, I am going back to the gang and going back to selling drugs." At the end of the visit, she left the prison crying.

Free Sex and Meet the Gang

Luis offered me one of his gang girls for a sex partner if I would let him have sex with Ramona during one of her visits. To do this, I would have had to sneak around the rules because such was strictly forbidden, but it would have been possible, had I desired. He described in great detail how beautiful or sexy many of the gang girls were and added, "If I tell a gang girl to have sex with someone, she will." He also told me how nice his gang was and how he would like me to meet them.

I turned down his offer, both with regard to the sexual liason and with regard to meeting the gang. Like a good salesman, he did not give up after my rejection. He said that he had already done this in X prison with a staff member there, that it had worked out well, and that we could do it easily here. I just had to work it out so that he and Ramona could have sexual intercourse during one of her visits, and he would then get me a gang girl of my choice (or at least one who fit my specifications regarding looks) for me to have sex with.

Even though I said "No," he may have had the gang try to come visit me at the prison. I do not know if he just said this or if it was true. He told me, "I had the gang come by to visit you the other day, but they would not let them in." I did not want to meet his gang. The California street gangs are very brutal, killing many people and committing all sorts of crime. Although I worked with many gang members in the prison, such a structured situation – where there are guards present or nearby – is very different from meeting them in other ways. If I were to meet any of them outside the prison, who knows what might have happened to me? At first, I discounted Luis' statement about the gang coming to see me. I thought it was made up, just more of his manipulation, to get me to do the sex exchange. Or should I say "alleged" sex exchange because once he had sex with Ramona, would he really get a gang girl to have sex with someone? Or was it all bogus or perhaps a setup to get me to meet his gang on the outside and then have me beaten or killed? Luis was using creative thinking to further his dark-side needs, whatever they were (get me to like him and do favors for him, get me in a vulnerable spot where I could be blackmailed or killed, or who knows what?).

But something happened that made me think that the gang may have come to see me and been turned away by the prison staff. I had an appointment with a dentist in town, and the secretary, a Hispanic woman, called me at the prison to remind me of my appointment. However, the female guard who took all incoming phone calls told the secretary, "He does not work here any more." Was this a mistake, a desire not to deal with any phone calls except prison-related ones, or perhaps the gang had truly been there, so now any call from a Hispanic was suspect? I never found out.

I never took Luis up on his offers, but I learned that another staff member did, regarding the sexual arrangement. At least, he allowed Luis to have sex with Ramona. Whether or not he got sex from a Hispanic gang girl, I do not know. The dark-side creativity here is that Luis got to violate prison regulations and have sexual intercourse with his girlfriend, either by (a) trading the opportunity for a staff member to have sex with a gang girl or

(b) tricking the staff member into letting Luis have sex with Ramona and not coming through on his promise of sex for the staff member.

Also, it probably was good judgment on my part not to meet with Luis' gang. Another prisoner, who did cleanup in the therapists' offices, including mine, came across a book that a therapist had with her name and home address on the inside cover. Both he and Luis had her as a therapist. He asked Luis, "Do you like your therapist?"

Luis said, "No."

He asked, "Would you like to know where she lives?"

Luis said, "Yes."

So the prisoner gave Luis the therapist's home address. Shortly thereafter, someone did a drive-by shooting of her new van, parked in front of her house, as well as some of the cars parked right before and after it. No one was in the parked cars, fortunately. They were just parked in front of the houses. We all believed that it was Luis' gang that did the drive-by shooting.

On the Leyva

As a therapist, I try to have good relationships with all the prisoners so that they will be honest with me and I can help them to become crime-free. I got along well with all of them, helped in part because, unlike the guards, I do not demand that they do anything they do not want to do. My job does not include making them move from one place to another or stop watching television in the day room, and so on. However, this all came to a head with Luis when he tried to manipulate me on a certain occasion, and I resisted and let him know that I considered him manipulative.

He said to me about another prisoner, "He thinks I am manipulative. You don't think I am manipulative, do you?"

I said, "Are you kidding? You are one of the most manipulative people I have ever known," which was true.

Luis seemed surprised that his manipulation had not worked, and he said, "Fuck you, I'm never talking to you again."

Days later, when he passed me, he laughed and said, "You're on the 'leyva.'" This is a term Hispanic criminals used to indicate that you are being shunned, that no one in their group will talk to you or have anything to do with you. I have tried to look up the word and have asked many Hispanics about it, but no one knows anything about it. However, in the prison/criminal/gang culture, its meaning is known. Many cultures have ways of shunning a wrongdoer, showing that such behavior is not acceptable. It is a way that a culture defines what is deviant, what is rejected (Eisenman, 1991; Kelly & Clark, 2003; Tewksbury & Gagne, 2000). For example, among Hispanic gang members in prison, if you accept a cigarette from a Black prisoner, this is a serious offense and can get you put on the "leyva." In prison, racial and ethnic groups are separate and, basically, enemies. You are supposed to stick with your own group, according to the convict code. This code can be seen as creative, in that it helps the group to achieve solidarity and protection, or it could be seen as uncreative, in that it restricts information and learning from others.

Later, Luis did talk to me, and I said, "I thought you said you were never going to talk to me again."

His reply? "Fuck you."

I was trying to show him that words have meaning and that one should be careful about saying things just because that is how you feel at the moment, but I doubt he got my meaning. Later on, he was talking to me again. He did things mainly to manipulate, so what he said may or may not have been true in any given instance. He used words to manipulate and get what he wanted. He was very good at it. He used his creativity for his selfish, dark-side purposes with little regard for who he hurt.

BILLY, ANOTHER GREAT MANIPULATOR

Billy is a Black, 18 years old, and a member of the Crips gang. He sold drugs, mostly cocaine, under the direction of a man known as "Blue," which is the Crips' color. He did whatever "Blue" told him to do. Had "Blue" told him to kill someone, he would have. I write about Billy in my latest book (Eisenman, 2007), calling him Roy in Chapter 7 about sex offenders and Billy in Chapter 16 about his life and his time in prison when I knew him. Billy was full of rage owing to the horrible life he had led: no parents most of his life, raped by an uncle when he was very young, sent from placement to placement, and so on. He had a list of 56 people he intended to kill when he got out of prison. We got along extremely well, and I wanted desperately to help him because he would be a horrible threat to society if he did not change. However, for all I know, I could have done something I did not even realize to offend him and become number 57 on his list. For example, the prison psychiatrist thought that his constant antisocial behavior might be due to brain damage and gave Billy an electroencephalogram (EEG) as a rough assessment of brain damage. Billy once asked me if the psychiatrist had any results from his EEG testing, and I told him that the EEG showed no signs of brain damage. Billy said, "You just saved his life." Had the psychiatrist found brain damage, Billy would either have added him to his list or killed him in the prison. Neither one seems like rational thinking/behavior to me. Billy was capable of low-level thinking but also was very clever and creative in attempts to get what he wanted – all this with that underlying rage and hatred of society. Almost all the prisoners hated authority, but Billy was prepared to carry out his hatred.

He also has a desire to kill people randomly at a mall when he gets out. He would use an Uzi submachine gun for this. If he is not killed at the first mall, he intends to go to a second mall and kill more, and he figures that he will be killed at the second mall. These two desires – to kill 56 people and to kill randomly at malls – are basically incompatible. You might be able to do one, but not both. However, his lack of clear thinking keeps him from seeing this. In any event, they are emotion-driven thoughts owing to his rage. I think that his rage is understandable, in a sense justifiable, in that he has had a horrible life. Who among us would not be like Billy if we had the same environmental background? At the same time, he has to be stopped from doing bad things, so I put a lot of effort into doing psychotherapy with him. However, it may be impossible to change someone who has his background. He was very good at swindling other prisoners, such as getting something from them for something promised in return but never delivering on his part of the bargain.

He was bisexual but seemed not to realize that he was partly homosexual and probably would punch you in the mouth if you said he was. However, he had been a male prostitute in Los Angeles, wearing a dress and soliciting men for sex. This came out in my psychotherapy with him. I doubt that the Crips knew about that part of his life. Had they known, they probably would not have admitted him to their gang or would either throw him out or kill him. He seemed to hate women, perhaps because he saw his mother die when he was three years old. His dad had already left, so it would make just as much sense to hate men, but perhaps witnessing the abandonment by his mother made him hate women. He would threaten to rape female staff, and he also would masturbate where female staff could see him. He denied that he wanted to be seen, but it was obvious to me that he did. This was a way of being hostile to female staff, a good example of the concept of passive aggressiveness, where you do something hostile to someone but in a somewhat passive way. So Billy succeeded in expressing hostility to female staff.

In some ways, it was difficult not to feel sorry for Billy, if you knew his background. In addition to all the horrible things about his life mentioned earlier, after his mother died, he had, finally, been placed in a group home where things seemed to work out. It was run by a Black woman and had youth of different ethnic and racial backgrounds. However, even though it was run by a Black woman, a social worker overseeing Billy decided that he "was not getting the Black experience" by being in this group home. Billy and the other kids there went swimming and surfing in the Pacific Ocean, listened to rock music, and did other things not consistent, in this social worker's eyes, with Black heritage. So, even though for the first time in his life Billy fit into a placement and was doing well, the social worker had Billy transferred out. This began a series of unsuccessful placements, including with the uncle who raped him, and the making of a dangerous criminal. It is a good example of why you should not let your political beliefs govern your professional judgment.

Billy used his ability to manipulate others to get whatever he wanted. He was very skilled at it and would do such things as make trades with other prisoners and get what they had to give him but never come through on his part of the bargain. He also manipulated staff to give him what he wanted. He tried this with me by being very honest at times, seemingly against his self-interest. But this set me up to believe him at other times when he was lying to me. However, since he had been so honest with me in the past, it was, at first, hard to believe that he was lying to me now. He was just brilliant – creative, I would say – in knowing how to use others to get what he wanted. Once again, this was creativity – but used for the dark side, not in a helpful way to anyone except the person doing the manipulating.

TOMMY, YET ANOTHER GREAT MANIPULATOR

Tommy is White and the leader of the Whites in our prison, a committed member of the Skinhead gang. Skinheads are neo-Nazis, who hate Blacks, Jews, and homosexuals and are known for their love of violence. Our prisoners broke down into White, Black, and Hispanic gangs, and each one had a prisoner leader. While many attained leadership by being the toughest, baddest prisoner in their racial/ethnic group, Tommy attained leadership of the Whites in the prison by being a bit smarter and more creative than many of the other prisoners. He, too, had excellent manipulation skills.

The psychiatrist liked him a lot, although I was more wary of Tommy. However, on one occasion as I was bringing one of my therapy groups back from my office to the main part of the prison, where their rooms were, they all walked in a line, one behind another, as though a guard were marching them back. This was required of them by the guards: "Get in line!" I let them walk back however they wanted. I remarked to them how they were lined up as though they were being led by a guard, to which Tommy said to me, "You are always dogging us down, just like the guards."

I said, "Do you really believe that?"

Tommy put his arm around my shoulder and gave me a hug and said, "You're OK, Eisenman."

It made me feel good. He had lowered my self-esteem and then granted me a raise. So the emotional, un-thought-out feeling would be to like Tommy because he made me feel good. Athletic coaches often do this with their players – criticizing or yelling at them to diminish their self-esteem and then raising it again. The emotional reaction is often that the players learn to love the coach.

A report on Tommy said that he was a major burglar, having done many big-time burglaries in several states. He had seen this report and was very proud of what it said. It was as if a professor read that someone called him nationally famous in his field for his research. The prisoners identified with being criminals. Most of them did not want to reform or at least had no idea how you might do it. So, by choice or by default, they were criminals, and they set out to be better burglars, robbers, child molesters, killers, and so on.

In one of his burglaries, Tommy had stolen a massive amount of valuable silver, which was never recovered. He intended to get it once he got out of prison. After I left the prison and went back into academia, one of the guards started befriending Tommy and eating lunch with him. This was amazing behavior. It was never done. The prisoners were taken to a prison cafeteria, where they were assigned seats and fed while being watched by guards. Someone suggested to me that this guard wanted to get in good with Tommy so that he could get some of the silver after Tommy got out. Of course, from Tommy's perspective, it was good to have a guard so interested in him. Tommy might get special privileges out of it. Whether he ever intended to share the silver with the guard, I do not know.

So just as he got me to feel emotionally positive toward him by lowering my self-esteem and then putting his arm around my shoulder, he was able to get the guard to feel good toward him with the promise of silver to come later. And he was able to get his fellow White prisoners to like him by appearing to be a good leader of the Whites, seeming like a bright person by claiming, falsely, to have a high IQ and by telling everyone what they wanted to hear (or what they needed to hear to make them good followers). This is another instance of malevolent creativity, that is, using one's creative abilities for evil and selfish purposes.

Tommy maintained the fiction that he was bright. He said that four reports said that he had a genius IQ. He said this so much that one of the therapists believed him and wrote it in one of her reports. I had read these reports. There were not four reports; there was one report that was mentioned four times in Tommy's file. And this report did not say that he had a genius IQ but that he had an IQ of 106, which is very average. However, this made Tommy bright for his peer group, the prisoners. Most of them tested out with below-average IQ's, that is, below 100. I got the therapist to correct the report, taking out the stuff about four reports and the genius IQ.

Tommy knew when to avoid being exposed. He had not graduated from high school, and a therapist arranged for him to take the GED exam so that he would have a high school equivalency, which could help him to get jobs when he was released. However, Tommy kept promising to take the test but would not show up for it despite the therapist arranging it just for him. I think Tommy knew that if he took and failed the test, he would be exposed as being not so smart. Also, it is possible that he did not want to be anything other than a burglar, so he did not need to worry about getting a high school degree.

Tommy liked to fight, or play fight, even during group psychotherapy. I saw him do it a few times. He always "beat" the others, but they were Whites who were in his prison gang (not necessarily Skinheads), and they might have let him win. The next thing I have to say is amazing: He got me to fight, or play-fight, him one time. Had you asked me, I would have said I would never do such a thing with a prisoner; they are too aggressive, it is too dangerous, and besides, it does not fit with my job duties. But Tommy begged me to do it, just to mess around with him. He came across like a little brother asking his big brother to play with him. So I agreed. We started wrestling. I grabbed his body and slammed it, rather gently, I think, into the wall several times. He put both his hands on the top of my head and pushed down hard. I do not know what he was trying to achieve, but I thought he might badly twist my neck. So I said to him, "We had better stop. I know I am not going to hurt you, but I do not know about you. You might hurt me." Fortunately, he stopped.

CLOSING REMARKS

Although criminals are often rigid in noncriminal life and incapable of solving problems effectively, these case studies show that they frequently do things that are novel and highly effective – in other words, creative – in their area of specialization – crime. Such confinement of creativity to a specific area is consistent with research showing that creativity is often domain-specific and thus does not negate the idea that criminals can be creative. Gamman and Raein (Chapter 9 of this volume) showed how criminals design novel "products" that are sometimes highly effective (successful crimes). The case studies in this chapter illustrate a further facet of the creativity of criminals: creativity in interpersonal relations. This involves finding novel and effective ways to manipulate others into assisting them in illegal activity. Their methods sometimes resemble those of scientists testing hypotheses through ingenious "experiments."

The effectiveness of the novelty criminals generate is enhanced by the fact that law enforcement officers, prison guards, and other personnel, in effect, the direct opponents of the criminals, may not display similar creativity but may be rigid or highly conventional and unable to react flexibly to novel situations. This is due in part to the fact that they are bound by narrow and strictly defined operational rules because this is seen as the best way to render prisoners' creativity ineffective. However, the red light case study shows that lack of flexibility in dealing with novel circumstances makes personnel highly vulnerable to unexpected or never previously observed behavior. Prisoners also display the ability to reverse roles and to transfer known principles to new situations. The case study of the raising and lowering of a prison psychologist's self-esteem by a prisoner who assumed a role similar to that of, for instance, a football coach suggests that workers in the corrective system may be highly susceptible to such novel applications of known principles.

REFERENCES

Dixon, S. (2009). *Dallas officer delayed NFL player as relative died. Yahoo Sports*, March 27. Available at http://sports.yahoo.com/nfl/news?slug=ap-player-stopped&prov=ap&type=lgns.

Eisenman, R. (1991). *From crime to creativity: Psychological and social factors in deviance*. Dubuque, IA: Kendall/Hunt.

Eisenman, R. (1992). Creativity in prisoners: Conduct disorders and psychotics. *Creativity Research Journal*, 5, 175–181.

(1999). Creative prisoners: Do they exist? *Creativity Research Journal*, 12, 205–210.

Eisenman, R. (2007). *Creativity, mental illness and crime*. Dubuque, IA: Kendall/Hunt.

Kelly, D. H. & Clarke, E. J. (2003). *Deviant behavior: A text-reader in the sociology of deviance*. New York: Worth.

Lyons, C. & Martin, B. (2009). *Abnormal psychology: Clinical and scientific perspectives,* 3rd ed. Redding, CA: BVT Publishing.

Morgan, C. D. & Murray, H. A. (1935). A method for investigating phantasies: The Thematic Apperception Test. *Archives of Neurology and Psychiatry,* 34, 289–306.

Tewksbury, R. & Gagne, P. (Eds.). (2000). *Deviance and deviants: An anthology.* Los Angeles: Roxbury.

12

So You Want to Become a Creative Genius? You *Must* Be Crazy!

DEAN KEITH SIMONTON

Please allow me to begin this chapter with an autobiographical observation: I have been conducting scientific research on creativity and genius – and especially creative genius – since the early 1970s. During the first quarter century of my career, I was often hard pressed to justify my research program (Simonton, 2002). Although the subject had once attracted the attention of such great psychologists as Francis Galton, James McKeen Cattell, Lewis M. Terman, and Edward L. Thorndike, the topic had become marginalized relative to mainstream research in psychology. Toward the end of the twentieth century, though, an unexpected event altered the status of my endeavors: the positive psychology movement. Martin Seligman, Mihaly Csikszentmihalyi, and others argued that it was time for psychologists to study human strengths and virtues rather than human weaknesses and vices (for instance, Seligman & Csikszentmihalyi, 2000). Besides suggesting new topics for psychological inquiry, the proponents of positive psychology also decided to co-opt already ongoing investigations as representative of the movement. Somewhat to my surprise, creativity, genius, and creative genius were added to the growing inventory of representative subjects for positive psychological studies. As a result, I began to receive invitations to give talks at positive psychology conferences and to write chapters for handbooks and anthologies devoted to the emerging field (for instance, Cassandro & Simonton, 2002).

Now I probably should not complain about seeing my life's work get enhanced attention. And I certainly relished the free trips to conferences and the additional publications in my curriculum vitae. Even so, I could not help but feel a little discomfort. It was as if I were an avid soccer player who had been suddenly recruited to become a place kicker in American football. My discomfort only grew when I realized that most positive psychologists tended to exhibit a special kind of "positivity bias" (cf. Bacon,

2005): Good things were expected to go with good things. The great human beings were those who scored the highest on all the human strengths and virtues. In this respect, the positive psychologists were following in the footsteps of Abraham Maslow (1970), the humanistic psychologist who had no problem identifying creative geniuses whom he deemed self-actualizers with all sorts of superlative traits.

Yet this presumption of universal greatness was to me most implausible. I was all too familiar with the personal stories of many great creative geniuses who were far from constituting exemplars of mental health and benevolent vitality. Indeed, the position of the positive psychologists seemed to be diametrically opposed to the recurrent concept of the "mad genius." Of course, this idea could be considered no more than an urban legend with no scientific foundation. To be sure, many researchers have published extensive lists of creative geniuses who have suffered from one or another severe mental illness (for instance, Prentky, 1980; Simonton, 1994). Still, it must be recognized that such long inventories by themselves prove nothing (Simonton, 2009). Since the advent of civilization, thousands of creative geniuses have left their marks on the annals of history (Murray, 2003). Hence, even if such geniuses had lower-than-average rates of psychopathology, it still would be possible to compile a large number of exceptions who were not so lucky. Consequently, it is necessary to collect and analyze actual data.

It is the purpose of this chapter to show that there is some grain of truth to the notion that you must be at least a little crazy to be a creative genius. Creative geniuses may not be the kinds of folks you normally would want as lovers, friends, in-laws, coworkers, or neighbors. At the same time, the research also suggests certain significant qualifications on the apparent linkage between genius-grade creativity and psychopathology. Before we can look at this literature, however, I first have to define what I mean by "creativity," "genius," and "creative genius."

DEFINITIONS

As will become immediately obvious, the definitions of the three key constructs suggest that creative genius would not be expected to be associated with mental illness. To begin with, "creativity" is usually defined as a process or ability that generates ideas or products that are both (a) original, novel, or surprising and (b) adaptive, functional, or workable (Simonton, 2000a). The first criterion merely separates what is generated from the routine or mundane, whereas the second criterion distinguishes the outcome from what might be considered insane, eccentric, or impractical. Thus this second criterion would seem to rule out on a priori grounds alone any association between creativity and psychopathology. For example, if someone consistently produces ideas or behaviors that are original, novel, or surprising but just as consistently nonadaptive, dysfunctional, or unworkable, then we might be inclined to consider that person to be mentally ill.

Unlike creativity, which enjoys a single generic definition, "genius" can be defined in two rather distinct ways (Simonton, 2009):

1. The *psychometric* definition conceives genius according individual performance on an IQ test. This definition goes back to Terman's (1925–1959) *Genetic Studies of Genius*, which identified as "geniuses" children who scored 140 or above on the Stanford-Binet intelligence scale. This criterion has even made it into the English dictionary, where a genius is defined as "a person who has an exceptionally high intelligence quotient, typically above 140" (American Heritage, 1992). Although such a definition does not make any direct reference to the mad genius question, I must point out that general intelligence exhibits a positive association with mental health (e.g., Simonton & Song, 2009). This relation will be returned to later in this chapter.
2. The *historiometric* definition conceives genius according to overt achievement in some culturally valued domain of creativity or leadership. This definition dates from Galton's (1869) *Hereditary Genius*. In this classic work, Galton conceived of genius in terms of achieved eminence or reputation, which he defined as "the opinion of contemporaries, revised by posterity" that indicates that an individual is "a leader of opinion, … an originator, … a man to whom the world deliberately acknowledges itself largely indebted" (p. 37). Given that the world will hardly acknowledge indebtedness to someone who is outright insane, the historiometric definition also would seem to deny the possibility that genius might be mad.

Last but not least, I must define "creative genius." Presumably, this definition would entail nothing more than combining the definition of "creativity" with the definition of "genius." However, because the latter features two alternative definitions, it would seem that we could end up with two rival conceptions of creative genius. On the one hand, we could call anyone a creative genius who (a) generates original and adaptive ideas or products and (b) scores high on an IQ test. This would be the "high-IQ creative genius." On the other hand, we could identify someone as a creative genius who (a) generates original and adaptive ideas or products and

(b) achieves eminence for the ideas or products thus generated. In other words, according to the latter definition, the creativity actually must assert so much impact on others that the creator becomes someone "to whom the world deliberately acknowledges itself largely indebted." This would be the "high-achievement creative genius."

For three reasons, I find the second of these two definitions preferable. First, not all creators who have achieved eminence for their contributions can claim genius-level IQs (Simonton, 2009). As a result, the first definition would seem to exclude too many outstanding creators. As a case in point, the physicist who received a Nobel Prize for his discovery of the transistor, the fundamental unit of modern electronics, did not qualify as a genius according to the IQ 140 definition (Simonton, 2009). Second, the alternative definition does not depend on assessment by an instrument that is not universally accepted as an indicator of anything other than the ability to do well on IQ tests. For instance, the person with the highest recorded IQ, Marilyn Vos Savant, with a score of 228, has not a single creative achievement to her credit worthy of the ascription of "genius" (Simonton, 2009). Third and last, the second definition is more consistent with other archetypal definitions of genius. For example, Enlightenment philosopher Immanuel Kant (1952 [1790]) affirmed that genius must produce work that is both *original* and *exemplary*, where the latter signifies that the work provides models worthy of emulation and admiration. Kant's definition therefore integrates the definition of creativity with Galton's historiometric definition of genius. Note, too, that the second, more integrated definition seems to disallow the existence of a mad genius. It is extremely unlikely that either contemporaries or posterity would find anything exemplary in the "ravings of a maniac."

But let us now turn to facts of the matter. These facts come from three distinct sources: (a) historiometric studies based on the quantitative analysis of biographic data concerning historic creators, (b) psychiatric studies of high-achieving creators that take advantage of clinical diagnoses, and (c) psychometric studies of contemporary creators that depend on the application of established assessment methods. I begin with the pro-madness thesis, then discuss the con-madness antithesis, and close with what I hope to be the sanest synthesis.

THESIS: CREATIVE GENIUS IS CRAZY

We have just settled on a definition of "creative genius" that combines the definition of "creativity" with the historiometric definition of "genius."

Creative geniuses generate original and exemplary products that are emulated and admired by contemporaries and posterity. Nevertheless, nothing in this integrated definition would lead us to believe that such great creators must be crazy. If anything, the definitions imply quite the contrary. Creative genius should be negatively correlated with psychopathology of any kind. There hence arises a curious paradox, for the empirical research appears to suggest a *positive* correlation! Consider the following five findings:

First, according to historiometric research, the rate and intensity of symptoms are generally higher among eminent creators than in the larger population (Ellis, 1926; Ludwig, 1995; Raskin, 1936). Although the differential is contingent on the definitions used, a rough estimate is that creative geniuses are about twice as likely to experience some mental disorder relative to reasonable comparison groups (Ludwig, 1995). Depression appears to be the most frequent symptom, along with such correlates as suicide and alcoholism (Goertzel, Goertzel, & Goertzel, 1978; Ludwig, 1990; Post, 1996). Even so, bipolar disorders and schizophrenia are not uncommon. Psychiatric investigations also appear to discover a higher rate and intensity of symptoms among highly creative individuals (Andreasen & Canter, 1974; Jamison, 1989). Once more, depression, alcoholism, and suicide seem to be the most frequent symptoms, although bipolar disorder may have a creative advantage over purely depressive disorder (Santosa et al., 2007). Finally, the psychometric results are consistent with the previous two sets of findings. Highly creative individuals score above average on several personality measures related to some degree of psychopathology (Barron, 1963; Eysenck, 1995; see also Shapiro & Weisberg, 1999). For example, creators receive elevated scores on the clinical scales of the Minnesota Multiphasic Personality Inventory (MMPI; Barron, 1963) and higher psychoticism scores on the Eysenck Personality Questionnaire (EPQ; Eysenck, 1994, 1995; Götz & Götz, 1979a; Pearson, 1983). Likewise, creativity is positively associated with schizotypy, a personality disposition that represents a kind of "normal" version of schizophrenia (Batey & Furnham, 2008; Cox & Leon, 1999; Fisher et al., 2004; Folley & Park, 2005; Kinney, Richards, Lowing, LeBlanc, & Zimbalist, 2001; Rawlings & Locarnini, 2008; Schuldberg, 2005).

Second, historiometric research suggests that more is better. On average, the greater the magnitude of achieved eminence as a creator, the higher is the expected rate and intensity of psychopathology or at least psychological "unease" (Ko & Kim, 2008; Ludwig, 1995). The effect size is by no means large, but it is positive rather than negative (cf. Simonton & Song, 2009).

Likewise, psychometric investigations show that the greater the magnitude of creativity exhibited, the higher the scores tend to be on scales suggestive of psychopathologic symptoms (Barron, 1963; Götz & Götz, 1979a, 1979b; Rushton, 1990; but see Chávez-Eakle, del Carmen Lara, & Cruz-Fuentes, 2006). Yet higher than average scores on these scales are positively correlated with personal characteristics that would seem to facilitate creativity. For instance, elevated scores on psychoticism are associated with independence and nonconformity, features that lend support to innovative activities (Eysenck, 1995). In addition, elevated scores are linked with the ability to generate unusual associative connections between ideas (Eysenck, 1994; Woody & Claridge, 1977; see also Tsakanikos & Claridge, 2005). Lastly, elevated scores on psychoticism are associated with the capacity for defocused attention (e.g., reduced negative priming or latent inhibition), thereby enabling ideas to enter the mind that normally would be filtered out during information processing (Eysenck, 1995; see also Abraham & Windmann, 2008; Burch, Hemsley, Pavelis, & Corr, 2006). Not only is a less restrictive mode of information processing positively correlated with (a) the ability to solve insight problems (Karimi, Windmann, Güntürkün, & Abraham, 2007) and (b) actual creative achievement (Carson, Peterson, & Higgins, 2003), but it is also associated with openness to experience, a cognitive inclination that is positively associated with creativity (Peterson & Carson, 2000; Peterson, Smith, & Carson, 2002; see also Miller & Tal, 2007; Strong et al., 2007).

Third, according to historiometric inquiries, familial lineages that generate the creative geniuses also tend to manifest a higher rate and intensity of psychopathologic symptoms (Jamison, 1993; Juda, 1949; Karlson, 1970). That is, the pedigrees of genius overlap the pedigrees of madness. Psychiatric research also supports the conclusion that outstanding creativity and psychopathology may coincide in the same family lines (Andreasen, 1987; Kinney et al., 2001; McNeil, 1971; Richards, Kinney, Lunde, Benet, & Merzel, 1988; Simeonova, Chang, Strong, & Ketter, 2005; see also Myerson & Boyle, 1941). Finally, the psychometric variables associated with psychopathology, such as psychoticism, also feature sizable heritability coefficients (Bouchard, 2004; Keller, Coventry, Heath, & Martin, 2005). The heritabilities are certainly high enough to account for the overlapping pedigrees of creativity and psychopathology. Therefore, to some extent, we can say that creative genius is not only born but also born mad.

Fourth, we must acknowledge that creative genius must be a product of nurture as well as nature. It is made as well as born. Yet, here too we discover a connection between creativity and psychopathology. For example, eminently creative individuals are more likely to come from highly unstable homes in which they experienced any of a number of traumatic events (Goertzel et al., 1978; Goertzel & Goertzel, 1962). Particularly conspicuous is the early loss of one or both parents (Eisenstadt, 1978; Roe, 1953; Silverman, 1974; but see Ludwig, 1995; Woodward, 1974). Even if the future genius did not suffer partial or complete orphanhood, he or she might be exposed to economic ups and downs, cognitive or physical disabilities, and other early experiential uncertainties or obstacles (Simonton, 1987). Of course, to some undetermined degree, these environmental influences also may reflect underlying genetic factors. Parents with prominent psychopathology are less prone to provide stable and conventional home environments for their children (Simonton, 2009).

Fifth and last, it always must be kept in mind that the life of a genuine creative genius is not always easy. Breakthrough ideas and unprecedented innovations are not always received with acclaim. It is no accident that revolutionary scientists who endeavor to overthrow the dominant disciplinary paradigm display more psychopathology than those who attempt to confirm and maintain that paradigm (Ko & Kim, 2008). Indeed, the sheer act of creation can be a source of extreme stress. The Social Readjustment Rating Questionnaire assigns 28 stress points for any "outstanding personal achievement" (Holmes & Rahe, 1967). This is about the same score given to "change in responsibilities at work," a "son or daughter leaving home," "trouble with in-laws," "wife begins or stops work," "begin or end school," or "change in living conditions." Just imagine what points should be credited to Darwin's *Origin of Species*, Kant's *Critique of Pure Reason*, Tolstoy's *War and Peace*, or Verdi's *Otello*! Strangely, even the fame and fortune that come your way when you make it big with an acclaimed masterpiece can come back to haunt you! The creative genius too often can succumb to the increased attention by resorting to alcoholism, drug abuse, and even suicide (Schaller, 1997). Not all of us are prepared to live our lives in fish bowls surrounded by critics and perhaps even paparazzi.

Taken altogether, these historiometric, psychiatric, and psychometric results suggest that creative genius really must be crazy. The more a person moves from everyday ("little-c") creativity to exceptional ("big-C") creativity, the higher are the odds that the individual will endure substantial psychopathology.

ANTITHESIS: CREATIVE GENIUS IS SANE

By this point, most positive and humanistic psychologists might feel strongly obliged to lodge a protest. Haven't I overlooked equally relevant empirical data that indicate that creativity and psychopathology are antithetical? Because the answer is affirmative, it is now time to treat the following five counterarguments:

First and foremost, out-and-out madness terminates creative genius. No empirical data are required to prove this point. When geniuses commit suicide or die of a drug overdose, they cease to be creative. Even those who do not take the ultimate exit but still surrender to unreserved insanity discover that their creativity likewise will vanish. Not only do we have no examples of products both original and exemplary emerging from the totally insane, but psychometric and psychiatric research shows that extreme mental illness yields a state of mind devoid of any creative capacity (Chávez-Eakle, del Carmen Lara, & Cruz-Fuentes, 2006; Ghadirian, Gregoire, & Kosmidis, 2001; Rothenberg, 1983; Rubinstein, 2008). The psychometric research may show that highly creative individuals tend to exhibit elevated scores on certain variables indicative of psychopathology, but these scores are never high enough to indicate genuine mental illness. Instead, the scores lie somewhere between the normal and abnormal ranges (Barron, 1963; Eysenck, 1995). Someone scoring at the optimal level for psychoticism or schizotypy is neither a psychotic nor a schizophrenic (see also Schuldberg, 2001). For example, although successful creative writers score higher than normal individuals on most clinical scales of the MMPI, and highly creative writers score higher still, scores for both groups remain below those received by psychotic samples (Barron, 1963). At these moderate levels, the individual will possess traits that actually can be considered adaptive rather than maladaptive from the standpoint of creative behavior.

Second, not only will full-blown madness stop genius in its tracks, but also such insanity will prevent it from appearing in the first place. This is so because creativity in most domains requires the acquisition of appropriate domain-specific expertise. This necessity is most often expressed as the "10-year rule" (Ericsson, 1996). It usually takes a full decade of study and practice to master the knowledge and skills necessary for world-class creative contributions. Although creators will vary in the precise amount of time required for this apprentice period (Kaufman & Kaufman, 2007; Simonton, 1991, 2000b), they cannot circumvent it altogether. Yet it is difficult to imagine how domain-specific expertise acquisition can take place in an intellect constrained by severe mental illness or emotional instability. In support of this conjecture, a study of 282 historic geniuses found that achieved eminence was positively correlated with mental health in childhood and adolescence (Simonton & Song, 2009). Moreover, early mental health was also conducive to accelerated intellectual development.

Interestingly, of all domains of achievement, it was the poets, dramatists, and novelists who were most likely to suffer from mental illness in their early years. One can argue that imaginative literature relies less heavily on an apprentice period in comparison with, say, composition or painting. In fact, another historiometric investigation found that poets were the least likely to have any kind of special training (Simonton, 1986).

Third, the historiometric literature indicates the rate and intensity of adulthood symptoms vary according to the particular domain in which creative genius is expressed (Ludwig, 1992; Post, 1994). For instance, psychopathology is more conspicuous for artistic geniuses than for scientific geniuses (Post, 1994; Raskin, 1936). Hence Ludwig (1995) found that 87 percent of great poets suffered psychopathology some time during their lives, whereas only 28 percent of the great natural scientists did so, a proportion closer to the population baseline (cf. Martindale, 1972). In general, "persons in professions that require more logical, objective, and formal forms of expression tend be more emotionally stable than those in professions that require more intuitive, subjective, and emotive forms" (Ludwig, 1998, p. 93). This conclusion is also supported by research both psychiatric (Andreasen & Canter, 1974; Jamison, 1989) and psychometric (Feist, 1998; Nettle, 2006; Preti & Vellante, 2007; see also Burch, Pavelis, Hemsley, & Corr, 2006; Ivcevic, 2007; Rawlings & Locarnini, 2008). The genius-madness relation is moderated by creative domain, and in some instances, the relation can become negligible or even nonexistent. Incidentally, the same contrast between logical, objective, and formal versus intuitive, subjective, and emotional creativity affects the developmental contrasts across geniuses who contribute to different domains (Simonton, 2009). The former come from much more stable and conventional home and educational environments, whereas the latter grow up in more unstable and unconventional settings (e.g., Berry, 1981; Martindale, 1972; Raskin, 1936; Simonton, 1986; see also Schaefer & Anastasi, 1968).

Fourth, even in those creative domains that seem to most favor some psychopathologic symptoms, there still will appear creative geniuses who show no mental illness of any kind during their entire lifetime (Ludwig, 1995; Post, 1994). This apparent mental health was characteristic of 13 percent of the poets in Ludwig's (1995) historiometric study. For other fields, the percentage will be even higher still, such as the natural sciences, to wit, 82 percent. To be sure, some unknown number of "normal" creative geniuses actually may be "closet abnormals," exhibiting pathologic symptoms too minor to show up in biographies. Even so, the same may be said of the comparison population. An untold number of them lead superficially mundane lives while being plagued by sundry personal demons. So the main conclusion remains: Mental illness cannot be taken as essential to creative genius.

Fifth, psychometric studies have found that creative individuals score high on certain additional characteristics that would seem to dampen the effects of any psychopathologic symptoms. In particular, creators display high levels of ego strength and self-sufficiency (Barron, 1963; Cattell & Butcher, 1968). Accordingly, they can exert metacognitive control over their symptoms, taking advantage of bizarre thoughts rather than having the bizarre thoughts take advantage of them. Furthermore, the capacity to exploit unusual ideas is supported by general intelligence. Although intelligence is not strongly correlated with creativity in the upper levels of the intelligence distribution, a certain minimal level of intelligence is required for exceptional creativity (Simonton, 2004). That threshold level is in the gifted range, roughly equivalent to an IQ of 120 or above. Creators do not necessarily have genius-grade IQs, but they do have sufficient information-processing power to select, modify, elaborate, and refine original ideas into creative contributions. To be specific, high intelligence probably helps to turn reduced latent inhibition from a deficit to an asset (Carson et al., 2003; see also Guastello, Guastello, & Hanson, 2004, for a possible role for emotional intelligence).

Psychoanalyst Kris (1952) once discussed how artistic creativity depended on "regression in the service of the ego." Although regression into "primary process" imagery obviously can go too far, this danger is mitigated if a strong intellect is in charge of the fantastic meanderings. Martindale (1990) conducted some fascinating historiometric and experimental research showing how this "controlled regression" process operates in diverse forms of artistic creativity, especially in literature. These episodes should no more undermine sanity than our daydreams and dreams during sleep. As soon as we become more alert, we can recognize the fantasies for what they are while concomitantly preserving those rare tidbits that seem worth the telling.

SYNTHESIS: CREATIVE GENIUS IS ECCENTRIC

We saw that the definition of creativity seemed to preclude the possibility of a connection between that construct and mental illness. The two definitions of genius also seem to negate any linkage between the two; the psychometric definition does so empirically (viz., the positive correlation between intelligence and mental health), and the historiometric definition does so analytically (viz., insanity cannot produce anything exemplary). We then looked at the historiometric, psychiatric, and psychometric research that has come up with five reasons why genius-grade creativity might be linked with psychopathology, at least to some degree. Nonetheless, these results then were immediately contradicted by five sets of findings from the same methodologic sources that indicate the opposite. So what is the true answer? Is creative genius crazy or not?

I think that the answer is "Yes." Or rather, "No." Creative genius is both sane and insane. This may seem to itself constitute a totally mad response, but I do not think that it is possible to give any other.

On the one hand, it should be immediately apparent by now that creative geniuses are not your average Joes or Janes. Take the positive association between high-level creativity and psychoticism (Eysenck, 1995): People who score high on psychoticism are not just more creative than the norm but also more aggressive, cold, unempathetic, antisocial, impulsive, impersonal, egocentric, and tough-minded; even worse, they often engage in more "overinclusive" or "allusive" thinking that at times can border on the weird. Even scientists, who are supposedly the least pathologic of creators, are far from representing exemplars of goodness. On the contrary, highly eminent scientists tend to be (a) withdrawn, skeptical, internally preoccupied, precise, and critical as well as (b) introspective, restrained, brooding, and solemn of manner (Cattell, 1963). Do these traits define the personality profile of the ideal lover, friend, in-law, coworker, or neighbor? I very much doubt it!

On the other hand, highly creative individuals must have strong virtues that mitigate the impact of their vices. I have already mentioned the importance of high intelligence and ego strength. Creative geniuses typically possess the cognitive and meta-cognitive resources to keep any pathologic tendencies in check. To be sure, in those domains of achievement that require the most originality, such as expressive poetry, these checks will not always be sufficient, so the tendencies sometimes cross the threshold into mental illness. Even so, most domains impose considerably more constraints on the creative imagination (Simonton, 2009b). Because creativity must be more logical, objective, formal, and conventional, geniuses in these domains do not have the pressures to descend so deeply into intuitive, subjective, emotive, and unconventional modes of thinking that verge on madness. It is for this reason that geniuses in the natural sciences tend to be more mentally healthy than in the social sciences; geniuses in the social sciences, more so than those in the humanities; and geniuses in the humanities, more so than those in the arts (Ludwig, 1998; Simonton,

2009). Naturally, geniuses who attain the highest eminence within their domains may have a higher likelihood of dipping over into some psychopathology from time to time. As we have seen, scientists who reject the received paradigm are more likely to experience more mental illness in comparison with their more conservative colleagues (Ko & Kim, 2008). And such revolutionaries tend to become more famous as well (see also Sulloway, 2009).

So perhaps it might be best to say that creative geniuses are more eccentric than crazy. That is, the typical creative genius is a bit off center, where the center is defined as complete normalcy – being just like "normal" people. Geniuses in some domains of creativity are more off center than those in other domains. And the greater the magnitude of creative achievement within any given domain, the greater will be the expected degree of cognitive and emotional eccentricity. Only in extreme cases will the eccentricity become so great that the ego will start to teeter-totter and perhaps even tip over the edge. Nevertheless, most creative geniuses most of the time will display an eccentricity that strays noticeably away from normalcy while stopping just short of the utterly crazy.

I suppose that a positive psychologist might take the position that this conclusion is actually fairly optimistic. The vast majority of creative geniuses in most domains somehow manage to carry out this delicate balancing act without going off the deep end. Perhaps so. But it still seems to me that extremely few creative geniuses of the highest order – and especially those in the arts – could ever serve as pure exemplars of mental health. However original and exemplary Van Gogh's paintings may be, I would not wish his tormented soul on my worst enemy. Additionally, if we accept that the greatest creators are more psychologically eccentric than lesser creators, then it becomes clear that the correlation of creative genius with human strengths and virtues can be negative rather than positive. This is so because these eccentricities too often correspond to human weaknesses and vices. In a certain way, a psychology of genius-grade creativity must be a *negative* psychology. To give the world enduring masterpieces, creative geniuses had to sell their souls to the devil.

REFERENCES

Abraham, A. & Windmann, S. (2008). Selective information processing advantages in creative cognition as a function of schizotypy. *Creativity Research Journal*, 20, 1–6.

American Heritage. (1992). *American Heritage Electronic Dictionary*, 3rd ed. Boston: Houghton Mifflin.

Andreasen, N. C. (1987). Creativity and mental illness: Prevalence rates in writers and their first degree relatives. *American Journal of Psychiatry*, 144, 1288–1292.

Andreasen, N. C. & Canter, A. (1974). The creative writer: Psychiatric symptoms and family history. *Comprehensive Psychiatry*, 15, 123–131.

Bacon, S. F. (2005). Positive psychology's two cultures. *Review of General Psychology*, 9, 181–192.

Barron, F. X. (1963). *Creativity and psychological health: Origins of personal vitality and creative freedom*. Princeton, NJ: Van Nostrand.

Batey, M. & Furnham, A. (2008). The relationship between measures of creativity and schizotypy. *Personality and Individual Differences*, 45, 816–821.

Berry, C. (1981). The Nobel scientists and the origins of scientific achievement. *British Journal of Sociology*, 32, 381–391.

Bouchard, T. J., Jr. (2004). Genetic influence on human psychological traits: A survey. *Current Directions in Psychological Science*, 13, 148–151.

Burch, G. S. J., Hemsley, D. R., Pavelis, C., & Corr, P. J. (2006). Personality, creativity and latent inhibition. *European Journal of Personality*, 20, 107–122.

Burch, G. S. J., Pavelis, C., Hemsley, D. R., & Corr, P. J. (2006). Schizotypy and creativity in visual artists. *British Journal of Psychology*, 97, 177–190.

Carson, S., Peterson, J. B., & Higgins, D. M. (2003). Decreased latent inhibition is associated with increased creative achievement in high-functioning individuals. *Journal of Personality and Social Psychology*, 85, 499–506.

Cassandro, V. J. & Simonton, D. K. (2002). Creativity and genius. In C. L. M. Keyes and J. Haidt (Eds.), *Flourishing: Positive psychology and the life well-lived* (pp. 163–183). Washington: American Psychological Association.

Cattell, R. B. (1963). The personality and motivation of the researcher from measurements of contemporaries and from biography. In C. W. Taylor and F. Barron (Eds.), *Scientific creativity: Its recognition and development* (pp. 119–131). New York: Wiley.

Cattell, R. B. & Butcher, H. J. (1968). *The prediction of achievement and creativity.* Indianapolis: Bobbs-Merrill.

Chávez-Eakle, R. A., del Carmen Lara, M., & Cruz-Fuentes, C. (2006). Personality: A possible bridge between creativity and psychopathology? *Creativity Research Journal*, 18, 27–38.

Cox, A. J. & Leon, J. L. (1999). Negative schizotypal traits in the relation of creativity to psychopathology. *Creativity Research Journal*, 12, 25–36.

Ericsson, K. A. (1996). The acquisition of expert performance: An introduction to some of the issues. In K. A. Ericsson (Ed.), *The road to expert performance: Empirical evidence from the arts and sciences, sports, and games* (pp. 1–50). Mahwah, NJ: Erlbaum.

Eisenstadt, J. M. (1978). Parental loss and genius. *American Psychologist*, 33, 211–223.

Ellis, H. (1926). *A study of British genius.* Revised edition. Boston: Houghton Mifflin.

Eysenck, H. J. (1994). Creativity and personality: Word association, Origence, and Psychoticism. *Creativity Research Journal*, 7, 209–216.

(1995). *Genius: The natural history of creativity.* Cambridge, England: Cambridge University Press.

Feist, G. J. (1998). A meta-analysis of personality in scientific and artistic creativity. *Personality and Social Psychology Review*, 2, 290–309.
Fisher, J. E., Mohanty, A., Herrington, J. D., Koven, N. S., Miller, G. A., & Heller, W. (2004). Neuropsychological evidence for dimensional schizotypy: Implications for creativity and psychopathology. *Journal of Research in Personality*, 38, 24–31.
Folley, B. S. & Park, S. (2005). Verbal creativity and schizotypal personality in relation to prefrontal hemispheric laterality: A behavioral and near-infrared optical imaging study. *Schizophrenia Research*, 80, 271–282.
Galton, F. (1869). *Hereditary genius: An inquiry into its laws and consequences*. London: Macmillan.
Ghadirian, A.-M., Gregoire, P., & Kosmidis, H. (2001). Creativity and the evolution of psychopathologies. *Creativity Research Journal*, 13, 145–148.
Goertzel, M. G., Goertzel, V., & Goertzel, T. G. (1978). *300 eminent personalities: A psychosocial analysis of the famous*. San Francisco: Jossey-Bass.
Goertzel, V. & Goertzel, M. G. (1962). *Cradles of eminence*. Boston: Little, Brown.
Götz, K. O. & Götz, K. (1979a). Personality characteristics of professional artists. *Perceptual and Motor Skills*, 49, 327–334.
(1979b). Personality characteristics of successful artists. *Perceptual and Motor Skills*, 49, 919–924.
Guastello, S. J., Guastello, D. D., & Hanson, C. A. (2004). Creativity, mood disorders, ond emotional intelligence. *Journal of Creative Behavior*, 38, 260–281.
Holmes, T. S. & Rahe, R. H. (1967). The social readjustment rating scale. *Journal of Psychosomatic Research*, 11, 213–218.
Ivcevic, Z. (2007). Artistic and everyday creativity: An act-frequency approach. *Journal of Creative Behavior*, 41, 271–290.
Jamison, K. R. (1989). Mood disorders and patterns of creativity in British writers and artists. *Psychiatry*, 52, 125–134.
Jamison, K. R. (1993). *Touched with fire: Manic-depressive illness and the artistic temperament*. New York: Free Press.
Juda, A. (1949). The relationship between highest mental capacity and psychic abnormalities. *American Journal of Psychiatry*, 106, 296–307.
Kant, I. (1952/1790). The critique of judgement. In R. M. Hutchins (Ed.), *Great books of the Western world*, Vol. 42 (pp. 459–613). Chicago: Encyclopaedia Britannica. (Original work published 1790.)
Karimi, Z., Windmann, S., Güntürkün, O., & Abraham, A. (2007). Insight problem solving in individuals with high versus low schizotypy. *Journal of Research in Personality*, 41, 473–480.
Karlson, J. I. (1970). Genetic association of giftedness and creativity with schizophrenia. *Hereditas*, 66, 177–182.
Kaufman, S. B. & Kaufman, J. C. (2007). Ten years to expertise, many more to greatness: An investigation of modern writers. *Journal of Creative Behavior*, 41, 114–124.
Keller, M. C., Coventry, W. L., Heath, A. C., & Martin, N. (2005). Widespread evidence for non-additive genetic variation in Cloninger's and Eysenck's personality dimensions using a twin plus sibling design. *Behavior Genetics*, 35, 707–721.

Kinney, D. K., Richards, R., Lowing, P.A., LeBlanc, D., & Zimbalist, M. E. (2001). Creativity in offspring of schizophrenic and control parents: An adoption study. *Creativity Research Journal*, 13, 17–25.
Ko, Y. & Kim, J. (2008). Scientific geniuses' psychopathology as a moderator in the relation between creative contribution types and eminence. *Creativity Research Journal*, 20, 251–261.
Kris, E. (1952). *Psychoanalytic explorations in art*. New York: International Universities Press.
Ludwig, A. M. (1990). Alcohol input and creative output. *British Journal of Addiction*, 85, 953–963.
(1992). Creative achievement and psychopathology: Comparison among professions. *American Journal of Psychotherapy*, 46, 330–356.
(1995). *The price of greatness: Resolving the creativity and madness controversy*. New York: Guilford Press.
(1998). Method and madness in the arts and sciences. *Creativity Research Journal*, 11, 93–101.
Martindale, C. (1972). Father absence, psychopathology, and poetic eminence. *Psychological Reports*, 31, 843–847.
(1990). *The clockwork muse: The predictability of artistic styles*. New York: Basic Books.
Maslow, A. H. (1970). *Motivation and personality*, 2nd ed. New York: Harper & Row.
McNeil, T. F. (1971). Prebirth and postbirth influence on the relationship between creative ability and recorded mental illness. *Journal of Psychology*, 39, 391–406.
Miller, G. F. & Tal, I. R. (2007). Schizotypy versus openness and intelligence as predictors of creativity. *Schizophrenia Research*, 93, 317–324.
Murray, C. (2003). *Human accomplishment: The pursuit of excellence in the arts and sciences, 800 B.C. to 1950*. New York: HarperCollins.
Myerson, A. & Boyle, R. D. (1941). The incidence of manic-depression psychosis in certain socially important families: Preliminary report. *American Journal of Psychiatry*, 98, 11–21.
Nettle, D. (2006). Schizotypy and mental health amongst poets, visual artists, and mathematicians. *Journal of Research in Personality*, 40, 876–890.
Pearson, P. (1983). Personality characteristics of cartoonists. *Personality and Individual Differences*, 4, 227–228.
Peterson, J. B. & Carson, S. (2000). Latent inhibition and openness to experience in a high-achieving student population. *Personality and Individual Differences*, 28, 323–332.
Peterson, J. B., Smith, K. W., & Carson, S. (2002). Openness and extraversion are associated with reduced latent inhibition: Replication and commentary. *Personality and Individual Differences*, 33, 1137–1147.
Post, F. (1994). Creativity and psychopathology: A study of 291 world-famous men. *British Journal of Psychiatry*, 165, 22–34.
Post, F. (1996). Verbal creativity, depression and alcoholism: An investigation of one hundred American and British writers. *British Journal of Psychiatry*, 168, 545–555.

Prentky, R. A. (1980). *Creativity and psychopathology: A neurocognitive perspective*. New York: Praeger.

Preti, A. & Vellante, M. (2007). Creativity and psychopathology: Higher rates of psychosis proneness and nonright-handedness among creative artists compared to same age and gender peers. *Journal of Nervous and Mental Disease*, 195, 837–845.

Raskin, E. A. (1936). Comparison of scientific and literary ability: A biographical study of eminent scientists and men of letters of the nineteenth century. *Journal of Abnormal and Social Psychology*, 31, 20–35.

Rawlings, D. & Locarnini, A. (2008). Dimensional schizotypy, autism, and unusual word associations in artists and scientists. *Journal of Research in Personality*, 42, 465–471.

Richards, R., Kinney, D. K., Lunde, I., Benet, M., & Merzel, A. P. C. (1988). Creativity in manic-depressives, cyclothymes, their normal relatives, and control subjects. *Journal of Abnormal Psychology*, 97, 281–288.

Roe, A. (1953). *The making of a scientist*. New York: Dodd, Mead.

Rothenberg, A. (1983). Psychopathology and creative cognition: A comparison of hospitalized patients, Nobel laureates, and controls. *Archives of General Psychiatry*, 40, 937–942.

Rubinstein, G. (2008). Are schizophrenic patients necessarily creative? A comparative study between three groups of psychiatric inpatients. *Personality and Individual Differences*, 45, 806–810.

Santosa, C. M., Strong, C. M., Nowakowska, C., Wang, P. W., Rennicke, C. M., & Ketter, T. A. (2007). Enhanced creativity in bipolar disorder patients: A controlled study. *Journal of Affective Disorders*, 100, 31–39.

Schaefer, C. E. & Anastasi, A. (1968). A biographical inventory for identifying creativity in adolescent boys. *Journal of Applied Psychology*, 58, 42–48.

Schaller, M. (1997). The psychological consequences of fame: Three tests of the self-consciousness hypothesis. *Journal of Personality*, 65, 291–309.

Schuldberg, D. (2001). Six subclinical spectrum traits in normal creativity. *Creativity Research Journal*, 13, 5–16.

(2005). Eysenck personality questionnaire scales and paper-and-pencil tests related to creativity. *Psychological Reports*, 97, 180–182.

Seligman, M. E. P. & Csikszentmihalyi, M. (Eds.). (2000). Positive psychology [Special issue]. *American Psychologist*, 55.

Shapiro, P. J. & Weisberg, R. W. (1999). Creativity and bipolar diathesis: Common behavioural and cognitive components. *Cognition & Emotion*, 13, 741–762.

Silverman, S. M. (1974). Parental loss and scientists. *Science Studies*, 4, 259–264.

Simeonova, D. I., Chang, K. D., Strong, C., & Ketter, T. A. (2005). Creativity in familial bipolar disorder. *Journal of Psychiatric Research*, 39, 623–631.

Simonton, D. K. (1986). Biographical typicality, eminence, and achievement style. *Journal of Creative Behavior*, 20, 14–22.

(1987). Developmental antecedents of achieved eminence. *Annals of Child Development*, 5, 131–169.

(1991). Emergence and realization of genius: The lives and works of 120 classical composers. *Journal of Personality and Social Psychology*, 61, 829–840.

(1994). *Greatness: Who makes history and why*. New York: Guilford Press.

(2000a). Creativity: Cognitive, developmental, personal, and social aspects. *American Psychologist*, 55, 151–158.

(2000b). Creative development as acquired expertise: Theoretical issues and an empirical test. *Developmental Review*, 20, 283–318.

(2002). It's absolutely impossible? A longitudinal study of one psychologist's response to conventional naysayers. In R. J. Sternberg (Ed.), *Psychologists defying the crowd: Stories of those who battled the establishment and won* (pp. 238–254). Washington: American Psychological Association.

(2004). *Creativity in science: Chance, logic, genius, and zeitgeist*. Cambridge, England: Cambridge University Press.

(2009). *Genius 101*. New York: Springer.

(2009). Varieties of (scientific) creativity: A hierarchical model of disposition, development, and achievement. *Perspectives on Psychological Science*, 4, 441–452.

Simonton, D. K. & Song, A. V. (2009). Eminence, IQ, physical and mental health, and achievement domain: Cox's 282 geniuses revisited. *Psychological Science*, 20, 429–434.

Strong, C. M., Nowakowska, C., Santosa, C. M., Wang, P. W., Kraemer, H. C., & Ketter, T. A. (2007). Temperament-creativity relationships in mood disorder patients, healthy controls and highly creative individuals. *Journal of Affective Disorders*, 100, 41–48.

Sulloway, F. J. (2009). Sources of scientific innovation: A meta-analytic approach. *Perspectives on Psychological Science*, 4, 453–459.

Terman, L. M. (1925–1959). *Genetic studies of genius* (5 vols.). Stanford, CA: Stanford University Press.

Tsakanikos, E. & Claridge, G. (2005). More words, less words: Verbal fluency as a function of "positive" and "negative" schizotypy. *Personality and Individual Differences*, 39, 705–713.

Woodward, W. R. (1974). Scientific genius and loss of a parent. *Science Studies*, 4, 265–277.

Woody, E. & Claridge, G. (1977). Psychoticism and thinking. *British Journal of Social and Clinical Psychology*, 16, 241–248.

13

Both Sides of the Coin? Personality, Deviance, and Creative Behavior

LUIS DANIEL GASCÓN AND JAMES C. KAUFMAN

Rupert Holmes wrote in the musical *The Mystery of Edwin Drood* (1979), "Would you not quite feel quite the fool of deception/To find the same face on both sides of the coin?." To elaborate on this a bit, consider Hannibal Lecter's escape from prison in *Silence of the Lambs*. He attacks and kills two guards. Rather than trying to run, he puts on a guard's uniform, dumps the guard down an elevator shaft, and places the guard's removed face onto his own. The responding officers assume that Lecter is actually the guard and put him in an ambulance – from which he escapes. Lecter is not only evil; he is also amazingly creative. Are his deviant behavior and creativity linked together as common traits, the way that a talented novelist also may write interesting e-mails? Or are they distinct entities in the same manner that a talented novelist also may make excellent birdcalls, cook tasty hash browns, or run a marathon? The relationship between creativity and deviant behavior – with the common ground of personality – is the subject of this chapter.

Personality is an immensely complicated facet of human psychology that is affected by heredity, social ties, environmental factors, biology, and the list goes on. Personality, in turn, affects human behavior in a variety of ways. Keeping Lecter's creative maneuvering in mind, the important questions to consider are (a) Does personality cause deviant behavior? and (b) Can personality predict future likelihood of involvement in criminal behavior? Researchers have indicated that, to a moderate degree, yes, personality can be used to predict future deviant and antisocial behavior and is relatively stable across the life course (Gudjonsson & Sigurdsson, 2004; Mak, Heaven, & Rummery, 2003; Schaeffer, Petras, Ialongo, Poduska, & Kellam, 2003). Others, however, suggest that personality is fairly unstable in childhood, is malleable through adolescence and early adulthood (Baltes, Lindenberger, & Staudinger, 1998), and does not crystallize until roughly age 30 (McCrae & Costa, 1990). Developmental research suggests that some correlates of personality do begin to solidify in adolescence (Caspi, Roberts, & Shiner, 2005), but, as we will show, there is reason to believe that personality remains relatively unstable until adulthood. Those traits most associated with deviant behavior are also correlates of creative behavior. But is creative potential directly related to deviant behavior? This question is more complex. Certainly, creativity and deviance are linked, and one way to understand this linkage is to understand their emergence in personality.

Literature in psychology and criminology share a common understanding of the psychological and behavioral characteristics deviant and creative individuals share (see Agnew, Brezina, Wright, & Cullen, 2002; George & Zhou, 2002; Halpern, 2003; Lynam & Miller, 2001). Creativity literature has stipulated that creativity is not merely artistic expression but rather a departure from traditional expectations that accomplishes an intended goal, is unique, is modifiable or adaptable, and is carried out to completion (Cropley, Kaufman, & Cropley, 2008). Impulsivity can be used in a similar fashion, as a coping strategy to reduce stress potentially caused by negative affect (Zuckerman, 1994), ranging from risky sports to deviant behavior (Roberti, 2004). These impulses can be further exacerbated by the presence of what Yochelson and Samenow (1976) call "cognitive distortions," which can color perception and, in turn, instigate deviant behavior. Creativity, in its cognitive form, like deviance, also can be termed a "problem-solving strategy" that aims at addressing a specific problem using creative solutions.

Creativity throughout youth and adolescence – in school and within peer groups – can be considered deviant given specific contexts and is often misidentified as deviant behavior, leading to mislabeling creative youth as "deviant," especially in cases of problem behavior in school (Halpern, 2003) (see Chapter 16 in this work). The aim here is to understand the covarying expressions of creativity and deviance in behavior through personality. This chapter is uniquely geared toward bridging the gap between criminology and psychology, which is part of an already growing body of literature but has yet to adequately explore this covariance.

In this chapter we will address several key issues by answering the following questions: What is personality? How does personality vary across demographic characteristics? What is a creative personality? How can creativity be misunderstood as deviant behavior? Also outlined will be the cognitive processes leading to divergent, deviant, and creative outcomes and what demographic characteristics are important for determining the onset of creativity and criminality.

PERSONALITY AND ITS DETERMINANTS

Personality research has centered largely on the identification of "traits" that shape human behavior. Five overarching traits or "factors" have been identified, known as the "Big Five" (Goldberg, 1992). The "Big Five" are often highly correlated with their prescribed behavior, though contextual factors do play a key role in determining behavior (Roberts, 2007; Stryker, 2007). Researchers tracing personality across the life course have suggested that personality is not susceptible to "context-bound" psychological, social, or cultural factors. Baltes, Lindenberger, and Staudinger (1998) have suggested that people become less amenable to personality changes – caused by social interactions or life events – such that personality and temperament lose their elasticity and gain stability into the adult years. The five factors include

Openness (O), or variety in experience, curiosity, unique ideas, imagination, adventurousness, and appreciation for the arts.

Conscientiousness (C), which accounts for such behavior as diligence, being goal-oriented, self-discipline, and planned or methodical behavior (as opposed to spontaneous behavior).

Extroversion (E), representing surgency, positive emotionality, energy, and stimulus-seeking behavior.

Agreeableness (A) measures compassion and cooperation.

Neuroticism (N), manifesting as generally unpleasant emotionality, characterized by anger, anxiety, depression, and vulnerability.

Research surrounding the degree to which each of these personality traits is expressed in behavior has produced a significant amount of literature (Costa & McCrae, 1992).

Age

Much attention has been paid to the continuity and change of personality traits as they relate to age. Temperament is a key component in the determination of personality and is thought to be innate. It is considered to be genetically determined and, along with facets of the individual character, constitutes personality (Rothbart, Ahadi, & Evans, 2000). Temperament is expressed in early life and is indicative of personality in adulthood (Romero, Luengo, & Sobral, 2001). This does not suggest, however, that personality in adulthood is an exact reflection of temperament in infancy. In fact, in infancy, temperament is relatively unstable (Lemery, Goldsmith,

Klinnert, & Mrazek, 1999). Only modest associations between temperament in infancy and personality in early adulthood are reported (Fraley, 1998), although temperament was found to predict later life outcomes, such as late marriage, downward mobility, and health-risk behavior in young adulthood (Caspi, Elder, & Herbener, 1990; Caspi et al., 1997). Certain types of psychopathology proved most consistent in terms of associations with later expressions of personality, as well as impulsivity, which was predictive of deviant behavior in adolescence (Kagan & Zentner, 1996). In addition to mental illness, factors such as educational performance, birth order, early parental loss, marginality, and the availability of role models can have a significant impact on antisocial behavior, personality disorders, creativity, and the degree of deviant behavior expressed throughout youth and adolescence (Simonton, 2000).

It is no secret that deviant behavior tends to peak from late childhood to middle adolescence and then begins to decrease in late adolescence to early adulthood. This peak at middle adolescence is where the divide between adolescent-limited and life-course persistence begins to form (Moffitt, 1993). The adolescent years mark a period of intense change; deviance, risk-taking, depression, and familial infighting surface more frequently in this period of development than in others (McCrae et al., 2002). Still, how can we account for the significant drop in deviant behavior after adolescence?

It may not be difficult to predict which personality traits are most likely to change and which are most likely to remain constant over the life course. Many researchers focus on changes across the life course (McCrae et al., 2000; Roberts, Walton, & Viechtbauer, 2006), and yet others focus on changes experienced during the more turbulent teenage period (McCrae et al., 2002; Roberts, Caspi, & Moffit, 2001). McCrae and colleagues (2000) found that across subjects, high-school-age youth exhibited modest declines in neuroticism (N), extroversion (E), and openness (O) and increases in agreeableness (A) and conscientiousness (C). Temperament was found to be particularly important in determining personality changes from childhood into adulthood. Robins, Trzesniewski, Tracy, Gosling, and Potter (2002) found that between the ages of 9 and 13 years, youth exhibited a steep decline in self-esteem. Romero, Luengo, and Sobral (2001) found that E was strongly related with deviant behavior among youth between the ages of 14 and 19 years; this trait was the most reliable predictor of antisocial behavior in the longitudinal analysis. The authors of this work assessed the participants twice over a two-year period among high school students, college attendees, and incarcerated boys and found that several elements of impulsivity were important for determining antisocial and deviant behavior among those in the sample.

Gender

The gender-delinquency debate is one of those topics that historically has garnered a considerable amount of attention. This literature has fairly recently begun to adopt the understanding that offending processes are similar among males and females, but rather it is the manner in which they are experienced and, in turn, expressed that differs (Piquero, Gover, MacDonald, & Piquero, 2005). Cauffman (2008) found that female deviance was consistently correlated with higher incidents of mental illness among offenders, which was not as pronounced among males. Twenty years ago, the amount of deviance among males was four times that of females. This gap is narrowing, however. Today, figures indicate that males offend only twice as much (Carrington, 2006; Cauffman, 2008).

In a study of a high school population, McCrae and colleagues (2000) found that both males and females decreased in those traits most associated with deviance – both N and E, in particular (Romero et al., 2001). Throughout this same period, researchers found that both males and females increased in levels of A and C, which indicates increases in responsibility and rule-abiding development. Overall, this period was marked by decreases in the traits associated with impulsivity and risk-taking behavior. One interesting finding to note, though, is the change in O, which is most associated with creativity. This trait, although decreasing along with N and E, did not follow as clear a pattern as the other traits.

In a longitudinal study including participants from 12 to 18 years of age, McCrae and colleagues (2002) found that N increased for females and O increased for both males and females. In the period from 12 to 16 years of age, though, O was the only trait that exhibited a measurable change, increasing among 43.5 percent of the population.

Some researchers have noted the importance of environmental factors in shaping personality throughout the various changes exhibited across the life course. In this case, family is the determining factor. In particular, skills, values, identity, and attitudes develop under environmental conditions, which then shape personality outcomes and, in turn, behavior (McCrae et al., 2000).

Family

Finn and colleagues (2001) studied 601 families and found that the effects of parental psychiatric disorders (e.g., depression and substance abuse), supportive parent-child communications, and household income contributed to personality pathways, which are associated with risky behavior (sensation-seeking behavior and social-deviance proneness). Thus overall family problems increased the likelihood that youth would become involved in deviant behavior. Having fewer than two supportive parents generally increased risk for deviant behavior, but this effect appeared stronger for boys than for girls. When combined with a parent with a mental disorder, the effects grew markedly, especially for girls, regardless of family income level. Even when those familial influences – including family risk factors such as instability, inconsistency, mental illness in parents, and alcoholism – were associated with deviance, female deviance proved to be markedly lower than males on average. Only when females were exposed to increased levels of deviant behavior via family history – history of mental illness and low parental support – did females approach males in the level of their deviance.[1]

Some researchers suggest that personality is influenced primarily by social environment, in particular, family life (Schaeffer et al., 2003), whereas others suggest that environment is often confused with parenting style, which has little do with environmental conditions (Johnson, Su, Gerstein, Shin, & Hoffman 1995). Of the two, parenting style is a more valid measure, given its concreteness, than family life, which does not lend itself so easily to assessment (Johnson et al., 1995). Personality research focused on the hereditary and biological origins of personality has found linkages between parent and child personality inside and outside the shared family environment. Measurements of family influence on child personality have found strong relationships. Digman (1980) found that child-rearing practices proved to be only marginally determinant of child personality traits. These reports have found that parenting style possibly could be confused or conflated with heredity, which may prove problematic in determining the source of the actual influence. McCrae and colleagues (2000) suggested that life experiences have little or no measurable effects on personality traits (Baltes et al., 1998). But are personality traits always the same or are

[1] The researchers found that family-based risk had a stronger influence on deviant behavior exhibited by youth at ages 13 to 14 years than among those aged 11 to 12 years (Finn et al., 2001).

they situational? Other researchers suggest that environment may play a big role or at least an interactive role with personality (e.g., see Caspi & Moffitt, 1991, 1993; Fleeson, 2004; Magnusson & Endler, 1977). Indeed, some studies show that the heritability of personality lies somewhere between 40 and 60 percent (Floderus-Myrhed, Pederson, & Rasmussen, 1980).

CREATIVITY AND DEVIANCE

Most research- and theory-based definitions of "creativity" boil down to two components. First, creativity must represent something different, new, or innovative. But it is not enough to just be different – creativity must also be appropriate to the task at hand. A creative response also must be useful and relevant (Kaufman, 2009). A number of studies have found increased levels of the trait O, above all other personality traits, among creative individuals (e.g., Dollinger, Urban, & James, 2004; Eysenck, 1993; Feist, 1998; McCrae, 1987). Eysenck (1993) distinguishes between creativity as an artistic style, which involves intelligence, and creativity as a personality trait. It is the latter that will be the focus here. Dollinger, Urban, and James (2004) found that among creative individuals (artists, painters, etc.), O was correlated with all measures of creativity, which supports the idea that creative individuals tend to rely on their imagination and unique ideas throughout the creative process, which involves generating unique solutions whereby the person approaches a particular dilemma from several unexpected or normally unseen angles. This amounts to thinking "around" rather than directly through a problem. People who do not employ creative solutions often stay within perceived parameters, hindering the generation of novel or path-breaking solutions. But this idea may be somewhat ambiguous. By thinking "around" a problem, creative individuals (assessed as having a high degree of O as a personality trait) employ a creative cognitive process when generating solutions. So, when confronted with a problem, whether it be a math problem or attempting to escape from jail, like Lecter, the individual generates creative solutions, solutions that exhibit some unique quality; that is, (a) they are relevant and achieve a specific goal, (b) they are new and original, (c) they are elegant (meaning that the product is fully worked out or well engineered), and (d) they are generalizable and adaptable. The latter, though, relates more to creative products and not so much to creativity as a process for the generation of solutions, although they are related.

When thinking about creativity and its connection to deviant behavior, though, we should identity just what exactly is creative about deviant behavior. It would be incorrect to suggest that all creative behavior is deviant, just as it is incorrect to suggest that all deviant behavior is creative. The judgment of creative/deviant acts is based not on whether the acts or products are right or wrong but rather on whether they fit the preceding criteria. Law serves the former purpose. Nonetheless, deviant behavior is a form of creative self-expression. Cropley et al. (2008) call this concept "malevolent creativity," distinguishing it from "benevolent" forms of creativity in the intended purpose. Such behavior is the product of a creative problem-solving process, and personality is the mechanism through which it is expressed. Although artworks may be creative, given that they are crafted employing innovative processes, the cognitive problem-solving process itself *is* creative. This is known as "creative adaptation," which is characterized by flexibility in thought and reflexivity and transformation of a person's environment (Meneely & Portillo, 2005).

Problem Solving

There are few things that distinguish routine problem solving (as a cognitive process) and creative problem solving. Still, the cognitive process involved in generating solutions is a normative one (Sternberg, 1999). There is nothing fanciful about the creative process. Although there is some disagreement (for instance, Bransford & Stein, 1984; Getzels & Csikszentmihalyi, 1976), sagacious creative thinkers are most productive when they employ solution-driven thinking for specific problems (Lubart 1994). Lubart (1994) suggests that there are four different ways that creativity can become part of the normal problem-solving process. Problem solving generally involves defining a problem, accessing relevant information, building a solution from that information, and evaluating and refining the proposed solution. Lubart (1994) breaks up each creative problem-solving technique into types. Type I involves the creative person performing one or more of the proposed steps more effectively than average. For instance, Hannibal Lecter, in planning his escape, had to be exceedingly methodical given the strictness of his incarceration. So, waiting for the most opportune moment, Lecter takes a pen and waits until food is brought into his cell, where the guard is attacked and killed. Certainly, Lecter's ability to craft a solution with limited time and resources is performed more effectively than normal. The amount of time spent on any one step or the number of times each step is performed significantly increases the creativity of problem-solving solutions as well. This process makes up type II. Lecter's incarceration undoubtedly afforded him a great deal of time to calculate, look for opportunities, craft and reformulate his escape plan over and over again, amounting to a very creative escape. Type III involves performing steps in a different sequence, which can either increase or limit creativity. Preoccupation with the evaluative process, for instance, can hamper idea production. Finally, type IV involves introducing a wholly different stage to the process that most people would not think to employ. For instance, this may involve enacting a divergent thinking activity that aids in creative idea generation. Lubart (1994), in addition to describing creative steps that add to an already existing problem-solving process, also outlines a four-stage creative process that, although it has similar elements, is meant to specifically generate creative solutions.

This process first involves preparation of a solution: problem analysis, information and material gathering, and initial working of a solution. Incubation follows this step. By actively processing the information, allowing ideas to "play" (employ ideational fluency), and taking time to ruminate, you are able to generate creative solutions more easily. Following incubation is the illumination stage. Without thinking of illumination as a process where the person is mystically struck by an idea, this process involves ideas coming into the conscious as cohering cognitive patterns. And finally, the creative person verifies the ideas generated by this process. If solutions are found to be unworkable, they return to earlier steps to reformulate their solutions (Lubart 1994). The key elements of this creative problem-solving process are those involving divergent and bisociative thinking (synthesizing or bringing together several arenas of thought) (Koestler, 1964). Let us explore these further.

Creative brains allow in a greater degree of incoming stimuli from the immediate surroundings (Peterson & Carson, 2000). This is the "musing" creative people undergo. "Latent inhibition" (LI), as it is known, is a cognitive mechanism that inhibits the perception of a considerable amount of stimuli in normal people. The trait openness (O), as discussed earlier, is associated with LI as well as divergent and creative thinking (McCrae, 1987). The latter trait is essentially the behavioral equivalent of LI. When employing cognitive problem-solving techniques, people with reduced LI are able to relate completely unrelated ideas, activating bisociative thinking (Amabile, 1983; Koestler 1964) that produces creative outcomes; the more unrelated they are, the more creative they are (Mednick, 1962). LI is related to both O and extroversion (E) (Peterson, Smith, & Carson, 2002) – the lower the levels of LI, the greater is the association. Peterson, Smith, and Carson (2002) found that reduced LI in highly intelligent individuals is correlated with higher levels of creativity. They suggest that intelligence may be used as a mechanism to handle the many different stimuli that a person with low levels of LI may be forced to encounter – intelligence may serve as a coping device, so to speak. A further possibility is that perhaps higher intelligence allows better management of potentially dangerous impulses. It seems that having reduced LI can be both a positive and a negative variable. What, then, are other implications of having low levels of LI?

Psychopathy, much like LI, also allows for "overinclusive thinking" (Burch, Hemsley, Pavelis, & Philip, 2006). But, whereas LI is characterized by the perception of normally undetectable stimuli, psychopathic people, in addition, are known for having no remorse and being shallow and manipulative, as well as egocentric (Miller, Lynam, & Leukfeld, 2003). Further, psychopathy is specifically associated with deviant behavior – drug use, deviance, aggression, and risky sexual activity (Miller et al., 2003) – which is not necessarily true of LI. Studies show that creativity correlates with some elements of psychopathy (Eysenck, 1993, 1995; Jamison, 1993; Ludwig, 1995), again owing to the presence of overinclusive thinking among both creative people and psychopaths caused by a weakened inhibitory device (Burch et al., 2006), although this association is not exclusive. Indeed, most creative people do not suffer from mental illness (Simonton, 2000). Whether considering psychopathy or low levels of LI, both facilitate fluency in thought and ideation, which, in turn, stimulates the "creative juices."

As discussed earlier, when "ideational fluency" is employed, the creative person is able to generate a variety of unconventional and original solutions (Wallach, 1985). The productive process can be broken up into two types of ideas: convergent and divergent ideas (Guilford, 1956). If you employ convergent thinking, you are simply trying to find the correct answer. But divergent thinking is used to produce numerous solutions. Although ideational fluency and divergent thinking are important for the creative process, they are not the same (Chan et al., 2001). Ideational fluency is involved in the cognitive problem-solving process (Eysenck, 1993). Without a steady flow of possible solutions, the creative process would be stifled. Ideational fluency is what gives creative solutions their breadth. But divergent thinking as a broader concept is the key to generating creative solutions (Glover, Bruning, & Plake, 1982).

Creativity and Mood

Another debate is whether being in a bad mood (officially known as "negative affect") will stimulate creativity. Some studies have found results that support this connection. A few have found that positive mood inhibits creative performance (see Kaufman, 2003, for a review), whereas other studies have found that negative mood either has no effect (for instance, Grawitch, Munz, & Kramer, 2003) on creativity or can enhance creative performance. Kaufmann and Vosburg (2002) looked at positive and negative mood in creative problem solving. Interestingly, they found that a positive mood led to better scores in early stages of idea production (similar to past findings, most recently Gasper, 2004). But a negative mood led to better scores in later stages. George and Zhou (2002) found that negative moods were related to higher levels of creativity (as measured by supervisor ratings) when rewards and recognition for creative work were salient.

An equally large body of research, however, has found that positive emotions and a good mood can have beneficial influences on creative performance. Several researchers, many of the projects led by Alice Isen (Estrada, Isen, & Young, 1994; Isen, Daubman, & Nowicki, 1987; Isen, Johnson, Mertz, & Robinson, 1985; Isen, Labroo, & Durlach, 2004; Montgomery, Hodges, & Kaufman, 2004), have conducted a series of studies in which they induced good mood in participants (typically through watching a comedic movie or receiving a small gift of candy) and then measured innovation/creativity (typically through problem-solving tasks or verbal creativity measures). People in good moods tend to show higher creativity than those in neutral or negative moods.

Similarly, Lynton and Salovey (1997) found that students in a good mood wrote better – constructed fiction and nonfiction – than students in a bad mood; unfortunately, they were unable to get reliable ratings for the creativity of the pieces. Schere (1998) found that both writers and artists showed improved mood after being creative within their own domain (there was no effect when writers created art or artists wrote).

Still other studies have found no relationship. Verhaeghen, Joormann, and Khan (2005) found that rumination served as a mediating variable between depression and creativity in college undergraduates. Self-reflective rumination was connected to both creative interests and behavior and depression – yet being in a current depressed mood was not associated with creativity. Consistent with their findings is Forgeard's (2008) finding that writers with unipolar depression were more likely to use words associated with cognitive thought (such as "know" or "understand") than either bipolar writers or the control group.

One criticism of this research could be that in nearly all studies, mood was induced. In other words, the moods were triggered by being asked to remember a happy or sad memory or being shown a funny or upsetting scene from a movie. Yet, typically, people experience moods based on their own thoughts, emotions, or spontaneously occurring life events. Amabile, Barsade, Mueller, and Staw (2005) studied the relationship between creativity and mood in organizational employees working on potentially creative products. They used the electronic event-sampling methodology based on earlier work by Csikszentmihalyi and Larson (1987), in which participants were e-mailed daily questionnaires about the day's events. These narratives then were coded for both affective and creative thought. In addition, the creative performances of these employees were rated by their peers on a monthly basis. Amabile et al. (2005) found significant results across their multiple measures that creative performance (self and peer evaluated) was positively related to being in a good mood. There was no relationship between creative performance and being in a bad mood.

Hirt, Levine, McDonald, Melton, and Martin (1997) argued for a hedonic contingency theory explanation for the positive mood-creativity relationship. People in a happy mood want to maintain their happy mood and are careful to behave in a way to stay happy. People in a sad mood, however, are not so careful because most activities are likely to improve their mood (Wegener & Petty, 2001). Therefore, people in a happy mood, when faced with a divergent thinking-type task, try to make the task as much fun and as enjoyable as possible by being more creative. Hirt, Devers, and McCrea (2008) manipulated people's beliefs in whether or not their moods could be changed. People typically believe moods are changeable, which makes sense. If you are generally in a good mood and someone kicks you in the shin or makes fun of your hair, you typically get into a bad mood. Indeed, with no manipulation, people generally were more creative if they were in a good mood. However, when people were convinced that their moods could be frozen, Hirt and colleagues found no connection between mood and creativity.

Related to a positive or negative mood is the idea of stress and anxiety. Several studies (Carlsson, 2002; Eysenck, 1995) have found that higher stress and anxiety are related to lower creativity. Carson and Runco (1999) found that students with better coping skills were more likely to be better creative problem solvers.

Criminal Thinking

As discussed earlier, is a significant portion of the academic literature dedicated to elucidating the cognitive process involved in creative problem solving. Similarly, there is a large of body of work that focuses on the cognitive process involved in "criminal" behavior. Specifically, we are referring to the work, most notably, of Yochelson and Samenow (1976) and Walters (1990). These authors viewed deviant behavior as the product of faulty logic by way of clouded judgment called "distorted thinking patterns." Yochelson and Samenow felt that deviant behavior resulted from flawed assumptions and decisions based on these distorted thinking patterns. Specifically, they outlined 52 "thinking errors" that lead to criminal behavior that are "mental processes required by the criminal to live his [or her] kind of life. They are 'errors' solely from the standpoint of society, and not from that of the criminal. For him [or her] these thinking patterns are indispensible to achieve objectives" (Yochelson & Samenow, 1976, p. 359) and lie along a continuum. Indeed, "they constitute his [or her] very fabric" (Yochelson & Samenow, 1976, p. 251).

Adding to this literature, Walters (1990), in his own work on the "criminal lifestyle," felt that deviance was influenced by several "person and situation" conditions. Basically, personal makeup (e.g., age, level of intelligence, emotional temperament) and social characteristics (e.g., social class, drug use, family relationships, intake of media violence) could significantly influence a person's likelihood of engaging in deviant behavior based on a combination of the preceding characteristics, which influence the person's perception of a given situation, creating a belief system that justifies criminal behavior and is reinforced by each inciting occasion (Walters, 1990). The "ABC's of human emotion," developed by Ellis (1962), illustrate how this process works. Creative responses start with an *A*ctivating event, leading to a specific *B*elief about how to react, which results in a *C*onsequent emotion. The more a person faces situations where he or she feels, given his or her distorted thinking, that deviant behavior is the only outlet or solution, the more conducive this behavior becomes for future deviance. In Walters's estimation, a specific attitude toward an event encourages behavior rather than the event itself. Thus it becomes a self-supporting system of criminality, contributing to its persistence and creating a criminal lifestyle – a lifestyle based on distorted thinking. "The lifestyle criminal finds the immediate gratification of crime more reinforcing than the long-term stability of conventional life" (Walters, 1990, p. 109). In addition to distorted thinking patterns, much like negative mood, stress can play a role in determining a person's likelihood of engaging in deviant acts that employ creative techniques.

Strain

Stress is a sign that change is needed. Change, or adaptation, works to alleviate the sensation of stress. For the immensely stressed, creative expression is an important coping strategy (Torrance, 1965). Sensitivity to stressors facilitates creative problem-solving strategies. As mentioned earlier, creative responses are typical reactions to negative affect (George & Zhou, 2002). This process follows Ellis' "ABC's," also discussed earlier.

From this perspective, the line between deviant and creative behavior is blurred. Both negate or contradict established modes of thought and behavior (Bower, 1999). A well-researched theory in criminology, namely, "strain theory," indicates that rational choice is not involved in the commission of crimes or the engagement in deviant behavior. Rather, when committing crimes, the impulse results from strain (Agnew, 2006), which, in this case, can be understood as stress. Much like stress, behavior resulting from strain is an attempt to reduce the sensation of strain. Although crime and deviant behavior are uncommon reactions to strain (Agnew, Brezina, Wright, & Cullen, 2002), it is important to understand how people are propelled toward deviant behavior as a result. Ultimately, personality determines whether or not people are likely to pursue deviant behavior as a strategy for coping with strain. People with increased levels of neuroticism (N) are most likely to perceive events as stressful. As a result, the person feels angry or upset and can respond in a deviant or antisocial manner (Agnew et al., 2002). People who feel strained are most likely to engage in deviant behavior when several conditions are present. If a person feels that he or she cannot employ legal or constructive outlets, if the costs of the deviant behavior seem low, if the person has a favorable disposition toward deviant behavior, if the person has low levels of self-restraint, or if the person is impulsive, he or she is more likely to become deviant (Agnew et al., 2002). Impulsivity, Agnew et al. (2002) highlight, is critical for determining how people will react to stress, strain, and negative moods. Impulsive people commonly exhibit several of the preceding factors that contribute to criminal responses to strain.

Impulsivity

"Impulsivity" (also known as "sensation-seeking behavior") is "defined by the seeking of varied, novel, complex, and intense sensations and experiences, and the willingness to take physical, social, legal, and financial risks for the sake of such experience" (Zuckerman, 1994, p. 27). Sensation seekers often become involved in risky behavior as a result of their disregard for consequences. Alcohol use, risky sexual behavior, gambling, and high-risk sports are just a few of these behaviors (Roberti, 2004). These impulsive behaviors at times can act as a coping strategy for stress (Agnew,

2006). Impulsive people are drawn toward social situations, peer groups, and individuals whose stimulus-seeking behavior parallels their own. This acts to reinforce their impulsive behavior, which is especially true of substance use (Roberti, 2004). High-risk situations and environments seem nonthreatening to sensation seekers. They often downplay risk and consequence and typically cannot discern between right and wrong (Roberti, 2004; Zuckerman, 1994). Thus, to them, there appear to be no negative consequences (Lynam & Miller, 2004).

The preference for increased stimuli essentially influences reactions and activities that favor deviant behavior. Impulsive behavior allows people to channel their need for stimulation (Farley, 1973). This is especially true in environments where socially acceptable methods for attaining stimuli are in short supply (Agnew et al., 2002). When exacerbated by stressors, impulsive people frequently respond with negative moods (i.e., depression, anger, or anxiety) (Lynam & Miller, 2004).

CONCLUSION

Whether the discussion focuses on children in school or criminal geniuses such as Hannibal Lecter, the point at which personality, deviance, and creativity meet is one that has been evaluated in both psychological and criminological literature for some time. Their converging elements, however, have not been expressly explored to any significant degree. We believe that this lack of research is unfortunate given their implications. Some may not immediately see the pertinence of looking for creativity in deviant acts or vice versa, but understanding this may shape the way we as an academic community approach creative and deviant people conceptually. Creativity throughout youth and adolescence – in school and within peer groups – is considered deviant given specific contexts. It is often misidentified as deviant behavior, leading to mislabeling creative youth as deviant, especially in cases of problem behavior in school (Halpern, 2003). This area of research may offer a deeper understanding of the psychological mechanisms that drive and propel behavior by understanding the covarying expressions of creativity and deviance in behavior through the personality. Whether it is through personality or through the expression of creativity in problem solving, we should appreciate the complexity of deviant behavior not for its criminal implications but for its quality as a creative adaptation to a person's environment that may be stressful or inhibitive of positive emotionality. This approach to understanding youth, personality, and cognition undoubtedly will open up new lines of psychological inquiry for the evaluation, clinical assessment, and treatment of people whose behavior challenges the conventions of conduct.

REFERENCES

Agnew, R. (2006). *Pressured into crime: An overview of general strain.* Los Angeles: Roxbury Press.

Agnew, R., Brezina, T., Wright, J., & Cullen, F. (2002). Strain, personality traits, and delinquency: Extending general strain theory. *Criminology*, 40, 43–71.

Amabile, T. M. (1983). *The social psychology of creativity.* New York: Springer-Verlag.

Amabile, T., Barsade, S., Mueller, J., & Staw, B. (2005). Affect and creativity at work. *Administrative Science Quarterly*, 50, 367–403.

Baltes, P., Lindenberger, U., & Staudinger, U. (1998). Life-span theory in developmental psychology. In W. Damon and R. M. Lerner (Eds.), *Handbook of child psychology*, 5th ed., Vol. 1 (pp. 1029 –1143). New York: Wiley.

Bower, R. (1999). Dangerous minds: Eminently creative people who have spent time in jail. *Creativity Research Journal*, 12, 3–13.

Bransford, J. D. & Stein, B. (1984). *The ideal problem solver: A guide for improving thinking, learning, and creativity.* New York: Freeman.

Burch, G., Hemsley, D., Pavelis, C., & Philip, C. (2006). Personality, creativity and latent inhibition. *European Journal of Personality*, 20, 107–122.

Carlsson, I. (2002). Anxiety and flexibility of defense related to high or low creativity. *Creativity Research Journal*, 14, 341–349.

Carrington, K. (2006). Does feminism spoil girls? Explanations for the official rises in female delinquency. *Australian and New Zealand Journal of Criminology*, 39, 34–53.

Carson, D. & Runco, M. (1999). Creative problem solving and problem finding in young adults: Interconnections with stress, hassles, and coping abilities. *The Journal of Creative Behavior*, 33, 167–190.

Caspi, A., & Moffitt, T. (1991). Individual differences are accentuated during periods of social change: The sample case of girls at puberty. *Journal of Personality and Social Psychology*, 61, 157–168.

Caspi, A. & Moffitt, T. (1993). When do individual differences matter? A paradoxical theory of personality coherence. *Psychological Inquiry*, 4, 247–271.

Caspi, A., Elder, G., & Herbener, E. (1990). Childhood personality and the prediction of life-course patterns. In L. N. Robins and M. Rutter (Eds.), *Straight and devious pathways from childhood to adulthood* (pp. 13–35). New York: Cambridge University Press.

Caspi, A., Begg, D., Dickson, N., Harrington, H., Langley, J., Moffitt, T., & Silva, P. (1997). Personality differences predict health-risk behaviors in young adulthood: Evidence from a longitudinal study. *Journal of Personality and Social Psychology*, 73, 1052–1063.

Caspi, A., Roberts, B., & Shiner, R. (2005). Personality development: Stability and change. *Annual Review of Psychology*, 56, 453–484.

Cauffman, E. (2008). Understanding the female offender. *Future of Children*, 18, 119–142.

Chan, D., Cheung, P-C., Lau, S., Wu, W., Kwong, J., and Li, W-L. (2001). Assessing ideational fluency in primary students in Hong Kong. *Creativity Research Journal*, 13, 359–365.

Costa, P. & McCrae, R. (1992). *Revised NEO personality inventory (NEO–PI–R) and NEO five-factor inventory (NEO–FFI) professional manual.* Odessa, FL: Psychological Assessment Resources.

Cropley, D. H., Kaufman, J. C., & Cropley, A. J. (2008). Malevolent creativity: A functional model of creativity in terrorism and crime. *Creativity Research Journal*, 20, 105–115.

Csikzentmihalyi, M. & Larson, R. W. (1987). Validity and reliability of the experience-sampling method. *Journal of Nervous and Mental Disease*, 175, 526–536.

Digman, J. (1980). Personality structure: Emergence of the five-factor model. *Annual Review of Psychology*, 41, 417–440.

Dollinger, S., Urban, K., & James, T. (2004). Creativity and openness: Further validation of two creative product measures. *Creativity Research Journal*, 16, 35–47.

Ellis, A. (1962). *Reason and emotion in psychotherapy.* Seacaucus, NJ: Lyle Stuart.

Estrada, C., Isen, A., & Young, M. (1994). Positive affect improves creative problem solving and influences reported source of practice satisfaction in physicians. *Motivation and Emotion*, 18, 285–299.

Eysenck, H. J. (1993). Creativity and personality: Suggestions for a theory. *Psychological Inquiry*, 4, 147–178.

(1995). *Genius: The natural history of creativity.* Cambridge: Cambridge University Press.

Farley, F. (1973). *A theory of delinquency.* Presented at the Annual Meeting of the American Psychological Association, Montreal, Canada.

Feist, G. (1998). A meta-analysis of personality in scientific and artistic creativity. *Personality and Social Psychology Review*, 2, 290–309.

Fleeson, W. (2004). Moving personality beyond the person-situation debate: The challege and the opportunity of within-person variability. *Current Directions in Psychological Science*, 13(2), 83–87.

Floderus-Myrhed, B., Pederson, N., & Rasmussen, I. (1980). Assessment of heritability for personality based on a short form of Eysenck Personality Inventory: A study of 12,898 twin pairs. *Behavior Genetics*, 10, 153–162.

Finn, P., Sharkansky, E., Brandt, K., & Turcotte, N. (2000). The effects of familial risk, personality, and expectancies on alcohol use and abuse. *Journal of Abnormal Psychology*, 109, 122–133.

Forgeard, M. (2008). Linguistic styles of eminent writers suffering from unipolar and bipolar mood disorder. *Creativity Research Journal*, 20, 81–92.

Fraley, C. (1998). Algorithms for model-based Gaussian hierarchical clustering. *Journal of Scientific Computing*, 20, 270–281.

Gasper, K. (2004). Permission to seek freely? The effect of happy and sad moods on generating old and new ideas. *Creativity Research Journal*, 16, 215–229.

George, J. & Zhou, J. (2002). Understanding when bad moods foster creativity and good ones don't. *Journal of Applied Psychology*, 87, 687–697.

Getzels, J. W. & Csikszentmihalyi, M. (1976). *The creative vision: A longitudinal study of problem-finding in art.* New York: Wiley-Interscience.

Glover, J., Bruning, R., & Plake, B. (1982). Distinctiveness of encoding and recall of text materials. *Journal of Educational Psychology*, 74, 522–534.

Goldberg, L. (1992). The development of markers for the big-five factor structure. *Psychological Assessment*, 4, 26–42.

Grawitch, M., Munz, D., & Kramer, T. (2003). Effects of member mood states on creative performance in temporary workgroups. *Group Dynamics: Theory, Research, and Practice*, 7, 41–54.

Gudjonsson, G. & Sigurdsson, F. (2004). Motivation for offending and personality. *Legal and Criminological Psychology*, 9, 69–81.

Guilford, J. P. (1956). The structure of intellect. *Psychological Bulletin*, 53, 267–293.

Halpern, D. (2003). *Thought and knowledge: An introduction to critical thinking*, 4th ed. Mahwah, NJ: Lawrence Erlbaum Associates.

Hirt, E., Devers, E., & McCrea, S. (2008). I want to be creative: Exploring the role of hedonic contingency theory in the positive mood-cognitive flexibility link. *Journal of Personality and Social Psychology*, 94, 214–230.

Hirt, E., Levine, G., McDonald, H., Melton, J., & Martin, L. (1997). The role of mood in quantitative and qualitative aspects of performance: Single or multiple mechanisms? *Journal of Experimental Social Psychology*, 33, 602–629.

Isen, A., Labroo, A., & Durlach, P. (2004). An influence of product and brand name on positive affect: Implicit and explicit measures. *Motivation and Emotion*, 28, 43–63.

Isen, A., Daubman, K., & Nowicki, G. (1987). Positive affect facilitates creative problem solving. *Journal of Personality and Social Psychology*, 52, 1122–1131.

Isen, A., Johnson, M., Mertz, E., & Robinson, G. (1985). The influence of positive affect on the unusualness of word associations. *Journal of Personality and Social Psychology*, 48, 1413–1426.

Jamison, K. R. (1993). *Touched with fire*. New York: Free Press.

Johnson, R., Su, S., Gerstein, D., Shin, H., & Hoffman, J. (1995). Parental influences on deviant behavior in early adolescence: A logistic response analysis of age- and gender-differentiated effects. *Journal of Quantitative Criminology*, 11, 167–193.

Kagan, J. & Zentner, M. (1996). Early childhood predictors of adult psychopathology. *Harvard Review of Psychiatry*, 3, 341–350.

Kaufman, J. C. (2003). The cost of the muse: Poets die young. *Death Studies*, 27, 813– 822.

(2009). *Creativity 101*. New York: Springer.

Kaufmann, G. & Vosburg, S. (2002). The effects of mood on early and late idea production. *Creativity Research Journal*, 14, 317–330.

Koestler, A. (1964). *The act of creation*. New York: Macmillan.

Lemery, K., Goldsmith, H., Klinnert, M., & Mrazek, D. (1999). Developmental models of infant and childhood temperament. *Developmental Psychology*, 35, 189–204.

Lubart, T. (1994). Creativity. In Robert Sternberg (Ed.), *Thinking and problem solving: Handbook of perception and cognition*, 2nd ed. New Haven, CT: Academic Press.

Ludwig, A. M. (1995). *The price of greatness: Resolving the creativity and madness controversy*. New York: Guilford Press.

Lynam, D. & Miller, J. (2001). Structural models of personality and their relation to antisocial behavior: A meta-analysis review. *Criminology*, 39, 765–798.

Lynam, D. & Miller, J. (2004). Personality pathways to impulsive behavior and their relations to deviance: Results from three samples. *Journal of Quantitative Criminology*, 20, 319–341.

Lynton, H. & Salovey, P. (1997). The effects of mood and expository writing. *Imagination, Cognition, and Personality*, 17, 95–110.

Magnusson, D. & Endler, N. S. (Eds.). (1977). *Personality at the crossroads: Current issues in interactional psychology*. Hillsdale, NJ: Erlbaum.

Mak, A., Heaven, P., & Rummery, A. (2003). The role of group identity and personality domains as indicators of self-reported delinquency. *Psychology, Crime & Law*, 9, 9–18.

McCrae, R. (1987). Creativity, divergent thinking, and openness to experience. *Journal of Personality and Social Psychology*, 52, 1258.

McCrae, R. & Costa, P. (1990). *Personality in adulthood*. New York: Guilford Press.

McCrae, R., Costa, P., Ostendorf, F., Angleitner, A., Hrebickova, M., Avia, M., et al. (2000). Nature over nurture: Temperament, personality, and life span development. *Journal of Personality and Social Psychology*, 78, 173–186.

McCrae, R., Costa, P., Terracciano, A., Parker, W., Mills, C., De Fruyt, F., *et al.* (2002). Personality trait development from age 12 to age 18: Longitudinal, cross-sectional, and cross-cultural analyses. *Journal of Personality and Social Psychology*, 83, 1456–1468.

Mednick, S. (1962). The associative basis of the creative process. *Psychological Review*, 69, 220–232.

Meneely, J. & Portillo, M. (2005). The adaptable mind in design: Relating personality, cognitive style, and creative performance. *Creativity Research Journal*, 17, 155–166.

Miller, J., Lynam, D., & Leukfeld, C. (2003). Examining antisocial behavior through the lens of the five factor model of personality. *Aggressive Behavior*, 29, 497–514.

Montgomery, D., Hodges, P., & Kaufman, J. (2004). An exploratory study of the relationship between mood states and creativity self-perceptions. *Creativity Research Journal*, 16, 341–344.

Peterson, J. B. & Carson, S. (2000). Latent inhibition and openness to experience in a high-achieving student population. *Personality and Individual Differences*, 28, 323–332.

Peterson, J., Smith, K., & Carson, S. (2002). Openness and extraversion are associated with reduced latent inhibition: Replication and commentary. *Personality and Individual Differences*, 33, 1137–1147.

Piquero, N., Gover, A., MacDonald, J., & Piquero, A. (2005). The influence of delinquent peers on delinquency: Does gender matter? *Youth Society*, 36, 251–275.

Roberti, J. (2004). A review of behavioral and biological correlates of sensation seeking. *Journal of Research in Personality*, 38, 256–279.

Robins, R., Trzesniewski, K., Tracy, J., Gosling, S., & Potter, J. (2002). Self-esteem across the lifespan. *Psychology and Aging*, 17, 423–434.

Romero, E., Luengo, M., & Sobral, J. (2001). Personality and antisocial behaviour: study of temperamental dimensions. *Personality and Individual Differences*, 31, 329–348.

Rothbart, M., Ahadi, S., & Evans, D. (2000). Temperament and personality: Origins and outcomes. *Journal of Personality and Social Psychology*, 78, 122–135.

Schaeffer, C., Petras, H., Ialongo, N., Poduska, J., & Kellam, S. (2003). Modeling growth in boys' aggressive behavior across elementary school: Links to later criminal involvement, conduct disorder, and antisocial personality disorder. *Developmental Psychology*, 39, 1020–1035.

Schere, J. J. (1998). *Effect of engaging in creative activity on the mood of artists and writers: An empirical test of flow theory.* PhD thesis, California School of Professional Psychology.

Simonton, D. (2000). Creativity: Cognitive, personal, developmental and social aspects. *American Psychologist*, 55, 151–158.

Sternberg, R. (1999). *Handbook of creativity.* Cambridge, England: Cambridge University Press.

Torrance, E. (1965). *Constructive behavior: Stress, personality, and mental health.* Belmont, CA: Wadsworth Publishing.

Verhaeghen, P., Joorman, J., & Khan, R. (2005). Why we sing the blues: The relation between self-reflective rumination, mood and creativity. *Emotion*, 5, 226–232.

Wallach, M. (1985). Creativity testing and giftedness. In F. D. Horowitz and M. O'Brien (Eds.), *The gifted and talented: Developmental perspectives* (pp. 99–123). Washington: American Psychological Association.

Walters, G. (1990). *The criminal lifestyle: Patterns of serious criminal conduct.* Newbury Park, CA: Sage.

Wegener, D. & Petty, R. (2001). *Theories of mood and cognition: A user's handbook.* Mahwah, NJ: Lawrence Erlbaum Associates.

Yochelson, S. & Samenow, S. (1976). *The criminal personality, Vol. 1: A profile for change.* New York: Jason Aronson.

Zuckerman, M. (1994). *Behavioral expressions and biosocial bases of sensation seeking.* New York: Cambridge Press.

14

Neurosis: The Dark Side of Emotional Creativity

JAMES R. AVERILL AND ELMA P. NUNLEY

The term "neurosis" was introduced in 1769 by Scottish physician William Cullen to refer to presumed nervous disorders in the absence of discernible neurologic defects. It gained wide currency during the first half of the twentieth century largely through the influence of Freud. Today, "neurosis" is no longer used as a technical term primarily because it is too broad for diagnostic and treatment purposes. Nevertheless, it is still used widely as a generic term for a wide range of disorders of primarily psychological origin. Carl Jung (1965) observed that frequently "people become neurotic when they content themselves with inadequate or wrong answers to the questions of life" (p. 140). This observation provides a good preliminary definition of neurosis. However, an important qualification is needed: Even more fundamental than contentment with inadequate or wrong answers are misdirected strivings for solutions. With this qualification in mind, we can ask: What kind of life questions lead to neurosis? And in what ways are neurotic answers inadequate or wrong? This chapter addresses these questions. Briefly stated, the kinds of life questions that occasion neuroses are those which (a) lead to emotional responses and (b) call for creative solutions. Neurosis results when an emotionally creative response miscarries.

REFLECTIONS ON THREE EARLY WORKS

Elsewhere (e.g., Averill, 1999; 2005; Averill & Nunley, 1992; Nunley & Averill, 1996) we have provided empirical support for emotional creativity, including laboratory research and clinical examples of emotional creativity gone awry. Here we take a different tack. Einstein once remarked that "originality is forgetting one's sources." This is perhaps more true in the social sciences than in Einstein's own field of theoretical physics. Generally, when a social scientist is convinced that he or she has something original to say about the human condition, a few hours in a good library will demonstrate differently. We therefore begin with three earlier authors who presented ideas central to the topic of creativity and neurosis, namely, Fyodor Dostoevsky (1821–1881), William James (1842–1910), and Otto Rank (1884–1939). For brevity, we focus on one work by each author: *Notes from Underground* (Dostoevsky, 1961 [1864]), *Varieties of Religious Experience* (James, 1961 [1902]), and *Art and Artist* (Rank, 1932).

Dostoevsky's *Notes from Underground*

Oatley (1999) has suggested that literature is a way of simulating emotions on the human brain. If Oatley's metaphor applies anywhere, it applies to the works of Dostoevsky, one of the giants of Russian literature.

"I am a sick man ... a mean man. There is nothing attractive about me. I think there is something wrong with my liver" (ellipses in the original). This is how Dostoevsky's "antihero" begins his *Notes from Underground.* "Underground" here means, in literal translation, "under the floorboards," where mice often dwell. The Underground Man compares himself to a mouse – but not just any mouse. The Underground Man believes that he "is guilty of being more intelligent than all those around me" (p. 95). One manifestation of this intelligence is a "heightened consciousness" or self-awareness that, paradoxically, makes him so subdued that he becomes more like a mouse than a man.

> Of course, the only thing left for it [the man as mouse] to do is to shrug its puny shoulders and affecting a scornful smile, scurry off ignominiously to its mousehole. And there, in its repulsive, evil smelling nest, the downtrodden, ridiculed mouse plunges into a cold, poisonous, and – most important – never-ending hatred. (Dostoevsky, 1961 [1864], p. 97)

Notes from Underground was written as Dostoevsky's wife lay dying in an adjacent room and as he was under financial pressure to meet a deadline for publication. It is a short work, but in it, Dostoevsky adumbrates many of the themes found in his later, more familiar novels. It is also of theoretical substance, often compared with works of Nietzsche and Kierkegaard.

In an introductory footnote Dostoevsky emphasized that the *Notes* are fiction but that people like the Underground Man "may, and indeed must, exist in our society." In a letter to his brother, he also asserted that the *Notes* would "be a forceful and candid thing; it will be the truth" (quoted by Mochulsky, 1967, p. 244). Dostoevsky clearly believed that the Underground Man represented an important aspect of human nature. And what is it about human nature that so concerned Dostoevsky? In the words of the Underground Man, "man is a creative animal, doomed to strive consciously toward a goal, engaged in full-time engineering, as it were, busy building himself roads that lead *somewhere – never mind where*.... The main thing is not *where* it goes but keeping the well-meaning babe at his engineering chores, thus saving him from the deadly snares of idleness" (p. 116, italics in original).[1]

Idleness or boredom may be a threat humans will do anything, no matter how crazy or unreasonable, to avoid. As is often the case, however, the real craziness comes not in the original threat but in the manner of avoidance. Escape from idleness can take two general forms: communion with others, as in friendship and love, and the pursuit of self-interest, which promotes independence and individuality. Dostoevsky saw life as a constant struggle between these two conflicting tendencies.

On several occasions, the Underground Man tried to make himself fall in love, even suffering "jealousy, violence, and all the trimming." Down deep, however, he did not believe his tribulations were real, and he felt like laughing. More fundamental than communion with others, the Underground Man asserted, is "our most important, most treasured possession: our individuality" (p. 113). Typically, when the Underground Man felt attracted to a person, he turned spiteful, and the more intense the attraction, the greater the spite. Not unexpectedly, others became spiteful to him in return. In this, he found a perverse pleasure. He would even have found pleasure, he claimed, in his face being slapped.

On one interpretation, it might seem that the Underground Man was simply masochistic, finding pleasure in humiliation and enjoyment in love's tribulations. But that would be too glib an interpretation. Recall Dostoevsky's observation that "man is a creative animal, doomed to strive consciously toward a goal." The operative word here is "consciously." By consciousness, Dostoevsky meant self-awareness – the ability to assess one's own experiences as they occur. On the stage or in the movies, people often find pleasure witnessing events that would be distasteful in real life. Through self-reflection, the Underground Man was witness to his own degradation. His "pleasure of despair" might best be interpreted not as a

[1] One might wonder to what extent the *Notes from Underground* is autobiographical. Perhaps the best that can be said is that the piece reflects in exaggerated form one side of Dostoevsky's character. One biographer (Steinberg, 1966) has described him as "constantly in a state of anxiety, tormented by everlasting fears, he consciously rejected all temptations of a quiet life with others and like others, and very early on withdrew into himself" (p. 9).

sign of masochism but as a misguided aesthetic experience – an example of emotional creativity gone awry.

William James's *Variety of Religious Experiences*

"When a person has an inborn genius for certain emotions, his life differs strangely from that of ordinary people, for none of their usual deterrents check him" (James, 1961 [1902], p. 215). Something similar could be said of genius in any field. But how does the life of an emotional genius differ from that of ordinary people? Is the difference always for the better? And what are the "deterrents" that check the emotions of ordinary people? We have seen intimations of answers to these questions in Dostoevsky's *Notes from Underground*. Dostoevsky was an emotional as well as literary genius, and his life – at least as exemplified by the Underground Man – did indeed differ strangely from that of ordinary people. The Underground Man, however, faced the dark side of emotional creativity.

At one time James also faced the dark side. As a young man, he aspired to be an artist and studied with the painter William Morris Hunt. Although not without talent, he decided (assisted by subterfuge from his father) that his future lay elsewhere. After further educational experiences in the United States and Europe, he received an MD degree in 1869 from Harvard University. Shortly thereafter, he fell into a depression marked by self-loathing, suicidal thoughts, and dreadful forebodings. The "sickness" lasted off and on for several years. In the *Varieties*, James described an episode from this period, which he ascribed, however, to an anonymous French writer. One evening at twilight, he related, "suddenly there fell upon me a horrible fear of my own existence.... Simultaneously there arose in my mind the image of a black-haired youth with greenish skin ... looking absolutely non-human." Terrified lest he become like that image, James "became a mass of quivering fear" (p. 138).

James' melancholy eventually subsided, in part through an act of will. On April 30, 1870, he made the following entry in his diary, referring to an episode similar to the one above but perhaps more mild:

> I think that yesterday was a crisis in my life. I finished the first part of Renouvier's second "Essais" and see no reason why his definition of Free Will – "the sustaining of a thought *because I choose to* when I might have other thoughts" – need be the definition of an illusion. At any rate, I will assume for the present – until next year – that it is no illusion. My first act of free will shall be to believe in free will. (McDermott, 1967, p. 7)

Of course, a person cannot simply will himself or herself out of a depressed state, at least not all at once. But James came to believe that "Such evil as this [melancholy] is curable, in principle at least upon the natural plane, for merely by modifying, either the self or the things, or both at once, the two terms may be made to fit, and all go merry as a marriage bell again" (p. 119). Put differently, a person can choose to change, often in small increments, one's circumstances, one's attitudes toward those circumstances, or both.[2]

When the change is for the better, and other criteria (to be discussed shortly) are met, we can speak of "emotional creativity." Creativity does not come easy, in the emotional any more than in other domain. Preparation is necessary, often accompanied by struggle and conflict. Then, outside conscious awareness, a period of incubation may follow. Finally, resolution of the problem may be achieved – the familiar "Eureka!" phenomenon. James described one such episode, which involved the struggles of a young man who suddenly gave up his religious faith on hearing a seemingly innocuous remark from his brother:

> How small an additional stimulus will overthrow the mind into a new state of equilibrium when the process of preparation and incubation has proceeded far enough. It is like the proverbial last straw added to the camel's burden, or that touch of a needle which makes the salt in a supersaturated fluid suddenly begin to crystalize out. [James, 1961 (1902), p. 151, ft 8]

Such sudden radical changes are not limited to religious experiences. "Falling in love also conforms frequently to this type," James observed, "a latent process of unconscious preparation often preceding a sudden awaking to the fact that the mischief is irretrievably done" (p. 152). People often feel "overcome" by emotion, but the feeling is in part illusion. Emotional transformations do not just happen, unbidden, any more than scientific or artistic insights just happen.

Shortly we will have more to say about emotional transformations, both creative and neurotic. For the moment, let us return to James' bout with melancholy that he resolved, in part, through an act of will or choice. For some people, whom James termed "healthy-minded," salutary choices in

[2] We are not here concerned with the hoary debate about free will. We make choices every day, from the trivial (e.g., what to have for lunch) to the meaningful (e.g., whom to marry), and such choices have consequences. This undeniable fact suffices for our purposes. Whether our choices are themselves "free" depends on how "freedom" is interpreted, an issue clearly beyond the scope of this chapter (see Dennett, 2003).

the face of adversity seem to come naturally. The healthy-minded person simply has "a constitutional incapacity for prolonged suffering" (p. 114). In the view of less benighted individuals, whom James labeled "sick souls," healthy-mindedness may seem "unspeakably blind and shallow." Conversely, to the healthy-minded, "the way of the sick soul seems unmanly and diseased … with their grubbing in rat holes instead of living in the light" (p. 140). Although unintended, this last is an apt description of Dostoevsky's Underground Man.

Biographies are seldom written about people who are, by temperament or good fortune, spared suffering. But healthy-mindedness does not have to be shallow. To illustrate, James cited the poet Walt Whitman as among the healthy-minded. Whitman felt a keen affinity for other people, derived great pleasures from the simple beauties of nature, and was unshakably optimistic. However, he did not live a life without struggle or conflict: "Do I contradict myself?" he asked in concluding his "Song of Myself," "Very well then I contradict myself (I contain multitudes.)" [Whitman, 1965 (1855), p. 88]. Few people are completely healthy-minded or completely sick-minded; most of us are full of contradictions but without the talents and resourcefulness of Whitman.

One source of self-contradiction is the conflicting desires for independence from and yet identification with others. We saw how this conflict was manifested in the neurotic behavior of Dostoevsky's Underground Man. James did not discuss the conflict in such dramatic terms, but its ramifications are evident in much that he wrote – and in his personal life.

Gale (1999) distinguishes between the "Promethean" James and the "mystical" James. The Promethean James prized his independence and extolled challenge and risk over comfort and safety; by contrast, the mystical James sought communion and harmony through self-surrender. Even more than Whitman's self, James' self contained multitudes.

Otto Rank's *Art and Artist*

Although not as well known as Dostoevsky and James, Otto Rank has been described as "artist, poet, psychotherapist, philosopher, mythologist, and educator" (Barbre, 1996). We include him here because he, more than anyone else, has explored the relation between creativity and neurosis, especially as related to the conflict between independence and communion.

In 1905, at the age of 21, with only a trade-school education, Rank sent Freud a manuscript, later published as *Der Künstler* (*The Artist*, Rank, 1907). In it, Rank attempted to explain artistic creativity using psychoanalytic principles. Freud was sufficiently impressed that he supported Rank's entry to the University of Vienna; there Rank received a Ph.D. in 1912 with a dissertation on the Lohengrin Saga. While at the university, Rank served as secretary of the Vienna Psychoanalytic Society, a post from which he was forced to resign in 1924 owing to theoretical disagreements with Freud. Rank subsequently moved to Paris and then New York, where he included among his clients and associates many artists and writers (two of the better known being Anaïs Nin and Henry Miller). An analysis of creativity remained a lifelong passion, culminating in his comprehensive *Art and Artist* (Rank, 1932).

Central to Rank's theorizing is the concept of "ideology." As humans, we are not blank slates at birth on which society can write any scenario, but neither do we possess a potent repertoire of inborn behaviors. Our biological impulses are broad and malleable. To survive, we must create realities in which to live. The blueprints for these realities are the ideals and moral codes that constitute an ideology. Some ideologies are comprehensive, encompassing broad aspects of a society. For example, capitalism and communism are ideologies that help to organize the production and distribution of goods, and Christianity, Islam, and Buddhism are ideologies that help to direct spiritual strivings. Not all ideologies are so broad in scope; for example, professions such as law and science have ideologies to guide the behavior of their members. We can even speak of ideologies idiosyncratic to the individual. As Rank would say, people "ideologize."

During socialization, people have available a range of ideologies handed down from prior generations. But socialization is never complete. Each individual and each generation must fashion its own ideologies to meet changing circumstances. This means that people are able to create their own realities within broad limits set by biology and the society into which they are born. Recognizing this, Rank saw creativity and its vicissitudes as more fundamental than sexuality and its vicissitudes, as postulated by Freud. This was one reason for the break between the two.

Like Dostoevsky and James, Rank also considered "will" to be a vital human characteristic, one with far-ranging ramifications. As explained by Rank:

> The individual will is a derivative of the biological life-impulse, but it is a purely human derivative. … [T]his differentiation between life-impulse and expression of will [is] the basic human problem *par excellence* since it comprises both the dualism of ego and species, of mortality and immortality, that is inherent in the individual, and all

> those creative tendencies which go beyond the mere function of propagation. (Rank, 1932, p. 84)

An early manifestation of will is familiar to every parent when, during the "terrible twos," a child resists inducements to conform. As children mature into adulthood, they continue to resist demands of all kinds, whether external from other people and circumstances or internal from their own desires and impulses. Such resistance is a negative manifestation of will. A positive manifestation is the striving of each person for individuality, as seen, for example, in self-assertion.

The striving for individuality begins at birth, when the infant is thrust from the security of the mother's womb. Birth, Rank speculated, is accompanied by diffuse feelings of anxiety that eventually differentiate into two poles that he termed "fear of life" and "fear of death." The terminology is odd, but the ideas are simple. Most people fear death. This fact would require little explanation, except that the concept of death can have various meanings. The most common meaning involves cessation of bodily functions; however, a loss of individuality is also a kind of death – a death of the self. Rank's concept of death-fear focuses primarily on the latter meaning, that is, a loss of individuality.

What about fear of life? To assert one's individuality, to live as an independent being, involves risk. Hence, living as an independent, unique individual also can be a source of fear. Not surprisingly, many people seek shelter from life's risks by conforming to the collective and its ideologies. This, however, is no real solution, for it can lead to death of the self. Throughout life, then, a person is faced with a struggle for independence (which evokes life-fear) and surrender to the collective (which evokes death-fear).

All people struggle to resolve the tension between the individual and the collective, between self-assertion and self-surrender, but the conflict is experienced as especially acute by the artist and the neurotic. (Rank used the term "artist" broadly to refer to any person who is creatively productive in any given field.) The artist and neurotic both strive for independence; they differ, however, in the way they resolve the conflict between individuality and conformity:

> So the struggle of the artist ... is really only an ideologized continuation of the individual struggle against the collective; and yet it is this very fact of the ideologization of purely psychical conflicts that marks the difference between the productive and unproductive types, the artist and the neurotic; for the neurotic's creative power, like the most primitive

> artist's, is always tied to his own self and exhausts itself in it, whereas the productive type succeeds in changing this purely subjective creative process into an objective one, which means that through ideologizing it he transfers it from his own self to his work. (Rank, 1932, p. 372)

As described earlier, people are born into a social reality. The average, well-adjusted person accepts as true the ideologies bequeathed by society; that is, his or her will is aligned with the ideals and moral codes of the group. The will of the average person thereby loses its creative edge.

Through stronger-than-average expressions of will, both neurotic and creative individuals develop their own ideologies, with idiosyncratic ideals and moral codes. Not surprisingly, this can be a source of fear. Neurotics, Rank speculated, show a predominance of life-fear that, as described earlier, is a fear of living independently, of relying on one's own resources for survival. Life-fear leads to a subversion of impulses (e.g., sexuality) and a flight from experience. Creative individuals, by contrast, show a preponderance of death-fear, of losing one's own identity in that of the group. This death-fear leads to attempts to accentuate and perpetuate the self through the constructions of new realities in the realms of art, science, business, interpersonal relationships, or wherever else a person's talents might lie.[3]

The preponderance of one type of fear over the other is only relative. Neurotics also fear death and attempt to create new realities for themselves. Unlike creative individuals, however, they cannot accept their realities as true. The neurotic's truth remains inauthentic, alien to the self as well as to the larger society. Creative individuals are more successful in this regard. They find their truth, which they then try to externalize, thereby modifying – for the better, they trust – the collective reality on which they depend, not only for resources, but ultimately for validation. In the words of Rank, "art is in the last resort anti-collectivist – it yet needs these collective ideologies, even if only to overcome them from time to time by the force of personality" (Rank, 1932, p. 18).

Although very different in background and approach, clear similarities exist in the views of Dostoevsky, James, and Rank. In particular, three themes stand out: (a) Conflict or struggle is a spur to both neurosis and creativity, (b) independence from and identification with others are basic but conflicting human needs, and (c) humans have some choice ("will") in determining how emotional conflicts are resolved – neurotically or creatively. We will return to these themes later in the chapter. But first, several

[3] Not all creative people would agree: "I don't want to achieve immortality through my work. I want to achieve it by not dying" (Woody Allen).

issues must be addressed. The focus of this chapter is on the ways that emotional creativity can go awry. This requires a description of the criteria by which creativity is assessed and an indication of how those criteria may apply to the emotions. We then describe two ways that emotional creativity can miscarry: (a) the misconstrual of emotional concepts and (b) the intrusion of extraneous factors, of which the conflicting needs for independence and communion are a prime example.[4]

CREATIVITY IN THE DOMAIN OF EMOTION

Csikszentmihalyi and Robinson (1986) wondered "what it would take to *create* talent in domains that are important to our survival, such as nurturance, wisdom, or frugality." Their conclusion: "Perhaps all it would take is agreement on the criteria of performance, and then – as if by magic – talent will reveal itself" (p. 271). Emotions are clearly important to our survival. But can we agree on the criteria for judging an emotional response as creative?

Criteria for Creativity

Originality is perhaps the most commonly mentioned criterion for creativity (see the earlier quote by Einstein). The concept of originality is, however, ambiguous. In one sense, "original" means unique or one of a kind; in another sense, it means having origins in the self. These two senses often overlap, but they also can conflict. For example, when people strongly identify with cultural norms or even with their own past accomplishments, what originates in the self may be conforming rather than different. To keep the two senses clear, we use "novelty" to refer to originality in the sense of uniqueness, and we use "authenticity" to refer to originality in the sense of self-originated.

[4] Various terms have been used to describe these conflicting tendencies; on the one side, for example, we find terms such as "individualism," "independence," "agency," "autonomy," and "self-assertion" and on the other side "collectivism," "interdependence," "communion," "intimacy," and "self-surrender." When relevant, we use whichever terms are favored by an author being cited. Otherwise, we use terms that colloquially fit the context. For example, we use "collectivism" when attachment is to a social group and "communion" when attachment is to another person. Needless to say, individual and group attachments may differ in important respects (Brewer & Gardner, 1996); however, our focus is on what they have in common (e.g., a sense of belonging and willingness for self-sacrifice).

In addition to being novel and authentic, a response must be of potential value to the individual or group if it is to be judged creative. We call this third criterion "effectiveness." Although easy to state, even trivially obvious, effectiveness is often difficult to evaluate. For example, a neurotic response may be an effective way of coping with threat in the short term but detrimental to interests of the individual in the long term, or even if effective for the individual in the long term, the response still may be detrimental to the interests of the broader society and hence judged as uncreative.

Applications to the Domain of Emotion

Nothing about the preceding criteria – novelty, authenticity, effectiveness – prevents their application to emotions – but not to all emotions equally. "Emotion" is a cluster concept. One emotional cluster consists of biologically based automatic responses over which we have little control, such as sudden fright. Another cluster consists of relatively undifferentiated states such as general excitement and depression. These, too, allow little opportunity for innovation and change.[5] Emotional creativity applies mostly to temporally bounded states that are recognized in ordinary language by such concepts as *anger*, *grief*, *love*, and *fear*. For simplicity, we will refer to these as "standard emotions."

And what, more precisely, is the meaning of "anger," "grief," "love," "fear," and the hundreds of other emotional concepts recognized in everyday English? Perhaps the first thing to note is that emotional concepts are "folk-theoretical" constructs. That is, they do not refer simply to behavior, but they also help to explain and legitimize behavior (e.g., "I did it *because* I was angry"). This means that emotional concepts are embedded in a broader network of ideas (normative beliefs and rules) about what it means to be emotional. We refer to this network of ideas as "folk theories of emotion" or, adapting the terminology of Rank, as "emotion ideologies."

[5] Discussions of creativity and psychopathology often focus on the fact that creative writers and artists are more prone to depression than are members of the general population (Andreason, 1987; Jamison, 1993; Richards, 1990). This is not our concern here. Depression per se is not subject to creative change, although creativity can be involved in its resolution. Recall, for example, William James' bout with depression, which he ameliorated, in part, through conscious decision. The following caveats also should be noted: For reasons that are not clear, poets tend to be more susceptible to depression than novelists; female poets more than male poets (Kaufman & Sexton, 2006); and, in contrast to artists and writers, creative scientists appear to be no more prone to depression than the general population (Ludwig, 1997).

Like ideologies, our folk theories of emotion describe not only what it is like to be in an emotional state but also what it *should be* like.

Recall James' statement that usual deterrents do not apply to people with a genius for emotion. We interpret "deterrents" broadly to mean the social norms – beliefs and rules – that make emotional concepts meaningful. Even with this broad interpretation, James' statement is incomplete or misleading in an important respect. The term "deterrent" has a negative connotation; that is, it focuses on the regulation rather than on the creation of emotions. This is too restrictive: The norms of emotion have a constitutive as well as regulative function; they help to make an emotion what it is.

To say that the normative beliefs and rules of emotion are constitutive as well as regulative does not mean that they specify in advance the precise nature of emotional responses. With few exceptions, standard emotions are complex syndromes; no single response, or type of response (i.e., thought, feeling, or action), is necessary or sufficient for the whole (Barrett, 2006). All that is implied in advance is (a) a normatively adequate instigation, (b) a disposition to respond in an admissible manner, and (c) an objective appropriate to the provocation. For example, the concept of anger implies (a) a wrong and (b) an urge to (c) correct the wrong. Similarly, the concept of fear implies (a) a danger and (b) an urge to (c) escape the danger. As illustrated in Figure 14.1, these relations are implicit in the emotional concept. Thus, to be angry at a good deed or to fear a benign event without special explanation is a logical contradiction, not simply an empirical oddity. Likewise, to be angry and not want to correct the wrong or to be frightened and not want to escape the danger (in the absence of countervailing considerations) involves a contradiction of terms.

Figure 14.1 depicts the three elements (instigation, responses, objective) implied by an emotional concept, as well as the embeddedness of emotional concepts within broader folk theories of emotion. Figure 14.1 also illustrates how non-normative or extraneous factors (e.g., illness or frustration) may influence the way a person interprets and responds to an instigation. We will have much more to say about such extraneous factors shortly. For the moment, we focus on the normative beliefs and rules that help to constitute emotional syndromes.

Table 14.1 lists some rules of anger, as gleaned from historical teachings, reports of everyday experience, and legal practices (Averill, 1982). Not listed are numerous beliefs about anger (some true and some fanciful) that help to make the concept of anger meaningful, for example, that anger is a biologically based impulse and hence universal (a belief, we suggest, that is more fanciful than true).

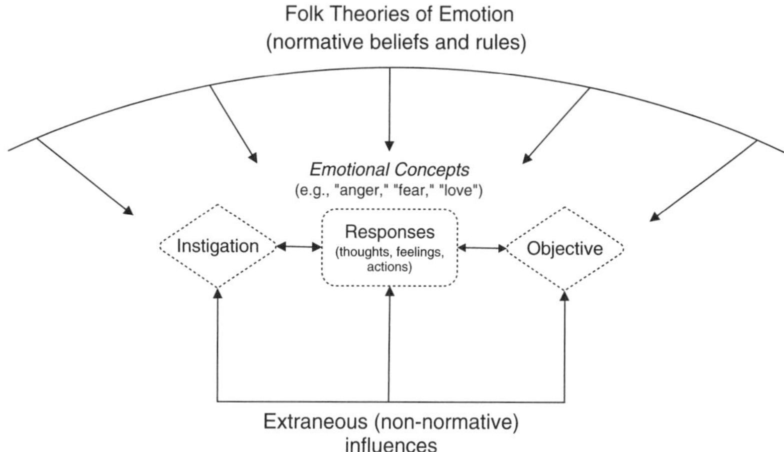

FIGURE 14.1. Emotional concepts accrue meaning within broader systems of constructs (folk theories of emotion), and they include as part of their meaning normatively admissible instigations, responses, and objectives. An actual emotional episode also can be influenced by a variety of extraneous factors so that the norms are honored more in the breach than in practice.

TABLE 14.1. *Some Beliefs and Rules about Anger, as Inferred from Historical Teachings, Legal Procedures, and Self-Reports of Everyday Experiences*

1. A person has the right (duty) to become angry at intentional wrongdoing or at unintentional misdeeds if those misdeeds are correctable (e.g., due to negligence, carelessness, or oversight).
2. Anger should be directed only at persons and, by extension, other entities (one's self, human institutions) that can be held responsible for their actions.
3. Anger should not be displaced on an innocent third party, nor should it be directed at the target for reasons other than the instigation.
4. The aim of anger should be to correct the situation, restore equity, and/or prevent recurrence, not to inflict injury or pain on the target nor to achieve selfish ends through intimidation.
5. The angry response should be proportional to the instigation; that is, it should not exceed what is necessary to correct the situation, restore equity, or prevent the instigation from happening again.
6. Anger should follow closely on the provocation and not endure longer than is needed to correct the situation (typically a few hours or days, at most).
7. Anger should involve commitment and resolve; that is, a person should not become angry unless appropriate follow-through is intended, circumstances permitting.

The rules presented in Table 14.1 may appear intuitively clear, even self-evident. At least, they should, if they have been internalized during the process of socialization. It is therefore instructive to contrast anger with *liget,* an emotion considered fundamental by the Ilongots, a head-hunting people who live in northern Luzon, the Philippines. Like anger, *liget* can be occasioned by insults, slights, and other affronts to the self, as well as by violations of accepted norms and practices. However, *liget* is based on a different set of cultural beliefs and follows different rules than does anger (Rosaldo, 1980). One of the most important expressions of *liget* is the taking of a head. The identity of the victim is of minor importance, for *liget* is not necessarily an act of revenge or the correction of some wrong; rather, the taking of a head is a way for a young man (it is a male prerogative) to establish his standing within the community. *Liget* also finds expression in giving as well as in taking life; for example, "concentrated" in sperm, it helps to make babies.

The anthropologic literature is replete with descriptions of emotional syndromes such as *liget* that differ in fundamental ways from standard emotions in our own culture (Mesquita, 2001). But we do not have to go across cultures to find examples of unusual emotional syndromes. Within any society, there are subcultural and sub-subcultural variations in emotion. This process of differentiation can be carried to ever smaller units until we reach the individual. Nor does the process ever stop. As individuals grow and circumstances change, so do the personal beliefs and rules that help to constitute their emotional experiences. If the person happens to be an emotional genius in James' sense and is sufficiently influential in other regards, he or she may help to establish a new set of norms and hence a new emotion within the culture. Something of this sort has been claimed for the poet Dante and the emergence of romantic love within Western cultures (Averill, 1985; Oatley, 2007).

The Misconstrual of Emotional Concepts

Rather than setting new standards, a person may misconstrue the normative beliefs and rules of an emotion in ways that are more neurotic than creative. The following is an example of misconstrued anger, as reported by a woman mired in an abusive relationship.

1. Never show that I am angry; hold it inside.
2. Never directly confront the person at whom I am angry.
3. It is allowed to express anger at one person to another person.
4. It is okay for someone else to tell the person about my anger; in fact, this is the preferred way.

5. When really angry, cry.
6. Never argue or confront.
7. Never make anyone else angry.
8. If I must direct my anger at someone, direct it at myself.

For whatever reasons, this woman did not seem to understand the concept of anger. She was like a tennis player who believes it is against the rules to hit the ball too hard over the net. Not surprisingly, she continually lost the game.

With regard to the criteria for creativity discussed earlier, the woman's behavior was novel in that it was contrary to the normative beliefs and rules of anger presented in Table 14.1. Her behavior, however, was clearly ineffective. It also was inauthentic – she was always playing a role of someone she thought she should be.

Dostoevsky's Underground Man provides a more dramatic example of failure to meet the criteria of creativity. With regard to the criterion of effectiveness: Living like a mouse, alienating all those around him, is not the best blueprint for success, no matter how success is conceived. For this reason alone, the Underground Man's behavior might be considered neurotic. The criteria of novelty and authenticity present more interesting issues.

The Underground Man pursues novelty by deliberately trying to be different. He claims that a person whose behavior is determined by the laws of nature, whether biological or social, or even by logical reasoning, is not a man, but an automaton: "… what do I care about the laws of nature and arithmetic if I have my reasons for disliking them?" (Dostoevsky, 1961 [1864], p. 99). A person's "most advantageous advantage" is his or her freedom to exercise his or her will, to go contrary to what others expect and what reason dictates. In the extreme, a person who feels completely determined "would go insane on purpose, just to be immune from reason" (p. 115).

The Underground Man strove for authenticity as well as novelty, but with uncertain success. He could never seem to decide who or what he actually is. "I'd feel better if I could only believe something of what I've written down here," he states. "But I swear I can't believe a single word of it. That is, I believe it in a way, but at the same time, I feel I'm lying like a son of a bitch" (p. 120).

To summarize, a person may fail to meet the criteria for creativity by misconstruing the beliefs and rules that make emotional concepts meaningful. In the process, standards can be set too high or too low to meet the criteria for creativity. Can the standard for effectiveness be set too high?

Without doubt: Perfectionism, the overzealous pursuit of excellence, is more a sign of neuroticism than creativity. Excesses in the pursuit of novelty (difference for difference sake) and authenticity (letting it all hang out) also can be signs of neuroticism. Still, aiming too high is less common a problem than aiming too low: Acceptance of mediocrity, conformity, and inauthenticity is too often the default choice of Rank's "average well-adjusted man."

NON-NORMATIVE SOURCES OF EMOTION

Earlier we indicated that there are two ways that emotional creativity can miscarry: (a) the misconstrual of normative beliefs and rules and (b) the intrusion of non-normative conditions (see Figure 14.1). We turn now to the second way. Specifically, we consider some extraneous factors that can lead to the misconstrual of emotional concepts. Ignorance owing to inadequate socialization (e.g., poor parenting) is sometimes at fault; however, neurotic behavior frequently occurs among people who "know better" – even among animals who cannot know better.

Neuroses in Animals

Can a dog be creative? Not in the relevant sense. Can a dog be neurotic? Yes, but not in the sense of creativity gone awry. Working in the laboratory of the Russian physiologist I. P. Pavlov, Shenger-Krestovnikova rewarded a hungry dog with food powder whenever a circle was presented and withheld the reward when an ellipse was presented. After learning to respond to the former and not to the latter, the difference between the two figures was gradually reduced so that the ellipse increasingly resembled the circle. When the circle and ellipse became nearly indistinguishable, the dog's behavior began to deteriorate, at first slowly and then abruptly. As described by Pavlov (1960 [1927]), "the hitherto quiet dog began to squeal in its stand, kept wriggling about, tore off with its teeth the apparatus for mechanical stimulation of the skin, and bit through the tubes connecting the animal's room with the observer, a behavior which had never happened before. On being taken into the experimental room the dog now barked violently, which was also contrary to its usual custom; in short it presented all the symptoms of a condition of acute neurosis" (p. 291).

Shenger-Krestovnikova's dog is not an isolated case. Similar results have been obtained with different species (e.g., rats, sheep, and monkeys) using a variety of conflict-inducing techniques (Cook, 1939). Humans, too, may exhibit neurotic-like symptoms when confronted with conflicting or ambiguous demands, and no adequate response is available (Mineka & Thomas, 1999).

Of course, people do not simply experience stress as a dog might; people are self-aware, interpreters of their own experiences. Such self-awareness allows increased flexibility in the way conflicts are resolved – creatively or neurotically (cf. Dostoevsky's Underground Man). The point we now wish to emphasize, however, is different; namely, although normative beliefs and rules may provide the logical framework for emotional reactions in humans, any particular episode may be determined, in part, by extraneous (i.e., non-normative) factors.

The Intrusion of Extraneous Factors

By "extraneous," we mean factors that fall outside the normative beliefs and rules that provide the logical framework for an emotional syndrome. The kind of conflict experienced by Shenger-Krestovnikova's dog is an example of a precipitating condition that, for obvious reasons, does not involve conceptually based beliefs and rules. Other examples include physiologic arousal from extraneous sources, food or sleep deprivation, hormonal imbalances, extreme heat or cold, and any of a wide variety of acute and chronic conditions. An emotional response also may be influenced by "ulterior motives," that is, by goals that are only tangentially related to the normatively prescribed objectives. For example, a person may become angry not to correct a wrong but to intimidate the target for personal advantage.

Ideally, the *actual* instigation to an emotion should conform to *normatively sanctioned* instigations, and the *actual* objective should conform to the *normatively sanctioned* objectives. For example, the "insult" that arouses anger should, in fact, be an insult and not, say, a legitimate correction; similarly, the objective of the response should, in fact, be to correct the wrong and not to gain an unrelated personal advantage. Often, however, extraneous factors intrude to make the situation less than ideal.

Often, extraneous factors exert their influence outside awareness, in which case the beliefs and rules that are normative for the emotion may be stretched and distorted to legitimize behavior that otherwise might appear inappropriate or even neurotic. For example, a husband who becomes angry at his wife over a trivial incident actually may be deflecting attention from misconduct on his part by shifting the blame to her for an unrelated offense. This does not mean, however, that the rationalization is an epiphenomenon of no causal influence on behavior. Neurotic behavior is not a one-time reaction to a stressful event. Neuroses develop over time, and what begins as a post hoc rationalization on one occasion may "grease the wheels" for repeat occurrences. Thus, blaming the wife on one occasion may develop into a pattern of spousal abuse.

THE CONFLICT BETWEEN INDIVIDUALISM AND COLLECTIVISM

With the preceding considerations in mind, we now return to an issue raised in our earlier reflections on Dostoevsky, James, and Rank, namely, the struggle between individualism and collectivism or, on the more interpersonal level, between independence from and communion with others. This dualism of human nature is the source of some of the most intractable and painful conflicts that people experience.[6] The following example of a woman we will call Nora is typical:

> A middle-aged professional woman, Nora came to counseling to help resolve an internal conflict she did not fully understand. Nora had been married and divorced twice by her early 30s. Both husbands were abusive, and she was left to raise three children as a single parent. After the children were grown, she lived alone and was, she thought, quite happy and contented. Nevertheless, she felt something was missing. When asked to picture what she desired in life, she focused almost exclusively on themes of communal relationships (e.g., weddings, home decorating, family, and the like).
>
> Nora's conflict became manifest when she met a man we will call Roger. Much to her dismay, the more she cared for Roger, and the more he expressed serious intentions toward her (e.g., speaking of marriage), the more ambivalent she became about the relationship. As the draw of intimacy increased, she became increasingly critical and even abusive toward Roger: She would pick on him over minor issues (e.g., the

[6] The conflict has deep biological as well as social roots. Species differ in the extent to which they live independently or communally. Among the great apes, for example, orangutans are more solitary than chimpanzees. Humans appear to be more like chimpanzees in their communal strivings, but they also evidence a desire for, and benefit from, solitude (Long & Averill, 2003). Cultures differ in the extent to which they reinforce these biological tendencies. For example, Western societies have been described as "individualistic" and Eastern societies as "collectivist" (for instance, Triandis, 1995). These societal differences have ramifications both for the emotional lives of individuals and for the criteria for assessing creativity (Averill, Chon, & Haan, 2001; Sundararajan & Averill, 2007).

way he spoke) or accuse him of infidelity (he traveled extensively on business).

Repeatedly Nora broke off the relationship with Roger. After each breakup, she felt miserable, called him and apologized, or she would wait several days for him to call her, and they would reconcile. Then the cycle would begin again.

Being an intelligent woman, Nora was fully aware of the destructiveness of her actions; yet she seemed unable to stop herself, or so she thought. Nora's prior experience in abusive relationships undoubtedly contributed to her ambivalence about becoming too close to Roger. But whatever the specifics of her case, her problem is by no means unique. Recall Dostoevsky's Underground Man. Whenever he felt attracted to another person, he became spiteful, and the stronger the attraction, the more spiteful he became. Dostoevsky did not attribute the Underground Man's dilemma to prior misfortunes; rather, he believed it manifested in exaggerated form a fundamental duality of human nature.

To many people, the goals of independence and communion, individualism and collectivism, might seem to fall at opposite ends of a continuum – the closer you approach one, the further you recede from the other. This is an oversimplification. People often feel most complete *as individuals* and are most willing to take risks when securely attached to another (Cassidy & Shaver, 1999). Even so, the conflicting desires for both independence and communion remain, never far below the surface (Bakan, 1966; Blatt, 2008). For some people, the conflict is resolved by retreat into one extreme or the other or a vacillation between the extremes. Still other people seek to avoid the conflict by identifying with an abstraction – an idealized other, say, who can be loved in absentia; with a social collective and its ideology or even humanity as a whole; or more abstractly still, with a deity that can love, and be loved, without limit. But whatever the resolution, the conflict never completely disappears, for it is fundamental to what we are as human beings. Like many intractable conflicts, the best "treatment" is often to recognize its nature, avoid the extremes, and use to advantage the challenges presented by any contending differences.

As we have seen, both Dostoevsky and James were acutely aware of the conflict between independence and communion, individuality and collectivism. But more than either Doestoevsky or James, Rank saw the roots of both creativity and neurosis in the intractable conflict between the individual and the collective. Recall that Rank considered collectivism, if carried to the extreme, to be a form of psychological death. But Rank also recognized that the "reality" in which we live is a hard-won product of previous generations. The creative person can succeed only by identifying, at least partially, with the collective. The problem is to free oneself from the past while yet contributing to and even transforming the collective reality. And so it is on the individual level: Only through communion with yet in independence from others can we transform the realities we have created for our selves.

In the conflict between the individual and the collective, Rank's emphasis was clearly on the individual. This emphasis was perhaps exaggerated by his personal history. During adolescence, the young Otto broke off spoken relations with his alcoholic father, disavowed his family name (Rosenfeld), and adopted Rank as his new surname. He was symbolically "reborn" under his new name. However, Rank also was critical of the hyperindividualism that characterizes modern Western societies. He explicitly recognized that creative individuals may use their talents to reinforce rather than modify the collective world view. Religious art during the Middle Ages is a good example. In painting the ceiling of the Sistine Chapel, for example, Michelangelo was not trying to overthrow religious orthodoxy of his day but to further it.

CONCLUDING OBSERVATIONS

In describing neurosis as emotional creativity gone awry, it might seem that we are being overly romantic – searching for meaning in the meaningless. This is not our intent. If neuroses are wrong answers to life's questions (to paraphrase Jung's observation cited earlier), creative individuals are more likely than the average person to give wrong as well as right answers. Indeed, for any given problem, there are many more ways to be wrong than right.

Strictly speaking, "neurosis" applies to behavior (answers), not to inherent characteristics of a person. Under relevant conditions, we are all capable of neuroses. It follows that people prone to neurotic behavior are as varied as people in general: Some are tall, others short; some are extraverted, others introverted; some are bright, others dull; and so forth. Neurotic behavior is similarly varied: Sometimes it is easily seen as creativity gone awry; other times it appears more like stupidity gone amok. But even when the latter description applies, creative elements are seldom completely lacking. Thus, without romanticizing a condition that is the source of considerable misery and pain, we believe that much can be learned from people as they try to cope with life's struggles, even when they give wrong answers.

REFERENCES

Andreasen, N. C. (1987). Creativity and mental illness: Prevalence rates in writers and their first-degree relatives. *American Journal of Psychiatry*, 144, 1288–1292.

Averill, J. R. (1982). *Anger and aggression: An essay on emotion*. New York: Springer-Verlag.

(1985). The social construction of emotion: With special reference to love. In K. Gergen and K. Davis (Eds.), *The social construction of the person* (pp. 89–109). New York: Springer-Verlag.

(1999). Individual differences in emotional creativity: Structure and correlates. *Journal of Personality*, 67, 331–371.

(2005). Emotions as mediators and as products of creative activity. In J. Kaufman and J. Baer (Eds.), *Creativity across domains: Faces of the muse* (pp. 225–243). Mahwah, NJ: Erlbaum.

Averill, J. R., Chon, K. K., & Haan, D. W. (2001). Emotions and creativity, East and West. *Asian Journal of Social Psychology*, 4, 165–183.

Averill, J. R. & Nunley, E. P. (1992). *Voyages of the heart: Living an emotionally creative life*. New York: Free Press.

Bakan, D. (1966). *The duality of human existence*. Boston: Beacon Press.

Barbre, C. (1996). Editor's Preface. In E. Menaker, *Separation, will, and creativity: The wisdom of Otto Rank*. Northvale, NJ: Jason Aronson.

Barrett, L. F. (2006). Solving the emotion paradox: Categorization and the experience of emotion. *Personality and Social Psychology Review*, 10, 20–46.

Blatt, S. J. (2008). *Polarities of experience*. Washington: American Psychological Association.

Brewer, M. B. & Gardner, W. (1996). Who is this "we"? Levels of collective identity and self representations. *Journal of Personality and Social Psychology*, 71, 83–93.

Cassidy, J. & Shaver, P. R. (Eds.). (1999). *Handbook of attachment: Theory, research and clinical applications*. New York: Guilford Press.

Cook, S. W. (1939). A survey of methods used to produce "experimental neurosis." *American Journal of Psychiatry*, 95, 1259–1276.

Csikszentmihalyi, M. & Robinson, R. E. (1986). Culture, time, and the development of talent. In R. J. Sternberg and J. E. Davidson (Eds.), *Conceptions of giftedness* (pp. 264–284). New York: Cambridge University Press.

Dennett, D. C. (2003). *Freedom evolves*. New York: Penguin Books

Dostoevsky, F. (1961). *Notes from underground* (A. R. MacAndrew, Trans.). New York: New American Library. (Original work published in 1864.)

Gale, R. M. (1999). *The divided self of William James*. New York: Cambridge University Press.

James, W. (1961). *Varieties of religious experience*. New York: Collier Books. (Original work published in 1902.)

Jamison, K. R. (1993). *Touched with fire*. New York: Free Press.

Jung, C. G. (1965). *Memories, dreams, reflections* (R. & C. Winston, Trans.). New York: Vintage Books.

Kaufman, J. C., & Sexton, J. D. (2006). Why doesn't the writing cure help poets? *Review of General Psychology*, 10, 268–282.

Long, C. R. & Averill, J. R. (2003). Solitude: An exploration of benefits of being alone. *Journal for the Theory of Social Behavior*, 33, 21–44.
Ludwig, A. M. (1997). Creative achievement and psychopathology: Comparison among professions. In M. A. Runco and R. Richards (Eds.), *Eminent creativity, everyday creativity, and health* (pp. 33–60). Greenwich, CT: Ablex.
McDermott, J. J. (Ed.). (1967). *The writings of William James*. New York: Modern Library.
Mesquita, B. (2001). Culture and emotion: Different approaches to the question. In T. J. Masyne and G. A. Bonanno (Eds.), *Emotions: Current issues and future directions* (pp. 214–250). New York: Guilford Press.
Mineka, S. & Thomas, C. (1999). Mechanisms of change in exposure therapy for anxiety disorders. In T. Dalgleish and M. J. Power (Eds.), *Handbook of cognition and emotion* (pp. 747–764). Chichester, England: Wiley.
Mochulsky, K. (1967). *Dostoevsky: His life and work* (M. A. Minihan, Trans.). Princeton, NJ: Princeton University Press.
Nunley, E. P. & Averill, J. R. (1996). Emotional creativity: Theoretical and applied aspects. In K. T. Kuehlwein and H. Rosen (Eds.), *Constructing realities: Meaning-making perspectives for psychotherapists* (pp. 223–251). San Francisco: Jossey-Bass.
Oatley, K. (1999). Fiction as cognitive and emotional simulation. *Review of General Psychology*, 3, 101–117.
(2007). Dante's love and the creation of a new poetry. *Psychology of Aesthetics, Creativity, and the Arts*, 1, 140–147.
Pavlov, I. P. (1960). *Conditioned reflexes* (G. V. Anrep, Trans. & Ed.). New York: Dover Publications. (Original work published 1927.)
Rank, O. (1907). *Der Künstler*. Vienna: Hugo Heller.
(1932). *Art and artist* (C. F. Atkinson, Trans.). New York: Alfred A. Knopf.
Richards, R. (1990). Everyday creativity, eminent creativity, and health. *Creativity Research Journal*, 3, 300–326.
Rosaldo, M. Z. (1980). *Knowledge and passion: Ilongot notions of self and social life*. Cambridge, England: Cambridge University Press.
Steinberg, A. (1966). *Dostoievsky*. London: Bowes & Bowes.
Sundararajan, L. & Averill, J. R. (2007). Creativity in the everyday: Culture, self, and emotions. In R. Richards (Ed.), *Everyday creativity and new views of human nature* (pp. 195–220). Washington: American Psychological Association.
Triandis, H. C. (1995). *Individualism and collectivism*. Boulder, CO: Westview Press.
Whitman, W. (1965). "Song of Myself." In H. W. Blodgett and S. Bradley (Eds.), *Leaves of grass*. New York: New York University Press. (Original work published in 1855.)

15

Dangling from a Tassel on the Fabric of Socially Constructed Reality: Reflections on the Creative Writing Process

LIANE GABORA AND NANCY HOLMES

Years ago, one of the authors of this chapter was explaining an unusual idea to a close friend and poetically admitted that the idea was "out there on the edge of the fabric of accepted reality." The friend laughed and said, "You're not just out there at the edge, you're swinging from a tassel!" We talked about how we both spent much of our lives "swinging from a tassel," and one of us inadvertently changed the metaphor from "swinging" to "dangling." It seems that when ideas are flowing, the creative process feels like swinging. When the ideas dry up, though, it can feel as if you are dangling alone in darkness.

This chapter begins with an investigation into experiences of depression, alienation, and self-abuse among the highly creative. After this journey to the dark side, it may be uplifting to see that Mother Nature may have a few tricks up her sleeve to minimize the extent to which we succumb to the negative aspects of creativity while still benefiting from its riches. Finally, we discuss another sobering aspect of creativity – the fact that many of our inventions are dangerous to ourselves, our planet, and the other living things we share it with – and discuss how a creation intimately reflects the structure of the worldview(s) of its creators. Although the discussion focuses primarily on creative writers, we believe that it is relevant to creativity in other domains, particularly the arts and, to a lesser extent, science, engineering, and business.

IN THE FERTILE SHADOWY SWAMPLANDS OF THE CREATIVE MIND

The tassel metaphor with which we began this chapter is not atypical of metaphors of the creative process. Things attached to ropes or strings figure prominently because they entail both freedom and constraint: the freedom to depart from the masses and the constraint that you cannot depart too far. As another example, a creative writing student recently told of how she once wrote a poem in which she was standing on a seashore with long strings attached to her fingers. At the end of each string was a bird, and the birds flew over the sea while she played and tugged at them with her fingers. Years later, in therapy, she had a sudden vivid memory of going through a traumatizing childhood event during which she had felt as if she had sprung apart into fragments, and all the fragments were birds. She believes that in writing the poem she tapped into this powerful memory of pain and loss. The poem exemplifies the tension between freedom (symbolized by the birds) and constraint (symbolized by the strings) that is intrinsic to creativity and illustrates as well how a work of art can have roots in the dark, fragmented places of the creator's psyche.

It is often suspect in critical circles to foreground biographic forces impinging on a work of art; critics tend to foreground social forces and the discourses of race, class, and gender as devices to understand art. Most artists prefer to say that the created work of art has a life of its own outside their lives – the story is the thing, not the storyteller. Nevertheless, they admit to drawing extensively from the wellspring of personal experience and to dredging up great pain in the process that they cannot control or deal with. Indeed, it is widely believed that creative individuals are more emotionally unstable and prone to affective disorders such as depression and bipolar disorder and have a higher incidence of schizophrenic tendencies than other segments of the population (Andreasen, 1987; Flaherty, 2005; Jamison, 1989, 1993). There is also evidence that they are more prone to suicide (Goodwin & Jamison, 1990) and to abuse drugs and alcohol (Goodwin, 1988, 1992; Ludwig, 1995; Norlander & Gustafson, 1996, 1997, 1998; Rothenberg, 1990b). Classic twentieth-century examples include the many mid-century American poets who wrote so-called confessional works and committed suicide, such as Sylvia Plath and Anne Sexton. Other famously creative individuals who committed suicide include writers Ernest Hemingway, Virginia Woolf, David Foster Wallace, and Thomas Disch; musicians Jimi Hendrix, Kurt Cobain, and Janice Joplin; painter Van Gogh; photographer Diane Arbus; abstract expressionist Mark Rothko; and mathematician Alan Turing. More recently, Heath Ledger seems to have gone so deeply into the "other" with his vivid portrayal of the sociopathic Joker in the latest Batman movie that he was unable to recoil from the darkness in himself. Novelist William Styron's memoir of his depression, *Darkness Visible*, provides a comprehensive list of suicidal and depressed artists (Styron, 1990, pp. 35–36) and also details his own struggle with suicidal thoughts and his eventual realization that most of his art had been tinged with his struggle for mental stability (pp. 78–79). Styron remarks that "[t]hrough the course of literature and art the theme of depression has run like a durable thread of woe" (p. 82). Thus art and its creation appear to have a powerful connection to mental illness, depression, and violent energies.

What comes first, the disturbance or the art? It is a chicken and the egg question. Some are convinced that it is the making of art that causes the disturbance. In an essay entitled, "The Keys to Dreamland," Northrop Frye (1963) notes that "[an author's] life may imitate literature in a way that may warp or even destroy his social personality" (p. 36). Advocates of this position believe that creative endeavors loosen the bonds that keep the pain we all feel at bay. As visual artist George Braque is widely quoted as having said, "Art is a wound turned to light." Artists must delve deeply into the subconscious or the intuitive, and frequently, dark associations and thoughts are brought to the surface. In nonartists, these feelings remain undisturbed and latent. They are not mined for material.

Others, however, are convinced that it is the disturbance that causes the art, that is, that the art arises from mental pain. A happy, well-adjusted person might not have as compelling a story as a damaged or wounded person or possibly have fewer resources of powerful emotion to draw on. Freud would have said it was the disturbance that caused the art but that the "disturbance" is not necessarily unique to the artist, just uniquely *available*. The artist is less liable to block or repress negative emotions and thus has more creative associations and self-permission to dwell in and explore them. A slightly more complex explanation for the relationship between creativity and mood disorders is that in a negative affective state one is more thwarted, more driven to solve a problem or express oneself, and thus one forges stronger associations in memory. Later on, when one returns to this negative affective state, one has access to a richer web of associations to draw on. Thus it is not a simple question of which causes the other; one enters a positive-feedback cycle in which the negative state inspires the art, but the desire to create art pulls one back into the (richly fertile) negative state.

A classic example of how darkly surprising the result can be is Mary Shelley's *Frankenstein*. Here, the creative artist delves deeply into the grave, into death itself, to create "life," which turns out to be a monster. The well-known feminist reading of this novel by Ellen Moers (1976) suggests that Shelley, a young woman of 19 in an era when childbirth was deeply associated with the death of the mother or infant, through her worldview was needing to understand her terrors and her anger around her pregnancies (Moers, 1976, pp. 91–99). Much literary theory about *Frankenstein* and other "gothic" novels, especially by women, theorize that this particular form of the novel is the result of women's worldviews entering the literary realm: "The Hispanic feminist theorist Gloria Anzaldúa has argued that one of the byproducts of being a woman in a patriarchy is social and cultural alienation, and that one of the consequences of being 'pushed out of the tribe' is the development of a heightened artistic sense or the drive to create cosmos out of chaos" (Hoevler, 2007, p. 62). Feminist critics have argued that *Frankenstein* and other late eighteenth-century and early nineteenth-century gothic novels illustrate this psychic strategy (Hoeveler, 2007, p. 62).

THE SELF-MADE WORLDVIEW

We believe that further insight into this issue can be gleaned by introducing the notion of a *worldview:* one's internal mental model of reality or distinctive way of "seeing and being in" the world. A human worldview is a unique tapestry of understanding that is *autopoietic* in that the whole emerges through interactions among the parts. It is also *self-mending* in the sense that just as injury to the body spontaneously evokes physiologic changes that bring about healing, events that are problematic or surprising or generate cognitive dissonance spontaneously evoke streams of thought that attempt to solve the problem or reconcile the dissonance (Gabora, 1999). One could say that creative works are the external manifestation of the self-mending aspect of a worldview. The painting, novel, or technological feat is the tangible evidence left behind of a mind's struggle to resolve a feeling of tension or imbalance or mend a gap in one's worldview.

One could say that a creator's understanding of the problem is honed as it is considered in the context of various facets of this worldview, and the worldview, in turn, transforms in response to ongoing shifts (ranging from imperceptible to revolutionary) in the conception of the problem (Gabora, 1999, under revision). A worldview is said to be "self-made" to the extent that its contents have been honed. In other words, individuals with self-made worldviews do not simply acquire knowledge; they make it their own, reframe it in their own terms, relate it to their own experiences, put their own slant on it, and adapt it to their needs and familiar modes of self-expression. The reclusive and radical American poet Emily Dickinson, who famously says "Tell all the Truth but tell it slant" (Dickinson, 1960, Poem 1129, line 1), is an example of a creative artist who completely reframed traditional poetics to convey her worldview of a godless universe, the nature of female passion, and various other unconventional social and philosophical concepts. As Dickinson keenly recognized, at the other extreme are individuals whose worldviews are not self-made at all but rather an inventory of socially transmitted information. (At a talk one of us recently gave, a member of the audience suggested that an individual at this end of the spectrum be referred to as a "world-made self.")

The notion of a self-made worldview is discussed at length elsewhere (Gabora, under revision); here, let us focus on how it relates to the dark side of creativity. Since individuals with self-made worldviews have a deeply engrained habit of thinking for themselves, their perspectives and behavior come to deviate from those of society at large. They tend to be perceived by some as interesting, whereas to others they are threatening or simply exasperating because they do everything their own way instead of the "right way." To the extent that they feel alienated from society, they have little interest in how it measures success, so time and energy go into the creative projects that are a source of not just passion in life but feelings of connection to something beyond oneself. While peers are ensuring themselves a place in society by rooting their worldviews ever deeper into the fabric of consensus reality, the self-made individual is "swinging from tassels" that have only the most tenuous link to worldly affairs. These projects often yield little in the way of immediate, well-defined outcomes, so the self-made individual may come across as someone with an unwarranted degree of confidence – someone with few tangible accomplishments who has not assimilated the "proper way" of doing things. Creative artists sometimes minimize their social and personal difficulties by consoling themselves with myths about creative people being "born geniuses," "eccentric," and so on.

While self-made individuals crave, like anyone does, to be welcomed and accepted and appreciated for who they are, a vicious cycle can set in, one that may set the pattern for the rest of their life. The more engrossed they become in creative projects, the less connected they feel, so the less effort goes toward worldly matters, so the more they deviate from norms and the less they "measure up," so the more they take solace in creative projects, a solace reinforced by the need for solitude in order to create (Piirto, 2005, p. 18). The tragic result is that although self-made individuals clearly have much to offer, they often do not live up to their potential, or if they do live up to their creative potential, their personal lives can be compromised. However, because they often dedicate their lives to tending and nurturing creative work – their tassel. If they *do* manage to climb up and haul it onboard, it may well be a thing of spectacular beauty quite unlike anything the world has seen before. Identifying self-made individuals, making them feel that they are not alone, and suggesting how they might carry out their projects or explore their ideas in ways that are consistent with society's aims would go a long way toward mending a wound in society and bestowing it with the rich gifts that such individuals have to give.

THE ADJACENT POSSIBLE

Creative individuals may be perceived as risk-takers, although, of course, a move that appears risky to one who is not intimately familiar with the domain may not be risky at all to one who knows it well. Creative types do not just learn about a domain through experience, but they extrapolate from experiences of *what is* to flesh out a framework for *what could be*. (Given how those threads look and feel and interact with other threads in the fabric of reality, what would they be like if they extended all the way out *here?*) This is sometimes called the "realm of potentiality" (Gabora & Aerts, 2005). Kauffman (2008) refers to it as the "adjacent possible."

Of course, some possibles are more adjacent than others; most people more readily conceive of painting a house a different color, for example, than of creating a world of fictional characters or developing a new branch of mathematics. We believe that Emily Dickinson dwells in the "deep end" of the adjacent possible. She is always gesturing toward the realm of potentiality: "I dwell in Possibility –/A fairer House than Prose –/More numerous of Windows –/Superior – for Doors –" (Dickinson, 1960, Poem 657, lines 1–4). Like many of her poems, this one ends with her characteristic punctuation mark, a dash, so that we are left dangling and swinging in some odd resonance of meaning and energy. Indeed, the nearly overwhelming number of dangling dashes here makes for a kinetic reading. She seems to use the dash as a way of suspending time and meaning over a mysterious void, as if she realizes she is "out there." A reader feels an intense reaching out for threads of connection, for what could be possible, the opening of windows of new perception and doors to new places. One could say that she created a poetic of "swinging from a tassel on the fabric of socially constructed reality." Dickinson shows the creative process as being one of intense connectivity and leaps through uncharted adjacent territory. However, the danger of making constant leaps into the unknown and unexplored is that she not only dwelt in possibility but she "lived on Dread –/To Those who know/The Stimulus there is/In Danger – Other impetus/Is numb – and Vitalless" (Dickinson, 1960, Poem 770, lines 1–5). The writer needs to take these risks or ends up in dull, dead space. Interestingly, when one's soul is spurred to take risks, she says, it goes "without the Spectre's aid/Were Challenging Despair" (lines 9–10). Although she is typically difficult here, she seems to suggest that leaping to fearful places, while keeping one in a state of dread and fear, is a challenge to despair of the soul – thus she lives *on* dread, not in it.

Creativity is also associated with "defocusing" (Ansburg & Hill, 2002). Perhaps one is just defocused with respect to consensus reality because the *focus* is on the adjacent possible (Gabora, 1999). That is, the self-made individual may have a blurred conception of what is actually going on around him or her while honing what could be. This is a vulnerable state. Being attuned to the halo of possibility associated with all things, events, and people may involve making the boundaries of the self more porous and fragile, being overly intuitive or empathic. Without wanting to overemphasize potentially simplistic psychobiographic assumptions, this could be one reason why Dickinson became a recluse, refusing to see anyone but close family and very few friends. Such people are vulnerable, too, in a more concrete sense; clearly, it is easier to pickpocket, or simply manipulate, someone who is gazing into the stars and contemplating the mysteries of the universe than someone who is alert to immediate danger. The incredibly prolific fiction writer P. G. Wodehouse lived so immersed in his fantasy world that he ended up an unwitting stooge of the Nazis (see Orwell's essay, "In Defence of P. G. Wodehouse"). Thus another dark side of creativity is that one is susceptible to not just affective disorders but also worldly dangers, and this may be directly related to the degree to which thoughts deviate from the here and now. To continue with our metaphor, the longer the string on which the tassel hangs, the larger is the arc that it carves out as you swing through the adjacent possible, and the less adjacent it is when you are not swinging but dangling.

THE ALLURE OF DARKNESS

Frye (1963) provides an insightful view of the writer's relationship to his or her material. The traditional conventions of literature and drama are comedy and tragedy – the conventions of literature have both a light and a dark side, as if in acknowledgment that imaginative life and its expression through literature have this duality. Frye says that the literary imagination is "vertical" in perspective – instead of looking out horizontally across the field of everyday life, the allure of great literature is that it plummets the depths and reaches for the heights of emotion and human action (Frye, 1963, p. 40), the two great halves of the imagination. More recent literary theory also posits this duality in the creative process itself. Theorist Julia Kristeva (1984) identifies creativity arising out of a tension between the semiotic (disrupting, fracturing) and the symbolic (ordering, linearity). Although some may quarrel with Kristeva's metaphorically gendering these drives, it is striking how often the metaphors of depth and height and order and chaos are used to talk about the creative process. Some artists speak of being struck by inspiration from above (hence the metaphor of the muse); others will speak, as Coleridge does, of mining deeply into dark energy. In Coleridge's "Kubla Khan," which is a great poem about the creative process, creative energy comes from a great chasm. Coleridge uses language that suggests that poetic energy derives from a dangerous, disruptive, and painful place: "savage," "enchanted," "demon," "wailing," and "haunted." However, the energy from this fountain of power is controlled and moderated. Coleridge calls the river that flows from this fountain of energy "Alph, the sacred river." There is little doubt that "Alph" denotes beginning or origin, but it also alludes to the "alphabet" or writing in particular. The sacred river of poetry has its origins in the demonic and savage fountain but is nevertheless bound by fences and gardens:

> So twice five miles of fertile ground
> With walls and towers were girdled round:
> And there were gardens bright with sinuous rills,
> Where blossomed many an incense-bearing tree;
> Coleridge, "Kubla Khan," lines 7–10

Those versed in prosody will note that the "twice five miles" of fences with the vertical towers and horizontal walls is a visual analogue of poetry's iambic pentameter. If you remember your scansion marks from school days, iambic pentameter is a weak beat (a horizontal mark) followed by a strong beat (a nearly vertical mark.) And just as the poem delivers this visual cue, the line changes from galloping tetrameter to orderly iambic pentameter. Thus the poem *enacts* the creation of a poem even as its topic is *about* the creation of a poem. The image of the "sinuous rills" takes us back once again to the strings and ropes of creative energy (strings that are later figured again with the dulcimer and the demonic poet's "floating hair"). Coleridge's image for the finished work of art is a "stately pleasure dome" that is built over the river as it plunges toward subterranean depths. Art, he proposes, is a balance between light and dark forces:

> The shadow of the dome of pleasure
> Floated midway on the waves;

Where was heard the mingled measure
From the fountain and the caves.
It was a miracle of rare device,
A sunny pleasure-dome with caves of ice!
Coleridge, "Kubla Khan," lines 31–36

While the work of art, that "miracle of rare device," delivers the balance between creative energy and constraining form, the author or creator personally may not maintain that balance. "Kubla Khan" does not end with an image of the glorious pleasure dome but with the image of the possessed poet of whom everyone should "Beware!" Coleridge, as his biographer Richard Holmes says, went through profound crises: "a collapsed marriage, a failed career, addiction to drugs, a disastrous love affair, and terrible moments of suicidal despair and sloth" (Holmes, 1982, p. v), and much of his work is unfinished. This raises the question of how artists deal with the consequences of being open to both ecstatic inspiration and deep mining into the darkness. Coleridge's image of the artist in full flight with that floating, dangling hair is one of demonic possession. Kristeva, in her book *Black Sun*, links depression and the creative process in a despairing cycle or feedback loop, positing that "loss, bereavement, and absence trigger the work of the imagination and nourish it permanently as much as they threaten it and spoil it" (Kristeva, 1984, p. 9). She suggests that the energy of loss at the heart of the creative process is both harmful and nurturing. There is no way to avoid damage when obeying the creative urge.

Interestingly, many critics have analyzed the consequence of emotions on the reader, going back to Aristotle's *Poetics* when he talks of the purging effect of tragedy. Northrop Frye's example comes from *King Lear* – when Gloucester's eyes are gouged out on stage, the audience is safe in the sense that they know they do not have to jump out of their seats and call the police; it is "just an act." The power of this scene, Frye says, is that the reader or the audience ideally becomes filled with "exuberant horror, full of the energy of repudiation" (Frye, 1963, p. 41). Susan Sontag in *Regarding the Pain of Others* suggests that Virginia Woolf felt that there was a similar moral purpose in looking at war photographs (Sontag, 2003, p. 6). However, as articulate and sensitive as all these writers are about the effect of violent or dark images on an audience, neither Aristotle, Sontag, nor Frye talks about the effect on the artist of imagining or witnessing horror. The inner effect on the artist of creating works that reveal pain, torture, and suffering is untouched. If the artist has rendered the scene or image convincingly, with pen and imagination, or has painted the flayed flesh of a victim, how is the artist affected? A reader or watcher can turn away or respond to an implied purpose for the work of art such as repudiating or protesting suffering, or simply acknowledging pain's human universality, or working up sympathy and tears. But what about the effect on the artist? The writer must, to some degree, internalize this horror in order to write about it convincingly. Does the artist who confronts horrors in the world or in the self need the consolation of self-medicating drugs or drink? Is sustained creative practice a dangerous act because, as Rothenberg (1990a, 1990b) suggests, creative people are unearthing unconscious processes? This process may be damaging to the self, but it also may be cathartic and cleansing, for in the telling of the story the writer's worldview is reforged into what may be a more coherent or encompassing internal reflection of the world. Margaret Atwood (2002), in her book, *Negotiating with Dead: A Writer on Writing*, speaks of the artist's "desire to make the risky trip to the Underworld" (p. 156) for the "story is in the dark" (p. 176). She has an entire chapter devoted to how it is "easy to go there, but hard to come back" (p. 180). Her metaphor of the journey to the underworld for this process underscores the social and personal value of the descent into the dark. Returning from the underworld with stories, with a message from the dead or with self-knowledge, is the payoff. William Styron (1990) ends his memoir with a subdued feeling of hope that artists will continue trying to see clearly "depression's dark wood" and finishes the book with a quote from Dante who, after reforging an entire universe of hell, purgatory, and heaven, says: "And so we came forth, and once again beheld the stars" (p. 84).

DIMINISHING THE DARK SIDE

Are there natural forces at work to minimize the negative aspects of creativity? A simplistic answer is that because, as discussed earlier, creative people tend to be more emotionally unstable and thus more likely to do themselves in with drugs, alcohol, or suicide, any genetic basis for their creative tendencies is less widely represented in successive generations. Indeed, studies indicate that creative people raise fewer children (Harrison, Moore, & Rucker, 1995). Thus there may well be selective forces that reduce creativity in human populations. However, such forces throw the baby out with the bathwater. In this section we discuss evidence for two natural processes that enable us to taste the fruits of creativity while eating as little as possible of the sour rind. The first operates at the level of the individual and the second at the level of a social group.

Adapting Our Mode of Thought to the Situation

Converging evidence suggests that we engage in two forms of thought or that thought lies on a spectrum from convergent or analytic to divergent or associative (Arieti, 1976; Ashby & Ell, 2002; Freud, 1949; Guilford, 1950; James, 1950 [1890]; Johnson-Laird, 1983; Kris, 1952; Neisser, 1963; Piaget, 1926; Rips, 2001; Sloman, 1996; Stanovich & West, 2000; Werner, 1948; Wundt, 1896). In analytic thought, memory activation is constrained enough to hone in and perform logical mental operations on the most clearly relevant aspects. Associative thought enables obscure (but potentially relevant) aspects of the situation to come into play. Thus, in an analytic mode of thought, the concept "GIANT" might only activate the notion of large size, whereas in an associative mode, the giants of fairytales might come to mind. This is sometimes referred to as the "dual-process theory of human cognition" (Chaiken & Trope, 1999; Evans & Frankish, 2009), and it is consistent with current theories of creative cognition (Finke, Ward, & Smith, 1992; Gabora, 1999, 2000, 2002, 2003; Smith, Ward, & Finke, 1995; Ward, Smith, & Finke, 1999). Associative processes are hypothesized to occur during idea generation, whereas analytic processes predominate during the refinement, implementation, and testing of an idea.

It has been proposed that during the Middle Upper Paleolithic we evolved the capacity to subconsciously shift between these modes depending on the situation by varying the specificity of the activated cognitive receptive field (Gabora, 2003, 2007; for similar ideas, see Howard-Jones & Murray, 2003; Martindale, 1995). This is referred to as "contextual focus"[1] because it requires the ability to focus or defocus attention in response to the context or situation one is in. Defocused attention, by diffusely activating a broad region of memory such that everything seems to be related in some way to everything else, is conducive to associative thought. Focused attention, by activating a narrow region of memory and treating items as distinct chunks that can be readily operated on, is conducive to analytic thought. Once it was possible to shrink or expand the field of attention and thereby tailor one's mode of thought to the demands of the current situation, tasks requiring either convergent thought (e.g., mathematical derivation), divergent thought (e.g., poetry), or both (e.g., technological invention) could be carried out more effectively. And once it was possible

[1] In neural net terms, contextual focus amounts to the capacity to spontaneously and subconsciously vary the shape of the activation function, flat for divergent thought and spiky for analytic thought.

to think like this, as with any new technology, human beings wanted to play with it: Art is an activity that constantly shifts from and plays between associative and analytic thought. Through the play of art, artists expand the bounds of these cognitive functions: A poet wants the listener or reader to think both giant (big) and giant (fairy tale) when the word is mentioned in a poem. As Rothenberg (1990b) shows, Dickinson delighted in using the double meanings of the words "cleaving" and "raveled" (pp. 86–87). When the individual is fixated or stuck, and progress is not forthcoming, defocusing attention enables the individual to enter a more divergent mode of thought, and working memory expands to include peripherally related elements of the situation. This continues until a potential solution is glimpsed, at which point attention becomes more focused and thought becomes more convergent, as befits the fine-tuning and manifestation of the creative work. Perhaps those who are particularly creative are working at both modes simultaneously. The artist certainly must both free-associate personal experiences and also reach to the art itself for its tools and conventions. A great artist has incredible facility in both, translating personal experience through conventions of the art – the more an artist knows about his or her craft, the more ways this can work. The more connotations a poet can cram into the word "giant" the better. More significantly, however, artists develop in themselves a sense of this double vision. Margaret Atwood (2002) devotes a full chapter in her book on writing to exploring the essential doubleness of creative artists. She quotes Nadine Gordimer as saying the following:

> Powers of observation heightened beyond the normal imply extraordinary disinvolvement: or rather the double process, excessive preoccupation and identification with the lives of others, and at the same time a monstrous detachment. … The tension between standing apart and being fully involved: that is what makes a writer. (quoted in Atwood, 2002, p. 29)

Atwood's book on writing, in fact, spends a great deal of time looking with a sort of horrified fascination at the detached and cold stance of the empassioned, devoted artist, the double life of being engaged in the world and necessarily outside it. This is another dark side of the creative life, that one is always at the service of the art, even in moments of terrible crisis. Many artists will tell you – as Atwood does (2002, pp. 120–121) – that in the midst of a great trauma, one small part of them is thinking, "How can I use this in my art?" This coldness or detachment, then, is one way artists protect themselves from the dark side.

In sum, there appears to be a duality at work in the creative process. If the contextual focus hypothesis is true, we are able to adapt our mode of thought to the situation we are in. When we are stumped, or need to express ourselves, or need to break out of a rut, we adapt ideas to new contexts and combine them in new ways using a highly creative but potentially emotionally overwhelming associative mode of thought. We then engage in a more even-keeled analytic mode of thought in which we fine-tune these strange new combinations. In this way, the fruits of one mode of thought provide the ingredients for the other, culminating in a more fine-grained internal model of the world. Thus we get maximal benefit from the bright side of creativity while minimizing its dark side, although often not without feeling some guilt at the application of the analytic mode on profound human feeling.

BATHING IN THE LIGHT OF CREATIVITY WITHOUT ACTUALLY BEING CREATIVE

Contextual focus operates at the level of the individual. A second way Mother Nature minimizes the dark side of creativity operates at the level of the social group. In a group of interacting individuals, only some need be creative. The rest can reap the benefits of the creator's ideas without having to withstand the dark aspects of creativity simply by copying, using, or admiring them. After all, few of us know how to build a computer or write a symphony or a novel, but they are nonetheless ours to use and enjoy when we please.

This can be seen clearly in EVOC, a computer model of how ideas evolve (Gabora, 2007, 2008a, 2008b; see also Gabora, 1995). EVOC consists of an artificial society of neural network–based agents that do not have genomes and neither die nor have offspring but that can invent, assess, imitate, and implement ideas for actions, and the fitness or utility of their actions thereby gradually increases. Agents have an unsophisticated but functional capacity to *mentally simulate* or assess the relative fitness of an action before actually implementing it (and this can be turned off). They are also able to invent strategically and intuitively, as opposed to randomly, building up "hunches" based on trends that worked in the past (and this too can be turned off). This is possible because of the integrated structure of the neural networks. What is interesting about EVOC for our purposes is that it is possible to vary the ratio of agents who are capable of inventing new actions as well as the degree to which these new actions are inventive, that is, deviate from what has come before. If none of the agents are capable of inventing new ideas for actions, what happens is absolutely nothing. One could say they all more or less stand around waiting for someone *else* to do something. No new actions come into existence, so their ability to imitate is squandered. However, if even a relatively small fraction of the agents *is* capable of inventing, each new invention spreads by imitation in waves throughout the artificial society, eventually reaching another creator, who puts another spin on it, and the set of actions implemented becomes fitter or more adapted over time (Leijnen & Gabora, 2009). Thus the set of actions executed by the artificial society evolves. This phenomenon in which a small group of innovators in form or style changes the course of the art is seen over and over again in literary and artistic history. A handful of early modernist painters and poets in the first decade of the 1900s transformed how poems were written and painters painted, meaning that imagism and free verse dominate mainstream poetry now and in painting cubism and abstraction are conventions in visual art. Some would argue that these destructive tendencies in art, to throw away the old and embrace the new, are yet another facet of the "dark side of creativity." As a choreographer (whose name we unfortunately forget) once said: "If you're not doing what your predecessors did, you're doing what your predecessors did."

SUSTAINABLE INVENTION EMERGES FROM A SUSTAINABLE WORLDVIEW

Some posit that manifestation of the creative drive is a deadening process, a means of dominating, of fencing things in and boxing them up, creating new conventions that some future innovator has to break, or to kill the creative energy and freeze it in a poem or painting. But, as commented on by Frye (1963, p. 38) and as seen in a poem such as "Kubla Khan," there is also a highly involuntary, unpredictable, and very much "alive" aspect to creativity.

The relationship between the controlling and out-of-control aspects of creativity was clarified for one of us at a regular spontaneous freestyle dance event in Brussels. There were many rules: You were not allowed to arrive late, were not allowed to talk, and so forth. This seemed unnecessarily harsh. After all, people who enjoy freestyle dance go to such places to *escape* rules! The organizer, however, had thought this through carefully. He explained that each rule had a specific purpose and contributed to the creation of a space – *un cadre*, or frame – within which something could grow that was not able to grow elsewhere in the world. This clearly *was* the case. By the end of the first hour, a strikingly altered state of mind reliably came over the dancers. We entered a different world, a world of silliness and glee, or of experiencing each other as having an angelic nature, or battling tooth-and-claw like prehistoric reptiles. The rules of the game had slightly restructured our worldviews in such a way that new possibilities could manifest.

This may have broad implications for creativity. Our creative expression reflects the voluntary and involuntary constraints we impose on how we go about weaving internal models of the external world. Artistic forms (narrative structure, poetic form, compositional fields and limits) may be inherent safety nets for artists as well as audience. The artistic forms order and shape the chaotic content whether in the world around us or from the depths of the subconscious. They are the ladders or ropes that help the artist in and out of the dark. Emily Dickinson is a prime example of a poet who broke every rule in the book in terms of traditional poetry yet did so in a relentless straightjacket of hymn meter and four-line stanzas; rule-bound, she wrote poetry that prefigures modernist experimental aesthetics by several decades. The rise of the gothic as a mode in literature has paralleled the rise of the industrial revolution and the scientific revolution and the demands of women and others for equality – an age in upheaval. We see humankind's dark treatment of humankind in most literature – magic/technology is portrayed as having a dark side throughout literature – magic lamps, Prospero's magic, and so forth.

These ideas about the relationship between constraint and freedom may have implications for building a sustainable world. Clearly, if our creative brains had not evolved, we would not have invented the vast array of different ways in which we are polluting, perhaps irreparably, our planet. Although we cannot curtail the involuntary, unpredictable nature of creativity, by weaving sustainable perspectives and practices deep into our worldviews we may alter the trajectories of creative thought processes on this planet in such a way as to nurture creative ideas that are in harmony with the world at large. Atwood, in the same chapter that details artist guilt over sacrificing human feeling to one's art, shows that artists' perspectives can end up providing huge social gains: "The eye is cold because it must be clear, and it is clear because its owner must look: he must look at everything. Then she must record" (2002, p. 121). Atwood's final pronoun points the way to how the inclusion of women into the formerly perceived male domain of creativity might alter ideas about the nature of creativity and its dark side. New literature by women employs other metaphors of creativity besides dangerous chasms and destructive breaking and crashing of old boxes. Women are slowly returning the imagery of birth, from a woman's perspective, to the discussion of creativity: Although the birth of a monster might have been 19-year-old Mary Shelley's dark fear in 1818, critic Pascale Sardin suggests that contemporary writers such as Nancy Houston, a Canadian novelist, are proposing new models of creative energy: "[I]n her *Creation Diary*, [Huston celebrates] the artistic possibilities contained in pregnancy and mothering" (Sardin, 2007, p. 164). Mothering and birth, though fraught with risks, can be positive and fertile metaphors for an organic and nurturing creative power.

CONCLUSIONS

This chapter began by outlining some evidence that creativity has a dark side; that is, creative individuals often lead tormented lives and are more prone to affective disorders, abuse of drugs and alcohol, and suicide. We noted that the creative individual has what we referred to as a "self-made worldview," and his or her focus is on the realm of what could be rather than the realm of what is.

The chapter also discussed theoretical and experimental evidence that we have evolved to minimize the dark side of creativity while capitalizing on the benefits. First, we engage in contextual focus; that is, we adapt our mode of thought to the situation we are in – convergent or analytic thought for most tasks and divergent or associative thought when we are stumped or need to break out of a rut. A second means by which the dark aspects of creativity are minimized is that only some individuals in a society are creative. The rest reap the benefits of creativity by copying the creators' ideas without having to face the drawbacks of being creative.

Finally, the chapter explored implications of the fact that if our creative brains had not evolved, we would not have invented the vast array of different ways in which we are polluting, perhaps irreparably, our planet. We posited that whether or not the creative ideas we nurture are in harmony with the well-being of our planet depends on the structure of our worldviews and the dynamical patterns they fall into for weaving narratives and interpreting situations.

We would like to end this chapter by inviting anyone who is swinging or dangling from a tassel at the edge of the fabric of consensus reality to look around at all the kindred "creative types" swinging or dangling from myriad other tassels. Don't wave at them – you might fall off! Just give them a warm, supportive smile as you swing by, hold on tight, and know as you climb your way up that tassel that you're not alone and that it is with you that the potential for human transformation resides.

REFERENCES

Andreasen, N. C. (1987). Creativity and mental illness: Prevalence rates in writers and their first degree relatives. *American Journal of Psychiatry*, 144, 1288–1292.

Ansburg, P. & Hill, K. (2003). Creative and analytic thinkers differ in their use of attentional resources. *Personality and Individual Differences*, 34, 1141–1152.

Arieti, S. (1976). *Creativity: The magic synthesis*. New York: Basic Books.

Ashby, F. G. & Ell, S. W. (2002). Single versus multiple systems of learning and memory. In J. Wixted and H. Pashler (Eds.), *Stevens' handbook of experimental psychology*, Vol. 4: *Methodology in experimental psychology*. New York: Wiley.

Atwood, M. (2002). *Negotiating with the dead: A writer on writing*. Cambridge, England: Cambridge University Press.

Chaiken, S. & Trope, Y. (1999). *Dual-process theories in social psychology*. New York: Guilford Press.

Coleridge, S. T. (1996 [1798]). "*Kubla Khan*." In Richard Holmes (Ed.), Coleridge: Selected poems (pp. 229–231). London: HarperCollins.

Dickinson, E. (1960). *The complete poems of Emily Dickinson*. Ed. Thomas H. Johnson. Boston: Little, Brown.

Evans, J. & Frankish, K. (2009). *In two minds: Dual processes and beyond*. New York: Oxford University Press.

Finke, R. A., Ward, T. B., & Smith, S. M. (1992). *Creative cognition: Theory, research, and applications*. Cambridge, MA: MIT Press.

Flaherty, A. W. (2005). Frontotemporal and dopaminergic control of idea generation and creative drive. *Journal of Comparative Neurology*, 493, 147–153.

Freud, S. (1949). *An outline of psychoanalysis*. New York: Norton.

Frye, N. (1963). The keys to dreamland. In *The educated imagination* (pp. 34–44). Concord, Ontario, Canada: House of Anansi.

Gabora, L. (1995). Meme and variations: A computer model of cultural evolution. In L. Nadel and D. Stein (Eds.), *Lectures in complex systems* (pp. 471–486). Reading MA: Addison-Wesley.

(1999). Weaving, bending, patching, mending the fabric of reality: A cognitive science perspective on worldview inconsistency. *Foundations of Science*, 3, 395–428.

(2000). Conceptual closure: Weaving memories into an interconnected worldview. In G. Van de Vijver and J. Chandler (Eds.), *Closure: Emergent organizations and their dynamics*. New York: New York Academy of Sciences.

(2002). Cognitive mechanisms underlying the creative process. In T. Hewett and T. Kavanagh (Eds.), *Proceedings of the fourth international conference on creativity and cognition* (pp. 126–133). Loughborough, UK: Loughborough University Press.

(2003). Contextual focus: A tentative cognitive explanation for the cultural transition of the middle/upper Paleolithic. In R. Alterman and D. Hirsch (Eds.), *Proceedings of the 25th annual meeting of the Cognitive Science Society.* Boston, MA: Lawrence Erlbaum Associates.

(2008a). EVOC: A computer model of cultural evolution. In V. Sloutsky, B. Love, and K. McRae (Eds.), *Proceedings of the 30th annual meeting of the Cognitive Science Society, Washington, DC, July 23–26.* North Salt Lake, UT: Sheridan Publishing.

(2008b). Modeling cultural dynamics. In *Proceedings of the Association for the Advancement of Artificial Intelligence (AAAI) Fall Symposium 1: Adaptive Agents in a Cultural Context, November 7–9, The Westin Arlington Gateway, Arlington VA* (pp. 18–25). Menlo Park, CA: AAAI Press.

Gabora, L. & Aerts, D. (2005). Evolution as context-driven actualization of potential: Toward an interdisciplinary theory of change of state. *Interdisciplinary Science Reviews*, 30(1), 69–88.

Goodwin, D. W. (1988). *Alcohol and the writer.* New York: Penguin.

(1992). Alcohol as muse. *American Journal of Psychotherapy*, 46, 422–433.

Goodwin, F. K. & Jamison, K. R. (1990). Alcohol and drug abuse in manic-depressive illness. In F. K. Goodwin and K. R. Jamison (Eds.), *Manic-depressive illness* (pp. 210–226). New York: Oxford University Press.

Guilford, P. J. (1950). Creativity. *American Psychologist*, 5, 444–454.

Hoeveler, D. L. (2007). Father, don't you see that I am dreaming? The female gothic and the creative process. In Diane Long Hoeveler and Donna Decker Schuster (Eds.), *Women's literary creativity and the female body* (pp. 43–46). New York: Palgrave Macmillan.

Holmes, R. (1982). *Coleridge.* Oxford, England: Oxford University Press.

Howard-Jones, P. A. & Murray, S. (2003). Ideational productivity, focus of attention, and context. *Creativity Research Journal*, 15, 153–166.

James, W. (1950 [1890]). *The principles of psychology.* New York: Dover.

Jamison, K. R. (1989). Mood disorders and patterns of creativity in writers and artists. *Psychiatry*, 52, 125–134.

(1993). *Touched by fire: Manic-depressive illness and the artistic temperament.* New York: Free Press.

Johnson-Laird, P. N. (1983). *Mental models.* Cambridge, MA: Harvard University Press.

Harrison, A., Moore, M., & Rucker, M. (1985). Further evidence on career and family compatibility among eminent women and men. *Archivo di Psicologia, Neurologia Psichiatria*, 46, 140–155.

Kauffman, S. (2008). *Reinventing the sacred.* New York: Basic Books.

Kris, E. (1952). *Psychoanalytic explorations in art.* New York: International Universities Press.

Kristeva, Julia. (1984). *Revolution in poetic language.* Trans. Margaret Waller. New York: Columbia University Press.

(1989 [1987]). *Black sun: Depression and melancholia.* Trans. Leon S. Roudiez. New York: Columbia University Press.

Leijnen, S. & Gabora, L. (2009). How creative should creators be to optimize the evolution of ideas? A computational model. *Electronic Proceedings in Theoretical Computer Science*, 9, 108–119.
Ludwig, A. M. (1995). *The price of greatness*. New York: Guilford Press.
Martindale, C. (1995). Creativity and connectionism. In S. M. Smith, T. B. Ward, and R. A. Finke (Eds.), *The creative cognition approach* (pp. 249–268). Cambridge, MA: MIT Press.
Moers, Ellen. (1976). *Literary women*. Garden City, NY: Doubleday.
Neisser, U. (1963). The multiplicity of thought. *British Journal of Psychology*, 54, 1–14.
Norlander, T. & Gustafson, R. (1996). Effects of alcohol on scientific thought during the incubation phase of the creative process. *Journal of Creative Behavior*, 30, 231–248.
Norlander, T. & Gustafson, R. (1997). Effects of alcohol on picture drawing during the verification phase of the creative process. *Creativity Research Journal*, 10, 355–362.
Norlander, T. & Gustafson, R. (1998). Effects of alcohol on a divergent figural fluency test during the illumination phase of the creative process. *Creativity Research Journal*, 11, 365–374.
Orwell, George. (1968 [1945]). In defense of P. G. Wodehouse. In Sonia Orwell and Ian Angus (Eds.), *The Collected Essays, Journalism and Letters of George Orwell: As I Please 1943–1945*, Vol. 3 (pp. 341–355). New York: Harcourt, Brace Jovanovich.
Piaget, J. (1926) *The language and thought of the child*. Kent, England: Harcourt Brace.
Piirto, J. (2005). The creative process in poets. In James C. Kaufman and John Baer (Eds.), *Creativity across domains: Faces of the muse* (pp. 1–22). Mahwah, NJ: Lawrence Erlbaum Associates.
Rips, L. (2001). Necessity and natural categories. *Psychological Bulletin*, 127, 827–852.
Rothenberg, A. (1990a). Creativity, mental health, and alcoholism. *Creativity Research Journal*, 3, 179–201.
(1990b). *Creativity and madness: New findings and old stereotypes*. Baltimore: Johns Hopkins University Press.
Sardin, P. (2007). Creation and procreation in Margaret Atwood's "Giving Birth": A narrative of doubles. In D. Long Hoeveler and D. Decker Schuster (Eds.), *Women's literary creativity and the female body* (pp. 163–192). New York: Palgrave Macmillan.
Sloman, S. (1996). The empirical case for two systems of reasoning. *Psychological Bulletin*, 9, 3–22.
Sontag, S. (2003). *Regarding the pain of others*. New York: Farrar, Straus and Giroux.
Smith, W. M., Ward, T. B., & Finke, R.A. (1995). *The creative cognition approach*. Cambridge, MA: MIT Press.
Stanovich, K. E. & West, R. F. (2000). Individual differences in reasoning: Implications for the rationality debate? *Behavioral and Brain Sciences*, 23, 645–726.

Styron, W. (1990). *Darkness visible: A memoir of madness.* New York: Random House.

Ward, T. B., Smith, S. M., & Finke, R. A. (1999). Creative cognition. In R. J. Sternberg (Ed.), *Handbook of creativity* (pp. 189–213). Cambridge, England: Cambridge University Press.

Werner, H. (1948). *Comparative psychology of mental development.* New York: International Universities Press.

Wundt, W. (1896). *Lectures on human and animal psychology.* New York: Macmillan.

16

Creativity in the Classroom: The Dark Side

ARTHUR J. CROPLEY

TEACHERS' AMBIVALENCE ABOUT CREATIVE CHILDREN

Ng and Smith (2004, p. 87) asked the question at the heart of this chapter: "Why is there a paradox in promoting creativity in the ... classroom?" Put simply, the paradox is that most teachers express strong approval of creativity *in theory*, as already shown over 30 years ago (Feldhusen & Treffinger, 1975) and repeated more recently by Runco, Johnson, and Bear (1993). However, *in practice*, the situation is different. Although they claim that they enjoy having creative children in their classroom, and indeed, as will be shown below, creative students are often very successful learners, teachers (Dawson, D'Andrea, Affinito, & Westby, 1999)

- dislike characteristics associated with creativity and
- not seldom express disapproval or even dislike of the students in their classes who are most creative or score highest on creativity tests.

As Westby and Dawson (1995) showed, many teachers who claimed to have a favorable view of creative children almost bizarrely described them as "conforming," something that Brady (1970) had already reported early in the modern creativity era. As Smith and Carlsson (2006, p. 222) put it, " ... teachers seem to have a confused picture of what is a favorite pupil and what is a creative pupil." When the teachers in the Westby and Dawson (1995) study were given adjectives describing traits more typical of what creative children are really like (e.g., risk-taking, curious), they said that they *disliked* such youngsters (see also Aljughaiman & Mowrer-Reynolds, 2005).

Similar findings have been reported consistently in a number of different countries and regions, including Africa, Australia, Eastern and Western Europe, the Middle East, and North America (e.g., Brandau et al.,

2007; Dawson et al., 1999; Howieson, 1984; Karwowski, 2007; Ng & Smith, 2004; Obuche, 1986; Oral & Guncer, 1993; Scott, 1999; Stone, 1980; Torrance, 1963a; Westby & Dawson, 1995).

This is also true of Eastern cultures. Teachers and parents in India reported favorable views of creativity but also linked several words associated with mental illness ("emotional," "impulsive") with creativity (Runco & Johnson, 2002). Tan (2003) found that student teachers in Singapore preferred students who had pleasant dispositions (such as being kind or friendly) to students who were more creative and risk-taking. Chan and Chan (1999) found that Chinese teachers associated student creativity with socially undesirable traits; they argued that in Chinese culture, nonconforming or expressive behavior can be interpreted as arrogant or rebellious. As in other studies that found that people who express positive attitudes to creativity may not understand what creativity really involves, Lau and Li (1996) repeated the by now familiar finding that students who were the most popular also were the ones most likely to be rated as creative. To summarize: Teachers are, at best, ambivalent about creativity in the classroom. Although they express admiration of it in theory, they often dislike it in practice.

Despite this paradox, the position adopted in this chapter is that not all the blame lies with the teachers. There are factors *inherent in creativity itself* that contribute to its own difficulties in the classroom; that is, aspects of creativity's dark side play a role in the paradox just outlined – creativity contains the seeds of its own unpopularity among teachers. These contributing factors will be outlined in the balance of this chapter, and suggestions will be made for what to do about the situation.

HOW IS CREATIVITY MANIFESTED IN THE CLASSROOM?

Creativity in the classroom involves teaching and learning based on *generation of novelty*. This involves processes such as recognizing problems and discrepancies in accepted content, looking at things in a different way, making unexpected links among apparently discrepant elements of information, and developing your own solutions to problems. It places high value on

- *cognitive processes* such as problem finding or going about solving problems in ways that differs from the usual,
- *personal properties* such as boldness and self-confidence,
- *motivational states* such as dissatisfaction with received wisdom or the drive to fill gaps in knowledge,

- *resistance to social pressure to conform* to classroom norms, and
- *generation of products* that are unexpected or different from what other students produce.

The extent to which creativity in the sense just outlined is the same as creativity in the aesthetic sense or is linked to creative production in the arts, literature, science, architecture, business, industry, and the like is not clear. In particular, it is unclear how well findings based on acclaimed "sublime" creativity can be transferred to the classroom, because it is obvious that very few school children win Nobel Prizes, have their works displayed in the Tate Gallery, or their music performed at the Sydney Opera House. Nonetheless, the approach just described is commonly referred to as involving "creativity," and the customary usage will be followed here.

The contrasting ("noncreative") approach to teaching and learning involves being quiet, neat, and orderly; memorizing prescribed content and regurgitating it accurately on demand; learning and repeatedly reapplying standard methods; taking care to remain within the accepted behavioral norms; and producing products that are along the lines expected by the teacher and other students (and parents, too, for that matter). This approach focuses on acquisition of existing facts; application of traditional methods; mastery of conventional tools and instruments; use of conventional logic; speed, formal correctness, and accuracy; and not rocking the boat. Despite what they say, this is what many teachers actually like.

A striking practical demonstration of the differences between the two approaches to teaching and learning is to be seen in the differences between mathematics teaching in Japanese secondary schools and in their American and German counterparts described in the now almost infamous Third International Mathematics and Science Study (TIMSS) study (Stigler & Hiebert, 1997). Analyses of videotapes showed that typical teaching behavior of German and American teachers was to start by presenting a problem to students, demonstrate a standard solution to this problem, require the students to memorize the solution, and then give them further problems of the same type so that they could reapply this solution in a cookbook manner. By contrast, Japanese teachers started by drawing students' attention to some issue in mathematics and challenging them to work out their own understanding of the problem, specify what they would regard as a solution, and then develop a solution along the lines they had just worked out. In a nutshell, the Japanese students spent their time "inventing, analysing and proving" (Stigler & Hiebert, 1997, p. 17), whereas the Americans and Germans spent theirs practicing routine procedures until they had perfected them.

Creativity-oriented teaching and learning are not just a luxury or a frill that take the place of "real" classroom teaching and learning. They facilitate not just "creative" activities but conventional learning too. In the TIMSS study just cited, for instance, the Japanese children were the third best mathematics achievers of students from the 41 countries in the project, whereas the Germans reached place 23 and the Americans place 28. Creativity-oriented teaching and learning lead to improved traditional learning (Ai, 1999), improved motivation and attitudes (Pleschovà, 2007), and greater personal well-being (Cropley, 1990). This has been known for close to half a century (for instance, Suchman, 1961).

ANTIPATHY OR INDIFFERENCE TO CREATIVITY

The effects just described seem to be the very things teachers would want. However, the evidence cited at the beginning of the chapter shows that many teachers dislike creativity or, at the very least, creative children. This has been well known almost from the beginning of the modern creativity era, although it may not have been discussed widely. Data in Torrance (1962, 1963b) showed nearly 50 years ago that in the United States at that time about 95 percent of natural science teachers, 98 percent of social studies teachers, and 85 percent of language teachers preferred students who displayed good knowledge of the accepted facts, paid attention in lessons, and worked with speed and accuracy. Only a handful preferred independent thinking, a critical attitude, the ability to decide for oneself, and similar properties.[1] Knowledge, speed, accuracy, and the like are, of course, highly praiseworthy, and there is no suggestion that teachers should not welcome them in students. However, they should not become so dominant that anything else is rejected.

Turning to higher education, Cropley and Cropley (2005) concluded that there is little support for creative students in colleges and universities either. It is true that there has been some effort in recent years to encourage creativity in these institutions: For instance, in the United States in 1990, the National Science Foundation (NSF) established the Engineering Coalition of Schools for Excellence and Leadership (ECSEL). This had the

[1] A note of caution is needed here: As, among others Ng and Smith (2004) and Craft (2005) have emphasized, neither the idea of what constitutes creativity nor of what constitutes desirable behaviour in students is culture-free, so that care should be exercised in generalizing from a European-North American perspective to other societies and cultural traditions. The contents of this chapter refer most obviously to the European-North American perspective.

goal of transforming undergraduate engineering education. However, a review of current practice throughout higher education in the United States conducted 10 years later (Fasko, 2000–2001) pointed out that the available information indicates that deliberate training in creativity is rare.

The problem is not confined to the United States. Although the European Union has established programs bearing the names of famous innovators such as SOCRATES or LEONARDO, it is astonishing that in the guidelines for the development of education in the European Community concepts such as "innovation" or "creativity" simply do not exist. To take a second example, at least until recently, the Max Planck Institute for Human Development, Germany's leading research institute for the development of talent in research in the social sciences had never supported a project on the topics of creativity or innovation. In a personal letter dated April 26, 2006, the office of the president of the Max Planck Society confirmed that the organization does not see creativity as a significant area of research.

What this means for individuals can be demonstrated with historical examples, although we should be careful about generalizing too freely from studies of sublime creativity involving acknowledged geniuses and earth-shaking novelty to everyday creativity in the classroom. Today, we know Evariste Galois as one of the most creative mathematicians who ever lived. His prodigious mathematical talent was already visible at school, but there was what would now be called a downside: He refused to pay serious attention to anything except mathematics. His teachers described him as "original," but they also judged him to be "singular," "withdrawn," even "bizarre." Tellingly, even his mathematics teacher, whom Galois greatly admired for having opened the door to new worlds for him, found his most-brilliant-ever student's failure to fit into the social framework unacceptable and turned against him. Galois eventually was forced to leave school, but despite his teachers' efforts, he succeeded in developing what is now known as "Galois theory." One of modern history's most revered creative thinkers, Albert Einstein, suffered a similar fate: His dissertation was rejected by the faculty at the Technische Hochschule in Vienna despite (or because of) the originality of his ideas. Rejected by the education system, he went on to publish the series of papers that led to the theory of relativity while working as a patent clerk and writing in his spare time at home. His professors literally encouraged him not to give up his day job!

Unease about creativity in school-level teaching and learning is not confined to teachers, nor is it a newly emerging phenomenon. In 1904, there were massive complaints from parents of high school students in the Australian state of Western Australia about the matriculation examination for admission to the University of Adelaide in the neighboring state of South Australia (there was at that time no university in Western Australia). The complaint was straightforward (e.g., Morning Herald, 1904): The university had changed its approach to examinations. The problem was that the university had suddenly set assignments such as "Make an evaluation of the historical accuracy of Sir Walter Scott's historical novels," whereas the protesting parents had expected something like "Explain what an anachronism is, and list and summarize three examples of anachronisms in the novel *Ivanhoe*." The complainants specifically criticized the fact that it was not possible to learn by heart the answer to such questions as the "Make an evaluation ..." example, and students thus were forced to use their own judgment and imagination, with the associated variability in answers, uncertainty about what constituted the "right" answer, possible subjective reactions by examiners, and – ultimately – risk. Protesting parents made it plain that they were not demanding an *easy* examination but rather one that was predictable and objective and thus, in their eyes, fair (and solvable by means of earnest hard work = rote learning).

Almost 100 years later, in 1996, the same university changed the criteria for admission to the medical school – although there are variations, in the main, students in Australia enter medical school directly from high school, and the number of applications far exceeds the number of places available. As a result, places traditionally go to students with the highest grades in the matriculation examination, regardless of other properties that may be relevant to being a doctor. The new criteria involved a combination of high school grades, scores on an aptitude test, and results of an interview. Among other things, the latter two procedures assessed problem-solving ability, communication skills, and ability to work in teams. There was a public outcry. Some candidates with extraordinarily good high school grades did not obtain a place, and the university was depicted in the press as being antiacademic. Some parents even went to the South Australian ombudsman (without success), although the procedure had been judged by educational theorists to be "based on cogent reasoning."

In 1996, too, the thrust of the objections was that (a) problem-solving ability and the like are ill-defined and subjective, (b) the new approach meant that what students needed to know could not be reduced to predefined factual knowledge that teachers know in advance and can pass on to students, and (c) the necessary qualities (problem solving, teamwork) cannot be acquired through honest toil over textbooks, whereas "the facts" of physics, chemistry, and biology can be. In both cases, the call was for exams with (a) highly defined solutions and (b) a clearly defined pathway to the solution (learning by heart). It seems that the kind of classroom learning teachers and students prefer had scarcely changed during the course of an entire century. In fact, in October 2006, the university announced that from 2007 onward greater emphasis would be given to traditional criteria.

Rejection of the introduction of even seemingly harmless – indeed highly beneficial – novelty is not confined to schools. In the 1840s, Austrian obstetrician Ignaz Semmelweiss dramatically reduced the incidence of death from puerperal fever in the lying-in hospital in Vienna simply by requiring the obstetricians under his supervision to wash their hands before touching women who had recently given birth. However, this novelty, although highly effective in reducing the death rate because it reduced cross-infection, was seen by other doctors as insulting because it implied that they were dirty and threatened their social role as saviors of the sick (even though, in reality, it increased their effectiveness in this role). Far from showing gratitude, Semmelweiss's colleagues labeled him a crackpot who was insulting their honor, and he was rejected and hunted into madness and early death. The death rate among the women patients returned to its earlier levels! Maintenance of the social order took precedence over saving lives by introducing novelty.

CREATIVITY AS A THREAT

The parents' misgivings in the two Australian examples given earlier are easy to understand. Most of the students involved in the two protests had spent years toiling over textbooks to acquire exact knowledge of clearly specified and closely defined factual material. Suddenly, the return on this investment of time and effort and all the emotional and social accompaniments of success or perceived failure were to depend on intangibles. The facts of biology or chemistry are the same for all candidates and do not depend on how well you get along with other people, the opinion or current mood of an examiner, or similar factors, and it seems to be possible to determine with a high degree of accuracy whether a particular candidate knows the facts and for different observers to agree on the extent of such knowledge. Furthermore, teachers know the facts in advance and can organize them and present them to students and check that they have learned them sufficiently well or prescribe remedial exercises if they have not. The whole thing is satisfyingly clear-cut.

From the teachers' point of view, they are the possessors of key knowledge and are experts in doling it out in appropriate portions and checking whether it has been swallowed and digested – the masters and mistresses of the situation. From the students' and parents' point of view, the task is concrete and clear-cut. They know in advance what is required (factual knowledge), how to acquire and display it, and how it will be evaluated. It is merely a matter of making the necessary amount of effort – a thoroughly satisfactory situation for all parties, except perhaps the future patients of the doctors. Stated briefly, creativity introduces uncertainty and risk into the classroom, especially for those with a vested interest in retaining the status quo, which turns out to be the majority of participants: teachers, parents, and students alike. In a certain sense, teachers' antagonism – and especially that of parents and students – is fully understandable, even in a way justified. For many of them, creativity is clearly a bad thing. What, then, is bad about it?

It is tempting to blame teachers for their resistance to creativity in the classroom, and this may well be justified to some extent. However, the problem is, to a considerable degree at least, *inherent in creativity itself* and is part of the dark side of creativity in the classroom. Creativity

- shakes the foundations of the received classroom order,
- brings uncertainty for pupils (and parents),
- questions the value of laboriously acquired knowledge and skills,
- threatens loss of status and authority for teachers, and
- weakens teachers' self-image.

It is scarcely surprising that many teachers (as well as parents and students themselves) regard it with suspicion. I will look more closely at some of these elements of the dark side in following sections.

A Threat to Received Knowledge

The core of creativity is novelty. Without something new, there is no creativity. Although novel techniques and methods, novel use of instruments and tools, novel ways of conceptualizing an area, and novel lines of attack on a problem also involve creativity, novelty is probably most obvious in the classroom in connection with knowledge and facts. For instance, Park and Jang (2005) concluded that the creativity of physicists depended on their knowledge of their field. In particular, it was connected with (a) recognition of gaps in existing knowledge, (b) identification of contradictions in such knowledge, and (c) a drive to round out incomplete knowledge.

Creativity also involves dissatisfaction with what already exists. Miller (1992) referred to Einstein's description of how his recognition that existing theories of thermodynamics were inadequate motivated him to develop the special theory of relativity and then the general theory. Einstein continued to be dissatisfied with his own theory and worked on it for much of the rest of his life. America's most distinguished inventor, Thomas Alva Edison, was never satisfied with his own inventions and, over the years, took out more than 100 patents on the electric light bulb alone. Mumford and Moertl (2003) described two case studies of innovation in social systems (management practice and student selection for admission to university) and concluded that both innovations were driven by "intense dissatisfaction" (p. 262) with the status quo. Thus, seeing that something is wrong with existing knowledge and being unwilling to accept the situation are core properties of the creative individual.

A Threat to the Teacher's Self-Image

A simple example of where this can lead in the classroom was seen in an Italian lesson where the teacher, who spoke Italian extremely well but had little knowledge of linguistics, was asked why the English word "sun" is *il sole* in Italian (masculine) but *die Sonne* (feminine) in German. How can the sun be simultaneously masculine and feminine? This led to an attempt by the curious and inquiring student to enter into a general discussion of how words acquire gender in the first place, especially in view of the fact that a word such as "milk" is masculine in Italian (*il latte*), French (*le lait*), and Latvian (*piens*) – although admittedly it is feminine in German (*die Milch*) – despite the fact that milk is obtained from *female* animals. Even more striking is that in ancient Rome the everyday word for penis was feminine and the word for vagina was masculine! The teacher, who had never looked at things this way before, was highly embarrassed by the question, which she could not answer.[2] In the past, her lack of knowledge had not been a problem because nobody had ever asked the question, but now she had been made to look inadequate.

For most teachers, transmitting standard knowledge in an easily understand manner is the essence of their job. Their knowledge is their stock in trade, and any threat to it is a serious matter. Furthermore, when teachers' knowledge has itself been acquired in a rote-learning manner and is

[2] This issue is the subject of debate in linguistics. Oversimplified, there are two broad explanations: (a) grammatical genders are leftovers of some ancient or traditional idea of the biological gender of objects versus (b) grammatical genders have nothing to do with biological or social gender, and are simply noun classes that reflect purely grammatical properties of particular words arising from their morphology or their historical linguistic origins.

largely parroted off by them, penetrating, unexpected, even challenging questions – no matter how innocently meant – are very threatening. They challenge teachers to look at their own material in a new way and give glimpses of the yawning abyss on whose edge they are standing. This may challenge not merely knowledge (cognition) but also teachers' self-esteem ("How poor I really am in my own specialty!"), as well as threatening the teacher's authority and status not only in relation to the creative student but also in the eyes of other students, too. Little wonder that this aspect of creativity arouses teachers' unease or dislike. Anything that places their pre-eminence in knowledge in question is dangerous.

A Threat to Good Order and Discipline

Creative children thrive on questioning received wisdom and tend to look at things from a different angle. This means that they may offer "strange" answers to teachers' questions or ask surprising or even odd questions of their own or go about a classroom task in an unexpected way. Cropley (2001) gave the example of a first grader who responded to the assignment to draw a human head in a drawing class by drawing the *inside* of a head, whereas every other child in the class knew enough to draw the outside without needing any instructions to that effect from the teacher. The boy then compounded the situation by asking for the teacher's help in correctly locating the uvula inside the throat cavity! This embarrassed the teacher – who initially could not make any sense out of the question – and caused great merriment among the other children, unleashing chaos in the otherwise orderly drawing lesson.

It is sometimes hard to distinguish between creativity in the classroom and disorderliness or disruptiveness or even sheer willful naughtiness. Creative children's attempts to understand things more deeply or from a different angle and express this via apparently strange questions, unexpected answers to the teacher's questions, apparently nonsensical remarks in classroom discussions, choice of exotic contents in classroom exercises, or selection of strange topics in homework or projects can disrupt lessons, and if not stopped by the teacher, they can seem to other students to involve toleration of misbehavior, thus encouraging these children to misbehave too. In short, creativity by its very nature represents a potential threat to good order in the classroom. Indeed, especially but not only in countries where there is strong emphasis on good order and respect for authority, teachers often see creative children as defiant, chaotic, or disruptive (Brandau et al., 2007; Karwowski, 2007).

Despite the high social value placed on the idea of creativity, the picture of the socially defiant, disruptive creative individual is not absurd, even when stated in positive terms as by, for instance, Moustakis (1977), who emphasized that creativity is the pathway to "living you own life your own way." Barron (1969) even concluded that creativity requires "resistance" to socialization, and Burkhardt (1985) took the theme of the individual against society further by arguing that the creative individual must fight against society's pathologic desire for sameness (*Gleichheitswahn*). Sternberg and Lubart (1995) called this fight "defying the crowd" and labeled the tendency of some individuals to resist society's pressure to conform "contrarianism" (p. 41).

Creative Students Can Be "Difficult"

Several comprehensive reviews of research on creativity and personality have appeared over the years, including, among numerous others, Dellas and Gaier (1970), Dacey (1989), and Eysenck (1997). There seems to be a stable set of personal characteristics that are related to creativity. Many of these characteristics are highly positive: autonomy, ego strength, tolerance of ambiguity, and openness, for instance. However, as usual, there is also the dark side. Characteristics associated with creativity also include lack of concern for social norms and antisocial attitudes, as well as psychopathologic tendencies (Andreasen, 1987; Jamison, 1993). To give an example of the latter, manic-depressive disturbances (mood fluctuations ranging from depression to heightened excitement) are six times more common in creative people than in the general public. Indeed, Schuldberg (2000–2001) concluded that creativity is linked with a number of subclinical patterns of personal adjustment (i.e., patterns of characteristics that in pronounced degrees are actively pathologic but at moderate levels are not).

Dellas and Gaier (1970) showed that the personalities of creative young people are similar to those of creative adults, and this is supported by studies focusing on children. Such studies have shown that creative children are significantly more introverted, more self-willed, less satisfied, and less controlled than children who display lower levels of creativity. In social situations, they are less willing to conform and less interested in making a good impression. The example of Galois extends the list to include being withdrawn and bizarre. To put it plainly and briefly, creative students sometimes can seem to teachers to be "weird," defiant, aggressive, self-centered, or antisocial, characteristics that make them disturbing, even threatening, and this is apparently part of being creative, at least in some people.[3]

WHAT IS TO BE DONE?

Within the framework of an educational discussion, the need for an educational solution springs immediately to mind. What is it, then, that teachers need to learn? The first problem is that they may believe that "creativity" is seen only in fine art, performing arts, literature, crafts, design, and the like, so they may see no place for it in "rigorous" disciplines such as science or mathematics and may dismiss it out of hand as irrelevant. They also may equate it with mere unfettered thinking – doing whatever you like regardless of accuracy, appropriateness, or effectiveness; that is, they may confuse creativity with what Cattell and Butcher (1968, p. 271) called "pseudo-creativity" (simply letting yourself go) or at best "quasi-creativity" (generating unusual ideas, it is true, but without reference to reality). Thus the first problem arises from teachers' misconception of creativity or the uncertainty arising from the fact that there are discrepancies between the everyday idea of creativity and the more closely defined understanding in technical discussions such as that of Cropley and Cropley (2005). In a nutshell, *creativity researchers have not succeeded in communicating a sufficiently tightly integrated but yet highly differentiated definition of creativity to teachers, parents, and students*. The solution is obvious: A more closely reasoned understanding of creativity needs to be worked out and communicated widely and effectively.

Amount and Kind of Divergence

Typically, we think of creativity in terms of the *amount* of novelty generated. Even in situations where novelty is unwelcome, such as in the behavior of a jumbo jet pilot during a landing or a brain surgeon during an operation, a certain amount of deviation from standard procedures can be tolerated without any great harm. In the classroom, a question that is mildly surprising or some other slightly unusual or unexpected behavior is unlikely to cause any serious problems. It is only when the amount of deviation from the customary becomes intolerably large that it is rejected.

[3] This is not to say that creative students really are "weird," but that they display personal characteristics that differ from those of less-creative classmates, and some of these deviations from the norm are in directions that disturb teachers or make them uneasy.

In other words, a little bit of creativity is acceptable, but too much may cause problems.

However, the *kind* of deviation is also important. Millward and Freeman (2002) made a distinction between change that stays *within* the limits of the existing social system (Cropley & Cropley [2009, p. 132] called this "orthodox" creativity) and change that challenges the system (i.e., "radical" creativity). Sternberg (2006) also distinguished between creativity that accepts existing paradigms and creativity that rejects them. From the point of view of the classroom, orthodox creativity (remaining within socially prescribed limits) involves deviating only in a way that the teacher and classmates can tolerate, whereas radical creativity involves venturing into the area of socially frowned-on ideas or actions. The deviation from the usual displayed by the boy who drew the inside of a head is a simple example of novelty that broke the paradigm: He could have drawn an orthodox head (i.e., from the outside) with a very large *amount* of deviation from the usual, such as a Martian head or one with three eyes, without serious consequences, but attacking the task from a previously unseen angle (at least in the case of the particular teacher) simply was too radical.

In a study with schoolboy soccer players, Herrmann (1987) taught his team to make totally unexpected moves, such as passing the ball straight to an opponent with a remark like, "Here. Have it if you want it," and then running past the opponent and calling for a return pass, which, to the consternation of opposing goalkeepers, often was forthcoming. Passing the ball and calling for a return pass does not in itself involve any deviation from the usual, but doing it in the particular way Herrmann's players did was extraordinary (radical) and caused outbursts of rage from opposing coaches, who found it so surprising that they denounced it as cheating! The fate of Evariste Galois is another example: A large *amount* of deviation from the norm in the direction of doing extra assignments and solving them in novel ways may well have been accepted, but going about this in a way not previously seen made him "strange" and "bizarre" despite the fact that his mathematics grades were exceptionally good. It is not just a matter of doing good work, but of doing it in ways that conform to teachers' expectations.

Glück, Ernst, and Unger (2002) showed that there are fairly systematic differences among teachers with regard to how they handle amount and kind of creativity and that these are related to the discipline they teach (e.g., art versus physics teachers). As a group, the former show a certain degree of tolerance of and even encourage originality, risk-taking, impulsivity, and nonconformity (moderate to large amounts of radical creativity), whereas as a group the latter prefer logical problem solving, responsibility, and reliability (small amounts of orthodox creativity or none at all).

This classification system can be expanded to take account of a further distinction. Research such as that of Simonton (1997) suggests that some societies are *product*-oriented (they focus on producing novel works such as art, literature, machines, and gadgets), whereas others are process-oriented (they focus on techniques, production and management procedures, etc.). Different communities of experts or specialists also may reflect this difference. Engineers, let us say, may place greatest value on product-oriented novelty; philosophers, on process-oriented novelty. Much the same may be true of teachers. An example would be the difference between those mother-tongue teachers who prefer students to produce large amounts of text (product orientation) and those who emphasize planning, correct grammar and syntax, checking for accuracy, and the like, even if productivity is low (process orientation).

These considerations suggest an analysis with three dimensions: amount of creativity, kind of creativity, and process versus product orientation. In schools, mathematics teachers, for instance, typically may be oriented toward processes and open to only low levels of novelty, as well as tolerating only orthodox novelty, whereas typical drama teachers may emphasize products showing high levels of radical novelty. Regardless of the subject they teach, individual teachers can be placed on a three-dimensional grid with eight extreme "types" ranging from the "Bohemian" (open for radical novelty, tolerant of a high level of divergence, and product-oriented) to the "traditionalist" (open only to orthodox novelty, tolerant of only low levels of divergence, and process-oriented). This helps to explain why one teacher may consider a child chaotic, rebellious, and destructive, whereas another may regard the same child as a breath of fresh air. It thus seems likely that teachers located in different areas of the three-dimensional space just outlined would require different kinds of training to equip them to foster creativity in their pupils while also needing a set of concepts that would give them a common language for discussing the differences in their points of view.

Understanding Creative Products

My purpose here is not to urge blind acceptance of any and all unexpected or uninhibited behavior. I am not trying to reduce creativity in the classroom to pseudo-creativity or quasi-creativity Ultimately, the proof of the pudding is in the eating – creativity should lead to creative *products*. However, teachers need to know how to ascertain whether school children's products are creative and in what way. This is not difficult with Galois, Einstein, or Edison because their work now enjoys widespread acclaim, although even here problems can arise, as attested to by the fact that Galois and Einstein had to wait years before society could grasp their creativity. But teachers work on a day-to-day basis with day-to-day products and need to be able to recognize the creativity (or lack of it) of such products more or less immediately. Furthermore, students and parents need to understand what kind of product is being sought and how to go about producing such products. Furthermore, "rules" for defining and producing creative products need to be couched in terms that do not simply require a new kind of blind conformity. Thus all participants in education need to be helped to develop a relatively down-to-earth but at the same time flexible and open-ended definition of the "creative" product.

Cropley (2005) and Cropley and Cropley (2005, 2009) have developed a system for recognizing creativity of products based on four *dimensions* of creativity (e.g., novelty, relevance and effectiveness, elegance, and genesis), *criteria* (e.g., problematization, internal elegance, and ideas going beyond the immediate problem), and *indicators* (e.g., diagnosis: drawing attention to shortcomings in what already exists; redirection: taking existing ideas in a new direction; and seminality: drawing attention to previously unnoticed problems). They also discussed in detail (Cropley & Cropley, 2009) how educational settings should be managed, that is, how teachers should behave in the classroom in guiding teaching and learning processes, in order to foster creativity in a goal-directed, differentiated, systematic manner rather than simply reducing the level of formality or rigor. However, a detailed presentation of this material would go beyond the limits of this chapter.

In closing, it can be said that the importance of creativity for the individual and society is widely accepted nowadays, and teachers typically report that they approve of it. However, many teachers at all levels do little to foster creativity in actual practice and even show dislike of creative children. This state of affairs is not merely the fault of teachers but is inherent in creativity itself; that is, it is part of the dark side. By its very nature, creativity involves questioning existing knowledge, doing things your own way, and being "difficult." In the classroom, such processes and states easily can encourage disorderliness and disruptiveness among other children, as well as threatening (even if unintentionally) teachers' stock in trade (expert knowledge) and challenging teachers' authority and self-image. Teachers' antipathy to creativity thus is scarcely surprising. To overcome this, teachers need better understanding of the process of generation of novelty and the nature of creative products.

REFERENCES

Ai, X. (1999). Creativity and academic achievement: An investigation of gender differences. *Creativity Research Journal*, 12, 329–327.

Aljughaiman, A. & Mowrer-Reynolds, E. (2005). Teachers' conceptions of creativity and creative students. *Journal of Creative Behavior*, 39, 17–34.

Andreasen, N. C. (1987). Creativity and mental illness: Prevalence rates in writers and their first degree relatives. *American Journal of Psychiatry*, 144, 1288–1292.

Barron, F. X. (1969). *Creative person and creative process*. New York: Holt, Rinehart & Winston.

Brady, E. B. (1970). The effects of creativity and intelligence on teacher ratings. *British Journal of Educational Psychology*, 40, 342–344.

Brandau, H., Daghofer, F., Hollerer, L., Kaschnitz, W., Kellner, K., Kirchmair, G., et al. (2007). The relationship between creativity, teacher ratings on behavior, age, and gender in pupils from seven to ten years. *Journal of Creative Behavior*, 41, 91–113.

Burkhardt, H. (1985). *Gleichheitswahn Parteienwahn* [Sameness psychosis]. Tübingen: Hohenrain.

Cattell, R. B. & Butcher, H. J. (1968). *The prediction of achievement and creativity*. New York: Bobbs-Merrill.

Chan, D. W. & Chan, L. K. (1999). Implicit theories of creativity: Teachers' perception of student characteristics in Hong Kong. *Creativity Research Journal*, 12, 185–195.

Craft, A. R. (2005). *Creativity in schools: Tensions and dilemmas*. London: Routledge Falmer.

Cropley, A. J. (1990). Creativity and mental health in everyday life. *Creativity Research Journal*, 3, 167–178.

(2001). *Creativity in education and learning*. London: Kogan Page.

(2005). *Creativity and problem-solving: Implications for classroom assessment* (24th Vernon-Wall Lecture, Glasgow, November 6, 2004). Leicester: British Psychological Society.

Cropley, A. J. & Cropley, D. H. (2009). *Fostering creativity: A diagnostic approach for higher education and organization*. Mahwah, NJ: Hampton Press.

Cropley, D. H. & Cropley, A. J. (2005). Engineering creativity: A systems concept of functional creativity. In J. C. Kaufman and J. Baer (Eds.), *Faces of the muse: How people think, work and act creatively in diverse domains* (pp. 169–185). Hillsdale, NJ: Lawrence Erlbaum.

Cropley, D. H. & Cropley, A. J. (2009). Recognizing and fostering creativity in design education. *International Journal of Technology and Design Education* (in press).

Dacey, J. S. (1989). *Fundamentals of creative thinking.* Lexington, MA: Lexington Books.

Dawson, V. L., D'Andrea, T., Affinito, R., & Westby, E. L. (1999). Predicting creative behavior: A reexamination of the divergence between traditional and teacher-defined concepts of creativity. *Creativity Research Journal*, 12, 57–66.

Dellas, M. & Gaier, E. L. (1970). Identification of creativity: The individual. *Psychological Bulletin*, 73, 55–73.

Eysenck, H. J. (1997). Creativity and personality. In M. A. Runco (Ed.), *The creativity research handbook*, Vol. 1 (pp. 41–66). Cresskill, NJ: Hampton Press.

Fasko, D. (2000–2001). Education and creativity. *Creativity Research Journal*, 13, 317–328.

Feldhusen, J. F. & Treffinger, D. J. (1975). Teachers' attitudes and practices in teaching creativity and problem solving to economically disadvantaged and minority children. *Psychological Reports*, 37, 1161–1162.

Glück, J., Ernst, R., & Unger, F. (2002). How creatives define creativity: Definitions reflect different types of creativity. *Creativity Research Journal*, 14, 55–67.

Herrmann, W. (1987). *Auswirkungen verschiedener Fussballtrainingsstile auf Leistungsmotivation* [Effects of different styles for coaching football on motivation]. Unpublished master's thesis, University of Hamburg.

Howieson, N. (1984). Is Western Australia neglecting the creative potential of its youth? Paper presented at the 1984 Annual Conference of the Australian Psychological Society, Perth, August 12–17.

Jamison, K. R. (1993). *Touched with fire: Depressive illness and the artistic temperament.* New York: Free Press.

Karwowksi, M. (2007). Teachers' nominations of students' creativity: Should we believe them? Are the nominations valid? *Social Sciences*, 2, 264–269.

Lau, S. & Li, W. L. (1996). Peer status and perceived creativity: Are popular children viewed by peers and teachers as creative? *Creativity Research Journal*, 9, 347–352.

Miller, A. I. (1992). Scientific creativity: A comparative study of Henri Poincaré and Albert Einstein. *Creativity Research Journal*, 5, 385–418.

Millward, L. J. & Freeman, H. (2002). Role expectations as constraints to innovation: The case of female managers. *Creativity Research Journal*, 14, 93–110.

Morning Herald. (1904). Adelaide University examinations. *Morning Herald*, October 15, 1904, p. 17.

Moustakis, C. E. (1977). *Creative life.* New York: Van Nostrand.

Mumford, M. D. & Moertl, P. (2003). Cases of social innovation: Lessons from two innovations in the 20th century. *Creativity Research Journal*, 13, 261–266.

Park, J. & Jang, K. (2005). Analysis of the actual scientific inquiries of physicists. Available at www.arxiv.org/abs/physics/0506191. Accessed September 17, 2006.

Ng, A. K. & Smith, J. (2004). Why is there a paradox in promoting creativity in the Asian classroom? In S. Lau, A. N. N. Hui, and G. Y. C. Ng (Eds.), *Creativity: When East meets West* (pp. 87–112). Singapore: World Scientific Publishing.

Obuche, N. M. (1986). The ideal pupil as perceived by Nigerian (Igbo) teachers and Torrance's creative personality. *International Review of Education*, 32, 191–196.

Oral, G. & Guncer, B. (1993). Relationship between creativity and nonconformity to school discipline as perceived by teachers of Turkish elementary school children, by controlling for their grade and sex. *Journal of Instructional Psychology*, 20, 208–214.

Pleschovà, G. (2007, January). Unusual assignments as a motivation tool. Paper presented at the conference Creativity or Conformity? Building Cultures of Creativity in Higher Education, University of Wales Institute, Cardiff, UK. Available at www.creativityconference.org/presented_papers/Pleschova_Unusual.doc. Accessed November 17, 2007.

Runco, M. A. & Johnson, D. J. (2002). Parents' and teachers' implicit theories of children's creativity: A cross-cultural perspective. *Creativity Research Journal*, 14, 427–438.

Runco, M., Johnson, D. J., & Bear, P. K. (1993). Parents' and teachers' implicit theories of children's creativity. *Child Study Journal*, 23, 91–113.

Schuldberg, D. (2000–2001). Six sub-clinical spectrum traits in normal creativity. *Creativity Research Journal*, 13, 5–16.

Scott, C. L. (1999). Teachers' biases toward creative children. *Creativity Research Journal*, 12, 321–328.

Simonton, D. K. (1997). Historiometric studies of creative genius. In M. A. Runco (Ed.), *The creativity research handbook*, Vol. 1 (pp. 3–28). Cresskill, NJ: Hampton Press.

Sternberg, R. J. (2006). The nature of creativity. *Creativity Research Journal*, 18, 87–98.

Sternberg, R. J. & Lubart, T. I. (1995). *Defying the crowd: Cultivating creativity in a culture of conformity*. New York: Free Press.

Stone, B. G. (1980). Relationship between creativity and classroom behavior. *Psychology in the Schools*, 17, 106–108.

Smith, G. J. W. & Carlsson, I. (2006). Creativity under the Northern Lights: Perspectives from Scandinavia. In J. C. Kaufman and R. J. Sternberg (Eds.), *International handbook of creativity* (pp. 202–234). New York: Cambridge University Press.

Stigler, J. W. & Hiebert, J. (1997). Understanding and improving mathematics instruction: An overview of the TIMSS video study. *Phi Delta Kappan*, 79, 14–21.

Suchman, J. R. (1961). Inquiry training: Building skills for autonomous discovery. *Merrill-Palmer Quarterly*, 7, 147–169.

Tan, A. G. (2003). Student teachers' perceptions of student behaviors for fostering creativity: A perspective on the academically low achievers. *Korean Journal of Thinking and Problem Solving*, 13, 59–71.

Torrance, E. P. (1962). *Guiding creative talent*. Englewood Cliffs, NJ: Prentice-Hall.

(1963a). The creative personality and the ideal pupil. *Teachers College Record*, 65, 220–226.

(1963b). *Education and the creative potential*. Minneapolis: University of Minnesota Press.

Westby, E. L. & Dawson, V. L. (1995). Creativity: Asset or burden in the classroom? *Creativity Research Journal*, 8, 1–10.

17

The Dark Side of Creativity and How to Combat It

ROBERT J. STERNBERG

CREATIVITY AND EVIL

Creativity involves producing ideas or products that are novel and high in quality or impact (Sternberg & Lubart, 1995; see also essays in Sternberg, 1999). On the face of it, many of the vexing problems that exist in the literature on creativity, such as how to recognize it or how to measure it, can be and have been addressed, if not totally resolved. There are other problems, however, that are even more vexing and that defy easy resolution. Was Joseph Mengele creative in devising novel medical procedures for torturing patients? What about Adolph Hitler and his cronies in devising novel means of mass extermination or Joseph Stalin in devising an elaborate series of prison camps into which were placed real and imagined political enemies? If the novelty criterion were the only one for deciding on levels of creativity, all these madmen would be called creative. But we distinguish between *originality*, which involves only novelty, and *creativity*, which involves quality or impact as well as novelty. Much of the time, quality and impact go hand in hand, but in the cases just cited, it is not obvious that they do. Mengele, Hitler, and Stalin all had great impact with their ideas, but the ideas were not good ones.

Or were they? Revisionist history in Russia is glorifying the contribution of Stalin to the history of the country, stating that however harsh his measures, they were necessary given the times. Incredibly as well, there are still neo-Nazis around the world who believe that Hitler was one of the best leaders, if not the best leader, of all time. According to these groups, therefore, Stalin and Hitler passed all the traditional tests for being labeled creative.

Creativity thus has an element of relativism, in the sense that how creative someone is depends on who is doing the judging (see

Csikszentmihalyi, 1996). Mozart's rival, Salieri, was judged during his lifetime to be more creative than he is today, whereas Van Gogh was judged by his contemporaries to be less creative than he is today. In the same way, the artwork of a first-grade student may be creative in the context of first-grade students but not in the context of professional artists. However, if creativity is contextual, does it somehow vitiate its importance as a set of cognitive and other abilities? Intelligence tests such as the Wechsler Adult Intelligence Scale (1997) are used, in suitably translated form, all around the world. Perhaps creativity is relative in a way intelligence is not. I doubt it. Just as the basic parameters of intelligence – the ability to learn and adapt to the environment (Sternberg & Detterman, 1986) – are the same everywhere, even though the particular behaviors that constitute adaptive behavior vary widely across cultures (Sternberg, 2004, 2007), so are the basic parameters of creativity – novelty and quality or impact. The dark side of creativity does not derive purely from the concept's relativity. When we speak of an "evil genius" such as Hitler or Mengele, we are generally referring to creativity being used for bad ends. One might hope that such examples would be limited to the evil geniuses of all time – the Hitlers and the Stalins – but that is far from clear. Today, numerous countries have armed themselves with nuclear weapons with the potential to cause massive destruction. The potential for damage is enormous, and moreover, it seems likely that it is just a matter of time before such weapons end up in the hands of terrorists, who have been quite ingenious – by their standards, creative – in devising ways of delivering destruction to innocent people. The intelligence and creativity of physicists and the states that have sponsored their work have made possible the creation of such weapons. Such intelligence and creativity also have created the global warming that is now threatening many life forms around the world, including our own. Indeed, intelligence and creativity, as traditionally defined, may be the tools by which we cause our own demise as a civilization and possibly as a species.

One could, of course, stipulate that intelligence and creativity exist only when they are used in pro-social ways. The problem here is that of who is doing the defining. Typically, any policy benefits some people but not others. Those who are benefited might view as pro-social the same policies that others view as antisocial. In Hitler's Germany, what was considered pro-social would turn most people's stomachs today. The comparison need not be with the past. In some cultures, suicide bombing may be viewed as an expression of intelligence – sacrificing one's life for a good cause – and creativity – finding a way to die that inflicts maximal damage on others. In other cultures, suicide bombing is viewed as totally reprehensible.

If creativity and intelligence both can lead to so much harm, is there some other construct that one would wish creative and/or intelligent people to possess that might deter them from using their abilities in destructive ways? I would argue that there is and that the construct is *wisdom.* We always should assess and teach for wisdom in conjunction with assessing and teaching for intelligence and creativity (Sternberg, Jarvin, & Grigorenko, 2009; Sternberg, Reznitskaya, & Jarvin, 2007).

WISDOM: THE BRIGHT SIDE

What Is Wisdom?

I define "wisdom" as the application of intelligence and creativity – in this chapter the emphasis is on creativity – to achieving the common good through a balance among (a) intrapersonal, (b) interpersonal, and (c) extrapersonal interests over the (a) short and (b) long terms in order to achieve a balance among (a) adaptation to existing environments, (b) shaping of existing environments, and (c) selection of new environments (see Sternberg, 1998, 2001a, 2003, and Sternberg & Jordan, 2005, for related views). Positive values are the values that are shared by the world's great ethical systems and religions – integrity, compassion, sincerity, honesty, reciprocity – and that historically have had universal appeal. Where those values have been attacked – and they have been in many instances in history – creativity and intelligence generally have been used for dark purposes, such as during the time of the Third Reich and in Darfur, among many other places, today.

Thus wisdom is not just about maximizing one's own or someone else's self-interest but is also about balancing various self-interests (intrapersonal) with the interests of others (interpersonal) and of other aspects of the context in which one lives (extrapersonal), such as one's city or country or environment or even God. Wisdom also involves creativity, in that the wise solution to a problem may be far from obvious. Creativity thus is a necessary but not sufficient condition for wisdom. One implication of this view is that when one applies intelligence and creativity alone, one may deliberately seek outcomes that are good for oneself and bad for others. In applying wisdom, one certainly may seek good ends for oneself, but one also seeks common good outcomes for others and institutions. If one's motivations are to maximize certain people's interests and minimize other people's, wisdom is not involved. In wisdom, one seeks a common good, realizing that this common good may be better for some than for others.

A terrorist may be intelligent, he or she may be creative, but the terrorist cannot be wise. Blowing up other people clearly is not for the good of the people who are blown up and is not intended to be.

Problems requiring wisdom always involve at least some element of each of intrapersonal, interpersonal, and extrapersonal interests. For example, one might decide that it is wise to take a particular teaching position, a decision that seemingly involves only one person. But many people typically are affected by an individual's decision to take a job – significant others, children, perhaps parents and friends. And the decision always has to be made in the context of what the whole range of available options is. Thus people have to know what the options are and what they mean. To be wise, one must know what one knows, know what one does not know, know what can be known, and know what cannot be known at a given time or place.

What kinds of considerations might be included under each of the three kinds of interests? Intrapersonal interests might include the desire to enhance one's popularity or prestige, to make more money, to learn more, to increase one's spiritual well-being, to increase one's power, and so forth. Interpersonal interests might be quite similar, except that they apply to other people rather than oneself. Extrapersonal interests might include contributing to the welfare of one's school, helping one's community, contributing to the well-being of one's country, serving God, and so forth. Different people balance these interests in different ways. At one extreme, a malevolent dictator might emphasize his or her own personal power and wealth; at the other extreme, a saint might emphasize only serving others and God.

Wisdom involves a balancing not only of the three kinds of interests but also of three possible courses of action in response to this balancing: adaptation of oneself or others to existing environments, shaping of environments in order to render them more compatible with oneself or others, and selection of new environments. In adaptation, the individual tries to find ways to conform to the existing environment that forms his or her context. Sometimes adaptation is the best course of action under a given set of circumstances. Typically, though, one seeks a balance between adaptation and shaping, realizing that fit to an environment requires not only changing oneself but also changing the environment. When an individual finds it impossible or at least implausible to attain such a fit, he or she may decide to select a new environment altogether, leaving, for example, a job, a community, a marriage, or whatever.

Wisdom manifests as a series of higher-order processes that typically are cyclic and can occur in a variety of orders. These processes include

(a) recognizing the existence of a problem, (b) defining the nature of the problem, (c) representing information about the problem, (d) formulating a strategy for solving the problem, (e) allocating resources to solution of a problem, (f) monitoring one's solution of the problem, and (f) evaluating feedback regarding that solution. In deciding about a teaching job, for example, one first has to see both taking the position and not taking it as viable options (problem recognition), then figure out exactly what taking or not taking the position would mean for oneself (defining the problem), then consider the costs and benefits to oneself and others of taking the position (representing information about the problem), and so forth.

Wisdom-Related Skills

Wisdom requires many distinct skills. First, wise judgments require knowledge regarding the topics about which one has to make judgments. This knowledge is of two kinds. "Formal" knowledge is the kind of knowledge one learns in school and through books. "Informal" knowledge is the kind of knowledge that is picked up through experience – that one learns along the path of life.

Second, wisdom requires analytic thinking, but it is not the kind of analytic thinking typically emphasized in schools or measured on tests of academic abilities and achievements. Rather, it is the analysis of real-world dilemmas where clean and neat abstractions often give way to messy and disorderly concrete interests. The kind of abstract analytic thinking that may lead to outstanding performance on a test such as the Raven Matrices, which presents figural reasoning items, will be of some but not much use in complex real-world dilemmas such as how to defuse the conflict between India and Pakistan.

Third, wise solutions are often creative ones, as King Solomon demonstrated in cleverly determining which of two women was truly the mother of a child. But the kind of crowd-defying, buy-low, sell-high attitude that leads to creative contributions does not in itself lead to wisdom. Creative people often tend toward extremes, although their later contributions may be more integrative, as pointed out by Gardner (1993). Creative thinking is often brash, whereas wise thinking is balanced. This is not to say that the same people cannot be both creative and wise. It is to say, however, that the kinds of thinking required to be creative and wise are different and thus will not necessarily be found in the same person. Moreover, teaching people to think creatively will not in and of itself teach them to think wisely.

It is important to note that although wise thinking must be, to some extent, creative, creative thinking (as discussed earlier) need not be wise. Wise thinking must be creative to some extent because it generates a novel and problem-relevant high-quality solution involving balancing of interests, and novelty and appropriate quality are the two hallmarks of creativity. But a solution can be creative – such as in solving a mathematical proof – but have no particular characteristics of wisdom. The proof involves no balancing of interests and no search for a common good. It is simply an intellectual problem involving creative thinking.

Fourth, practical thinking is closer to wisdom than are analytic and creative thinking, but again, it is not the same. Wisdom is a particular kind of practical thinking. It is practical thinking that (a) balances competing intrapersonal, interpersonal, and extrapersonal interests over the short and (b) long term and (c) balances adaptation to, shaping of, and selection of environments in (d) the service of a common good. Thus people can be good practical thinkers without being wise, but they cannot be wise without being good practical thinkers. Good practical thinking is necessary but not sufficient for the manifestation of wisdom.

Fifth, wisdom also seems to bear at least some relation to constructs such as social and emotional intelligence. There are also differences, however. Social intelligence can be applied to understanding and getting along with others to any ends for any purposes. Wisdom seeks out the good through a balancing of interests. Thus a salesperson who figures out how to sell a worthless product to a customer might do so by using social intelligence to understand the customer's wants but has not applied wisdom in the process. Emotional intelligence involves understanding, judging, and regulating emotions. These skills are an important part of wisdom. But making wise judgments requires going beyond the understanding, regulation, or judgment of emotions. It requires processing the information to achieve a balance of interests and formulating a judgment that makes effective use of the information to achieve a common good

Perhaps the most salient difference among constructs is that wisdom is applied toward the achievement of ends that are perceived as yielding a common good, whereas the various kinds of intelligences may be applied deliberately toward achieving either good ends or bad ones, at least for some of the parties involved. Interestingly, the conception of wisdom proposed here is substantially closer to Chinese conceptions of intelligence than to American conceptions (Yang & Sternberg, 1997a, 1997b). Indeed, one of the words used in Chinese to characterize intelligence is the same as the word used to characterize wisdom.

Foolishness

Foolishness is the absence of wisdom (Sternberg, 2002c). Smart and creative people can be foolish and, indeed, are at times especially susceptible to foolishness if they have very high opinions of themselves and their thought processes. Foolishness thus can be part of the dark side of creativity and intelligence. Foolish people are susceptible to six fallacies in thinking.

The "fallacy of egocentrism" occurs when an individual starts to think that the world centers around him or her. In life, it is all about that individual. Other people come to be seen merely as tools in the attainment of the person's goals. Why would smart people think egocentrically when one would expect that egocentrism would be a stage out of which they would have passed many years before? The reason is, I believe, that conventionally smart people have been so highly rewarded for being smart that they lose sight of their own limitations. Wisdom requires one to know what one does know and does not know. Smart people often lose sight of what they do not know, leading to the second fallacy.

The "fallacy of omniscience" results from having available at one's disposal essentially any knowledge one might want that is, in fact, knowable. With a phone call, a powerful leader can have almost any kind of knowledge made available to him or her. At the same time, people look up to the powerful leader as extremely knowledgeable or even close to all-knowing. The powerful leader then may come to believe that he or she really is all-knowing. So may his or her staff, as illustrated by Irving Janis (1972) in his analysis of victims of groupthink. In case after case, brilliant government officials made the most foolish of decisions, in part, because they believed they knew much more than they did.

The "fallacy of omnipotence" results from the extreme power one wields. In certain domains, one essentially can do almost whatever one wants to do. The risk is that the individual will start to overgeneralize and believe that this high level of power applies in all domains.

The "fallacy of invulnerability" comes from the presence of the illusion of complete protection, such as from a huge staff. People and especially leaders seem to have many friends ready to protect them at a moment's notice. The leaders may shield themselves from individuals who are anything less than sycophantic. The problem, pointed out by Harry Truman, is that high-powered (Washington) leaders who want friends ought to buy themselves a dog. As soon as things turn bad, many of the individuals who once seemed to be friends prove to be anything but that.

The "fallacy of unrealistic optimism" results when people think that because they are so smart or creative, the ideas they have inevitably will turn out well. George W. Bush's invasion of Iraq appears at this time to have been an example, and his "mission accomplished" banner certainly was. Bravado replaced common sense and wisdom.

The "fallacy of ethical disengagement" results when people believe that ethics are important – for other people. The creative accounting at Enron, Worldcom, Arthur Andersen, and various other failed firms was indicative of this fallacy.

In terms of the balance theory of wisdom, foolishness always involves interests going out of balance. Usually, the individual places self-interest way above other interests. But not always. Neville Chamberlain truly may have believed that he was doing the best for Great Britain. In ignoring the interests of all the other countries that were being crushed under Hitler's brutal rein, though, he was ignoring the common good and, as it turned out, the long-term good of his own country.

Similarly, occasionally people sacrifice everything for another individual, only to be crushed by their own foolishness. The "classic" case is that of the prolonged war between Greece and Troy. Was Helen of Troy worth the war? Many wars have started over slights or humiliations, and the interests of the slighted or humiliated have taken precedence over the interests of the thousands who have then been sacrificed to avenge the slight. There are those who believe that the war in Chechnya resulted in part from the humiliation suffered by the Russian army in the earlier war in Chechnya. Certainly, events in post–World War I Europe contributed to Germany's humiliation after that war, thereby setting the stage for World War II.

Wisdom involves a balancing not only of the three kinds of interests but also of three possible courses of action in response to this balancing: adaptation of oneself or others to existing environments, shaping of environments to render them more compatible with oneself or others, and selection of new environments. Foolishness is reflected in actions that represents poor use and balance of these processes. Wars are examples of shaping of the environment that often have proved to be of little avail. What, for example, did the Hundred Years War have to show for itself in the end? Or, for that matter, the more recent Cold War? National leaders shaped environments in ways that caused great harm, suffering, and distress. In much of the world, they are continuing to do so.

Not only does foolishness derive from inappropriate shaping of the environment, but one also can adapt to a tyrannical environment to save one's own skin, only to find oneself paying the ultimate price. An example of this principle is shown in a quotation by Pastor Martin Niemöller:

> In Germany first they came for the communists
> and I did not speak out –
> because I was not a communist.
> Then they came for the Jews
> and I did not speak out –
> because I was not a Jew.
> Then they came for the trade unionists
> and I did not speak out –
> because I was not a trade unionist.
> Then they came for the Catholics
> and I did not speak out –
> because I was a Protestant.
> Then they came for me –
> and there was no one left
> to speak out for me.

DEVELOPING WISE THINKING

There are several reasons why schools should seriously consider including instruction in wisdom-related skills in the school curriculum.

Why Should Wisdom Be Included in the School Curriculum?

The development of wisdom is beneficial because the judgments it yields can improve quality of life and conduct. Knowledge can and indeed must accompany wisdom. People need knowledge to draw on in rendering judgments – knowledge of human nature, of life circumstances, or of strategies that succeed and strategies that fail. Although knowledge is necessary for wisdom, it is not sufficient for it. Merely having knowledge does not entail its use in judging rightly, soundly, or justly. Many highly knowledgeable individuals lead lives that are unhappy. Some of them make decisions that are poor or even reprehensible. This century provides many examples of such decisions.

First, as noted earlier, intelligence and creativity, as well as knowledge, are insufficient for wisdom or seeking of the common good. Wisdom seems a better vehicle for the attainment of the common good. Second, wisdom provides a mindful and considered way to enter considered and deliberative values into important judgments. One cannot be wise and at the same time impulsive or mindless in one's judgments.

Third, wisdom represents an avenue to creating a better, more harmonious world. Malevolent dictators may be knowledgeable and even be creative and intelligent, at least with regard to the maintenance of their own power. Given the definition of wisdom, however, it would be hard to argue they were wise. Fourth and finally, students, who later will become parents and leaders are always part of a greater community and hence will benefit from learning to judge rightly, soundly, or justly on behalf of their community.

If the future is plagued with conflict and turmoil, this instability does not simply reside *out there somewhere*; it resides and has its origin *in ourselves*. For all these reasons, we endorse teaching students not only to recall facts and to think critically (and even creatively) about the content of the subjects they learn but also to think wisely about it too.

It is impossible to speak of wisdom outside the context of a set of values that in combination may lead one to a moral stance or, in Kohlberg's (1983) view, stage. The same can be said of all practical intelligence: Behavior is viewed as practically intelligent as a function of what is valued in a societal/cultural context. Values mediate how one balances interests and responses and collectively contribute even to how one defines a common good. The intersection of wisdom with the moral domain can be seen in the overlap between the notion of wisdom presented here and the notion of moral reasoning as it applies in the two highest stages (4 and 5) of Kohlberg's (1983) theory. Wisdom also involves caring for others as well as oneself, along the lines suggested by Gilligan (1982). At the same time, wisdom is broader than moral reasoning. It applies to any human problem involving a balance of intrapersonal, interpersonal, and extrapersonal interests, whether or not moral issues are at stake.

Procedures to Follow in Teaching for Wisdom

Wise thinking can be developed. How? There are several procedures a teacher can follow in teaching for wisdom (Sternberg, 2001b). First, students should read classic works of literature and philosophy (whether Western or otherwise) to learn and reflect on the wisdom of the sages. The rush to dump classic works in favor of modern works would make sense only if the wisdom these modern works had to impart equaled or exceeded that of the classic works.

Second, students would be engaged in class discussions, projects, and essays that encouraged them to discuss the lessons they have learned from these works and how they can be applied to their own lives and the lives of others. A particular emphasis would be placed on the development of dialogical and dialectical thinking. Dialogical thinking involves thinkers understanding significant problems from multiple points of view and understanding how others legitimately could conceive of things in a way that is quite different from their own. Dialectical thinking involves thinkers understanding that ideas and the paradigms under which they fall evolve and keep evolving not only from the past to the present but also from the present to the future, as noted by Georg Hegel.

Third, students would need to study not only "truth," as we know it, but values. The idea would not be to force-feed a set of values but to encourage students reflectively to develop their own values.

Fourth, such instruction would place an increased emphasis on critical, creative, and practical thinking in the service of good ends – ends that benefit not only the individual doing the thinking but others as well. All these types of thinking would be valued, not just critical thinking of the kind that leads to a higher IQ.

Fifth, students would be encouraged to think about how almost everything they study might be used for better or worse ends and to realize that the ends to which knowledge is put *do* matter.

Finally, teachers would realize that the only way they could develop wisdom in their students would be to serve as role models of wisdom themselves. A role model of wisdom will, I believe, take a much more Socratic approach to teaching than teachers customarily do. Students often want large quantities of information spoon-fed or even force-fed to them. They then attempt to memorize this material for exams, only to forget it soon thereafter. In a wisdom-based approach to teaching, students will need to take a more active role in constructing their learning. But a wisdom-based approach is not tantamount to a constructivist approach to learning. Students have not achieved or even come close to achieving wisdom when they merely have constructed their own learning. Rather, they must be able not only to construct knowledge from their own point of view but also to construct and sometimes reconstruct it from the point of view of others. Constructivism from only a single point of view can lead to egocentric rather than balanced understanding.

We have constructed a program for teaching for wisdom in the context of American History (Reznitskaya & Sternberg, 2004; Sternberg, Jarvin, & Reznitskaya, 2008; Sternberg, Reznitskaya, & Jarvin, 2007). The program attempts to apply principles such as developing dialogical and dialectical thinking to instruction of middle-school students. For example, students might come to see that what one group views as settlers, another group views as invaders or that the same economic policies that might be viewed favorably at one time might be viewed unfavorably at another.

CONCLUSION

Creativity has a dark side. So does intelligence. Our schools teach children in ways that seem largely oblivious to the dark sides to which knowledge, intelligence, and creativity can be put. The Harry Potter series is perhaps among the best set of children's books for teaching how intellectual skills and knowledge may be put to bad use, but unless they start appearing in mandated curriculum materials, they are unlikely to be taught in many schools. The world is right now paying for the dark side of creativity and intelligence – through global warming, disappearance of the ozone layer, proliferation of nuclear weapons, terrorism, the increasingly uneven income distribution, and many other problems. As a society, we could do something about it if we chose to teach for wisdom (Sternberg, 2002a, 2002b). Regrettably, to date, our society has lacked the wisdom to teach for wisdom. We are paying and will continue to pay the consequences.

REFERENCES

Amabile, T. M. (1996). *Creativity in context.* Boulder, CO: Westview.

Csikszentmihalyi, M. (1996). *Creativity: Flow and the psychology of discovery and invention.* New York: HarperCollins.

Flynn, J. R. (1987). Massive IQ gains in 14 nations: What IQ tests really measure. *Psychological Bulletin*, 101, 171–191.

Gardner, H. (1993). *Creating minds.* New York: Basic Books.

Gilligan, C. (1982). *In a different voice: Psychological theory and women's development.* Cambridge, MA: Harvard University Press.

Janis, I. L. (1972). *Victims of groupthink.* Boston: Houghton Mifflin.

Kohlberg, L. (1983). *The psychology of moral development.* New York: Harper & Row.

Neisser, U. (Ed.). (1998). *The rising curve.* Washington: American Psychological Association.

Niu, W. & Sternberg, R. J. (2001). Cultural influences on artistic creativity and its evaluation. *International Journal of Psychology*, 36, 225–241.

(2002). Contemporary studies on the concept of creativity: The East and the West. *Journal of Creative Behavior*, 36, 269–288.

Reznitskaya, A. & Sternberg, R. J. (2004). Teaching students to make wise judgments: The "teaching for wisdom" program. In P. A. Linley and S. Joseph (Eds.), *Positive psychology in practice* (pp. 181–196). New York: Wiley.

Sternberg, R. J. (1997). *Successful intelligence.* New York: Plume.

(1998). A balance theory of wisdom. *Review of General Psychology*, 2, 347–365

(Ed.). (1999). *Handbook of creativity.* New York: Cambridge University Press.

(2001a). What is the common thread of creativity? Its dialectical relation to intelligence and wisdom. In R. J. Sternberg and N. Dess, (Eds.), Special section on creativity. *American Psychologist*, 56, 360–362.

(2001b). Why schools should teach for wisdom: The balance theory of wisdom in educational settings. *Educational Psychologist*, 36, 227–245.

(2002a). It's not just what you know but how you use it: Teaching for wisdom in our schools. *Education Week*, 22, 42, 53.

(2002b). It's not what you know but how you use it: Teaching for wisdom. *Chronicle of Higher Education*, 48, B20.

(2002c). Smart people are not stupid, but they sure can be foolish: The imbalance theory of foolishness. In R. J. Sternberg (Ed.), *Why smart people can be so stupid* (pp. 232–242). New Haven, CT: Yale University Press.

(2003). *Wisdom, intelligence, and creativity synthesized*. New York: Cambridge University Press.

(2004). Culture and intelligence. *American Psychologist*, 59, 325–338.

(2007). Intelligence and culture. In S. Kitayama and D. Cohen (Eds.), *Handbook of cultural psychology* (pp. 547–568). New York: Guilford Press.

Sternberg, R. J. & Detterman, D. K. (Eds.). (1986). *What is intelligence?* Norwood, NJ: Ablex.

Sternberg, R. J., Jarvin, L., & Grigorenko, E. L. (2009). *Teaching for wisdom, intelligence, creativity, and success*. Thousand Oaks, CA: Corwin.

Sternberg, R. J. & Jordan, J. (Eds.). (2005). *Handbook of wisdom: Psychological perspective*. New York: Cambridge University Press.

Sternberg, R. J. & Lubart, T. I. (1995). *Defying the crowd: Cultivating creativity in a culture of conformity*. New York: Free Press.

Sternberg, R. J., Jarvin, L., & Reznitskaya, A. (2008). Teaching for wisdom through history: Infusing wise thinking skills in the school curriculum. In M. Ferrari (Ed.), *Teaching for wisdom: Cross-cultural perspectives on developing wisdom*. New York: Springer.

Sternberg, R. J., Reznitskaya, A., & Jarvin, L. (2007). Teaching for wisdom: What matters is not just what students know, but how they use it. *London Review of Education*, 5, 143–158.

Wechsler, D. A. (1997). *Wechsler Adult Intelligence Scale*, 3rd ed. (WAIS-III). San Antonio, TX: Psychological Corporation.

Yang, S. & Sternberg, R. J. (1997a). Conceptions of intelligence in ancient Chinese philosophy. *Journal of Theoretical and Philosophical Psychology*, 17, 101–119.

Yang, S. & Sternberg, R. J. (1997b). Taiwanese Chinese people's conceptions of intelligence. *Intelligence*, 25, 21–36.

18

A Systems Engineering Approach to Counterterrorism

AMIHUD HARI

TERRORISM AS CREATIVITY

Terrorism is "the systematic use of violence to create a general climate of fear in a population and thereby to bring about a particular political objective" (Encyclopaedia Britannica, 2005). Terrorism has a long history, and it affects almost every nation on earth: The terrorist activities of September 11, 2001 (abbreviated here as 9/11) brought this home with particular force. Terrorist actions such as 9/11 have two properties that are of particular interest for the present discussion: They must surprise the people against whom they are directed (otherwise the intended targets will implement appropriate prevention or avoidance measures), and they must be effective. If they do not have any concrete effect (such as killing people), they are a failure and even may lead to loss of resources for no gain, "gain" being understood in terms of dealing out death and destruction. This means that in order to cause a climate of fear, the malevolent products of terrorists must satisfy the two basic criteria of creativity (novelty and effectiveness). Thus they are an example of the dark side of creativity – indeed, because they deliberately seek to cause harm, of malevolent creativity.

Unlike most people and organizations that generate effective novelty, terrorists function more or less outside the conventional moral system. In terms of Sternberg's position (Chapter 17 of this volume), they do not concern themselves with the common good (although terrorists often claim that they are pursuing a higher-order common good, even in the societies they claim to be defending their work is often rejected or condemned), so they are not affected by moral considerations. Even in war, nations usually pay at least lip service to the "rules of war" and seek through

I am grateful for the support provided by Gordon Institute for System Engineering in the Technion Haifa, Israel.

"rules of engagement" to avoid harming innocent bystanders, although there are notable exceptions such as the allied bombing of the German civilian populace in World War II. This means that the creativity of terrorists represents a special form of malevolent creativity – one that is free of moral constraints.

Creative Products

Terrorists are continually changing their ways and means in, unpalatable as it is to say it, a very creative manner, as 9/11 shows. Thus a deep understanding of creativity is required to understand the way they are creating the next threat and to block their activities. Since the effects their malevolent creativity achieves (i.e., its products) are crucial for success or failure (from the point of view of the terrorists), understanding the creativity of terrorists requires an extended understanding of creative *products*. Cropley and Cropley (2005) have proposed an appropriate model of creative products founded on the concept of creativity in engineering, basing it on the idea of "functional" creativity. A bridge built by civil engineers must, for instance, not only be original and surprising in design (novel), but it also must solve the problem successfully of how to transport vehicles across a river (effectiveness). A nonfunctional product that is novel but ineffective is at best aesthetic. A product that is effective but not novel is routine. There may well be a place for both in creativity theory, but a terrorist product that does not cause death and destruction is useless (from the terrorists' point of view), no matter how novel it is, whereas terrorists who stick to a single product become predictable, no matter how effective the product is, and are likely to have a short career.

The concept of functional creativity goes beyond mere novelty and effectiveness to incorporate two further principles that are used in this chapter to analyze the malevolent creativity of terrorists. These are elegance and genesis (Cropley and Cropley originally referred to the latter as "generalizability"). In the present context, an "elegant" product is one that achieves its effective surprise in a smooth, neat, and (of particular importance for antiterrorist agencies) economical way. A "generic" product is one that draws attention to previously unnoticed weaknesses (seminality), suggests new ways of solving old problems (germinality), or transfers directly to different situations (Cropley & Cropley, 2005). While novelty and effectiveness are sufficient for a solution to be creative, in business settings, elegance and genesis add value to a new solution, for instance, by making it difficult for rivals to emulate or nullify it or by subtracting value from rival solutions, for instance, by making a whole class of competing solutions obsolete. To take a simple example, the development of the transistor not only added effective novelty to the area of portable radio construction but also ultimately revolutionized communications technology (genesis) and subtracted value from the vacuum tube, despite the fact that vacuum tubes continued to be capable of doing the job they were developed for, although no longer used.

Cropley, Kaufman, and Cropley (2008) drew attention to a further property of functional solutions. They are highly susceptible to the effects of time because the passage of time usually means loss of novelty, and where effectiveness depends on surprise, loss of novelty frequently leads to loss of effectiveness. Cropley, Kaufman, and Cropley (2008) called this effect "decay" of novelty/effectiveness. D. H. Cropley (Chapter 19 of this volume) gives the example of the thwarting of the 9/11 terrorists' planned use of flight UA93 to attack either the White House or the Pentagon. Once the passengers on that flight heard about the World Trade Center attacks, that is, once novelty had seriously decayed, they were in a position successfully to oppose the planned further attack, albeit at the cost of their own lives.

The problem for the users of malevolent creativity is that they do not wish to conceal their novelty from public knowledge: On the contrary, they often wish it to become as widely known as possible, for instance, to achieve the general climate of fear referred to in the opening paragraph. This means that, as in the UA93 example just cited, the novelty of their actions often decays very rapidly. Terrorists thus must constantly generate further effective novelty. The same is true of countermeasures: Their life cycle is very short. They must involve fast, effective, adaptive solutions to deal with continuously changing conditions. Organizations seeking to engineer antiterror solutions have to be very creative to remain effective because terrorists continuously change their methods. Thus the malevolent creativity of terrorists can be regarded as a process of extremely flexible, rapidly changing generation of effective novelty in the face of competition from a rival (antiterrorism agencies). The terrorists, however, are not constrained by working from a highly stable, immobile infrastructure such as extensive physical plant, a body of career managers, control by government or other regulators, or the demands of shareholders, as traditional businesses are. Terrorist organizations use this freedom to plan and perform their operations.

OPPOSING TERRORISTS' MALEVOLENT CREATIVITY

Thinking of terrorism as malevolent creativity sheds light on creative ways of combating it. Counterterrorist agencies need to see their activities in the context of competing functional creativity. Terrorists and counterterrorists are two creative agencies competing with each other to develop functionally creative products that outperform their opponents' products, add value to their own products, or subtract value from their opponents' products. This applies to products that are physical engineering devices and objects (e.g., metal detectors) as well as products that are systems, services, and processes. The concept of functional creativity dictates that counterterrorism must, at a minimum, continuously generate effective novelty in order to stay ahead of the competition (the terrorist). Furthermore, by understanding the terrorist product in terms of the characteristics of functional creativity, it is possible to tailor counterterrorist solutions to maximize their effectiveness and even to subtract value from the terrorist product.

Many counterterrorist approaches focus only on problem solving. Creativity theory, however, emphasizes creative problem *finding*. This includes re-examination of the nature of the problem and asking whether the right problem is being addressed. This is akin to the difference between verification and validation in engineering. Verification asks, "Are we solving the problem right?" whereas validation asks, "Are we solving the right problem?" A problem-finding approach makes it possible to see combating terrorism in a new light. The following example from Tibi (2003) demonstrates this.

Passengers, airport operators, and aviation companies are all forced to invest substantial resources and time in order to prevent hijackings. But is the problem of terrorists hijacking passenger aircraft really one of preventing them from getting guns onto the aircraft? Or is it really a problem of negating the danger posed by a terrorist who has succeeded in getting a gun onto an aircraft? The former focuses attention on things like metal detectors and security screening, whereas the latter might focus attention on arming other passengers as a means of negating the effect of an armed terrorist. In the event of a hijacking, the "autoimmune" concept is based on enlisting the passengers to foil the event rather than trying to prevent the hijacking in the first place. Both approaches are directed at solving the underlying problem of hijacking, yet they generate radically different solutions, some of which (like metal detectors) have already experienced very substantial decay of novelty and are not 100 percent effective, in any case, so they are easy for terrorists to counteract. The metal detector also gives potential terrorists ample opportunity to study their competitors and devise their own creative ways of subtracting value from (nullifying) their competitor's efforts.

A solution to the newly defined problem might, for example, involve providing nonlethal weapons to all passengers. While radical, it is certainly original and surprising (not least for the terrorist). Arguably, this "autoimmune" aircraft solution would have stopped the 9/11 events within seconds of the first terrorist brandishing his box cutter and saved many lives. The purpose of this example is not to suggest an actual solution but to illustrate the kinds of thinking and analysis, based on concepts of creativity, that would yield other real, workable solutions. Such solutions, realistically, may work only once because of novelty decay. It is no longer so much the case that the price of peace is eternal vigilance; rather, it is now the case that the price of survival is eternal creativity.

Counterterrorists also face an interesting variant of the moral issues discussed previously in order to avoid their own creativity becoming dark. Western cultures generally are not prepared to compromise fundamental values such as freedom of transportation, freedom of communication (the right to know), legal systems founded on the presumption of innocence and trial by jury, the right to meet, and the right to privacy, especially in business and financial issues. Public opinion in the West still protests and opposes any attempt to compromise these values in order to prevent terror. Examples include objections to activities such as building security fences to segregate populations, preventative searches of people and property without due cause, pre-emptive investigations, profiling, and preventive arrests. It may well, of course, be right to oppose such measures, but that does not alter the facts of the uneven playing field on which the two organizations compete. Thus the creativity of counterterrorists is restricted by constraints that the malevolently creative can ignore.

A SYSTEMS ENGINEERING–ORIENTED APPROACH TO FINDING SOLUTIONS

The efforts of the International Council on Systems Engineering (INCOSE) to modify the SE processes to develop antiterror solutions are very impressive (INCOSE, 2002, 2003, 2004, 2005). However, cases have arisen where an antiterror solution-development team simply refused to use the SE guidelines as required by the SE standards and handbooks because of the urgency of the problems. They claimed that standard SE processes do not meet the special characteristics of antiterror solutions development outlined earlier and especially that they do not display the required urgency. Comments such as "We have to save lives here; there is no time for the 26 standard views of DODAF documents" were encountered (DODAF is the

U.S. Department of Defense Architecture Framework) (DODAF, 2004). Responding to this problem, Hari and Weiss (1996) proposed a 10-step approach to designing solutions that they called the "integrated customer-driven design method" (ICDM). This integrates creativity-fostering techniques such as brainstorming (Gordon, 1961; Osborn, 1957) and TRIZ (Theory of Inventive Problem Solving) (Altshuller, 1984).

In the past, novel products and systems frequently were designed by a single person who possessed all the know-how needed. With the information explosion, the possibility of a single person designing a novel complex system alone has been practically eliminated, and an integrated product development team (IPT) is needed (Clausing, 1994). The tools developed by the design theory and methodology community and by ICDM are aimed at assisting and coordinating the activities of an IPT in the development of a new product or a new system. In counterterrorism, a methodology is required that will generate rapid and constantly changing solutions. A telling factor is the need for continuous creativity aimed at solving the "right" problem. Such approaches are referred to in SE as "agile."

According to the *American Heritage Dictionary of the English Language*, "agile" is defined as an ability to move in a quick and easy fashion; active (Houghton Mifflin, 1976). Key practices of agile SE were published by Wilson and Mooz (2003), who defined it as

> ... rapid user and stakeholder requirements management, including concept selection, architecture development, system integration, verification, and validation in a development environment characterized by swift adaptation to changes, non-hierarchical baseline management, and a notable absence of low-value bureaucracy.

The features that distinguish agile SE from traditional SE are speed and adaptability. A deep discussion on agility is found in Dove (2001). He discusses agility from the broader enterprise and organizational viewpoint, including a set of tools for analyzing, measuring, and designing change-proficient business practices and strategies. The seven key practices of agile SE can be summarized as

1. The project team understands, respects, and works (behaves) within a defined systems engineering process.
2. The project is executed as fast as possible with minimum down time or staff diversion to other priorities during the project.
3. All key players are physically or virtually colocated. Other contributors are available online.

4. There is a strong bias for automatically generated electronic documentation. Engineers rely on their tools and their "electronic engineering notebooks" to record decision rationales. Artifacts and documentation for operations and replication are done only if necessary, not to support an existing bureaucracy or policy.
5. Baseline management and change control are by formal, oral agreement based on "make a promise, keep a promise" discipline, and players hold each other accountable. Control gates are settled with a handshake.
6. Opportunity exploration and risk reduction are accomplished by expert consultation and rapid model verification, coupled with close customer collaboration. Software development is done in a rapid development environment, whereas hardware is developed in a multidisciplined model shop.
7. A culture of constructive confrontation pervades the project organization. Issues are actively sought. Anyone can identify an issue and pass it on to the most likely solver. No issue is left unresolved (the team takes ownership for success; it is never "someone else's responsibility").

The Antiterror Solution Workshop

The desire to satisfy these requirements while complying with SE standards and processes motivated the development of a special five-day workshop. The participants included some of the most creative experts in a wide range of areas. The focus of the workshop was on an immediate, painful, and relevant problem. Israel experienced a series of terror attacks with many civilian casualties during the years 2003–2004. In one of them, a suicide bomber had recently blown up a bus in Haifa, Israel, and 14 people, most of them children, had been murdered; one of them was the son of a colleague. The urgency of the problem created a feeling of a mission, excitement, devotion, and persistence.

The effort started with preparatory meetings. The first one included decisions on the methodology, the problems to focus on, the time frame, general instructions, and boundaries and constraints of the expected solutions. A half-day "awareness day" was then carried out. During this, the representative of the customers described the needs and the challenges, the organizers described the methodology, and the president of the organization gave the motivation and declared the management commitment to the process. The participants were arranged in four teams – a team for each terror problem that was to be solved. In a second meeting, the team structure was finalized, and customer representatives were allocated to each of the teams. In this preparation meeting, background material also was selected and sent to the team members. Logistic preparation, budgets, and some other formal arrangements also were finalized.

The workshop meetings took place in the organization's training facility, which includes a plenum hall, four syndicate rooms, and other facilities. The team meetings were scheduled for five consecutive Tuesdays. This allowed team members to continue with their regular jobs. The workshop structure also allowed team members to go through some reading and Internet search activities between the meetings. Each day was opened with a short session of methodologic and general instructions; then the teams dispersed to the syndicate rooms for the team sessions. Toward the end of the day, the teams returned to the plenum hall to present their outcomes to the other teams for discussion and for decision making for the next meeting as well as conclusions.

The workshops were accompanied and supported by an organizational consultant, who observed the whole process, interviewed team members and customer representatives, and helped the facilitators with advice and lessons learned. The process was structured but flexible. Methodology was tailored to the special requirements of the process and each team's unique characteristics. For example, two teams found that their solutions were mutually linked, and these teams initiated additional joint sessions. A series of terror events in Israel encouraged organization of another workshop to solve other terror problems in 2004.

The workshops yielded several conceptual and technological solutions to the major problems. Some examples for such concepts include

- Autoimmune concept for airplane hijacking
- Self-checking at the bus door
- A fence with no fence
- Real-time intelligence for terror events

As a result of the lessons learned in these workshops, research was initiated to develop, study, and formalize the counterterror agile system engineering process.

In all, 30 teams of experienced engineers were assigned to develop creative antiterror solutions; 19 of them served as research groups, and 11 served as control groups. All 30 teams applied the 10 steps of ICDM step by step. The teams met 14 times, once a week for 3 hours of training, consulting, and sharing their progress, and continued applying the process during the days between meetings. Data were measured and collected on several aspects of the work, such as time investment, performance, effectiveness, novelty, elegance, generalizability, design quality, and levels of ICDM methodology performance. The research teams and the control teams performed their tasks at the same time but did not know about each other. The subjects of the projects include ports protection, bus protection, border pass systems, portable police barriers, containers protection, water reservoirs protection, and terror-intent forensic incrimination.

Results indicated that

1. Using agile SE processes, two to three months from a need identification to implementation of a solution is more than enough time.
2. In order to achieve reasonably good results, a team should invest 100 to 170 hours per team member. To achieve very good results, the team needs to invest more then 200 hours per person, which is questionable from an economic point of view.
3. The creative activities of ICDM encourage the teams to be very creative and to create many ideas and concepts.
4. The screening tools of ICDM help to reduce the number of ideas and concepts to a manageable number. As a result, the screening tools of ICDM help to identify the best ideas and concepts rapidly and efficiently.
5. Incentives help the teams to create more ideas and more primary concepts.
6. Final concepts exhibit a high level of novelty and effectiveness.
7. Final concepts also achieve a high level of elegance.
8. The generic quality of products is low.

An enormous amount of effort is being invested to initiate rapid, creative, and effective methods of combating terrorist malevolent creativity. One of these efforts was the establishment of workshops that offered a semistructured environment for the creation of new ideas and conceptual solutions by highly motivated teams. This chapter presented such a process and discussed the special ingredients and features of agile systems engineering as applied to antiterror solutions and the application of the model of functional creativity in the context of combating terrorism.

REFERENCES

Altshuller, G. S. (1984). *Creativity as an exact science.* New York: Gordon & Breach.

Clausing, D. (1994). *Total quality development.* New York: ASME Press.

Cropley, D. H. & Cropley, A. J. (2005). Engineering creativity: A systems concept of functional creativity. In J. C. Kaufman and J. Baer (Eds.), *Creativity across domains: Faces of the muse* (pp. 169–185). Hillsdale, NJ: Lawrence Erlbaum.

Cropley, D. H., Kaufmann, J., & Cropley, A. J. (2008). Malevolent creativity: A functional model of creativity in terrorism and crime, *Creativity Research Journal*, 20, 105–115.

DODAF. (2004). *DoD architecture framework*, Version 1.0, Vol. 1, February 9,. Washington D.C., 83 pp.

Dove, R. (2001). *Response ability: The language, structure and culture of the agile enterprise*. New York: Wiley.

Encyclopædia Britannica. "Terrorism." In *Encyclopedia Brittanica*. Available at http://www.britannica.com. Accessed May 13, 2005.

Gordon, W. J. J. (1961). *Synectics, the development of creative capacity.* New York: Harper.

Hari, A. & Weiss, M. P. (1996). ICDM – an inclusive method for customer-driven conceptual design. In *Proceeding of the 2nd ASI Annual Total Product Development*, November 1996, Pomona CA (pp. 721–747).

Houghton Mifflin. (1976). *American Heritage Dictionary of the English Language*. Boston: Houghton Mifflin.

INCOSE. (2002). Mackey, W. F., Pyster, A., Crisp, H., Cropley, D., Mayian, S., Raza, S., Cropley, A. The role of systems engineering in combating terrorism. In *INCOSE 2002 – 12th Annual International Symposium Proceedings*, Las Vegas, NV.

(2003). Mackey, W. F., Crisp, H., Cropley, D., Long, J., Mayian, S., Raza, S. The role of systems engineering in combating terrorism. In *INCOSE 2003 – 13th Annual International Symposium Proceedings*, Washington, D.C.

(2004). Mackey, W. F., Long, J., Ewald, W., Weinmann, I., Zonnenshain, A., Gianni, B. Recent systems development and legal efforts to secure national borders in the US, Europe, Israel, and Iraq. In INCOSE *2004 – 14th Annual International Symposium Proceedings*, Toulouse, France.

(2005). Mackey, W. F., Sutton, S. J., Long, J., Wright, D. M., Zonnenshain, A., Ewald, W. Will current international counterterrorism strategy reduce or eradicate terrorism? A debate on the issues. In INCOSE *2005 – 15th Annual International Symposium Proceedings*, Rochester, NY.

Osborn, A. F. (1957). *Applied imagination: Principles and procedures of creative thinking.* New York: Charles Scribner's Sons.

Tibi, D. Y. (2003). Autoimmune concept for dealing with the problem of airplane hijacking. Paper presented at the Technologies, Systems, and Architecture for Transnational Defense Conference, AeroSense, SPIE, Orlando, Florida, April.

Wilson, M. A. & Mooz, H. (2003). Agile systems engineering for rapid project solution development. In *INCOSE 2003 – 13th Annual International Symposium Proceedings*, Washington, D.C.: INCOSE.

19

Malevolent Innovation: Opposing the Dark Side of Creativity

DAVID H. CROPLEY

Cropley (2005) and Cropley, Kaufman, and Cropley (2008) explored the notion that creativity might be employed with the deliberate intention of causing harm or damage to others (e.g., McLaren, 1993; James, Clark, & Cropanzano, 1999) by focusing on acts of terrorism. One of the starkest examples of such *malevolent* creativity was seen in the terrorist attacks of September 11, 2001 (9/11). Judged against the criteria of a functionally creative product developed by Cropley and Cropley (2005) – namely, novelty, relevance and effectiveness, elegance and generalizability – Cropley et al. (2008) argued that terrorists, such as those involved in the 9/11 attacks, exploit creativity to help them achieve their goals. Whether used consciously or unconsciously, creativity is as much a weapon for terrorists as it is for business executives.

Cropley et al. (2008) also, however, explored the notion of "decay" in relation to creativity. In essence, every creative product, process, or service, once implemented, sows the seeds of its own destruction. In the case of the 9/11 terrorists, the very novelty that was so spectacularly successful in the Twin Towers and Pentagon attacks had, by the time of the United Airlines (UA93) hijacking, decayed to the point that UA93's passengers responded quite differently, possibly quite creatively, and with some success. The effectiveness of the terrorist attack on UA93 was significantly diminished in comparison with the other attacks on 9/11 (if we assume that, as is generally thought to be the case, the terrorists intended to crash the plane into either the White House or the U.S. Capitol). Cropley et al. (2008) argued that by linking novelty and effectiveness in this way, valuable insights can be gained for the practice of counterterrorism. This chapter takes the discussion of malevolent creativity a step further, with the goal of developing additional insights into what might be done to counteract the use of creativity with the intention of causing damage or harm to others.

ESTABLISHING A CONCEPT OF MALEVOLENT CREATIVITY

I discussed the concept of creativity as a tool that might be used deliberately to enhance the actions of terrorists in 2005 (Cropley, 2005). That article drew parallels between the results of creativity as a competitive enabler in business and its usefulness in the domains of terrorism/counterterrorism. I argued that the same competitive benefits that businesses hope to draw on through creative products are also available to people and organizations with less benevolent motives. It is clear that while creativity normally is regarded as a tool for enabling positive, affirming change, there is no reason why it cannot be used for negative, destructive ends. Terrorists are, in the words of Benjamin and Simon (2002), "genuinely creative, and their ingenuity and desire to inflict massive casualties will continue to drive them."

In the earlier article (Cropley, 2005), I focused principally on the terrorist "product" – the outcome of actions taken by the terrorist. This includes hijackings, suicide bombings, roadside bombings using improvised explosive devices (IEDs), and other acts of terror. A principal conclusion of the article was that novelty, as a key prerequisite of creative products, is vital to and indeed enhances the effectiveness of the product. The article also concluded that novelty, and therefore effectiveness, decays from a peak when the product is first introduced into its "market" to lower levels simply with the passage of time. The article did not examine or attempt to analyze the range of personal, social, and environmental factors that also impact on creativity and creative potential. In other words, the focus was on the *product* exclusively among the four *P*s (Process, Person, Product, and Press) first proposed by Barron (1969) and Rhodes (1961). Cropley et al. (2008) extended the concept of malevolent creativity further. While the discussion continued to focus predominantly on the product (the criminal act), the article also touched on some of the personal and noncognitive aspects that might be linked to malevolent creativity.

Whether malevolent creativity is defined only in relation to acts of terror or more generally in relation to all acts with intentional negative consequences, it is apparent that a deeper understanding of creativity with the deliberate intention of causing harm or damage to others will be achieved only by studying not only the product but also the person, process, and press. This is consistent with the view expressed by Runco (Chapter 2 of this volume) that creativity is best understood without consideration of products. Furthermore, in the same way that creativity in a conventional, benevolent sense is the driver and enabler of innovation, it follows that malevolent creativity is also the driver and enabler of malevolent innovation. Therefore, to understand malevolent applications of creativity and innovation and to gain insights into how these may be mitigated or eliminated, it is necessary to focus broadly on the general process of innovation and the social and psychological dimensions that influence it, subsequently applying the insights gained to an analysis of malevolent innovation.

CREATIVITY AND ITS ROLE IN THE PROCESS OF INNOVATION

Before turning to the specifics of malevolent creativity and innovation, it is first necessary to revisit the relationship between creativity and innovation in a conventional context. In business, commerce, manufacturing, and marketing, for instance, it has become almost axiomatic that creativity and innovation are the keys to meeting the challenges of the early twenty-first century arising from technological advances, social change, globalization, climate change, and the like. Buzan (2007, p. vii) stated that "it is a globally accepted awareness that right now any individual, company or country wishing to survive in the twenty-first century must develop the brain's seemingly infinite capacity to create and to innovate." He also drew attention to initiatives in various countries to "raise the level of national creativity" as a means for ensuring growth in "today's increasingly competitive global marketplace." Florida (2004) tied the strength of the world's largest economy, the United States, directly to creativity by attributing its success to its openness to new ideas and its ability to attract creative people to work within its environment. The global financial crisis, the effects of which began to make themselves felt late in 2008, only reinforces the importance of creativity to recovering this prosperity. As part of the "European Year of Creativity and Innovation," José Manuel Barroso, president of the European Commission, stated in May 2009 (Barroso, 2009)

> Creativity is a crucial component of our capacity to innovate. And innovation is a key factor not just to become more competitive, but also to improve our quality of life and the sustainability of our development.
>
> The progress of societies depends on innovation and creative people: these two elements contribute to collective and individual well-being, ensure long and sustainable economic growth and can provide new answers to the current financial, economic and social crisis.

In other words, the notion that creativity and innovation are, in effect, drivers of positive, beneficial, and desirable change is entrenched in our collective consciousness. Creativity and innovation therefore are instinctively regarded as good.

However, as Anderson (1992, p. 40) pointed out, harnessing creativity presents special difficulties:

> Creativity is the gift and discipline that provides the competitive edge – in marketing, production, finance, and all of the other aspects in an organization. Firms and managers crave it. Awards are given for it. Incentives encourage and cajole it. But it is still the most elusive weapon in an executive's arsenal.

Thus, although there may well be widespread, in-principle acceptance of the importance of creativity, not to mention its fundamentally positive nature, the crucial practical questions that continue to challenge us are (a) how to recognize it in practical settings such as a manufacturer, business, or market and (b) how to shape such environments in ways that promote generation of effective and useful novelty and its subsequent implementation in practice, the two steps that together define the process of innovation. However, Anderson also might have added that the benefits that creativity offers are open to abuse. Greed, avarice, and ambition can tilt the positive benefits of creativity from economic well-being and a competitive edge to economic ruin.

A Differentiated Approach

The original surge in modern interest in creativity was set in motion by the so-called "Sputnik shock" in 1957, when the Western world's engineers were judged to have been beaten in the first event in the space race by the engineers of the Soviet Union. Thus the initial focus of the modern creativity era was not artistic creativity but practical, or what Cropley and Cropley (2005, p. 169) called "functional" creativity. The focus of thinking was not traditional aesthetic questions of truth and beauty but pragmatic issues of how to promote national welfare through production of useful machines, tools, technological devices, appliances, production and distribution systems, and so on (regrettably, especially weapons).

However, the discussions that followed immediately on the Sputnik shock and dominated psychological thinking for the next 50 years were strongly shaped by the ideas of Guilford, which were already well known among specialists, especially in psychometrics (e.g., Guilford, 1950), as well as by the thinking of Torrance (e.g., Torrance, 1962, 1963), an educator whose ideas achieved their greatest impact in elementary school classrooms.

Furthermore, the more philosophical discussions of what creativity is for came to be dominated by humanistic writers (e.g., Maslow, 1973; May, 1976; Rogers, 1961), who saw its value as lying in its perceived beneficial effects on personal growth, self-actualization, and similar aspects of individual well-being. The result was that the creativity discussion came to be dominated by questions of recognizing, measuring, and fostering creative thinking in the classroom, and the purpose of fostering creativity came to be seen as the personal development of individuals. Promotion of creativity came to be seen as a matter of encouraging divergent thinking, above all among schoolchildren, in order to promote individual development. Such an approach runs the risk of becoming mere "glorification of individuals" (Boden, 1994, p. 4).

One result of this was that *products* came to be neglected or evaluated purely from the point of view of degree of divergence from the conventional, and such divergence often was treated as inherently good. A child who produced a surprising drawing was regarded as "creative" regardless of whether the drawing satisfied aesthetic or practical criteria or even made any sense at all. Of course, there is no doubt that divergent thinking plays a major role in creativity – Runco (1991) has reviewed this role extensively – but on its own, it cannot account for functional creativity. Plucker and Renzulli (1999) summarized a substantial number of research studies in which products were a central focus. However, their interest was in psychological testing, and they saw the study of products as a response to a "perceived need for external criteria to which researchers could compare other methods of measuring creativity" (Plucker & Renzulli, 1999, p. 44). In other words, products were little more than a tool for looking at other issues. Looked at from a practical point of view, mere divergence and self-expression are likely to lead only to "pseudo-creativity" (e.g., Cattell & Butcher, 1968, p. 271) or at best "quasi-creativity" (Heinelt, 1974). The former involves novelty deriving only from nonconformity, lack of discipline, blind rejection of what already exists, and simply letting oneself go. The latter has many of the elements of genuine creativity – such as a high level of fantasy – but only a tenuous connection with reality, that is, a lack of practical usefulness. An example would be the novelty generated in daydreams.

In recent years, however, discussions once again have become more practical. Horenstein (2002, p. 2) emphasized practical, useful creativity involving "devices or systems that *perform tasks or solve problems* [emphasis added]." Burghardt (1995, p. 4) made the distinction even more explicit: He saw engineering and technological creativity as "creativity *with a purpose* [emphasis added]," whereas creativity in fine art and the like is "creativity with *no functional purpose* [emphasis added]." Such creativity directly promotes social welfare through its contribution to the emergence of new machines, structures, and processes in such areas as engineering, health care, agriculture, and even law enforcement. For instance, economic theory suggests that returns on investments in rich countries should have been lower during the second half of the twentieth century than during the first half because the stock of capital was rising faster than the workforce. However, the fact is that they were considerably higher. The decisive factor that defeated the law of diminishing returns and added greatly to an explosion of human material welfare was the *addition to the system of new knowledge and technology*, that is, creativity. In fact, at the turn of the century, creative products were accounting for more than half the economic growth (Economist Technology Quarterly, 2002, p. 13).

It is this practical view of creativity, focusing on functional purpose and problem solving, that opens a door to the dark side of creativity. Put simply, how is creativity to be understood if the functional purpose to which creative solutions are applied is to cause harm to others?

THE SIX *PS* OF CREATIVITY

Useful, practical, *benevolent*, products – especially ones that can be produced and/or marketed successfully – are what business and industry are interested in. How are organizations to be managed to promote the development of such products? The traditional model of creativity in psychology is the four *P*s approach: The social/psychological factors involved in creativity are the person, the process, the product, and the influence of the surrounding environment (press), as originally proposed by Barron (1969) and Rhodes (1961). This offers a starting point for developing an answer to the question just asked. However, Cropley and Cropley (2008) argued for a more differentiated discussion of noncognitive factors by subdividing person into *personal properties*, *motivation*, and *feelings*, thus looking at creativity from the point of view of a *six* Ps model: "Process," "Personal Motivation," "Personal Properties," "Personal Feelings," "Product," and "Press." The manager's task then seems disarmingly straightforward: Help people master processes that lead to effectively novel products, motivate people to carry out such processes, support personality traits that help them do this, make sure that they feel good about developing effective novelty, recognize "good" products, and provide appropriate rewards for such products.

The Paradoxes of Innovation

Unfortunately, identifying facilitatory or inhibitory cognitive processes, personal characteristics, motives, and feelings and identifying environmental conditions that promote creativity and innovation turn out to be less straightforward than might have been hoped. Psychological research (e.g., McMullan, 1978) has shown that the human properties and environmental conditions involved in innovation are not necessarily universally favorable or unfavorable – something that is facilitatory under some circumstances may be inhibitory under others. Such apparently contradictory findings led Cropley (1997) to refer to the whole area of creativity as a "bundle of paradoxes" (p. 8).

For the sake of brevity and simplicity, the paradoxes of creativity are reduced here to a series of bipolar dimensions that summarize the paradox for each of the six *P*s. For instance, production of effective novelty is fostered by a family of cognitive processes that can be subsumed under the heading "divergent" (e.g., making broad associations, recognizing surprising links, etc.) but also by a family of essentially "convergent" processes (e.g., homing in on the best answer, testing the practical effectiveness and feasibility of a trial solution), even though these appear to be diametric opposites. This paradox of creative processes will be presented here via the shorthand of "divergent versus convergent thinking." In the case of personal properties, innovation is facilitated by a cluster of traits such as tolerance of ambiguity and inner-directedness, as well as by an apparently contradictory cluster involving properties such as eagerness to eliminate ambiguity and willingness to go along with others. These two clusters are summarized as involving the bipolar dimension of "innovative versus adaptive personal properties."

In the case of motivation, the paradoxes are summarized under "proactive versus reactive motivation." The individual is sometimes prompted to act by internal motives such as dissatisfaction with the status quo and by identifying problems oneself (proactively), sometimes by external factors such as pressure from a manager to solve an already existing problem (reactively). Feelings may be "generative" or "conserving" – for instance, an individual may feel excited about the prospect of generating something novel but also may sometimes feel frightened and wish only to preserve as much as possible of the status quo. In the case of products, both creative and routine by-products are required (a product has to be novel, but it also has to work), yielding the dimension "creative versus routine products," and both high- and low-demand properties of the work environment facilitate innovation. Sometimes giving people their head may be most favorable to innovation, sometimes insisting that they produce the goods. The paradoxes of each *P* are summarized in Table 19.1, which also gives further, more specific examples of what each dichotomy involves.

The existence of these paradoxes – seemingly contradictory bipolar dimensions that may favor creativity under some circumstances but inhibit it under others – presents both benevolent and malevolent creativity with certain challenges. Logically, for benevolent creativity, the challenge is to adapt the organization and individual in such a way as to conform to the facilitatory pole of each dimension and avoid the inhibitory pole. In the case of malevolent creativity, the challenge for counterterrorism is the opposite – how can we force the inhibitory pole of each dimension onto terrorists and others who seek to use creativity for malevolent purposes?

TABLE 19.1. *The paradoxes of the six Ps of innovation*

P	Paradox	
Process	*Divergent thinking versus convergent thinking*	
	Involves: • Conceptualizing a situation broadly • Asking unexpected questions • Making remote associations • Problem finding and restructuring • Generating solution criteria • Communicating a situation in a general way	Involves: • Conceptualizing a situation precisely • Accepting the way a situation is presented • Reapplying the already known • Recognizing familiar patterns in material • Working according to existing criteria • Communicating a situation to others clearly and precisely
Personal properties	*Innovative personality versus adaptive personality*	
	A person is: • Tolerant of ambiguity • Flexible • Independent • Nonconforming • Open-minded	A person is: • Eager to eliminate ambiguity • Inclined to do things in known ways • Eager to win the agreement of others • Inclined to go along with others • Closed-minded

P	Paradox	
Motivation	*Proactive motivation versus reactive motivation*	
	A person is driven by: • The urge to go it alone • Risk-taking • Low drive for closure • Drive to seek the new/surprising	A person is driven by: • The urge to cooperate with others • Risk avoidance • Drive for rapid closure • Drive to avoid the new/ surprising
Feelings	*Generative feelings versus conserving feelings*	
	A person feels: • Pleasure in finding a novel solution • Excitement in the face of • uncertainty • Optimism when problems arise • The desire to do more when successful • Enjoyment of challenge when unsuccessful	A person feels: • Pleasure in already having an easy solution • Anxiety in the face of uncertainty • Pessimism if problems arise • Relief and feeling of closure when successful • Disappointment and discouragement when unsuccessful
Product	*Creative product versus routine product*	
	A product is: • Novel • Elegant • Seminal • Germinal	A product is: • Relevant (matches task specification) • Correct • Effective
Press	*Low management demand versus high management demand*	
	Management: • Defines tasks broadly • Assigns responsibilities loosely • Offers opportunities for acquiring broad knowledge and skills • Makes time for analyzing and ruminating • Is open to and rewards novelty • Delays sanctions against lack of success • Protects those who don't conform • Stands up to external pressure	Management: • Defines tasks narrowly • Assigns highly specific responsibility • Insists on deep specialized knowledge • Demands rapid solutions • Is suspicious of novelty • Rewards "not rocking the boat" • Quickly sanctions lack of success • Sidelines/ridicules those who don't conform • Gives in to external pressure

The Phase Approach

The simultaneous importance of mutually contradictory processes, motivational states, personal properties, and feelings; the importance of products being both new and yet also fitting in with what already exists; and the need for both high and low demand in the environment raise considerable difficulties for people such as managers who wish to establish an environment that will promote production and exploitation of effective novelty. They must promote, for instance, accuracy and effectiveness because innovations must work properly or their firm will risk serious harm. Accuracy and effectiveness involve convergent thinking, adaptive personal properties, conserving feelings, extrinsic motivation, routine products, and high environmental demand. However, they also must foster generation of variety and perception of possible applications of such novelty, which involve divergent thinking, innovative personal properties, generative feelings, intrinsic motivation, surprising products, and low environmental demand. Thus managers face the seemingly impossible task of combining fire and ice.

The answer to how this is to be done is provided by a phase approach: Contradictory poles of the paradoxes really are both of central importance, but *not simultaneously* – apparently contradictory processes, subproducts, human factors, or environmental presses play their key role *in different phases* of the process of innovation. The influence of certain environmental conditions waxes and wanes in importance depending on what phase of the innovation process is currently active. Particular human properties may foster production of effective novelty in one phase but inhibit it in another. For instance, the personal trait of nonconformity or the process of unfettered thinking may together foster seeing problems and getting novel ideas about what to do about them in situations where coming up with something new is required but inhibit painstaking verification of the value of ideas or effective communication in situations where the primary task is to link novelty to the requirements of the real world in ways that are understandable and acceptable to users (such as marketing people or customers).

What is needed is a phase model that sorts out the sequence of steps involved. The "classical" approach is that of Wallas (1926), who originally proposed seven phases, although over the years this came to be reduced to four: information, incubation, illumination, and verification. However, Cropley and Cropley (2008) argued for seven phases that they labeled "preparation," "activation," "generation," "illumination," "verification," "communication," and "validation." The first five phases involve production of effective novelty and thus are concerned, in essence, with creativity as it is typically understood in the dominant psychological/educational discussion. The last two phases involve applying or exploiting the novelty and thus, in a sense, are the phases where creativity fuses with the real world to become innovation. These phases do not necessarily form a lock-step progression of completely distinct stages. There are interactions, false starts, restarts, early breakoffs, and the like that have been referred to by Shaw (1989) as involving "loops."

Thus, for instance, in the phases of activation and generation, it is important to think divergently, but in the phases of validation and verification, it is important to think convergently (see Table 19.2). To take a second example, a highly demanding management style may facilitate innovation in the phases of communication and validation but inhibit it during preparation, activation, and generation. What is needed is an environment that makes it easy for people to function in either way *at the right time.* Martindale (1989, p. 228) referred to this process of moving backwards and forwards from one pole of a paradox to the other in the course of generation and exploitation of effective novelty as "oscillation." Koberg and Bagnall (1991, p. 38) referred to "alternating psychobehavioral waves." In cricket-playing countries, people who can oscillate or alternate would be described in everyday language as "all-rounders," whereas in baseball terms, until recently they would have been known as "switch hitters."

When the six *P*s are mapped onto the seven phases, the result is a differentiated model of the creativity/innovation process that specifies more precisely (a) the different mental actions that are central to innovation, (b) the sequence of steps (phases) leading to an innovation (*process*), (c) what *personal properties*, *motives*, and *feelings* are of central importance in each step (*person*), and (d) what kind of sub*product* the actors need to generate in each step. Armed with this insight, the model then identifies (e) environmental properties – especially management behaviors (*press*) – that will either inhibit or foster innovation in each phase of the process. Table 19.2 shows the pole of each paradox that is of core importance in each phase.

It is important to note that the entries in each cell (e.g., "convergent thinking" in the cell specifying the core process in the phase of preparation) are not meant to imply that the process, personal property, motivational state, pattern of feelings, intermediate product, or kind of environment mentioned in a cell is exclusively involved in the phase in question. For instance, in the example given (the process in the phase of

TABLE 19.2. *Paradoxical social-psychological dimensions and the phases of innovation*

Dimension Phase	Process	Motivation	Personal properties	Feelings	Product	Press
Preparation	Convergent	Mixed	Adaptive	Conserving	Routine	High
Activation	Divergent	Proactive	Innovative	Generative	Creative	Low
Generation	Divergent	Proactive	Innovative	Generative	Creative	Low
Illumination	Convergent	Proactive	Innovative	Generative	Creative	Low
Verification	Convergent	Mixed	Adaptive	Conserving	Routine	High
Communication	Mixed	Reactive	Adaptive	Conserving	Routine	High
Validation	Convergent	Reactive	Adaptive	Conserving	Routine	High

preparation), divergent thinking (making unexpected combinations, seeing surprising implications, etc.) also may play a role, in addition to the convergent thinking (acquiring factual information, reasoning logically) mentioned in the table. However, the process of convergent thinking is of *predominant* importance in this cell: The main thing here is to acquire broad and accurate mastery of what is already known. In the same way, in the phase of generation, a certain degree of pressure from the environment to produce a result (high environmental demand) also may be facilitatory, in addition to the low demand mentioned here, but the *core* quality of the environment in this phase is that it provides freedom from pressure to find a quick solution (low demand).

The Six *P*s of Malevolent Innovation

In the same way that (benevolent) creativity is better understood in the context of the broader process of (benevolent) innovation (see Table 19.2), and drawing on the idea that benevolent creativity can be contrasted with its misapplication, in the form of malevolent creativity, I now return to the idea of malevolent innovation. In particular, if we can understand (benevolent) creativity better by examining not only the product but also the person, process, and press, it follows that we can gain deeper insights into malevolent innovation in the same way. It is a reasonable hypothesis that the elements that either inhibit or foster benevolent creativity also foster or inhibit malevolent creativity. Similarly, the phases through which an individual and/or organization proceeds as an idea is first conceived and then exploited are the same irrespective of the intended purpose of the result – good or bad. This view is consistent with Runco's argument (Chapter 2 of this volume) that creativity can or indeed should, he claims, be examined without reference to products because in his view the process of creativity is neutral and independent of the benevolent or malevolent nature of the product.

The rationale is that if a particular pole of each social-psychological dimension (see Table 19.2) is ideal for (benevolent) innovation, then it is also ideal for malevolent innovation. If I were advising a firm about how to improve its innovation on the basis of this model, I would say, for example, "When you are in the phase of generation, you should endeavor to create a low-demand environment" (i.e., the cell in Table 19.2 that shows the intersection of the "generation" phase and the "press" dimension). In the case of malevolent innovation, however, since the aim of counterterrorist activities is to *inhibit* rather than facilitate innovation, the reverse it true.

To counteract the malevolent innovation of terrorists, for example, it is necessary to promote conditions that are known to be *bad* for creativity. To counter malevolent innovation, I would advise: "When terrorists are in the phase of generation, their malevolent innovation process is enhanced by a low-demand environment. Therefore, to disrupt this phase, counter-terrorist organizations would seek to reverse, or disrupt, or interfere with the 'Press', to make the phase as ineffective as possible." This would be achieved, for example, by forcing a high-demand environment on the terrorists (e.g., by constant harassment).[1]

Further examples help to illustrate the manner in which the phase model of innovation may be applied to opposing the dark side of creativity. One element of a low-demand press, which is favorable for the generation phase of creativity, among others, is the opportunity to acquire broad knowledge and skills. Thus society must seek to deny this opportunity to terrorists. The importance of knowledge can be seen in the case of the 9/11 terrorists, who lived in the United States prior to their attack; they attended flying schools to develop the skills they needed and were able to visit airports and observe security procedures in everyday use. We need to ask the question: "How could these opportunities have been denied to the terrorists?" Keeping in mind that we are seeking ways to limit the opportunity for terrorists to acquire broad skills and knowledge (i.e., preparation) without knowing exactly what these might be, lawful societies are faced with a difficult task. On the other hand, in the case of benevolent activities, we also do not know exactly what might be useful and beneficial. We only know that if we increase and encourage opportunities to acquire broad skills and knowledge, then these might be useful at some point. The question is, therefore, how to deny terrorists and potential terrorists opportunities to acquire broad knowledge and skills (without imposing a solution that is as bad or, indeed, worse than the problem it is trying to solve because, for instance, it unduly restricts the everyday freedom of ordinary members of the public).

In the generation phase, divergent thinking is a desirable facilitatory dimension. In a benevolent context, a company might, for example, encourage the use of techniques such as brainstorming, as well as encouraging individuals to ask unexpected questions, look for unusual combinations of ideas, and so forth. How do we disrupt or inhibit divergent

[1] Some of the suggested strategies that would result from promoting the mirror image of the conditions that foster creativity may be draconian or restrictive. However, in order to remain within the limits of the present chapter, I will not attempt to analyze the moral or social implications here.

thinking in potential terrorists? In fact, two approaches to opposing the dark side of creativity emerge. We can either interrupt or inhibit what is known to be favorable in a given phase, or we can actively encourage the pole that we know is unfavorable in a given phase. In this current example, where divergent thinking is favorable and facilitatory, the latter approach to counteracting malevolent innovation requires us to examine how we actively encourage *convergent* thinking among terrorists? This leads to an important dilemma associated with using the phase model of innovation for counterterrorism. Unlike conventional, benevolent situations, we have to assume that we have little or no direct control over the individuals and organizations seeking to undertake malevolent innovation. Unlike a company seeking to develop an innovative new product, we cannot send the terrorists on an *anti*brainstorming workshop! Thus we must find ways to achieve the desired effect of disrupting the malevolent innovation process *indirectly* – whether by inhibition of what is favorable or encouragement of what is unfavorable.

Given the constellation of seven phases and six dimensions in innovation (see Table 19.2), it is also hard to set up different conditions to disrupt every possible combination of phase and dimension. I have already stated that conditions that favor one phase typically inhibit another, and vice versa. Thus, rather than attempting to monitor where terrorists are in the innovation process and adapting the dimensions accordingly, as we would attempt to do in a benevolent situation, it makes more sense to try to insert one or more *barriers* across points in the innovation process in the hope that these will prove difficult, if not impossible, for malevolent innovators to cross. Table 19.3 highlights the phases and dimensions of the malevolent innovation process and illustrates the concepts of phase barriers to malevolent innovation. The barriers are marked by the vertical bold lines between "Preparation" and "Activation," between "Generation" and "Illumination," and between "Verification" and "Communication."

An approach to identifying where these barriers should be placed is to examine each dimension and decide which pole of the dimension is more open to disruption (either by inhibition of the favorable condition or encouragement of the unfavorable condition). For example, is it easier to disrupt convergent thinking or divergent thinking in our situation, where we have only indirect control over what the malevolent innovators do? Once we establish which pole of each dimension is the most susceptible to disruption, we then can match this with the ideal constellations in Table 19.3 to find the phase or phases most likely to be affected by barrier(s) to malevolent innovation.

TABLE 19.3. *The (malevolent) innovation phases and dimensions with potential phase barriers*

			→ → Invention → →				→ Exploitation →	
	Phase	**Preparation**	**Activation**	**Generation**	**Illumination**	**Verification**	**Communication**	**Validation**
Dimension	**Poles**	Knowledge, problem recognition	Problem definition, refinement	Many candidate solutions	A few promising solutions	A single optimal solution	A working prototype	A successful product
Process Thinking Style	Convergent versus Divergent	Convergent	Divergent	Divergent	Convergent	Convergent	Mixed	Convergent
Motivation	Reactive versus Proactive	Mixed	Proactive	Proactive	Proactive	Mixed	Reactive	Reactive
Personal Properties	Adaptive versus Innovative	Adaptive	Innovative	Innovative	Innovative	Adaptive	Adaptive	Adaptive
Feelings	Conserving versus Generative	Conserving	Generative	Generative	Generative	Conserving	Conserving	Conserving
Product Phase output	Routine versus Creative	Routine	Creative	Creative	Creative	Routine	Routine	Routine
Press Organizational climate	High Demand versus Low Demand	High	Low	Low	Low	High	High	High

The approach to disrupting malevolent innovation presents some interesting challenges. In the same way that most of the literature on creativity has an assumed benevolent focus, the literature also has focused on ways to help people enhance their ability to think divergently, be suitably motivated, etc. We are now looking at ways to do the opposite – to inhibit the ability of people to think divergently, for example – we are interested in what might be called "anticreativity." The discussion is complicated by the fact that we lack direct control over the subjects of interest. Is it possible to foster a particular kind of thinking, or a particular motivation, or certain feelings, or indeed a particular organizational climate indirectly? Can we remotely manipulate how terrorists think in order to make them less effective innovators?

GENERAL PRINCIPLES FOR DISRUPTING MALEVOLENT INNOVATION

The model of innovation summarized in Table 19.3 suggests two fundamental approaches to disrupting malevolent innovation:

- Phase blocks
- Dimensions blocks.

The former approach, already touched on, seeks to identify ways of disrupting the flow of the malevolent innovation process from one phase to the next (i.e., it is based on the columns of Table 19.3 – "Preparation," "Activation," "Generation," "Illumination," "Verification," "Communication," and "Validation"). The latter seeks to identify social-psychological dimensions that are most amenable to disruption, that is, the rows of Table 19.3 – "Thinking Processes," "Motivation," "Feelings," and the like).

It makes sense that the further we proceed along the path of innovation, the closer we get to a working product. Terrorists take advantage of the first phase, preparation, by developing required skills and collecting intelligence about their intended target, much in the manner of the 9/11 terrorists. The preparation phase therefore seems to offer potential for nipping malevolent innovation in the bud. At the same time, we must assume that preparation manifests itself to varying degrees. Even if we limit the malevolent innovators' opportunities for preparation, they still can proceed, albeit less well equipped for malevolent innovation. The preparation phase therefore seems to offer potential primarily in terms of weakening but not blocking malevolent innovation. The verification phase seems to offer the next opportunity for blocking the malevolent innovator. We know that terrorists frequently conduct trials of their intended method of attack. The bombers who attacked London in July 2005 rehearsed their attacks in a form of verification intended to confirm that their "solution" was indeed the single, best method of attack. How do we block this verification phase and thus disrupt the malevolent innovator? The final phase that offers an opportunity to block the malevolent innovator is the communication phase. Involving wider communication of the product, this phase requires the malevolent innovator to broaden the base of those involved, with the risk that "competitors" (e.g., counterterrorism agencies) will learn of it before it can be fully exploited. How can this communication phase be disrupted?

These three phases offer scope for blocking the malevolent innovation process (see Table 19.3) because they require interaction between the innovators and the wider world. Preparation requires that malevolent innovators immerse themselves in the environment they are targeting. Verification requires that the malevolent innovator rehearse the malevolent product in a realistic setting. Communication requires that malevolent innovators "advertise" their product. To block malevolent innovation in these phases requires strategies that limit the ability of the malevolent innovator, in this case a terrorist, to immerse himself or herself in the target environment. The concept of "phase blocks" tells us *when* in the process to apply strategies for disrupting malevolent innovation. The question of *how* to disrupt malevolent innovation – whether inhibiting the favorable or encouraging the unfavorable – is addressed by considering "dimension blocks."

Blocking Dimensions

Blocking "dimensions" (see Tables 19.2 and 19.3) focuses on the disruption of process, motivation, feelings, and the like. If we start by looking at the dimensions of the three phases identified earlier, one fact stands out. The phases of preparation, verification, and communication have nearly identical favorable dimensions. This suggests that an approach based on the following strategies would have potential to block the three key phases identified in the preceding section when combined with other generic phase-blocking strategies described in the preceding section:

- *Disrupting convergent thinking.* Convergent thinking is favorable to innovation in the three phases of concern. Of the two strategies – inhibiting the favorable or encouraging the unfavorable – it seems to make most sense to try to inhibit the terrorists' ability to think convergently.

- *Inhibiting reactive motivation.* In the three phases of interest, mixed or reactive motivation is facilitatory. Therefore, the most promising line of attack is to attempt to inhibit reactive motivation in order to disrupt malevolent innovation. This might be achieved, for example, by interfering with the ability of terrorists to collaborate and cooperate with each other (see Table 19.1).
- *Inhibiting adaptive personal properties.* In the three phases of interest, adaptive personal properties favor innovation. Therefore, to disrupt malevolent innovation, we must seek to interfere with the elimination of ambiguity, the development of consensus among terrorists, and so on.
- *Inhibiting conserving feelings*, such as anxiety in the face of uncertainty, or *encouraging unfavorable generative feelings*, such as excitement or unrealistic optimism.
- *Inhibiting the creation of routine, concrete products.* In the three phases of interest, the facilitatory focus is on relevant, correct, and effective products. Inhibiting this might involve, for example, restricting the opportunities for terrorists to test their products, as the July 2005 London bombers were able to do.
- *Encouraging a low-demand environmental press.* In the three target phases, a high-demand press is facilitatory. Encouraging the opposite, unfavorable low-demand press might involve removing sources of pressure, encouraging nonconformity, and so on.

For each dimension, the task of blocking malevolent innovation may be achieved either by inhibiting the favorable or encouraging the unfavorable, or possibly a combination of both. Regardless of the approach, there are challenges that remain to be addressed. If, for example, we wish to disrupt favorable thinking in the verification phase (favorable in this case is convergent thinking), it seems intuitively unwise to actively encourage terrorists to improve their ability to think divergently. The dilemma is that some of our strategies, while blocking one phase or dimension, actually could improve the malevolent innovator's capability in a different phase. The conservative approach is therefore probably to focus on inhibiting the favorable rather than encouraging the unfavorable – however, this is clearly an area where further research is required. Whichever approach is adopted, key questions also remain to be answered – how exactly can a dimension be inhibited, especially where direct control and influence may be limited?

REFERENCES

Anderson, J. V. (1992). Weirder than fiction: The reality and myths of creativity. *Academy of Management Executive*, 6, 40–47.

Barron, F. X. (1969). *Creative person and creative process*. New York: Holt, Rinehart & Winston.

Barroso, J.-M. (2009). Message to the European Commission Conference: Can creativity be measured? Brussels, May 2009.

Benjamin, D. & Simon, S. (2002). *The age of sacred terror*. New York: Random House.

Boden, M. A. (1994). Introduction. In M. A. Boden (Ed.), *Dimensions of creativity* (pp. 1–8). Cambridge, MA: MIT Press.

Burghardt, M. D. (1995). *Introduction to the engineering profession*, 2nd ed. Reading, MA: Addison-Wesley.

Buzan, A. (2007). Foreword. In S. C. Lundin and J. Tan (Eds.), *CATS: The nine lives of innovation* (pp. iv–viii). Spring Hill, Queensland, Australia: Management Press.

Cattell, R. B. & Butcher, H. J. (1968). *The prediction of achievement and creativity*. New York: Bobbs-Merrill.

Cropley, A. J. (1997). Creativity: A bundle of paradoxes. *Gifted and Talented International*, 12, 8–14.

Cropley, D. H. (2005). Eleven principles of creativity and terrorism. Science, Engineering & Technology Summit on Counter-Terrorism Technology, 4th Homeland Security Summit and Homeland Exposition, Canberra.

Cropley, D. H. & Cropley, A. J. (2005). Engineering creativity: A systems concept of functional creativity. In J. C. Kaufman and J. Baer (Eds.), *Faces of the muse: How people think, work and act creatively in diverse domains* (pp. 169–185). Hillsdale, NJ: Lawrence Erlbaum.

(2008). Elements of a universal aesthetic of creativity. *Psychology of Aesthetics, Creativity and the Arts*, 3, 155–161.

Cropley, D. H., Kaufmann, J., & Cropley, A. J. (2008). Malevolent creativity: A functional model of creativity in terrorism and crime. *Creativity Research Journal*, 20, 105–115.

Economist Technology Quarterly. (2002). Thanksgiving for innovation. *Economist Technology Quarterly*, September 21, pp. 13–14.

Florida, R. (2004). America's looming creativity crisis. *Harvard Business Review*, 82, 122–136.

Guilford, J. P. (1950). Creativity. *American Psychologist*, 5, 444–454.

Heinelt, G. (1974). *Kreative Lehrer/kreative Schüler* [Creative teachers/creative students]. Freiburg: Herder.

Horenstein, M. N. (2002). *Design concepts for engineers*, 2nd ed. Upper Saddle River, NJ: Prentice-Hall.

James, K., Clark, K., & Cropanzano, R. (1999). Positive and negative creativity in groups, institutions, and organizations: A model and theoretical extension. *Creativity Research Journal*, 12, 211–227.

Koberg, D. & Bagnall, J. (1991). *The universal traveler: A soft systems guide to creativity, problem solving and the process of reaching goals*. Menlo Park, CA: Crisp Publications.

McLaren, R. B. (1993). The dark side of creativity. *Creativity Research Journal*, 6, 137–144.
McMullan, W. E. (1978). Creative individuals: Paradoxical personages. *Journal of Creative Behavior*, 10, 265–275.
Martindale, C. (1989). Personality, situation, and creativity. In J. A. Glover, R. R. Ronning, and C. R. Reynolds (Eds.), *Handbook of creativity* (pp. 211–228). New York: Plenum Press.
Maslow, A. H. (1973). Creativity in self-actualizing people. In A. Rothenberg and C. R. Hausman (Eds.), *The creative question* (pp. 86–92). Durham, NC: Duke University Press.
May, R. (1976). *The courage to create*. New York: Bantam Books.
Plucker, J. A. & Renzulli, J. S. (1999). Psychometric approaches to the study of human creativity. In R. J. Sternberg (Ed.), *Handbook of creativity* (pp. 35–61). New York: Cambridge University Press.
Rhodes, M. (1961). An analysis of creativity. *Phi Delta Kappan*, 42, 305–310.
Rogers, C. R. (1961). *On becoming a person*. Boston: Houghton Mifflin.
Runco, M. (1991). *Divergent thinking*. Norwood, NJ: Ablex.
Shaw, M. P. (1989). The Eureka process: A structure for the creative experience in science and engineering. *Creativity Research Journal*, 2, 286–298.
Torrance, E. P. (1962). *Goals for guiding creative talent*. Englewood Cliffs, NJ: Prentice-Hall.
(1963). *Education and the creative potential*. Minneapolis: University of Minnesota Press.
Wallas, G. (1926). *The art of thought*. New York: Harcourt Brace.

20

Summary – The Dark Side of Creativity: A Differentiated Model

DAVID H. CROPLEY

Chapter 1 of this volume drew attention to a general failure by society to recognize the existence of the dark side of creativity. Subsequent chapters looked at the ways in which creativity can be manifested in forms that are neither positive nor beneficial. This dark side of creativity (McLaren, 1993) has attracted other labels, such as "negative creativity" (James & Taylor, Chapter 3 of this volume) and "malevolent creativity" (D. H. Cropley, Chapter 19 of this volume). (The difference between these two concepts will be discussed in greater detail below.) Leaving aside the precise meanings of the terms used, one thing is clear: Creativity can be and sometimes is used with the deliberate intention of causing harm or damage to others. Furthermore, even creativity that is intended to be entirely benevolent and positive in outcome may have unintended or unforeseen negative consequences – what begins with good intentions may end with harmful outcomes. To take an example, the discoveries of Jenner and Pasteur in the field of immunology, although extremely beneficial for all humankind, undoubtedly opened the door to the concept of biological warfare.

The dark side need not involve deliberate intent to do evil. People may have benevolent motives but be unaware of or unable or unwilling to anticipate the negative consequences of their creativity. Some creative workers with fundamentally benevolent intentions may even go so far as to blind themselves deliberately to the dark side of their work perhaps because of their fascination with or unquestioning belief in what they are doing, or their political or religious convictions, or through deception or coercion (see Zaitseva, Chapter 4 of this volume, and Hecht, Chapter 5 of this volume).

A failure to recognize the existence of the dark side – or a simple undifferentiated understanding of it – is dangerous for individuals, organizations, and society. It opens the doorway to manipulation, deception, exploitation, fraud, crime, and terrorism. As Eisenman (Chapter 11 of this volume) pointed out, criminals may show high levels of creativity in carrying out actions that are often bad for other people and intended to be so (i.e., malevolent). Negative creativity is not necessarily trivial and does not always occur at the lowest "routine" level of creativity defined by Cropley and Cropley (2005). As Gamman and Raein (Chapter 9 of this volume) emphasized, some negative creativity possesses the "Wow!" factor. The effective novelty generated by terrorists (the most notable example being the 9/11 attacks) shows that malevolent creativity can do tremendous harm and have a devastating impact on a society. Furthermore, the people who become involved in generating negative creativity are not necessarily monsters of evil, as Zaitseva and Hecht (Chapters 4 and 5 of this volume) showed, whereas undoubted monsters of evil are not necessarily recognized as such by all observers (see Sternberg, Chapter 17 of this volume).

The goal of this book was to gather essays representing disparate fields of study (including, but not limited to, psychology, criminal justice, sociology, engineering, education, history, and design) and with different areas of focus (again including, but not limited to, personality development, mental health, deviant behavior, law enforcement, and counterterrorism) to illustrate the nature of the dark side of creativity, to examine its variants, and to draw attention to its dangers. The ultimate aim was to determine how to prevent the negative consequences of creativity or to protect societies from these undesirable and indeed frequently harmful outcomes. In drawing the book to a close, it is now appropriate to synthesize a framework to aid in doing this.

In the preceding chapters a broad picture of the ways in which the dark side of creativity is conceived, incubates, evolves, and emerges in real settings has been developed. This involves not only the outcome, or "product," of creativity but at least three other dimensions [the others, first proposed by Barron (1955) and Rhodes (1961), being "person," "process," and "press"]. Not only is there a dark side to the product, or the outcome, of creativity, as has just been pointed out, but also to its impact on the person engaged in creative acts and behaviors, to the process leading to creativity, and finally, to the press, or environment, in which creativity takes place.

Any attempt to study this dark side of creativity is complicated by the fact that it may be very difficult to reach universal agreement on what constitutes a harmful or damaging or, more generally, negative outcome. A simple way to understand this is to recall the public demonstrations of joy in some countries that greeted news of the 9/11 attacks. As repugnant as that may seem, it demonstrates that the well-known aphorism "One person's terrorist is another's freedom fighter" is an accurate expression of the dilemma involved in seeking to understand the dark side of creativity. Thus moral and ethical issues are also important in understanding the dark side of creativity. Criteria of what is a positive outcome and what a negative one are needed. Sternberg (Chapter 17 of this volume) suggested that the answer is "wisdom," which manifests itself in concern for the common good.

These moral and ethical aspects of the dark side also shed light on the impact of creativity at the level of the individual, or person. If the essence of creativity is going against the crowd, taking risks and deviating from the routine, and strengthening the development of a unique identity, then creativity, of course, can facilitate personality development and promote mental health. It can, however, also reach a point where these positive traits cross a line and become antisocial or pathologic, manifesting themselves in manipulation, maladjustment, neurosis, crime, and even terrorism. Much the same can be said of the dark side of the process of creativity. As A. J. Cropley (Chapter 16 of this volume) pointed out, creativity involves essentially destructive processes such as questioning received wisdom or rejecting what already exists. These are regarded as good and desirable, that is to say, as positive or falling on the bright side, when they foster personal growth, but when they go wrong, they lead to disorder or chaos. Thus what is needed is a system for understanding where and how creativity crosses to the dark side.

DEFINING CREATIVITY: NOVELTY AND USEFULNESS

If the widely used definitions of creativity that regard novelty and usefulness as its core criteria (see, e.g., Sternberg & Lubart, 1999) are accepted, then the question must first be asked: "Useful for what and for whom?" The term "usefulness" implies that creativity is undertaken with some particular purpose in mind. The purpose is often captured through the idea of problem solving. Indeed, "creative problem solving" is a common phrase and is associated with the application of techniques for the generation of novel ideas. Well-known examples of these include "brainstorming," devised by Alex Osborn in the early 1950s (Osborn, 1953), and "synectics," formulated by William Gordon in the same decade (Gordon, 1961).

The problems that people seek to solve through the application of these techniques and methods and a large range of others (see, e.g., Higgins, 1994) may be conceptualized more generally as needs. In a conventional sense, the need might, for example, be that of a motorist for a more fuel-efficient automobile, the need of a society for a means of reducing air pollution produced by internal combustion engines, or the need of a doctor for a means to "see" inside a patient's body. The various solutions to these needs, respectively, an electronic fuel injector, a catalytic converter, and a magnetic resonance imaging (MRI) machine, would, when first introduced, have been seen as novel – that is to say, original and new – and continue to be seen as useful and/or effective in addressing the need today.

It is also a widely held belief nowadays that creativity and the process of exploiting creativity – innovation – are essential ingredients of competitive businesses. Whether this innovation takes the form of small improvements to what already exists (typically referred to as "incremental" innovation) (see, e.g., Christensen, 1997, or Sternberg, Kaufman, & Pretz, 2002) or of radical changes to the status quo (usually called "disruptive" innovation) (see also Christensen, 1997), there can be no doubt that recognizing and responding to the needs of customers, in the sense of solving their problems through the generation of effective, novel solutions, is a key activity for businesses. Organizations that are good at this activity prosper, whereas those which are not may stagnate or perish.

In 2002, the *Economist Technology Quarterly* reinforced this fact, pointing out that at the turn of the twenty-first century, more than half of economic growth is accounted for by creative products. Indeed, creativity has been described as the most important economic resource of the twenty-first century (Florida, 2002). Pilzer (1991) described the concept of "economic alchemy," whereby novel technologies continue to override the limitations of finite resources. Creativity and innovation in the automotive industry, for example, continue to improve the fuel efficiency of automobiles and in so doing reduce dependence on oil. This has the effect of extending the life of that finite resource. Pilzer argued that societies are not constrained by finite resources, provided that technological creativity and innovation continue to drive businesses. Thus it is apparent that creativity can be extremely "useful," a highly positive aspect.

CREATIVITY AND COMPETITION

Does this competitive model apply only to businesses? "Competition" can be conceived of more broadly by recognizing that opposing armies, for example, are engaged in a form of competition. Similarly, opposing sporting teams are competing in a more readily recognizable way. Students may be in competition for a good grade or the teacher's time and attention. It is also possible to think of doctors as competing with diseases, in this case for the health of people, or even law enforcement agencies as competing with criminals. These examples open up a somewhat different perspective on the positive aspect of usefulness. It is easy to see, in a business context – for example, two rival manufacturers competing to sell washing machines – that usefulness means the same thing for both parties. Usefulness is about providing customers with clean clothes. It is about performing a function. If a novel idea, for example, using an electric motor to agitate a container full of clothes rather than manual labor, is also useful (in this case, the task is performed more effectively by a motor than by a human), then this creative idea is both new and useful and offers a competitive advantage. Both rival manufacturers wish to provide their customers with a machine that helps in the process of washing clothing, and both seek to do this effectively, efficiently, and at an affordable cost. The one that can do so most efficiently, and most effectively, and at the lowest cost typically will capture the lion's share of the market. There do not seem to be any problems of negative or malevolent creativity here.

However, what about the case of a law enforcement agency competing with criminals? In this case, the competition is of a fundamentally different nature. One party, the police, is seeking to do something that most people would have no hesitation in categorizing as laudable, desirable, and good, whereas the other party, the criminals, is seeking to do something that most would regard as undesirable or, indeed, illegal and overtly bad. In this example, it is now no longer the case that the two competitors share the same basic benevolent objective (i.e., to satisfy a customer need). Rather, one competitor is doing something regarded as good or benevolent, whereas the other is doing something bad or malevolent. Whether this latter example is labeled "negative creativity," in contrast to the positive, benevolent creativity embodied in the example of the competing businesses, or "malevolent creativity," we must examine and seek to understand what it is that makes the process and the outcomes of some creative activities desirable and good and others bad.

A DARK SIDE TO CREATIVITY

A good starting point is to return to the key criteria of creativity – novelty and usefulness. Novelty presents fewer problems. It is widely agreed that novelty captures the notion that something is original and new. More colloquially, it might be said that a novel solution to a problem has "never been seen before," in contrast to a solution that is already well known. This is not to say that an established solution is not desirable. It is possible to speak of "routine" solutions, whose primary criterion is that they are effective – they solve the problem – even if they lack novelty. Effectiveness, or usefulness, however presents a moral dilemma that manifests itself in some of the examples cited earlier. Moving from the idea of rival businesses competing with each other to meet a customer need and returning to the idea of law enforcement agencies competing with criminals or even security forces competing with terrorists begins to reveal the problem.

While it might be said casually that "most people" would regard the idea of hijacking a plane and crashing it into a building as bad, if not overtly evil, and therefore not at all useful or effective, it cannot be denied that there are some people who would see this situation differently. There is no doubt that the 9/11 hijackers believed that what they were doing served some noble purpose and that, in the light of what actually happened, it was highly useful and effective. That their method of attack on that day was also, by definition, surprising and therefore highly novel – commercial airliners had not been hijacked and crashed into buildings previously – is not in question. Similarly, the conman who devises a new method for defrauding an organization or the thief who finds a new way to defeat a security system may develop solutions that exhibit high degrees of novelty, and presumably, they do these things because they solve a problem that the criminal has – in this case, the desire to obtain more money. This leads to a situation in which it seems that the current lexicon of creativity is not fully equipped to describe these situations and that the lack of a term to classify these cases – where the goal of the creative process is to achieve harmful, illegal, or immoral ends – hinders the ability to analyze them and take action against them.

THE MANY FACES OF THE DARK SIDE

Two pairs of concepts have already been articulated in the field of creativity and help to make sense of this dark side of creativity. James and Taylor (Chapter 3 of this volume) use the term "negative" creativity, in contrast to "positive" creativity, to describe the undesirable, or indeed harmful, consequences of creativity. These terms provide a more general classification of creativity with respect to the nature of the outcome, or product. Good products and outcomes, in other words, those which are beneficial and affirming, are labeled "positive." Those which are undesirable, harmful, and/or damaging are negative. A more differentiated classification of product and outcome is yielded by the pair of terms "malevolent" creativity and "benevolent" creativity. Coming into use more recently than positive and negative creativity (D. H. Cropley, Chapter 19 of this volume; Cropley, Kaufman, & Cropley, 2008), these terms provide a second, more explicit and more precise level of classification.

The critical factor that differentiates malevolent creativity from negative creativity is the *intent* of the actor. Malevolent creativity must involve not only a harmful or damaging outcome or product but also a deliberate intent to cause harm or damage. Negative creativity, by contrast, may feature no deliberate intent. In the case of negative creativity, the harmful or damaging outcomes may be merely an unfortunate by-product, such as the discovery of microorganisms leading to germ warfare.

At least two factors therefore are relevant to understanding the dark side of creativity. The first is the product or outcome of the activity. This is typically the generation of an effective or useful, novel solution to a problem that, in the case of negative creativity, does harm to at least some people. The second is the intent of the actor – that is, the individual or possibly the organization generating the effective novelty. The division of positive and negative creativity according to its benevolence or malevolence makes it possible to look simultaneously not only at the product (the outcome of the creativity) but also at the person [the intentions of the individual(s) generating the effective novelty in question]. Table 20.1 identifies the primary differentiator for the dark side of creativity. In straightforward terms, bad outcomes/products arising from the process of generation of effective novelty are labeled "negative creativity," and good outcomes/products are labeled "positive creativity."

TABLE 20.1. *Negative-positive creativity and product*

Product/outcome	Primary label
Bad	Negative
Good	Positive

TABLE 20.2. *Outcome and intent – malevolent creativity*

Product/outcome	Intent	Secondary label
Bad	Malevolent	Conscious malevolence
Good	Malevolent	Failed malevolence
Bad	Benevolent	Failed benevolence
Good	Benevolent	Conscious benevolence

Taking account of the actor's intentions as well as the outcome (i.e., looking at person as well as product) expands the available classifications of creativity, including those representative of the dark side, from two categories to four. This serves a purpose that is more than merely technical. In particular, it makes it possible to turn attention from the output of the creative process or activity to its inputs and indeed to the process itself. Table 20.2 adds the intent of the actor in the creative process to the nature of the product or outcome of Table 20.1. This permits more precise differentiation than is possible when using the labels "positive" and "negative." When a creative process, for example, the development of a novel form of terrorist attack (such as the attacks on 9/11 previously mentioned) results in an outcome that is undeniably negative, it now can be further examined and an attempt made to understand the intent of the actor(s). Where the intent is deliberately to cause harm to others, as was the case on 9/11, the label "negative" creativity is replaced with "consciously malevolent creativity."

The terrorists in question set out to create a novel "solution" to their problem that would, if successful (i.e., effective and useful), undeniably and without any shadow of a doubt result in the deaths of many innocent people and the widespread destruction of property. Because it was both novel and effective, the product was creative, and because of the evil intent, it was not merely negative creativity but consciously malevolent creativity. The negative outcome was not the result of an accidental set of circumstances, nor was it an unfortunate by-product of an activity that had positive intent. Where this is the case, in other words, where the intention is to do good but something goes awry, it is possible to speak of "failed benevolence" (good intent, bad outcome).

Similarly, when benevolent intent results in a positive outcome or product, then the label "positive" creativity is replaced with "consciously benevolent creativity." However, addition of the factor intent also now acknowledges the possibility that malevolent intent may – through no fault of the actor, whose intentions were bad – result in a positive outcome. In this latter case, the label "failed malevolence" now would be used. In other words, in comparison with Table 20.1, there are two possible situations in which the result is positive and two possible cases where the result is negative. Table 20.2 allows these cases to be expressed with greater precision.

Table 20.2 illustrates the value to be gained in the more differentiated understanding that results from an analysis of the dark side of creativity. At a primary level, negative creativity recognizes that the product of the creative process may be bad. The invention of the internal combustion engine, for example, has led to pollution and millions of premature deaths in automobile accidents and is an example of negative creativity. However, it seems certain that Karl Benz, who designed and built the first four-stroke engine, did not do so with the intent of polluting the environment or killing people but that he hoped to do good. Thus, in a more differentiated analysis, an appropriate secondary label for this invention, at least with respect to the polluting/safety aspects of the engine, would be "failed benevolence." The negative aspects of the invention are unintended and unforeseen consequences of the solution to the primary problem that the device was created to solve.

THE FOUR *P*'S OF CREATIVITY AND THE DARK SIDE

The addition of the factor intent has enriched understanding of the dark side of creativity. Negative outcomes may be deliberate, but they also may happen, as it were, accidentally. Ironically, at least in theory, it also would be possible for positive outcomes to happen accidentally. However, the literature on creativity points to other factors that could further enhance understanding and lead to a more highly differentiated model of creativity. As has already been pointed out, the traditional model of creativity in psychology is the four *P*s approach: person, process, product and the influence of the surrounding environment (press). Person covers a range of factors, including motivation (such as willingness to take risks or, more central for the present discussion, desire to do harm or to do good), feelings, and other personal properties (see Gascon and Kaufman, Chapter 13 of this volume). For present purposes, this factor will be used to refer to intent. The factor product is what we have already referred to under the same name or, alternatively, as "outcome." If process and press are now added to the table of factors leading to creativity, we expand the available categorizations from four (see Table 20.2) to eight (Table 20.3).

For the purpose of differentiating the dark side more precisely, process and press will be treated together as representative of factors that influence what happens between the formation of an intent and the realization of the end product. These will be categorized again using two poles. Either the process and press act to support the activity for which a useful, novel product is the output, or they act to undermine it. The former will be labeled "supportive" and the latter "obstructive."

Table 20.3 introduces four new categorizations that are distinct from those discussed in the preceding section. In Table 20.2, on the dark side of the creativity ledger, conscious malevolence and failed benevolence both

TABLE 20.3. *Product, person, process, and press – types of malevolent creativity*

Product	Person (intent)	Process/press	Secondary label
Bad	Malevolent	Supportive	Conscious malevolence
Good	Malevolent	Supportive	Failed malevolence
Bad	Benevolent	Supportive	Failed benevolence
Good	Benevolent	Supportive	Conscious benevolence
Bad	Malevolent	Obstructive	Resilient malevolence
Good	Malevolent	Obstructive	Frustrated malevolence
Bad	Benevolent	Obstructive	Frustrated benevolence
Good	Benevolent	Obstructive	Resilient benevolence

lead to an outcome or product that is negative but arise from an intent that is, respectively, malevolent and benevolent. In Table 20.3, the addition of process/press now distinguishes between creative activities that take place in circumstances that are either supportive of the intent or that act against it. Thus, while intent may be malevolent and a negative outcome may result, two pathways to this result can be conceived of. One arises from a situation where both the process and the press act in concert with the intent, whereas the other arises from a situation where process and press act in opposition to the intent. Put more plainly, malevolent intent that achieves a negative outcome despite the process and press is "resilient" malevolence, in contrast to conscious malevolence that succeeds because of the process and press.

The terrorist attacks on 9/11 again help to understand the different forms of the dark side of creativity. It can be argued that the hijackers of the aircraft involved in the Twin Towers attacks and the Pentagon attack succeeded despite an obstructive environment (press). In other words, the normal security measures that were part of the environment in which those attacks were made were directed against the terrorists but failed to prevent them. The creativity of the attacks therefore was not only intentionally harmful but also resilient enough not to be deterred by a hostile press (security measures aimed at thwarting terrorism). It is interesting, however, to note that the attack on United Airlines Flight 93 (UA93) did not possess the same resilience. It may be argued that the reason for this "failure" of the terrorist attack was that it was no longer novel (and therefore no longer creative to the same degree as the other attacks). When the passengers on UA93 fought back, this obstructive environment overcame the malevolence of the terrorist attack and turned it into frustrated malevolence. In this case, it must be admitted that there is a degree of relativity in this discussion. The terrorist attack still was successful, particularly because it murdered the people on board the flight, but it was clearly not nearly as successful as is generally believed was the intent. Thanks to the bravery of the people on board, the UA93 attack did not succeed to the degree that it might have.

DEALING WITH THE DARK SIDE

The latter example paves the way for a final question: "So what?" Why is it necessary, important, and/or useful to develop a more precise, more highly differentiated model of the dark side of creativity? Is it not sufficient to recognize that creativity – the generation of effective or useful novelty – sometimes can lead to bad outcomes? There are two answers to these questions. First, it is entirely consistent with the progress of science to seek to understand a phenomenon in progressively greater detail. The contrast between negative and positive creativity opens our eyes to the fact that creativity does not have to be only about beneficial, desirable self-actualization. Creativity is an ingredient of competitive success, but its contribution to the success of one side in competitive situations is not necessarily confined to activities or outcomes that are inherently good. Second, the more precise and more highly differentiated the model of the dark side of creativity, the greater is the likelihood of finding ways of counteracting it. In the same way that the positive aspects of creativity are highly valued, for example, in business – a great deal of time and effort are spent trying to enhance the creativity of individuals and organizations – time and effort need to be invested in learning how to minimize the impact of the dark side. Whether this is used to prevent terrorist attacks, or to prevent criminal acts, or simply to guard against the accidental negative consequences of a new technology, a detailed model of the dark side of creativity is the first step in equipping society to deal with it.

The four factors that characterize the dark side of creativity – product, person, and process/press – allow formulation of more specific approaches to counteracting the dark side. The example of the 9/11 attacks highlights the potentially disruptive impact that an obstructive press might play with regard to frustrating malevolent creativity. With the benefit of hindsight, how might the outcome on September 11, 2001, have differed if a more obstructive press (e.g., tighter airport security) had existed? By the same token, strategies that do not focus on product alone but attempt to disrupt person (including evildoers' negative intent) or process may offer opportunities to turn a negative outcome into a positive one. Sternberg (Chapter 17 of this volume) offers a concrete approach. While accepting that creativity can be used for bad ends, he suggests that "wisdom" is a construct that might be taught, in conjunction with creativity (and intelligence), to eliminate the dark side of creativity. Sternberg's approach suggests that by focusing on the person, through the construct of wisdom, it might be possible to succeed in deterring the dark side of creativity.

It is also clear that there is a class of effects that falls outside the framework just described. The essence of Table 20.3 is focused on what might be called the "primary" product of creativity – that is, the problem to be solved or the need to be satisfied. There is, however, also what might be called a "secondary" product, or by-product. This is the impact of the creative activity [with its primary product, the associated intent of the actor(s), and the role of the means, or process, and the environment, or press] on the actor(s). In other words, a fifth dimension of the dark side of creativity is a fifth *P* – "price" (or "cost"). Hari (Chapter 18 of this volume), Jasper (Chapter 6 of this volume), and Simonton (Chapter 12 of this volume) give clear examples of this dimension. Hari understands cost literally, namely, in terms of financial resources consumed. Jasper uses the example of area bombing in contrast to precision bombing to highlight elements of the innovation dilemma. Put simply, creative ideas offer the possibility of attractive rewards, but these may come at a cost to the innovator. Simonton's discussion of creative genius and mental illness highlights the personal, psychological cost that may be associated with creativity.

CONCLUDING REMARKS

The concept of a dark side to creativity, at least explicitly stated, is fairly new. It arises when attention is turned away from studies of creativity based on outcome measures that focus on positive ideas, solutions, products, and outcomes to outcome measures that focus on negatives. Acts of terrorism, as well as fraud, theft, and deceit, bring into focus the fact that creativity is by no means limited to the production of useful or effective novelty for universally positive purposes. James and Taylor (e.g., Chapter 3 of this volume) address the qualitative dilemma this poses by recognizing that while the decision of what is good or bad requires a subjective judgment, where a creative product achieves an outcome that is good for some but bad for many, it is not unreasonable to label this as negative. Negative outcomes or products in a general sense that result from creativity provide a starting point for studying the dark side of creativity. If the intent of the actor is added, then it becomes possible to differentiate more precisely the nature and kind of dark-side creativity involved.

Once other social and psychological factors are added to this model – simplistically the person and the press – then additional categorizations of the dark side of creativity are possible. Thus the dark side is first characterized by the nature of the outcome. Bad outcomes – at least those which are bad for the majority – resulting from the generation of effective or useful novelty give rise to negative creativity. If the nature of the intent of the actor is added to the model, then it is possible to speak of "malevolent" creativity resulting from intentionally harmful effective novelty. Where the intent was positive but the outcome was negative, creativity that is unintentionally (or perhaps accidentally) malevolent can be distinguished and called "failed benevolence." If a dimension to capture the nature of the process and press that support the generation of effective novelty is added, the most differentiated model of the dark side of creativity is achieved. In this case, a supportive environment reinforces the deliberate production of harmful, effective novelty. There may be cases, however, where intentionally harmful effective novelty succeeds despite attempts to frustrate it. In this obstructive environment, the result is resilient malevolence.

Thus creativity has two basic sides – the bright and the dark. The three dimensions discussed result in eight specific manifestations of creativity. Four of these can lead to negative, undesirable, and/or harmful outcomes and involve the dark side of creativity. Each of these four instances of the dark side, however, occurs through a different combination of factors, meaning that some of the negative outcomes are deliberate and some are unintended or accidental. Understanding these four faces of the dark side of creativity offers insights into how these negative consequences of the generation of effective novelty might be overcome.

REFERENCES

Barron, F. X. (1955). The disposition towards originality. *Journal of Abnormal and Social Psychology*, 51, 478–485.

Christensen, C. M. (1997). *The innovator's dilemma*. Boston, MA: Harvard Business School Press.

Cropley, D. H. & Cropley, A. J. (2005). Engineering creativity: A systems concept of functional creativity. In J. C. Kaufman and J. Baer (Eds.), *Faces of the muse: How people think, work and act creatively in diverse domains* (pp. 169–185). Hillsdale, NJ: Lawrence Erlbaum.

Cropley, D. H., Kaufman, J. C., & Cropley, A. J. (2008). Malevolent creativity: A functional model of creativity in terrorism and crime. *Creativity Research Journal*, 20, 105–115.

Economist Technology Quarterly. (2002). Thanksgiving for innovation. *Economist Technology Quarterly*, September 21, pp. 13–14.
Florida, R. (2002). *The rise of the creative class.* New York: Basic Books.
Gordon, W. J. (1961). *Synectics.* New York: Harper.
Higgins, J. M. (1994). *101 creative problem solving techniques – The handbook of new ideas for business.* Winter Park, FL: New Management Publishing Company.
McLaren, R. B. (1993). The dark side of creativity. *Creativity Research Journal*, 6, 137–144.
Osborn, A. F. (1953). *Applied imagination.* New York: Scribner's.
Pilzer, P. Z. (1991). *Unlimited wealth.* New York: Crown Publishers.
Rhodes, M. (1961). An analysis of creativity. *Phi Delta Kappan*, 42, 305–310.
Sternberg, R. J., Kaufman, J. C., & Pretz, J. E. (2002). *The creativity conundrum.* Philadelphia: Psychology Press.
Sternberg, R. J. & Lubart, T. I. (1999). The concept of creativity: Prospects and paradigms. In R. J. Sternberg (Ed.), *Handbook of creativity* (pp. 3–15). New York: Cambridge University Press.

Index